#38 Aggressors & Strugglers I

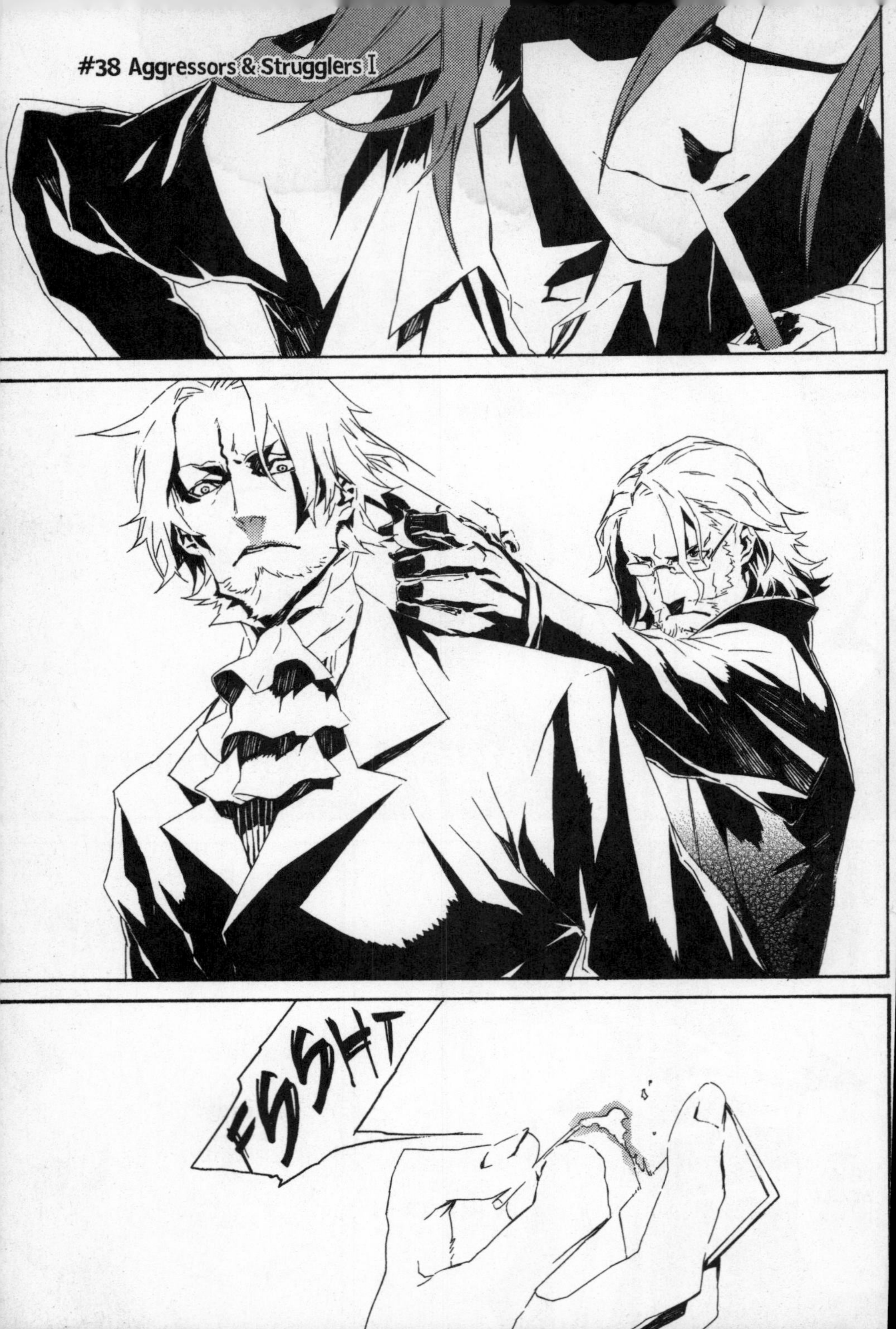
FSSHT

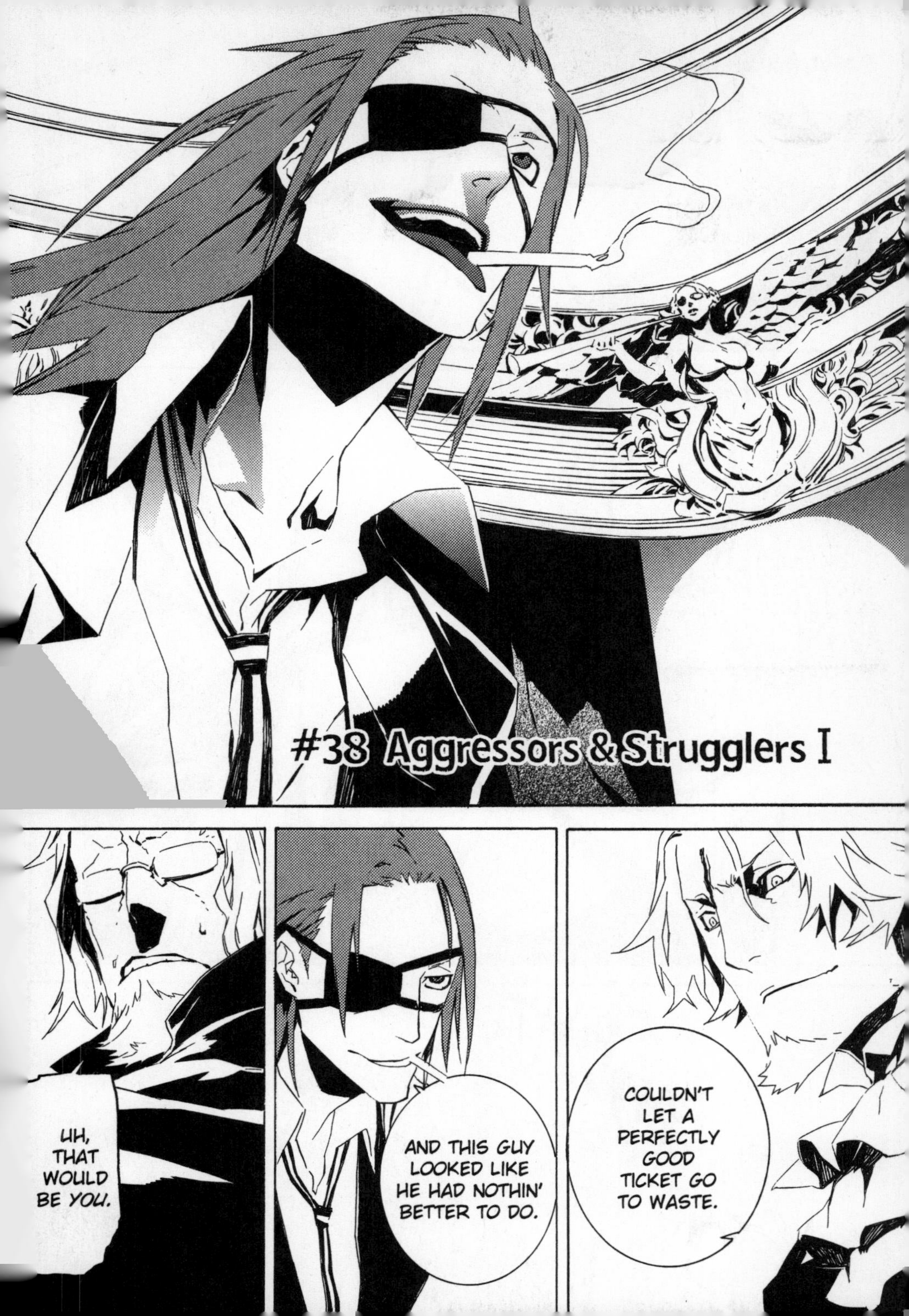
#38 Aggressors & Strugglers I
COULDN'T LET A PERFECTLY GOOD TICKET GO TO WASTE.
AND THIS GUY LOOKED LIKE HE HAD NOTHIN' BETTER TO DO.
UH, THAT WOULD BE *YOU*.

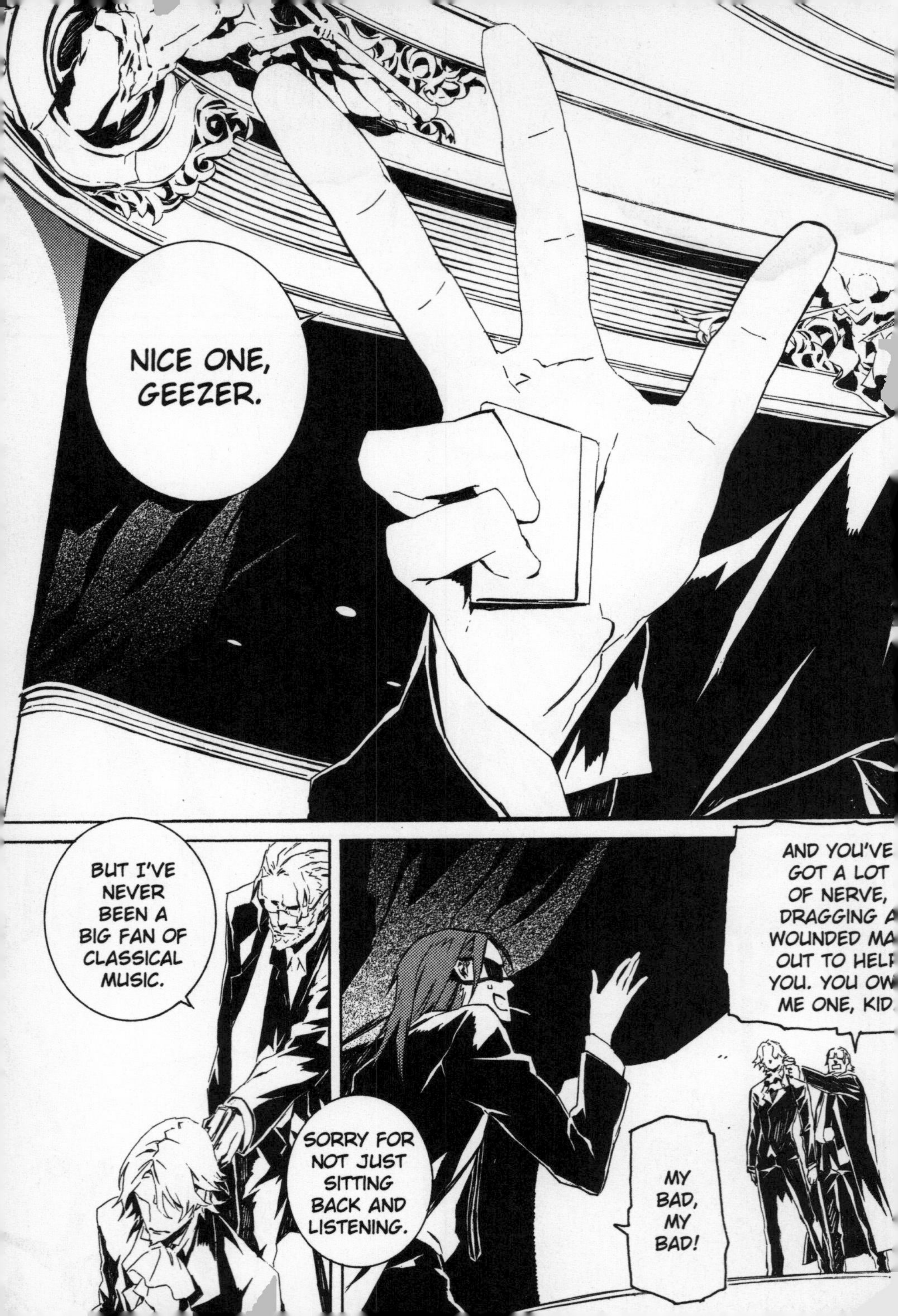
NICE ONE, GEEZER.
AND YOU'VE GOT A LOT OF NERVE, DRAGGING A WOUNDED MA OUT TO HELP YOU. YOU OW ME ONE, KID.
MY BAD, MY BAD!
SORRY FOR NOT JUST SITTING BACK AND LISTENING.
BUT I'VE NEVER BEEN A BIG FAN OF CLASSICAL MUSIC.

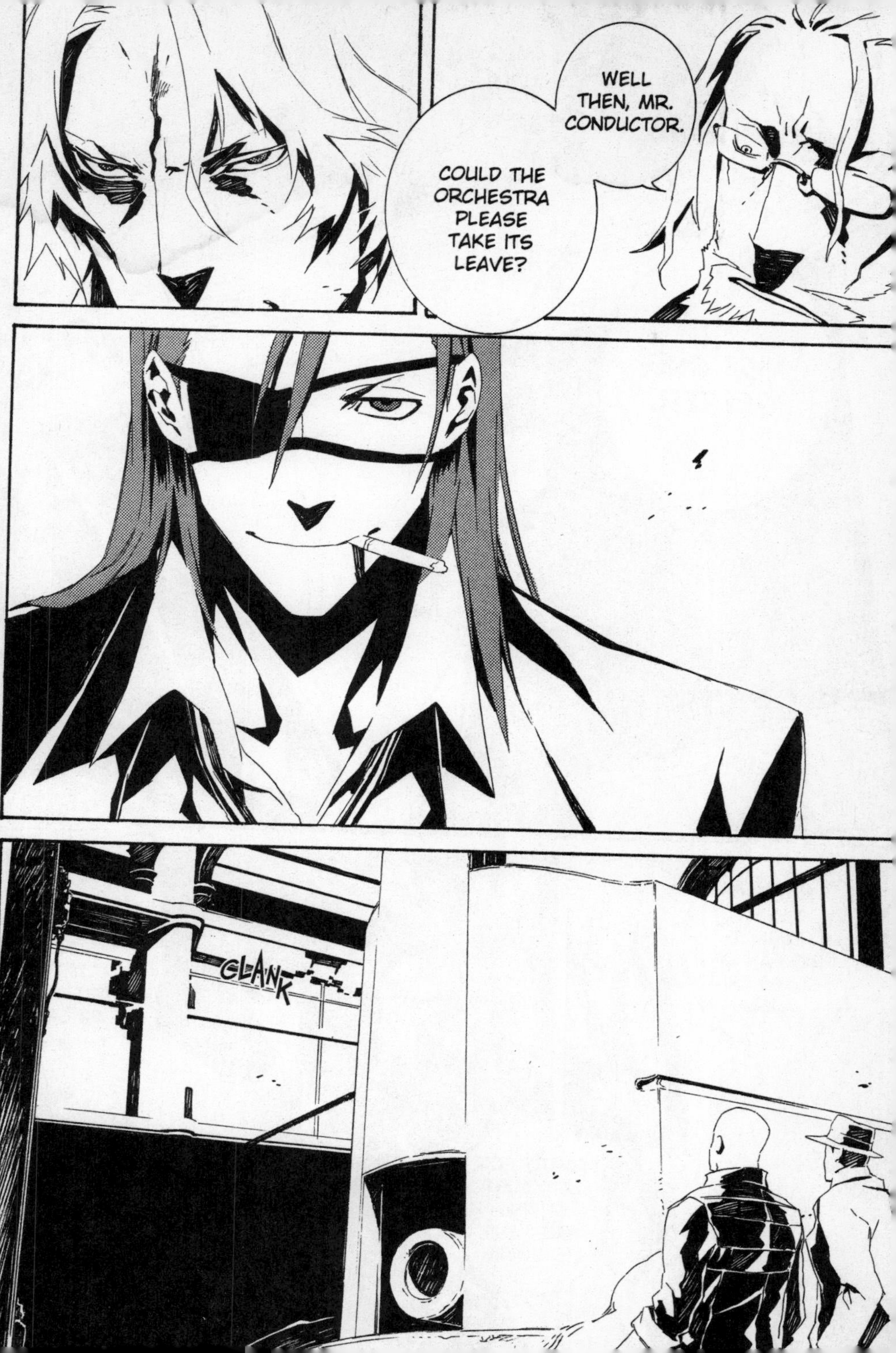
WELL THEN, MR. CONDUCTOR.
COULD THE ORCHESTRA PLEASE TAKE ITS LEAVE?
CLANK

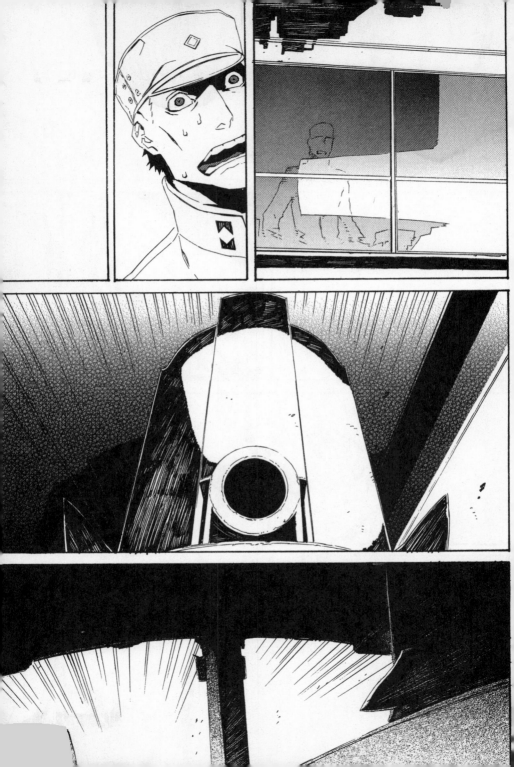

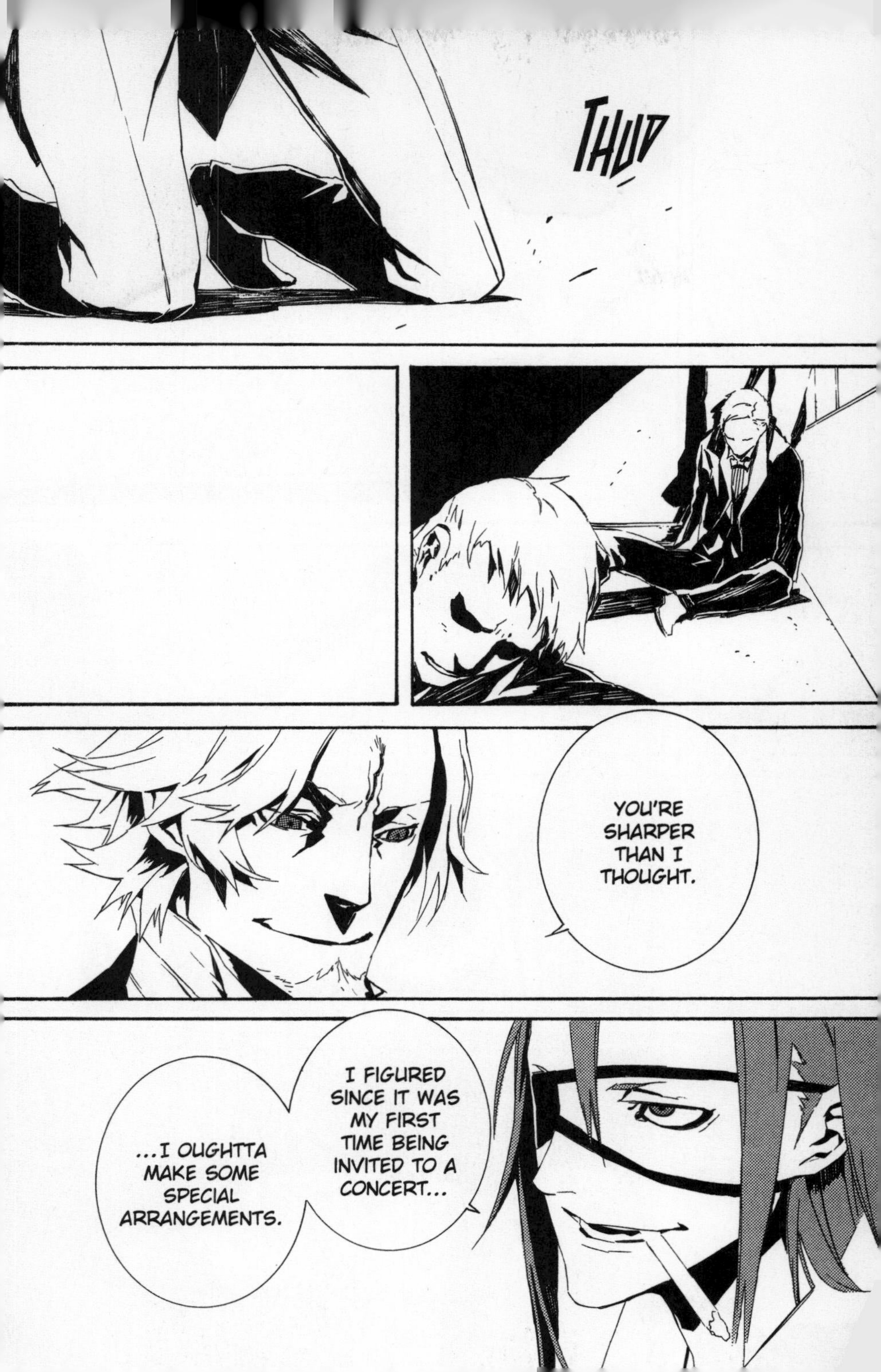
THUD
YOU'RE SHARPER THAN I THOUGHT.
I FIGURED SINCE IT WAS MY FIRST TIME BEING INVITED TO A CONCERT...
...I OUGHTTA MAKE SOME SPECIAL ARRANGEMENTS.

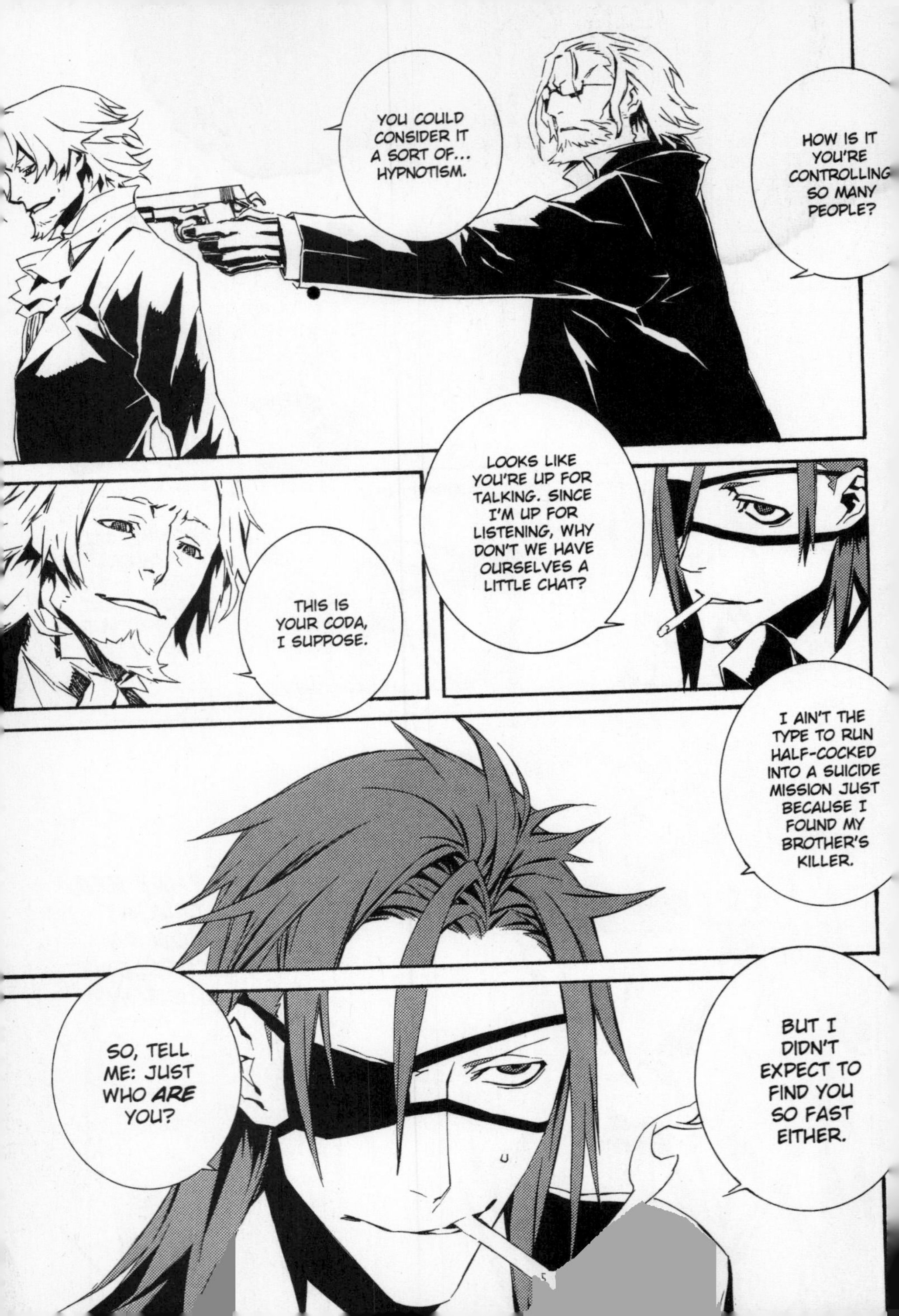
HOW IS IT YOU'RE CONTROLLING SO MANY PEOPLE?
YOU COULD CONSIDER IT A SORT OF... HYPNOTISM.
LOOKS LIKE YOU'RE UP FOR TALKING. SINCE I'M UP FOR LISTENING, WHY DON'T WE HAVE OURSELVES A LITTLE CHAT?
THIS IS YOUR CODA, I SUPPOSE.
I AIN'T THE TYPE TO RUN HALF-COCKED INTO A SUICIDE MISSION JUST BECAUSE I FOUND MY BROTHER'S KILLER.
BUT I DIDN'T EXPECT TO FIND YOU SO FAST EITHER.
SO, TELL ME: JUST WHO *ARE* YOU?

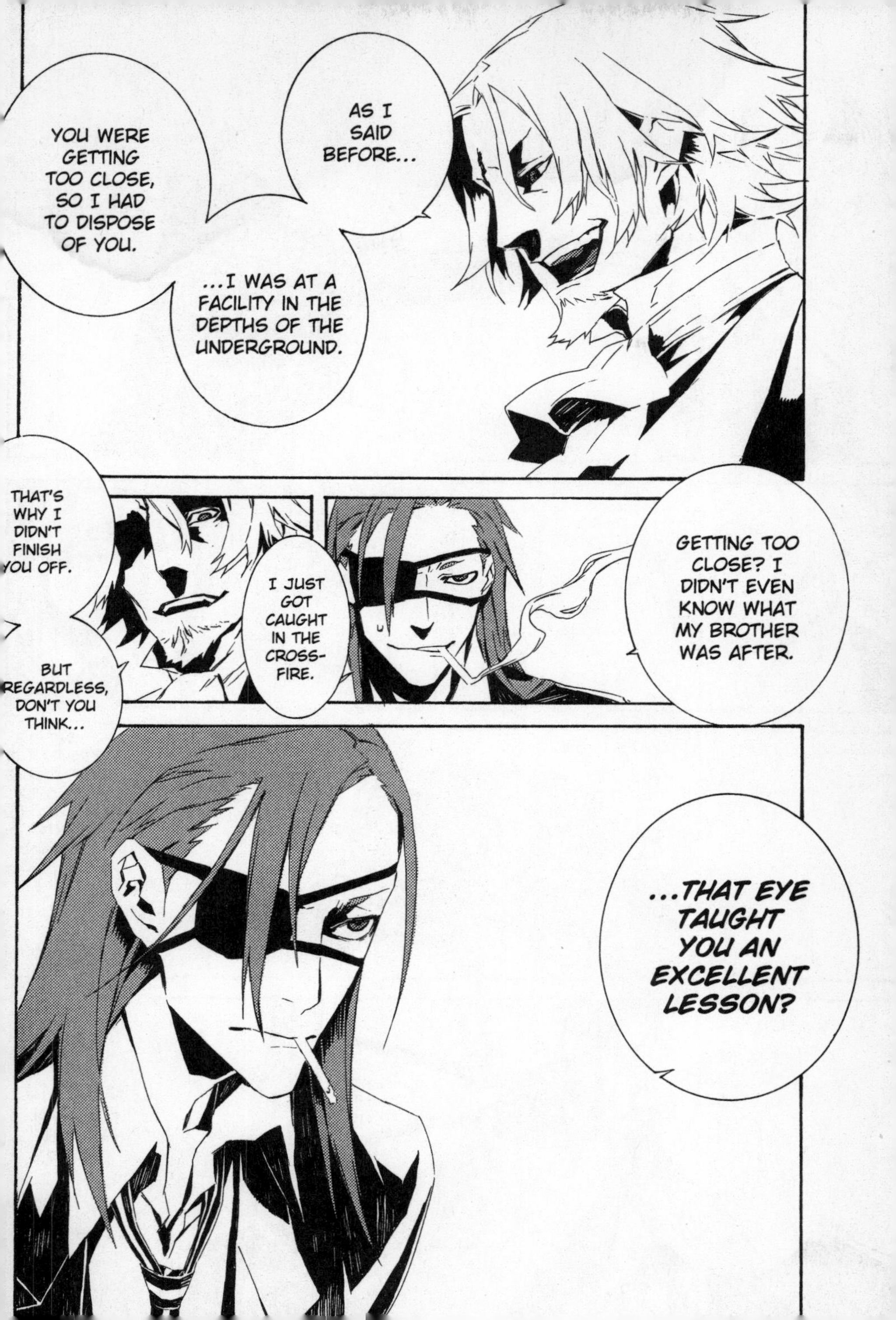
AS I SAID BEFORE...
...I WAS AT A FACILITY IN THE DEPTHS OF THE UNDERGROUND.
YOU WERE GETTING TOO CLOSE, SO I HAD TO DISPOSE OF YOU.
GETTING TOO CLOSE? I DIDN'T EVEN KNOW WHAT MY BROTHER WAS AFTER.
I JUST GOT CAUGHT IN THE CROSS-FIRE.
THAT'S WHY I DIDN'T FINISH YOU OFF.
BUT REGARDLESS, DON'T YOU THINK...
...THAT EYE TAUGHT YOU AN EXCELLENT LESSON?

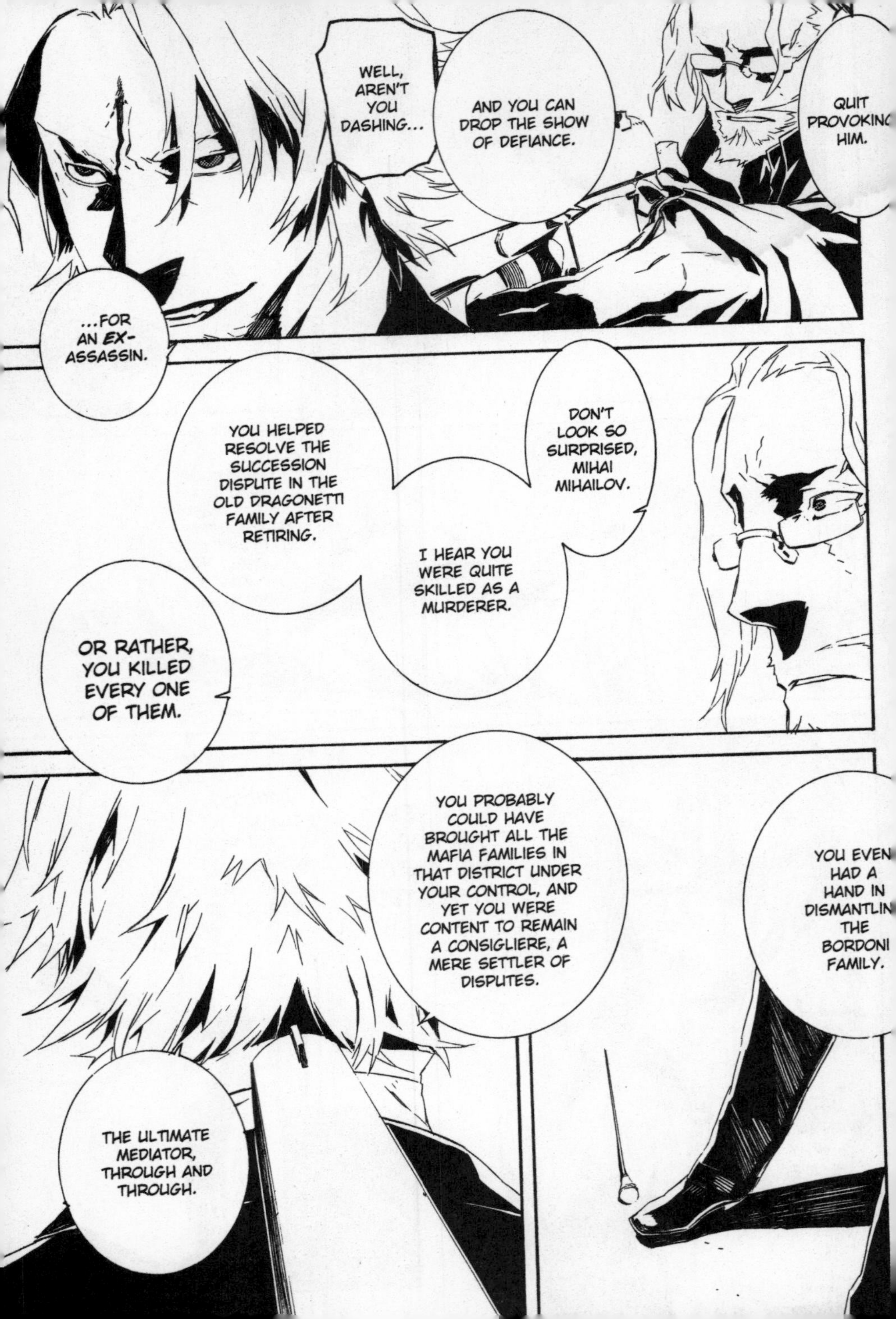
QUIT PROVOKING HIM.
AND YOU CAN DROP THE SHOW OF DEFIANCE.
WELL, AREN'T YOU DASHING...
...FOR AN *EX*-ASSASSIN.
DON'T LOOK SO SURPRISED, MIHAI MIHAILOV.
YOU HELPED RESOLVE THE SUCCESSION DISPUTE IN THE OLD DRAGONETTI FAMILY AFTER RETIRING.
I HEAR YOU WERE QUITE SKILLED AS A MURDERER.
OR RATHER, YOU KILLED EVERY ONE OF THEM.
YOU EVEN HAD A HAND IN DISMANTLIN THE BORDONI FAMILY.
YOU PROBABLY COULD HAVE BROUGHT ALL THE MAFIA FAMILIES IN THAT DISTRICT UNDER YOUR CONTROL, AND YET YOU WERE CONTENT TO REMAIN A CONSIGLIERE, A MERE SETTLER OF DISPUTES.
THE ULTIMATE MEDIATOR, THROUGH AND THROUGH.

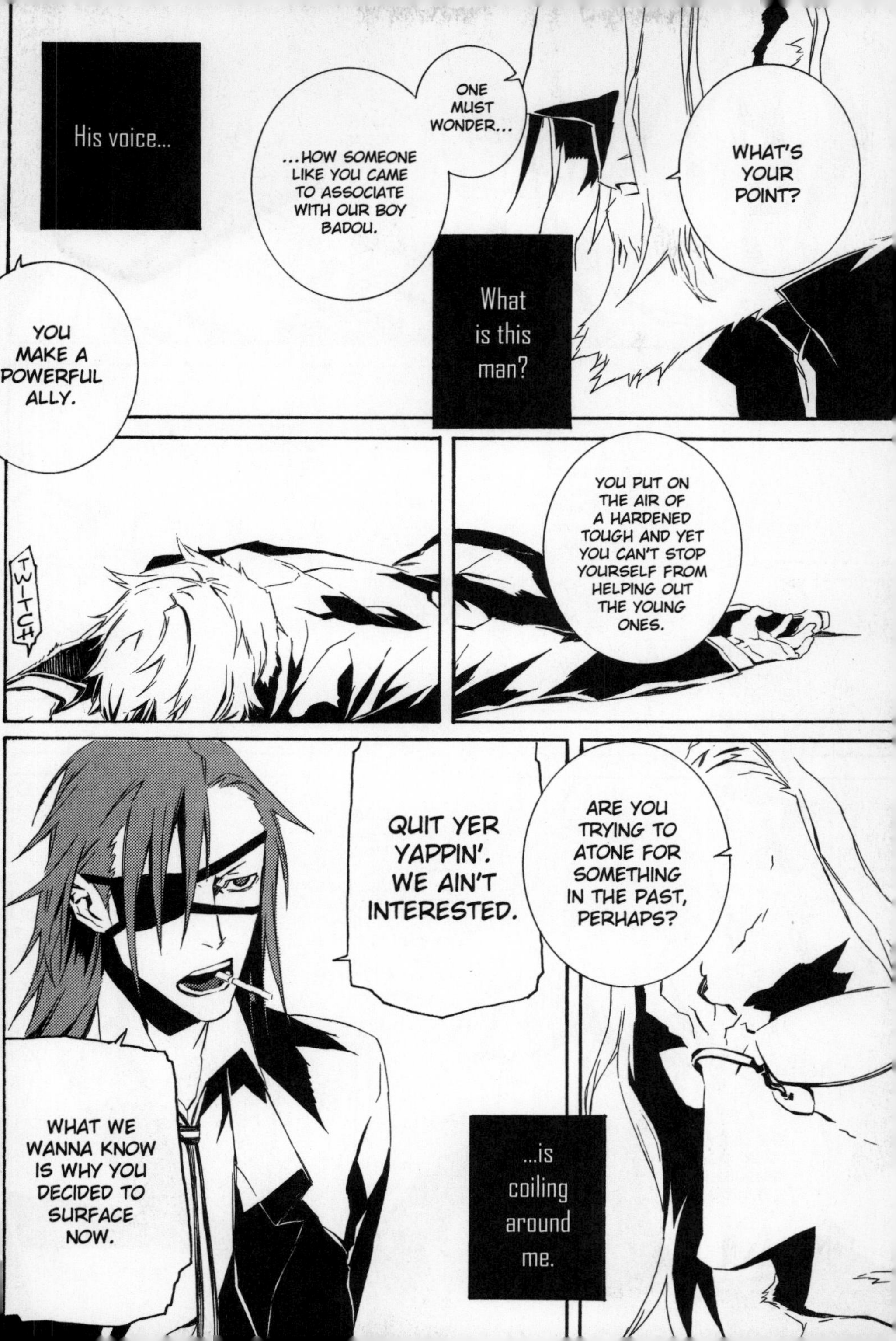
WHAT'S YOUR POINT?
ONE MUST WONDER...
...HOW SOMEONE LIKE YOU CAME TO ASSOCIATE WITH OUR BOY BADOU.
His voice...
What is this man?
YOU MAKE A POWERFUL ALLY.
YOU PUT ON THE AIR OF A HARDENED TOUGH AND YET YOU CAN'T STOP YOURSELF FROM HELPING OUT THE YOUNG ONES.
TWITCH
ARE YOU TRYING TO ATONE FOR SOMETHING IN THE PAST, PERHAPS?
...is coiling around me.
QUIT YER YAPPIN'. WE AIN'T INTERESTED.
WHAT WE WANNA KNOW IS WHY YOU DECIDED TO SURFACE NOW.

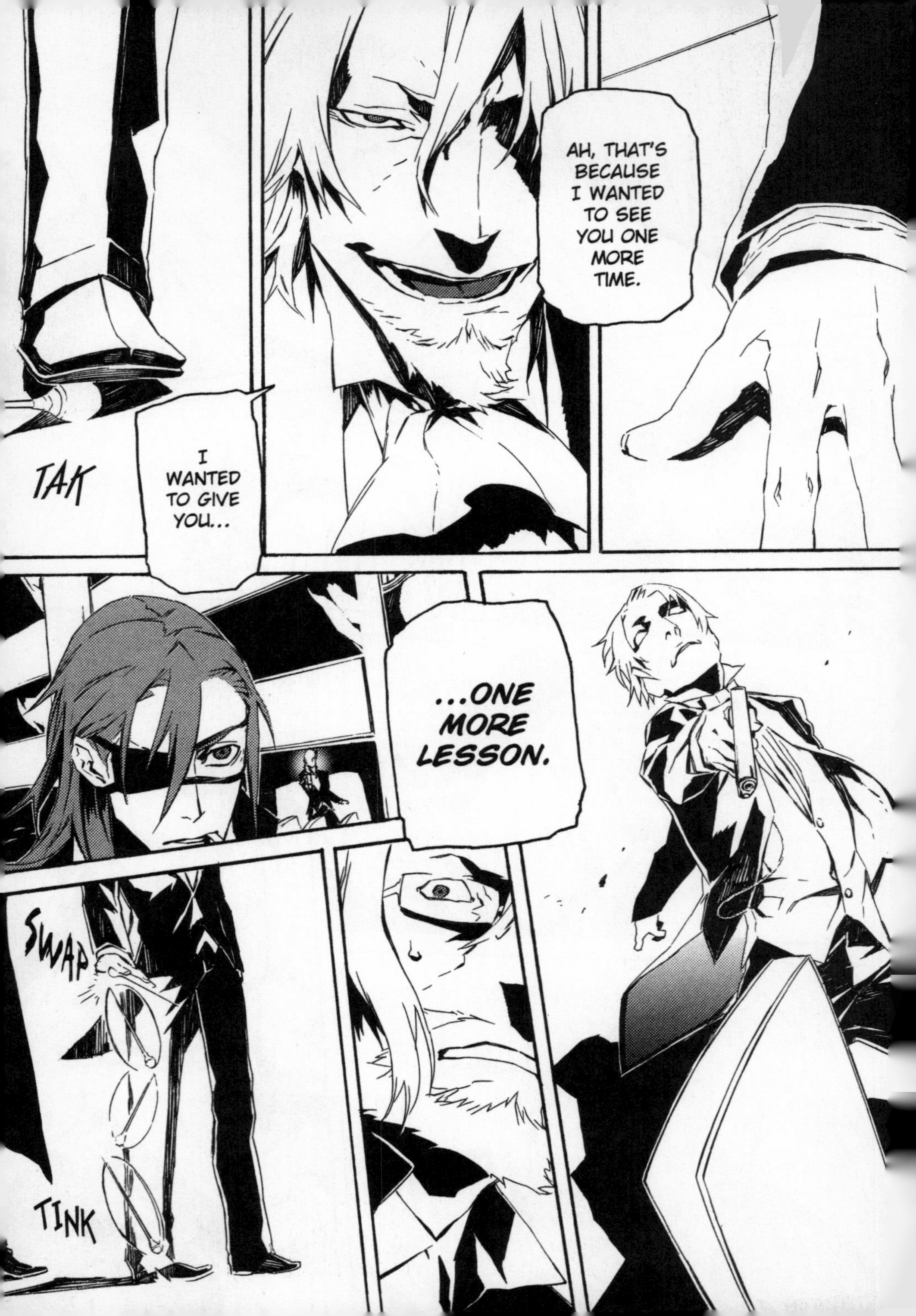
AH, THAT'S BECAUSE I WANTED TO SEE YOU ONE MORE TIME.
I WANTED TO GIVE YOU...
TAK
...ONE MORE LESSON.
SWAP
TINK

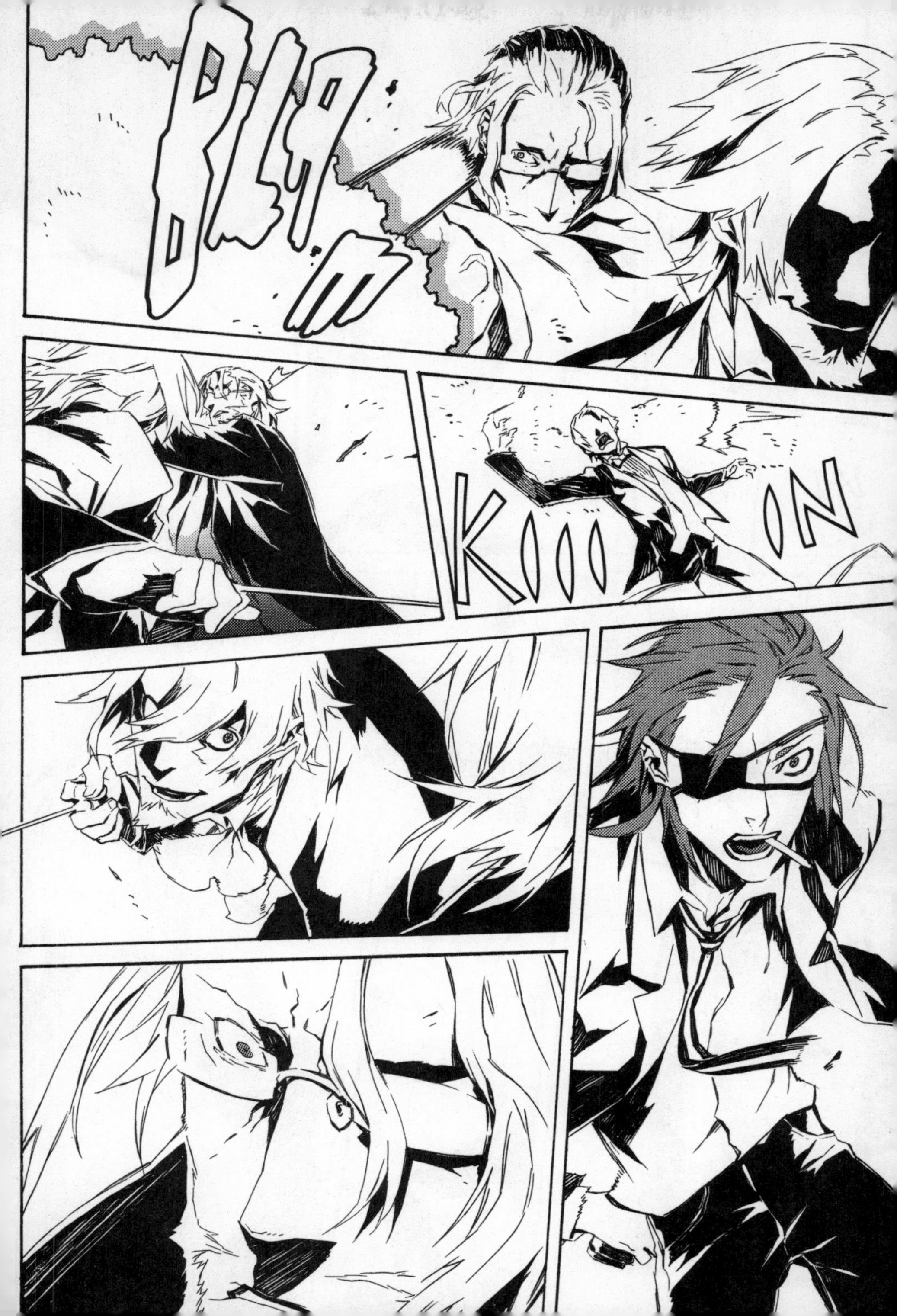
BLAM
KIIIIN

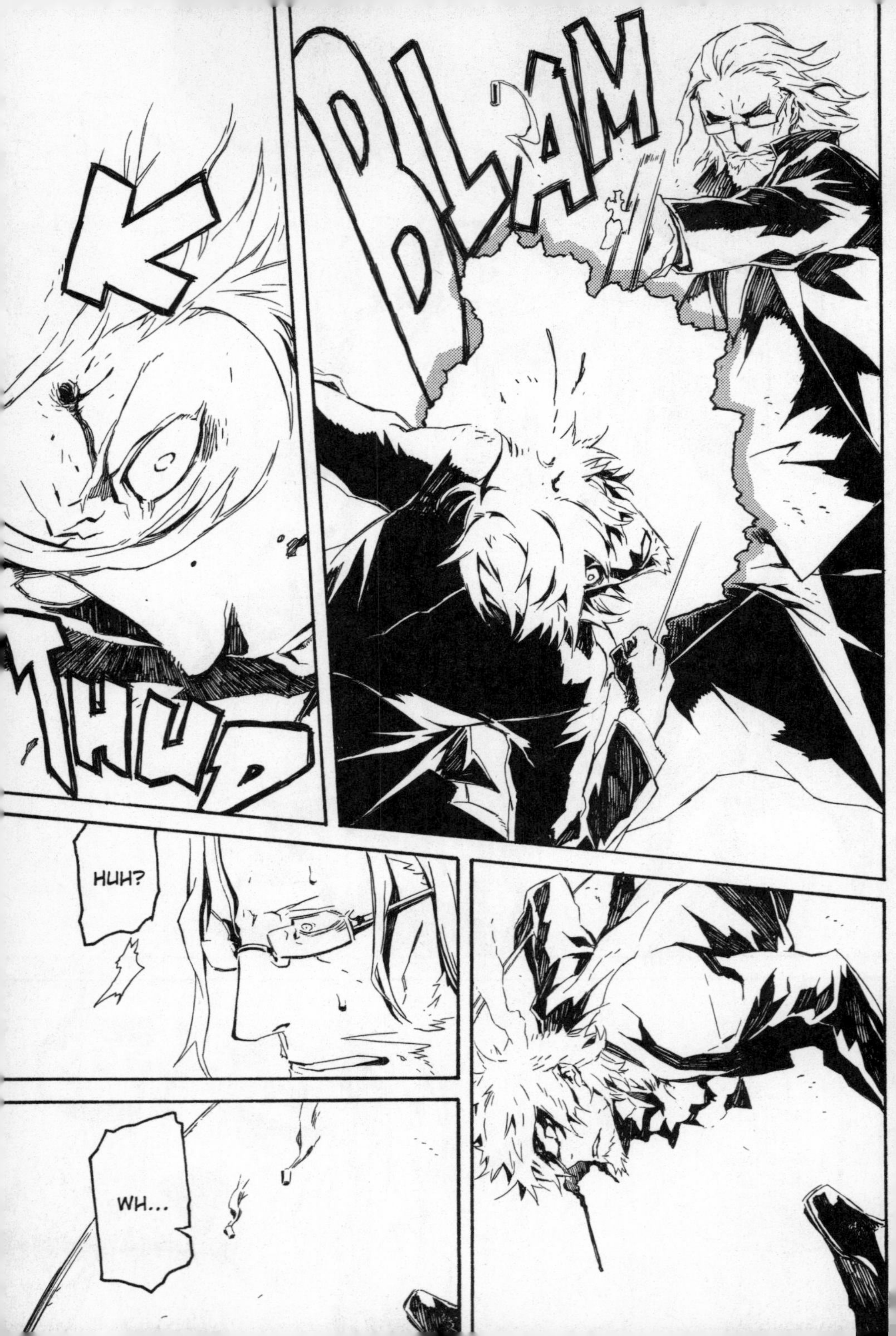
BLAM
K
THUD
HUH?
WH...

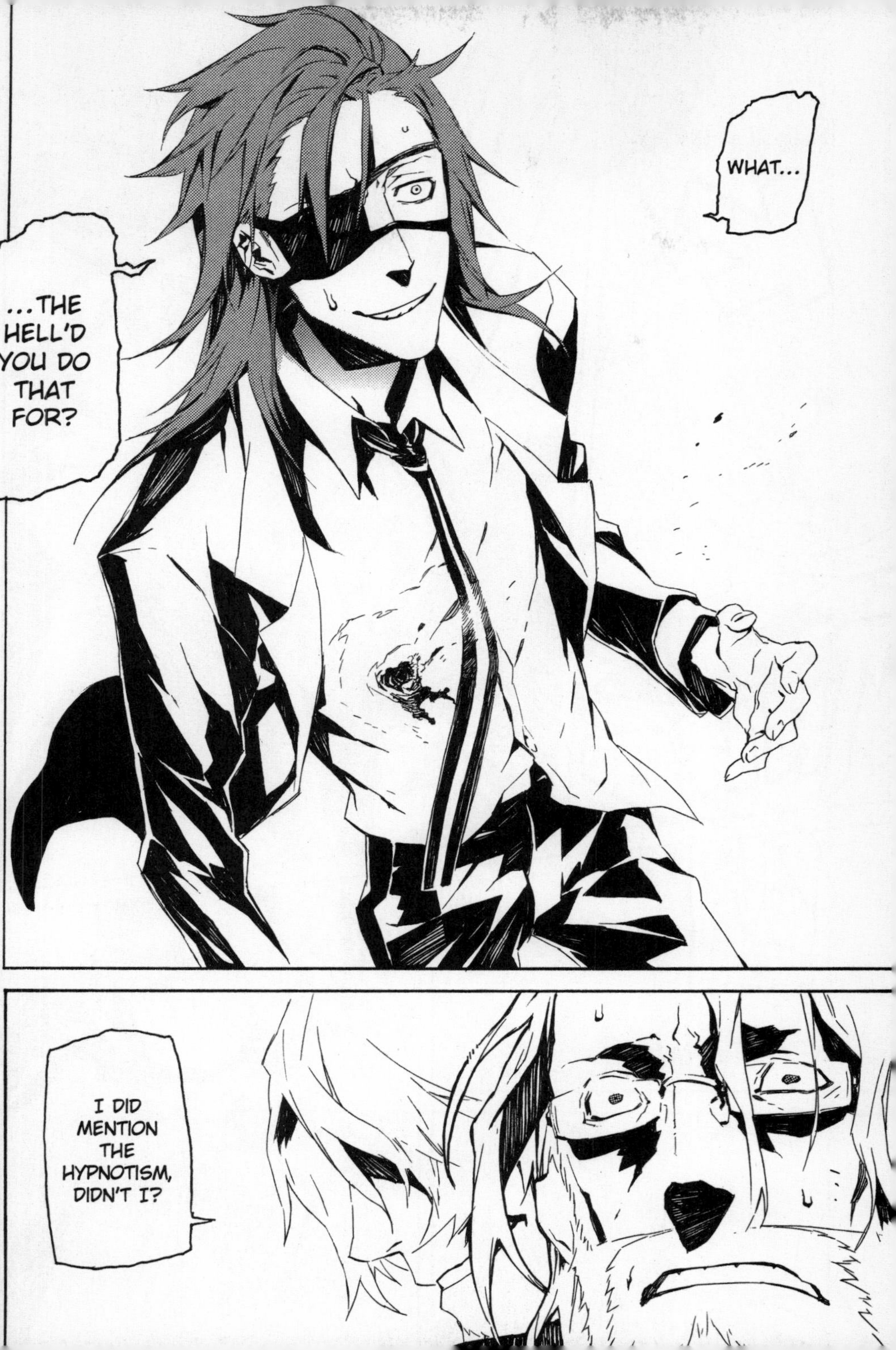
WHAT...
...THE HELL'D YOU DO THAT FOR?
I DID MENTION THE HYPNOTISM, DIDN'T I?

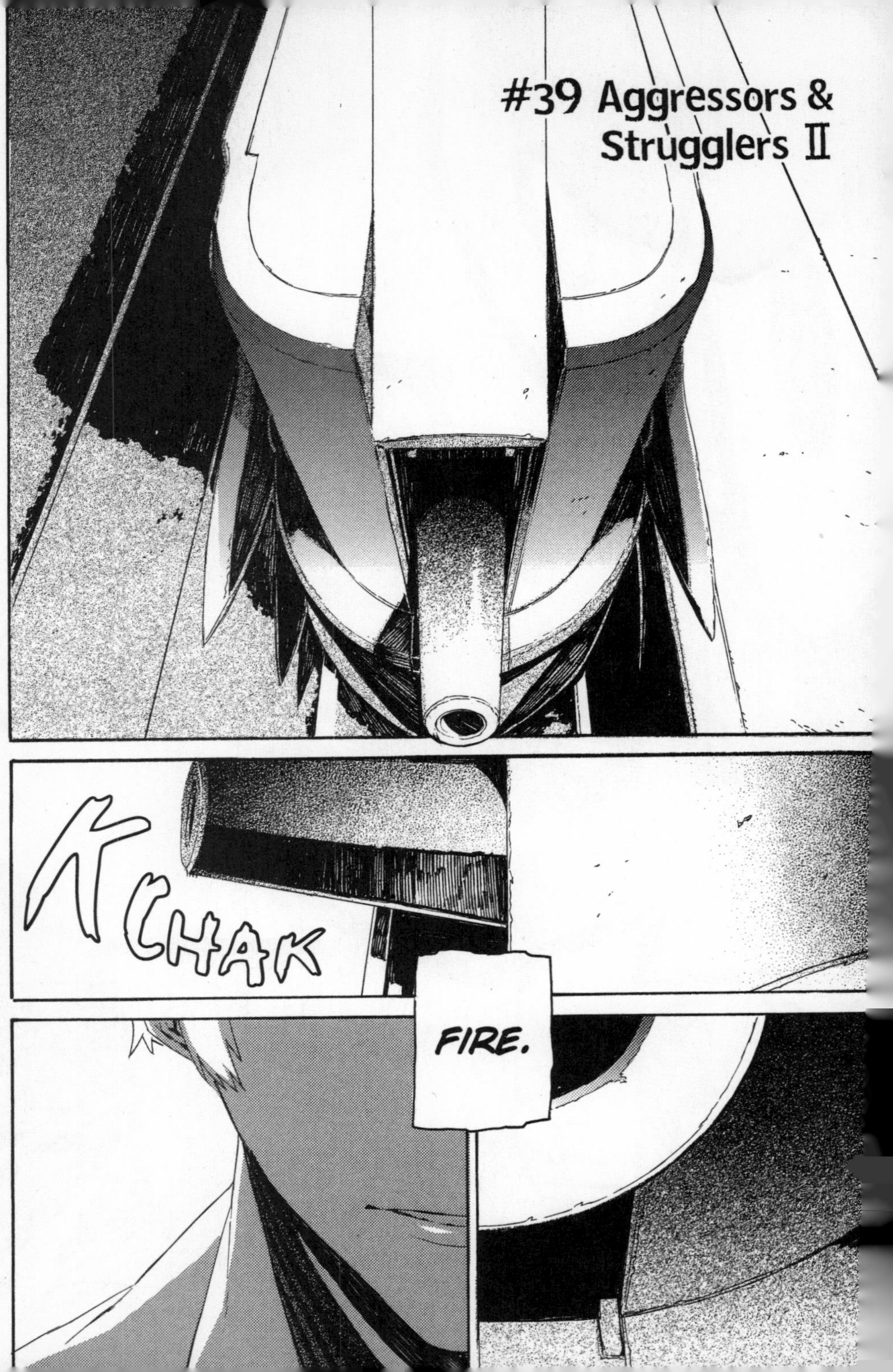
#39 Aggressors & Strugglers Ⅱ
KCHAK
FIRE.

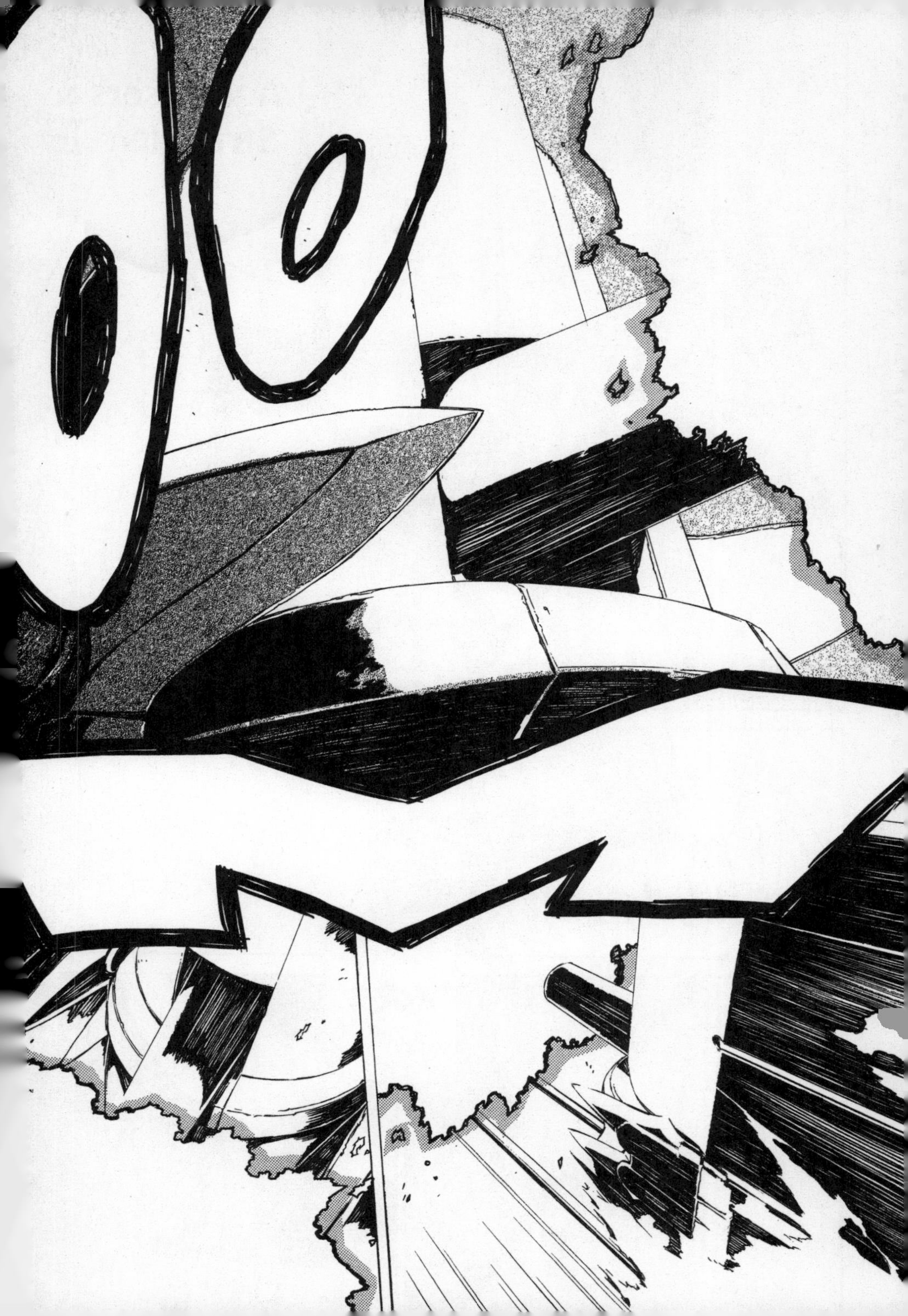

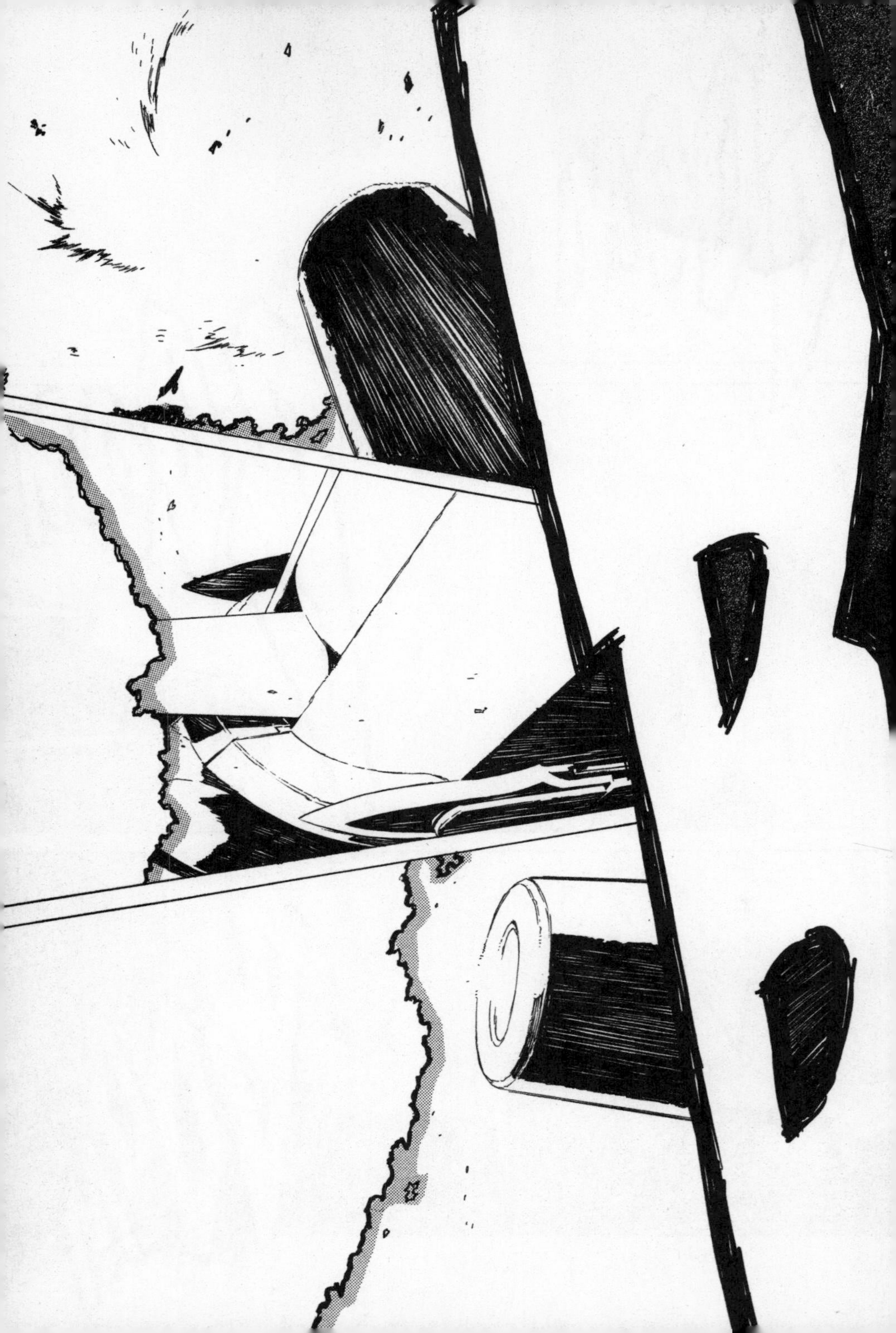

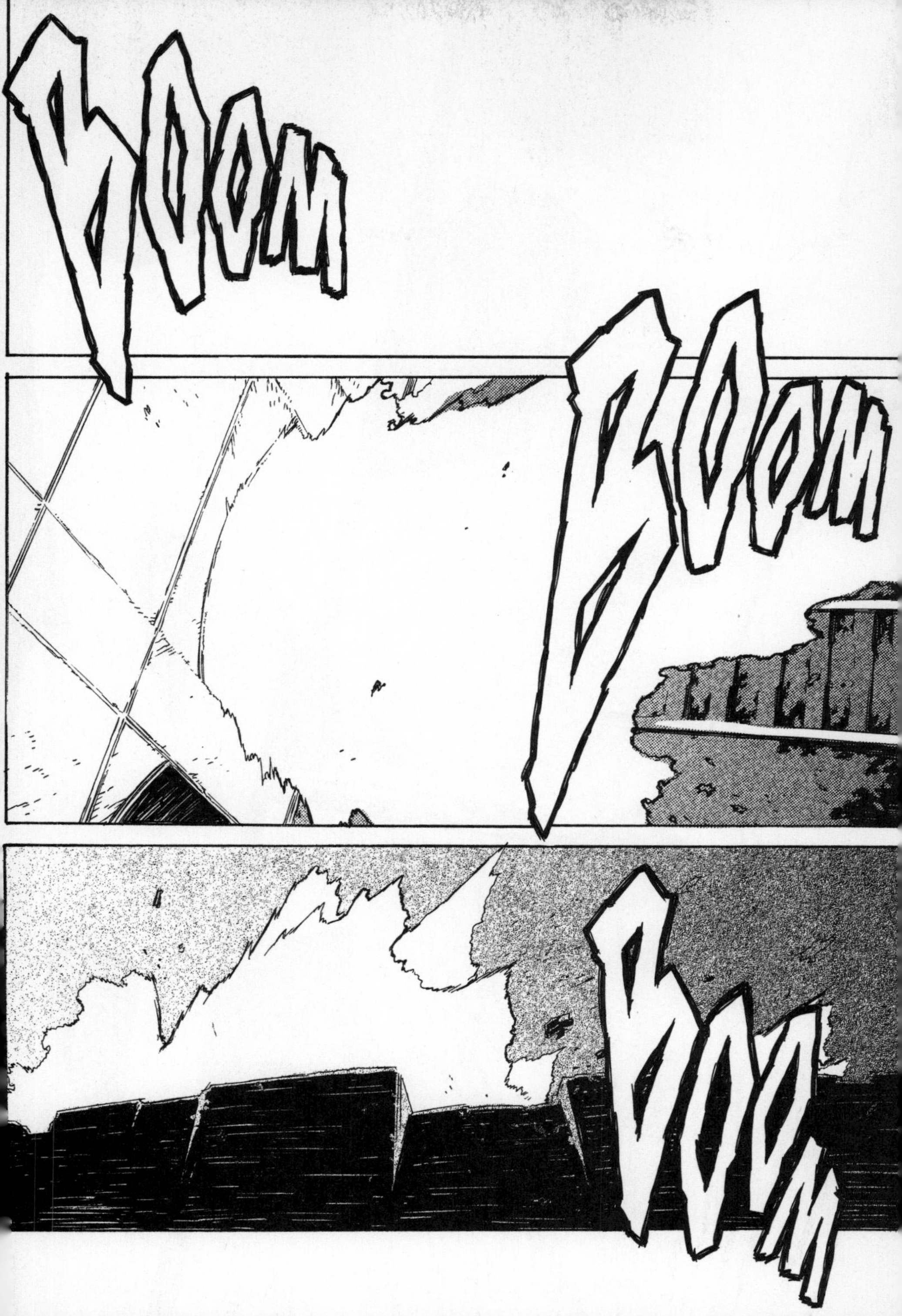
BOOM
BOOM
BOOM

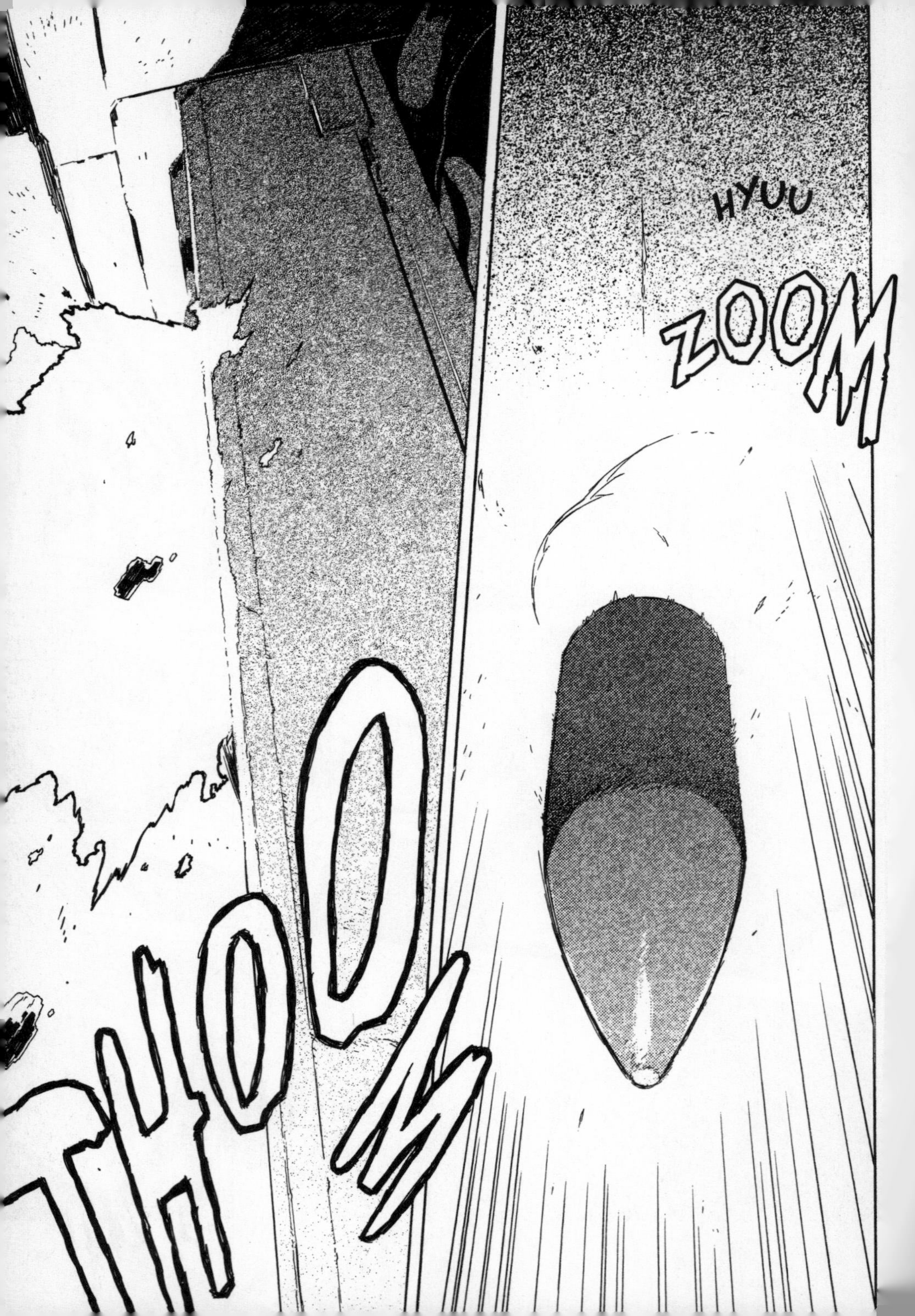
HYUU
ZOOM
THOOM

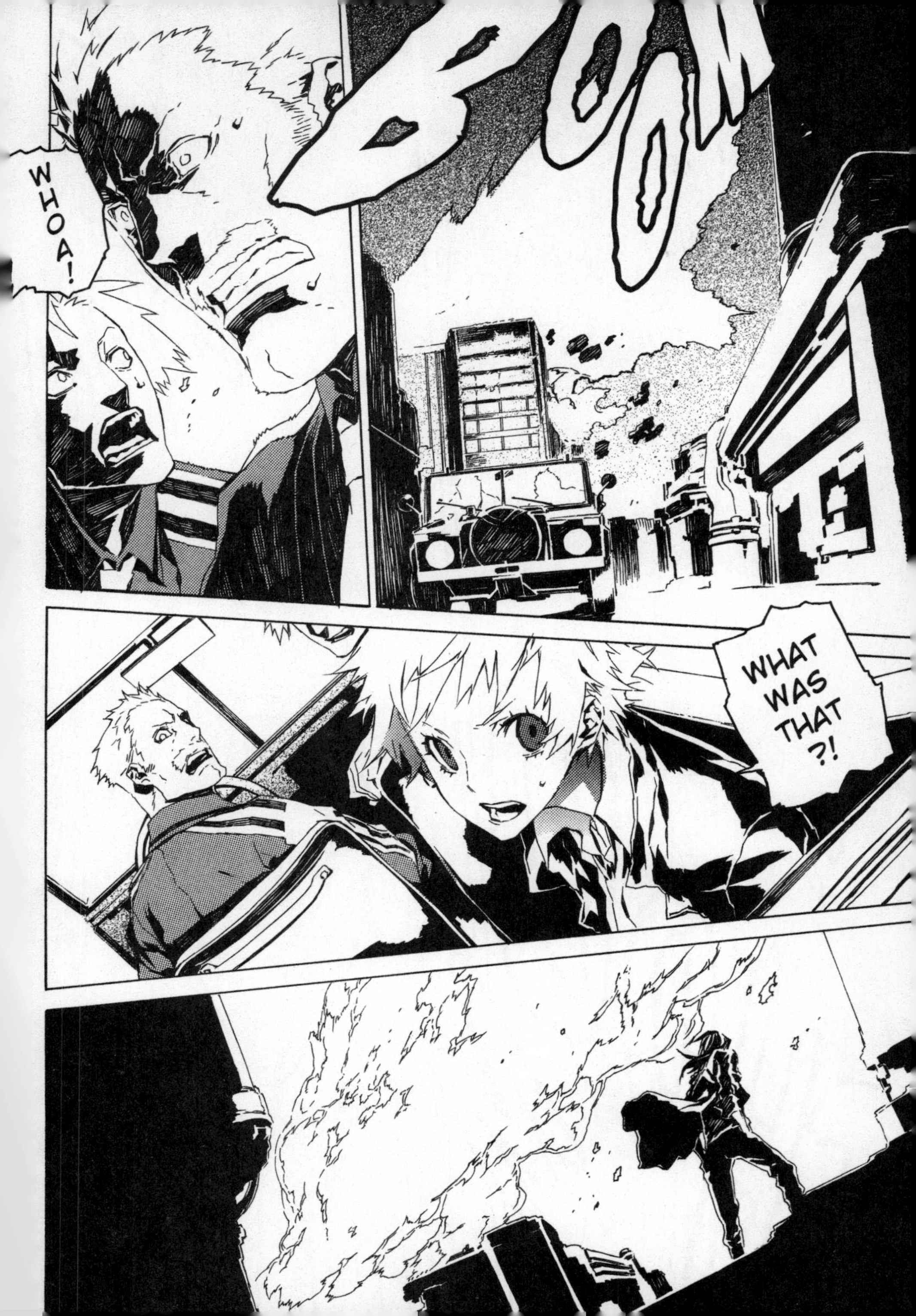
BOOM
WHOA!
WHAT WAS THAT ?!

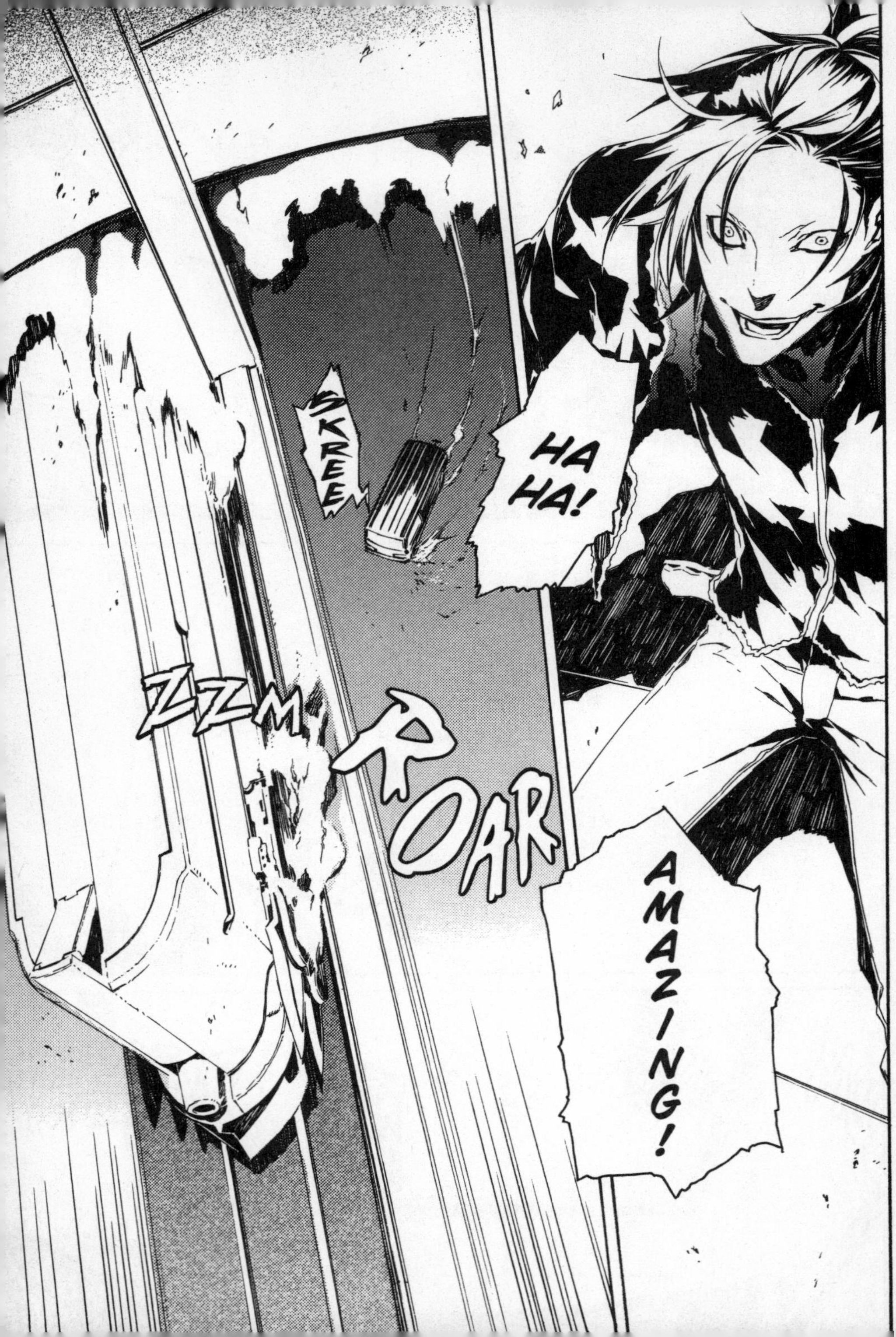
HA HA!
AMAZING!
SKREE
ZZM
ROAR

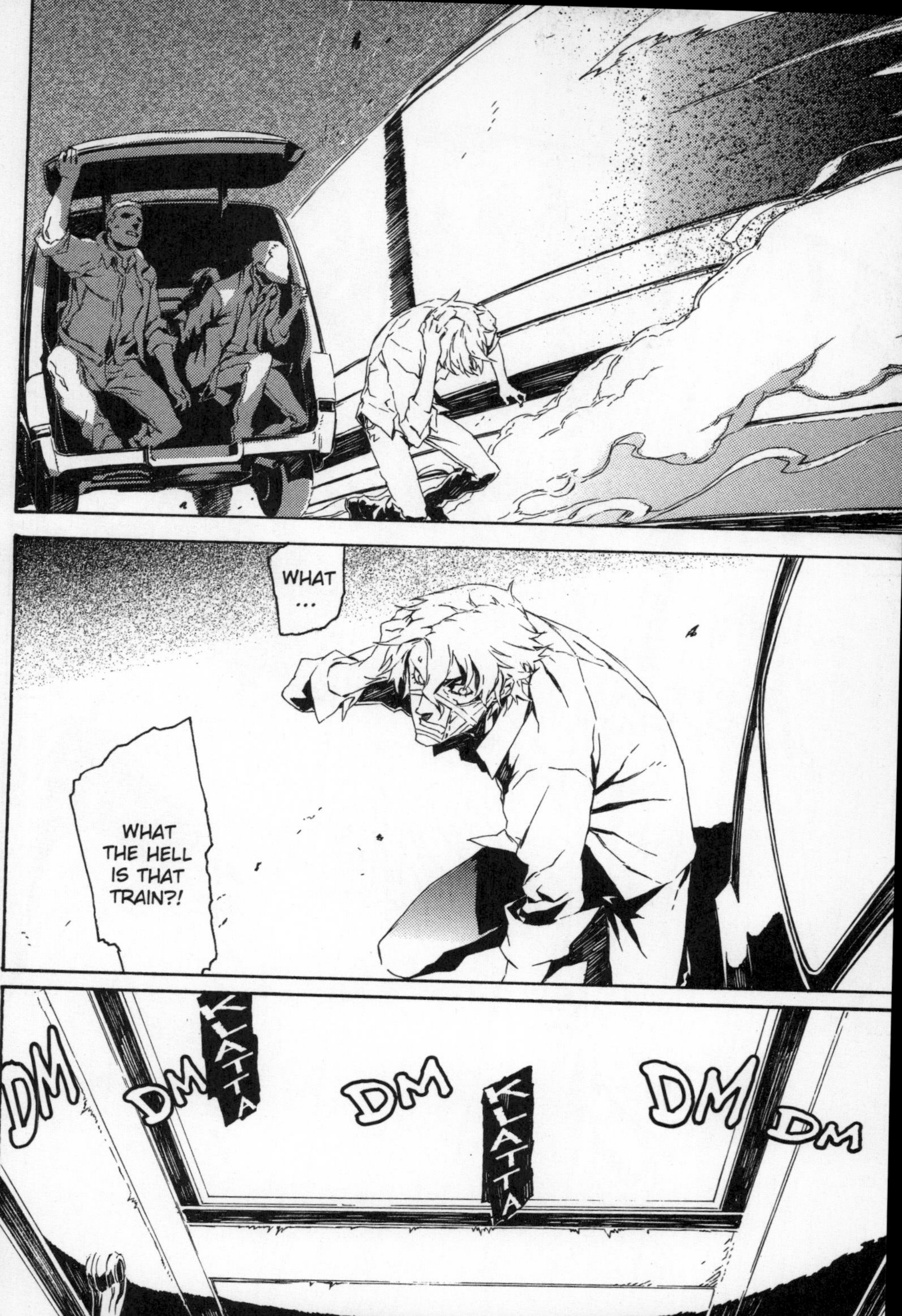
WHAT ...
WHAT THE HELL IS THAT TRAIN?!
DM DM
KLATTA
DM
KLATTA
DM
DM

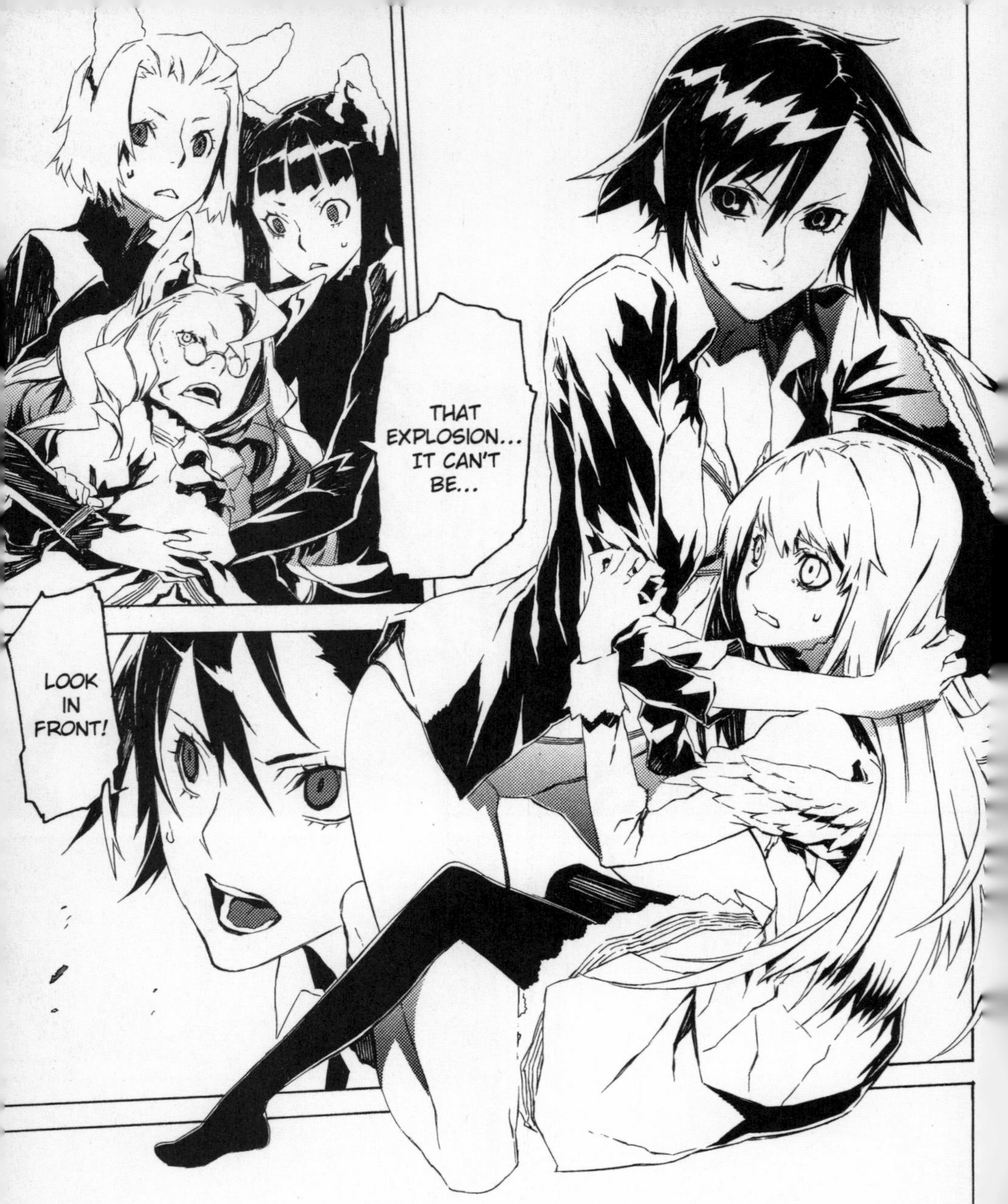
THAT EXPLOSION... IT CAN'T BE...
LOOK IN FRONT!

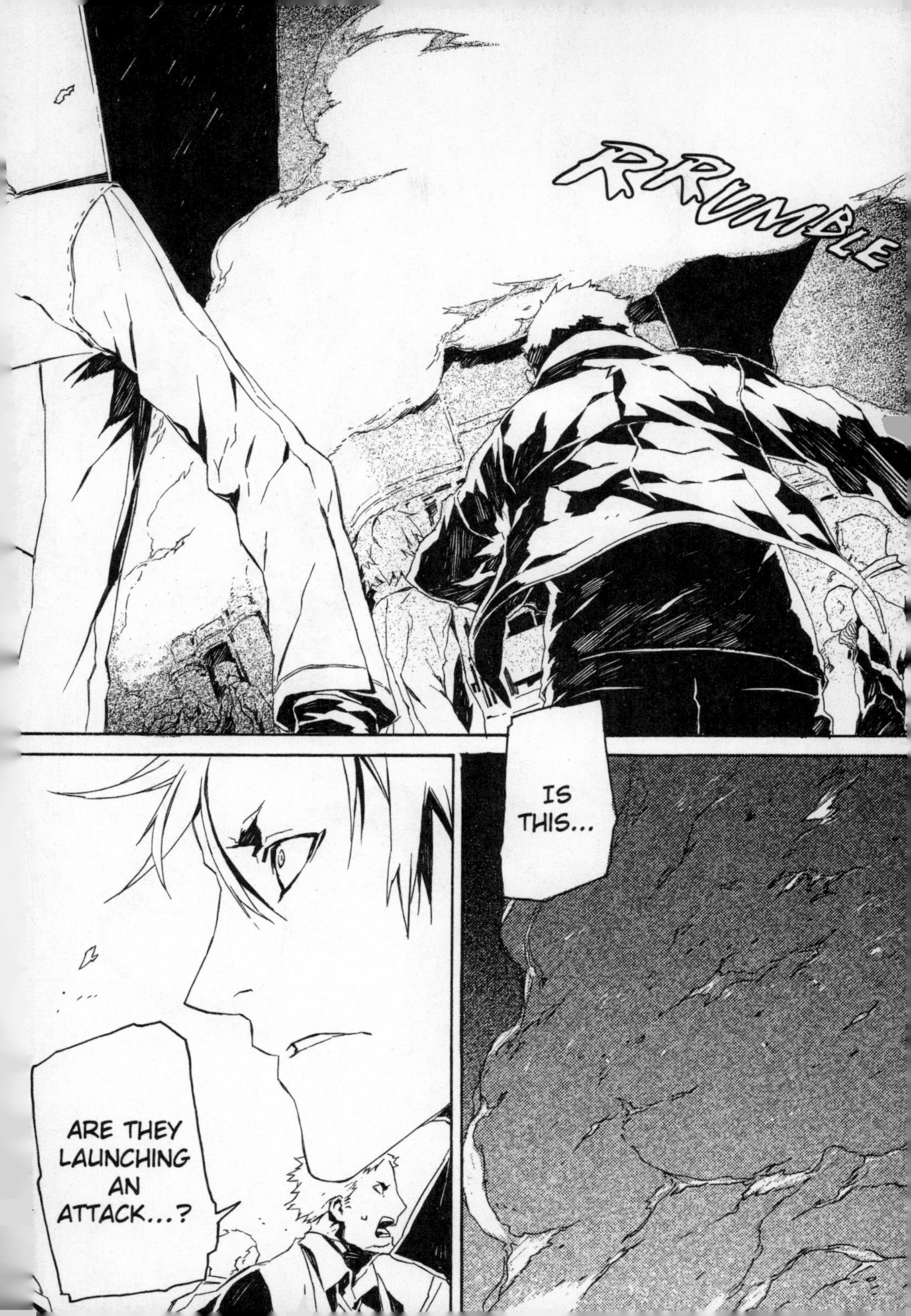
RRUMBLE
IS THIS...
ARE THEY LAUNCHING AN ATTACK...?

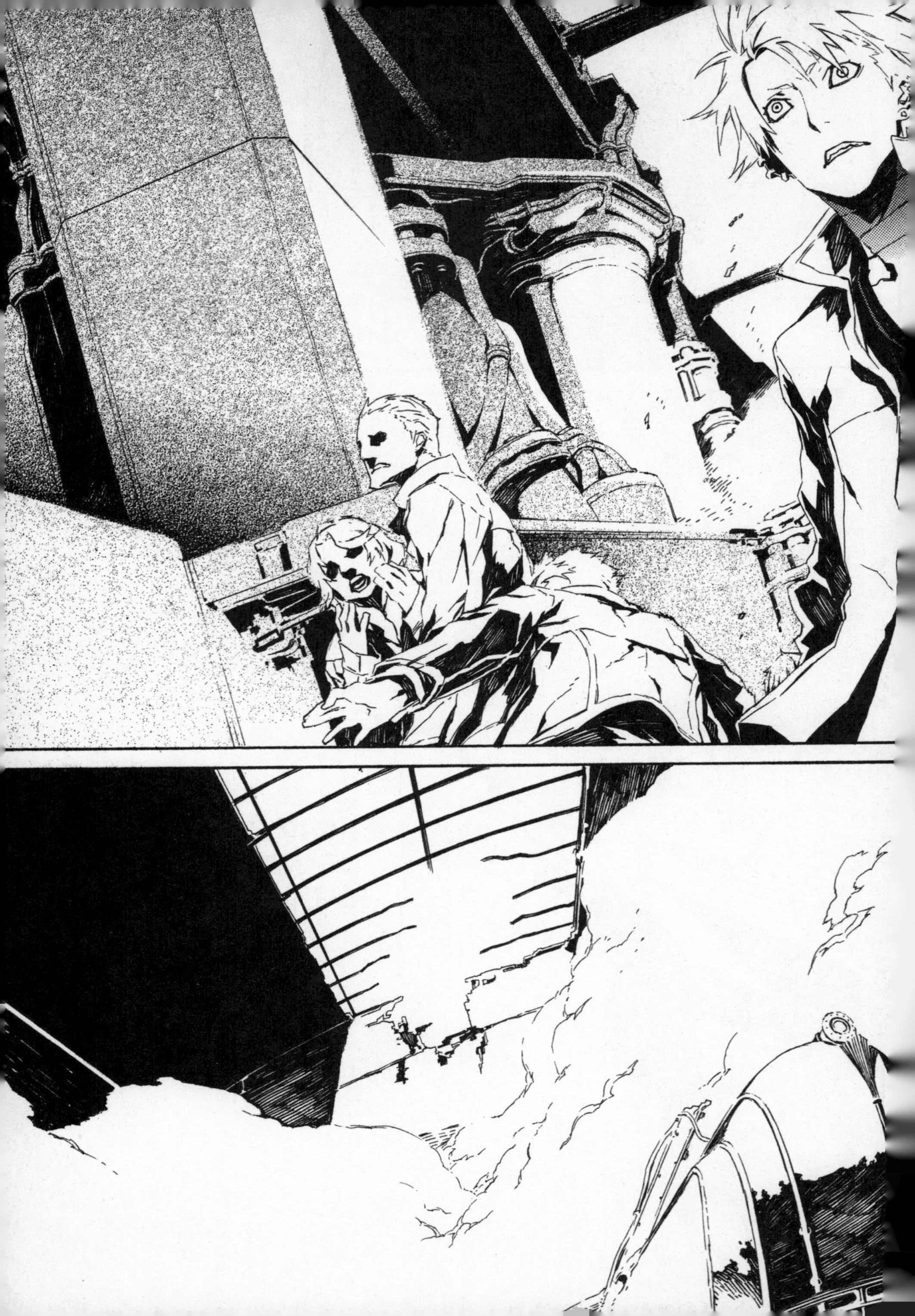

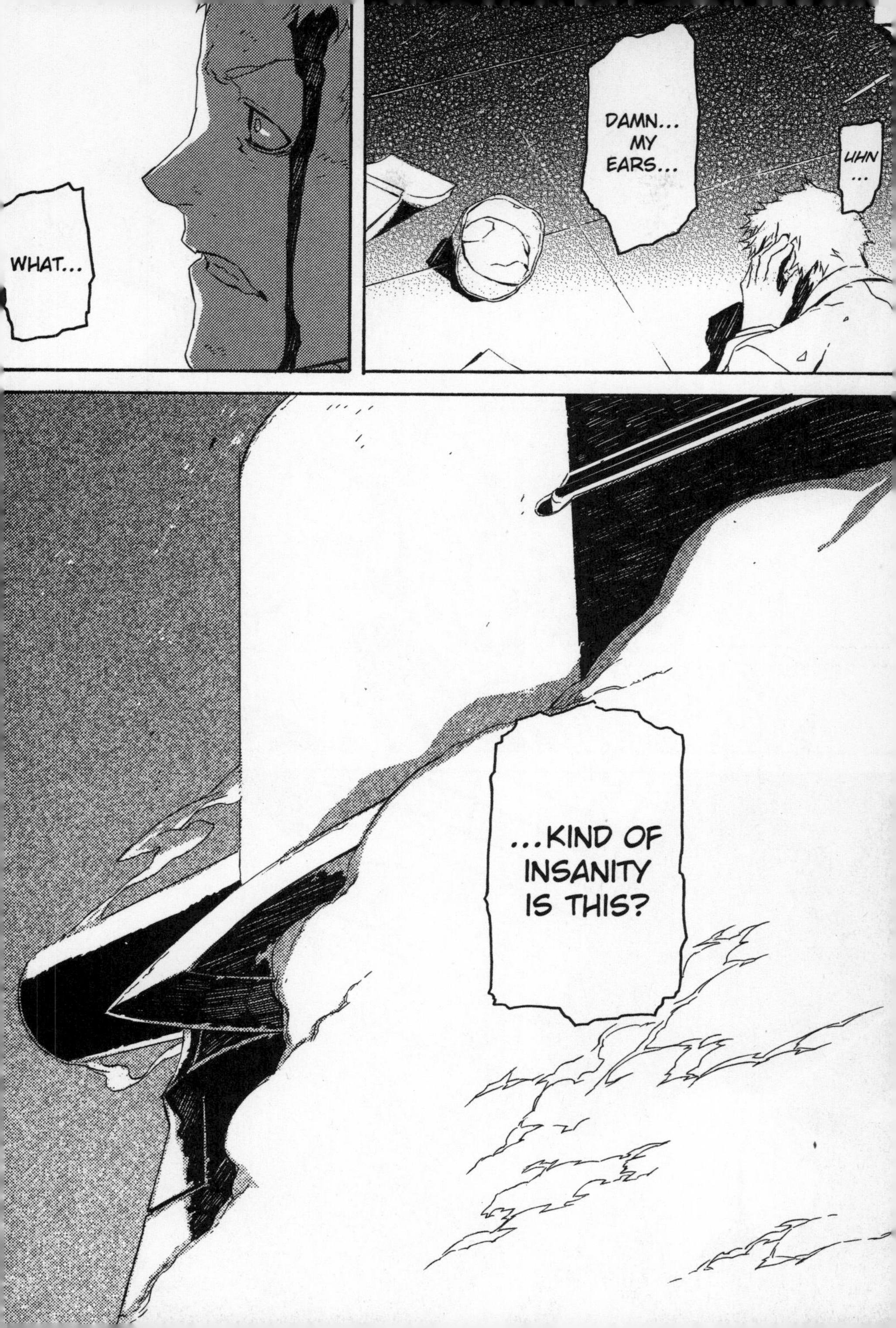
UHN...
DAMN... MY EARS...
WHAT...
...KIND OF INSANITY IS THIS?

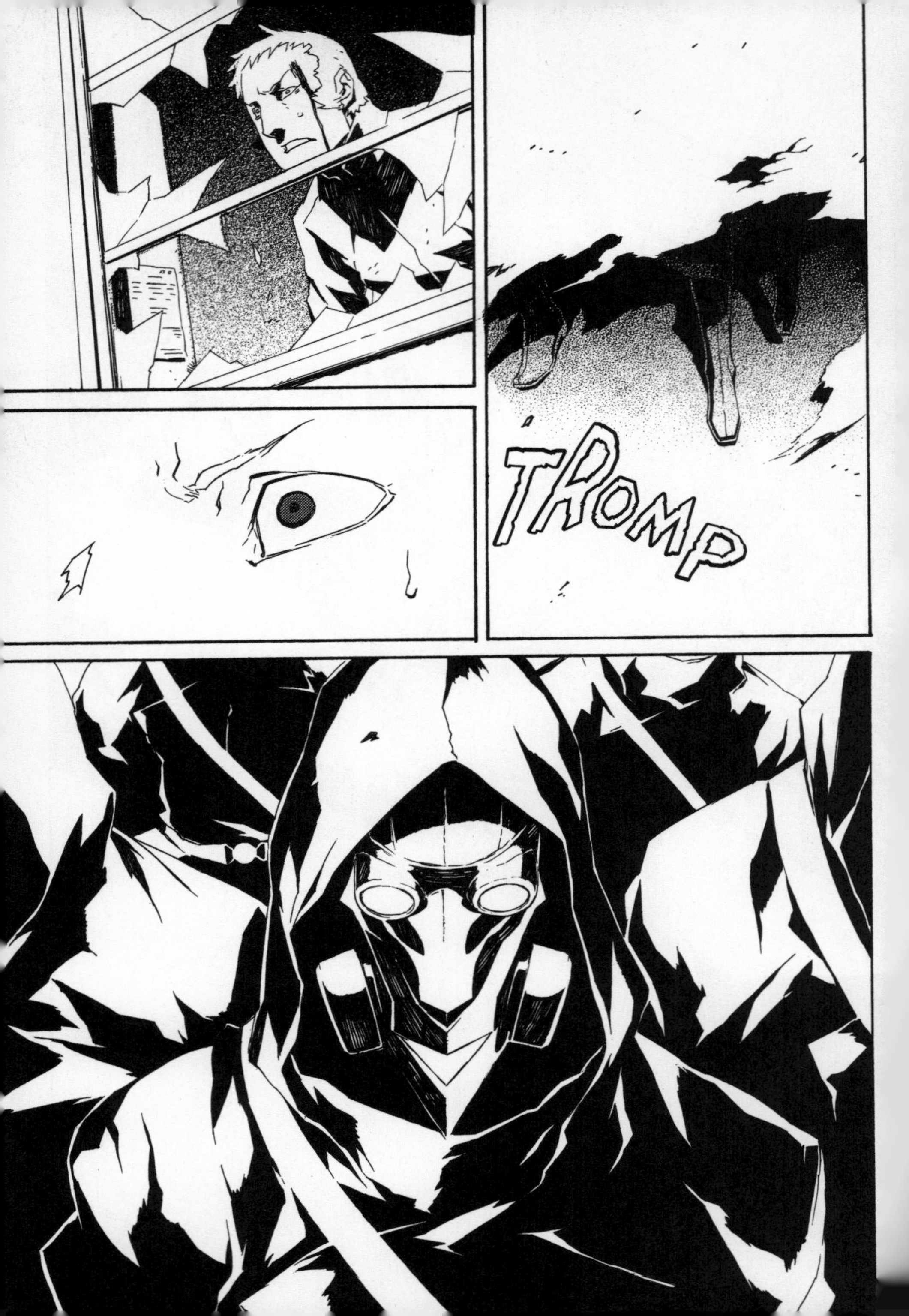
TROMP

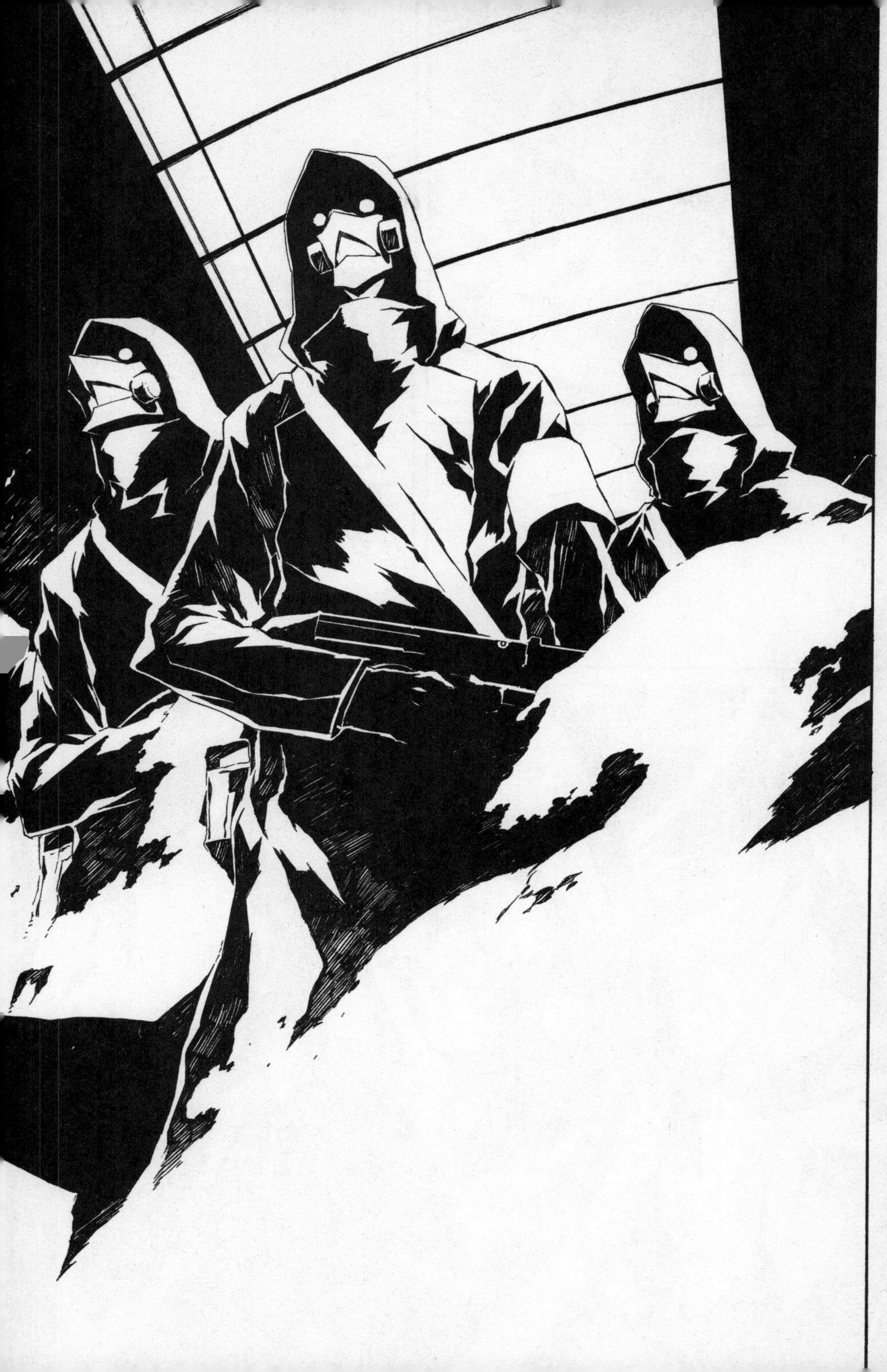

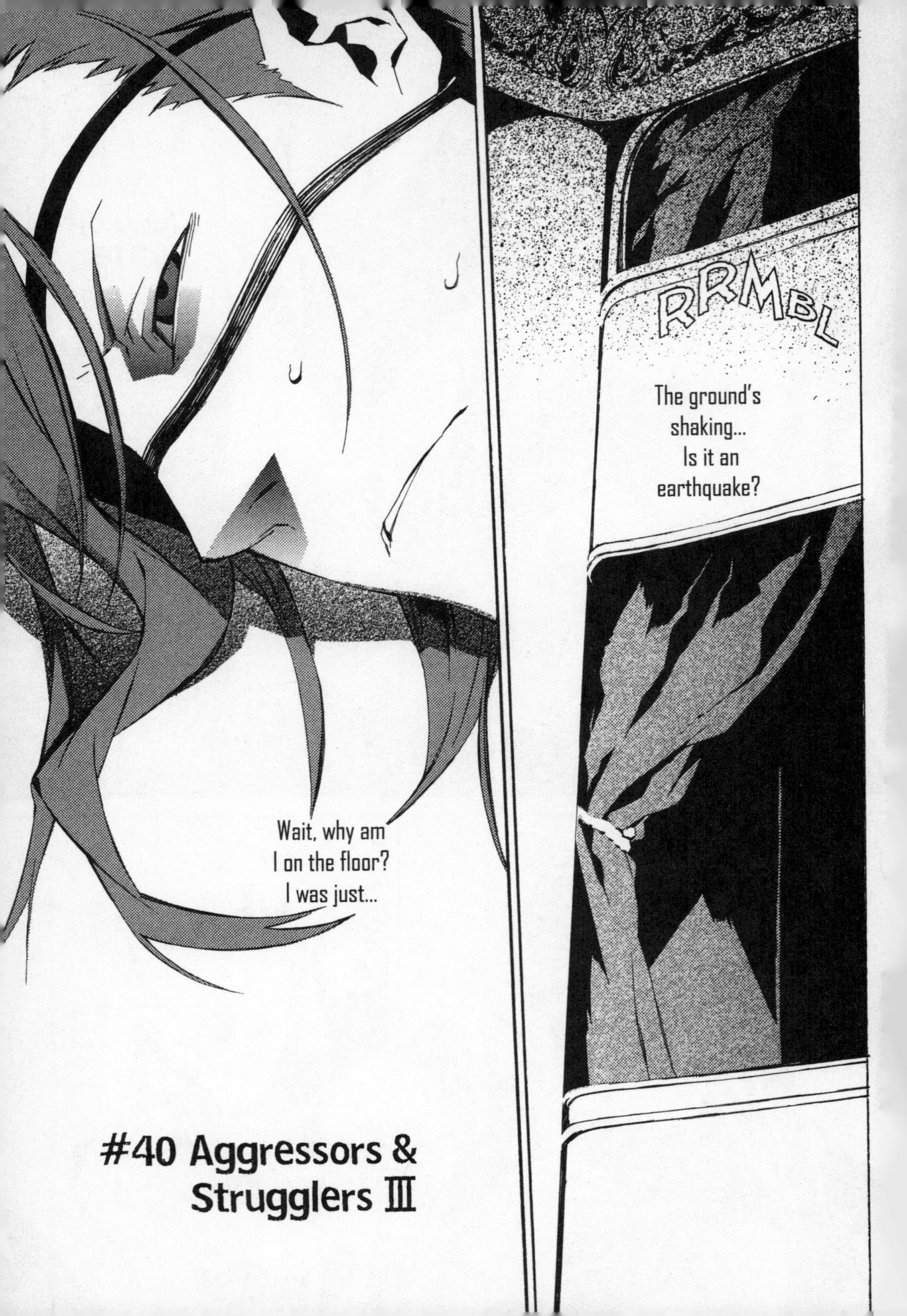
RRMBL
The ground's shaking... Is it an earthquake?
Wait, why am I on the floor? I was just...

#40 Aggressors & Strugglers Ⅲ

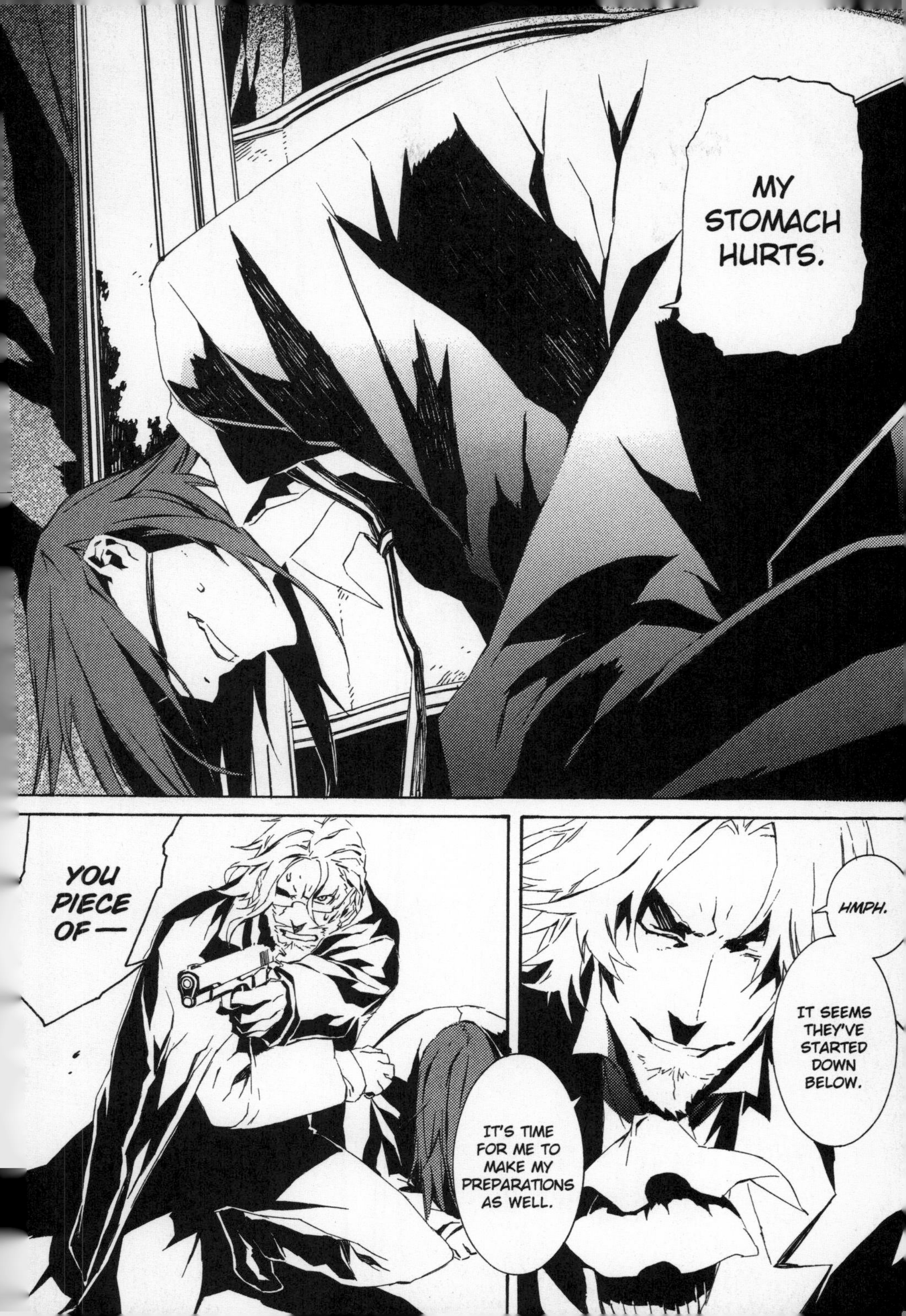
MY STOMACH HURTS.
HMPH.
IT SEEMS THEY'VE STARTED DOWN BELOW.
IT'S TIME FOR ME TO MAKE MY PREPARATIONS AS WELL.
YOU PIECE OF—

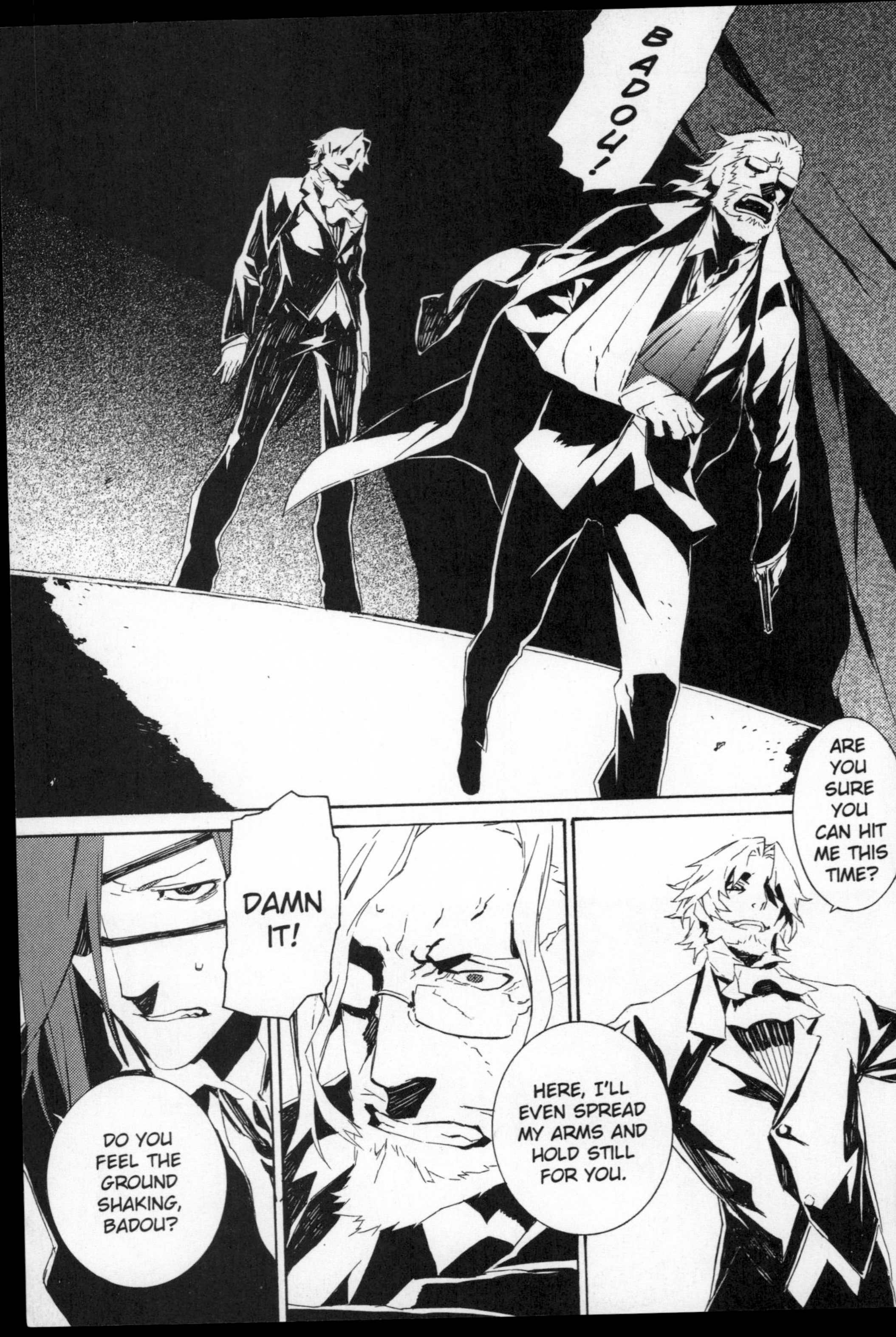
BADOU!
ARE YOU SURE YOU CAN HIT ME THIS TIME?
HERE, I'LL EVEN SPREAD MY ARMS AND HOLD STILL FOR YOU.
DAMN IT!
DO YOU FEEL THE GROUND SHAKING, BADOU?

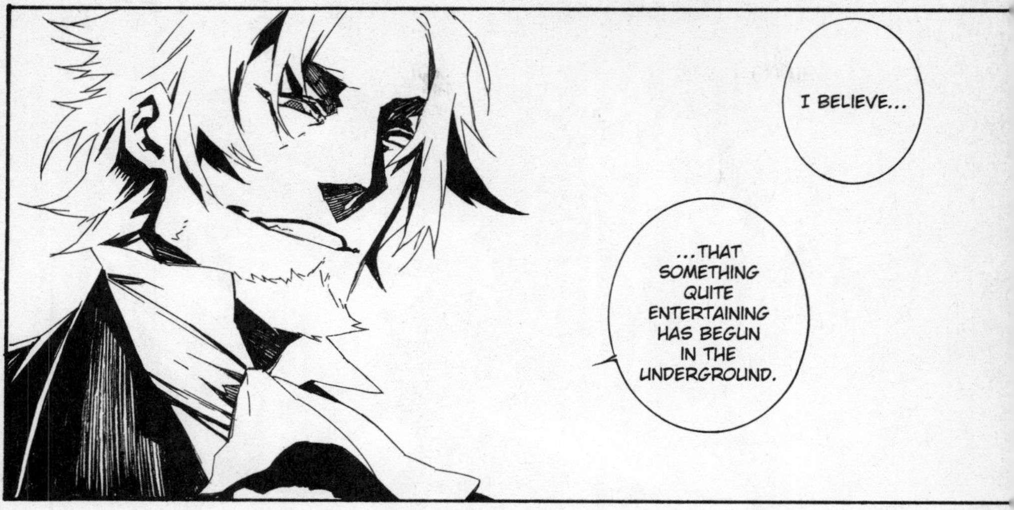
I BELIEVE...
...THAT SOMETHING QUITE ENTERTAINING HAS BEGUN IN THE UNDERGROUND.

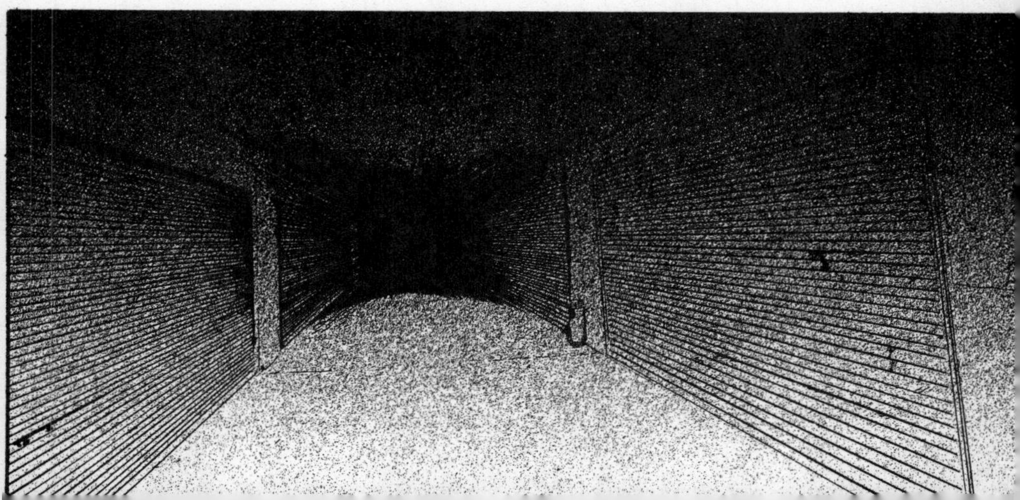

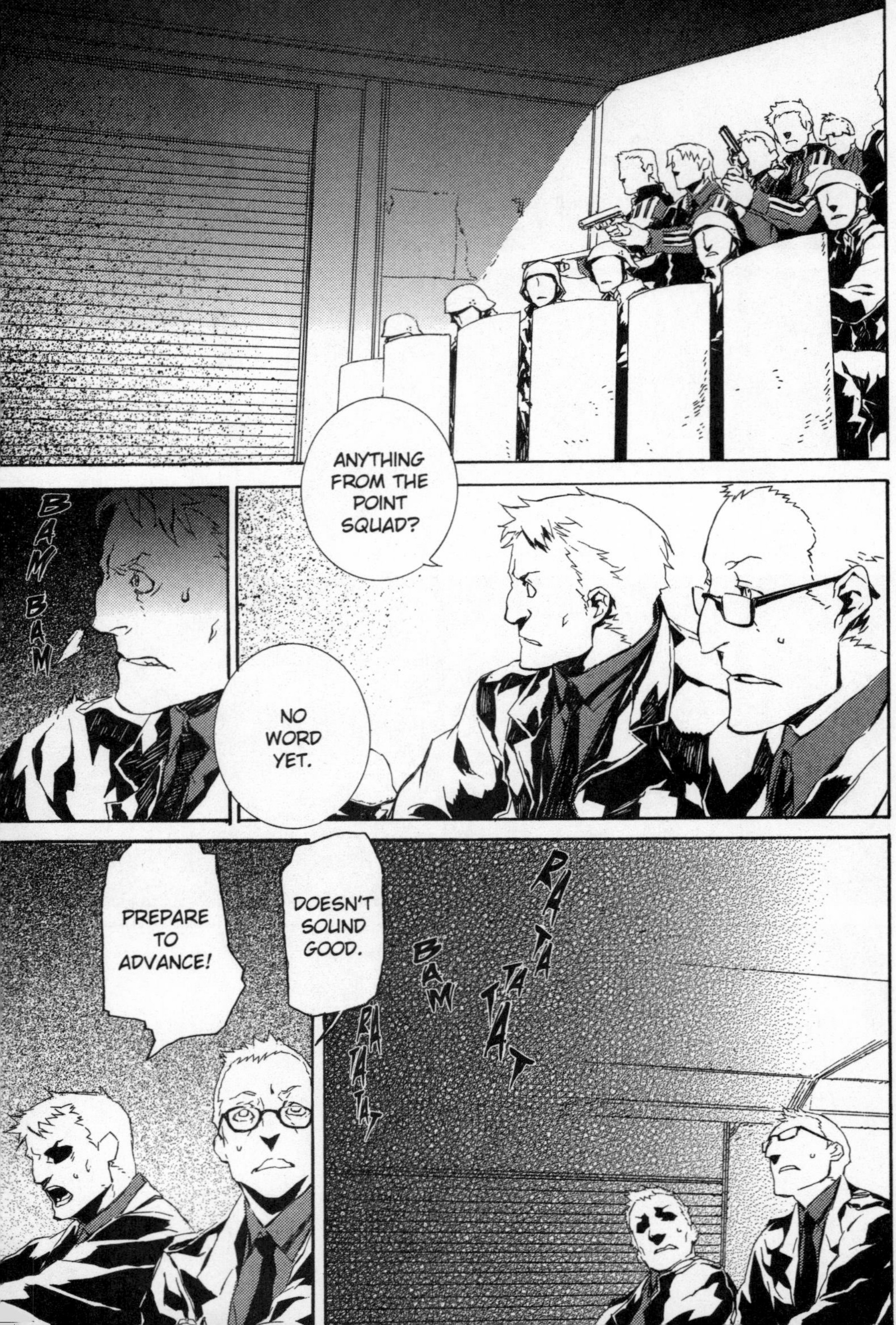
ANYTHING FROM THE POINT SQUAD?
NO WORD YET.
BAM BAM BAM
RATATATAT
BAM
RATATATAT
DOESN'T SOUND GOOD.
PREPARE TO ADVANCE!

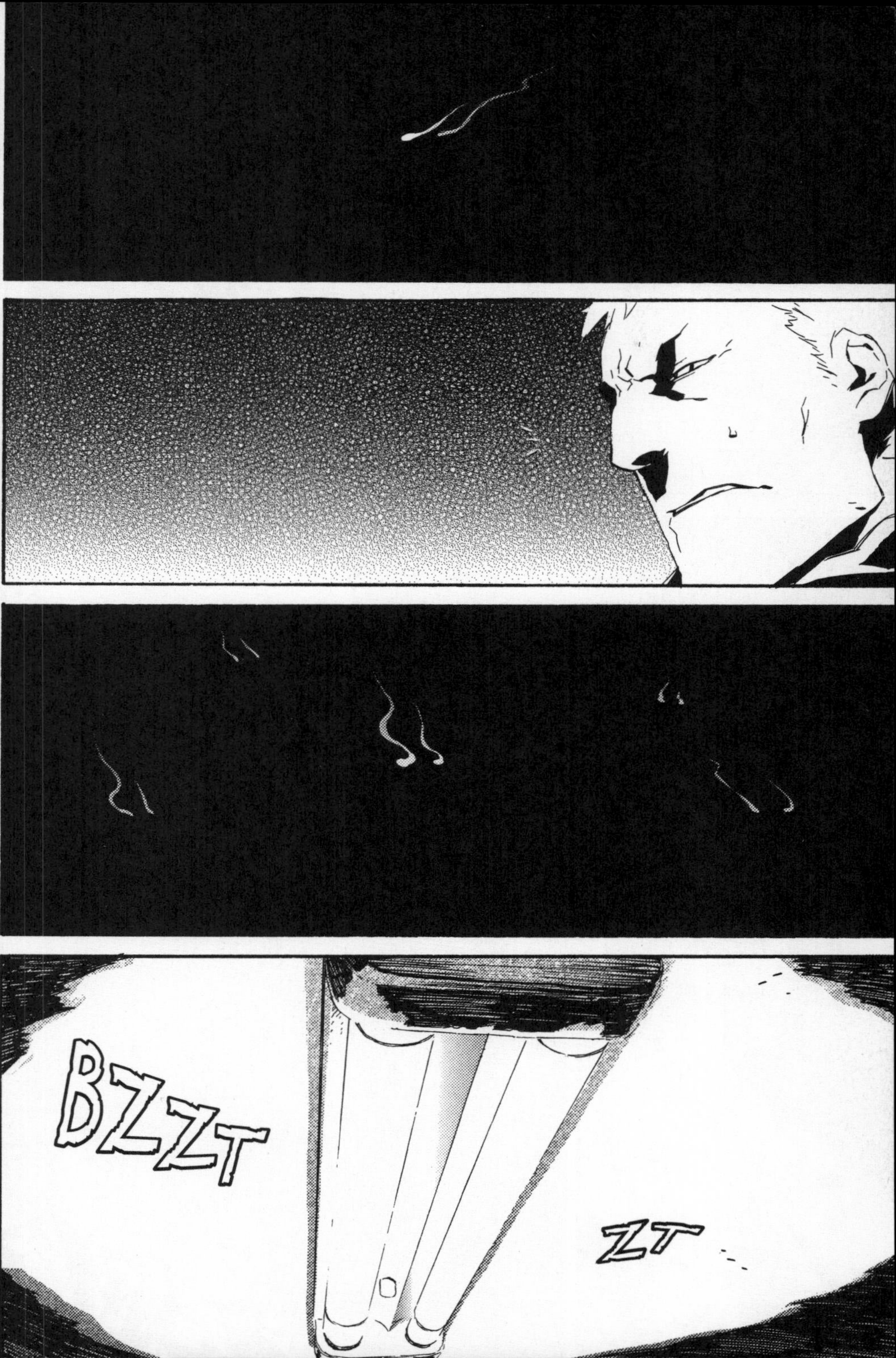
BZZZT
ZT...

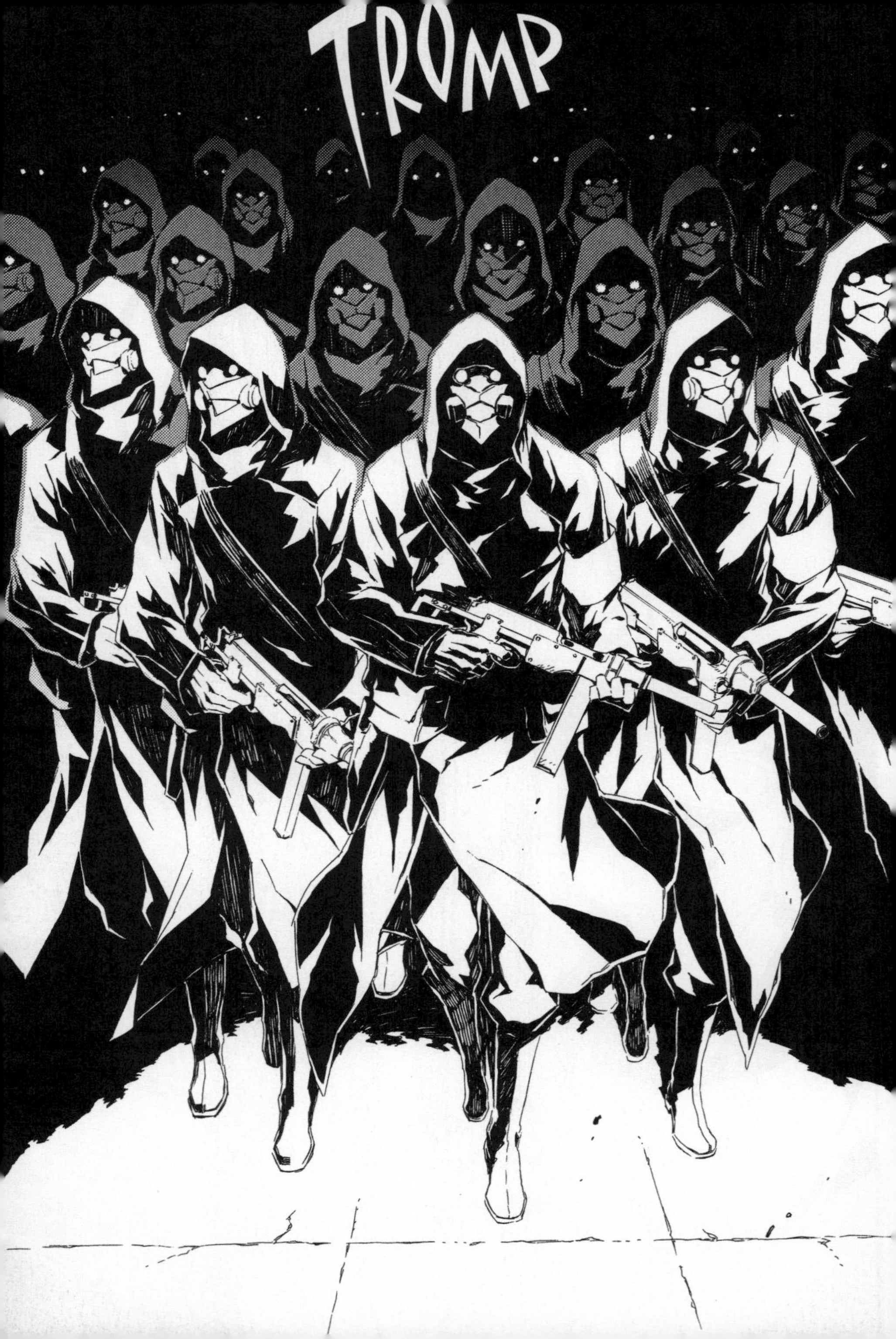
TROMP

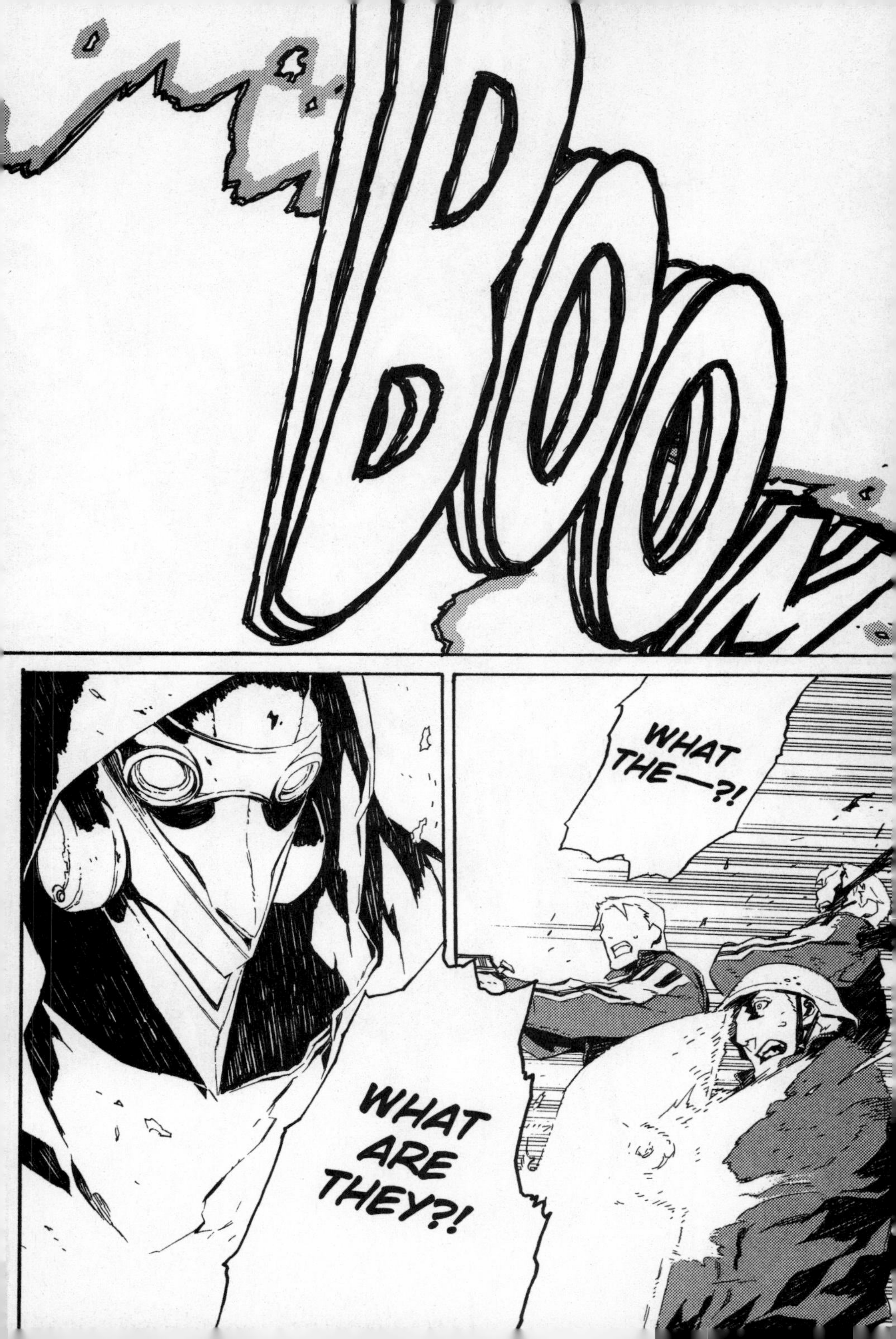
BOOOM
WHAT THE—?!
WHAT ARE THEY?!

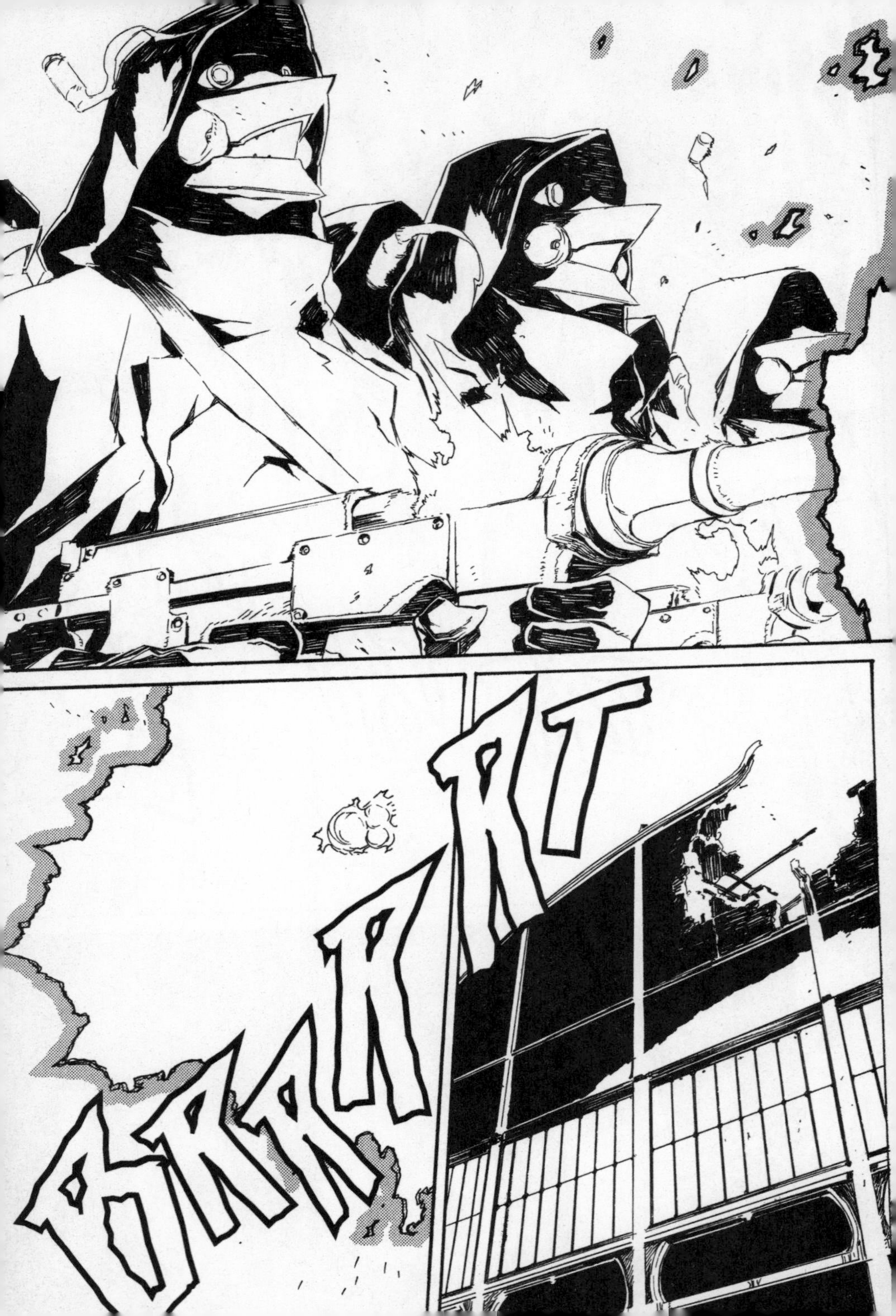
BRRRRT

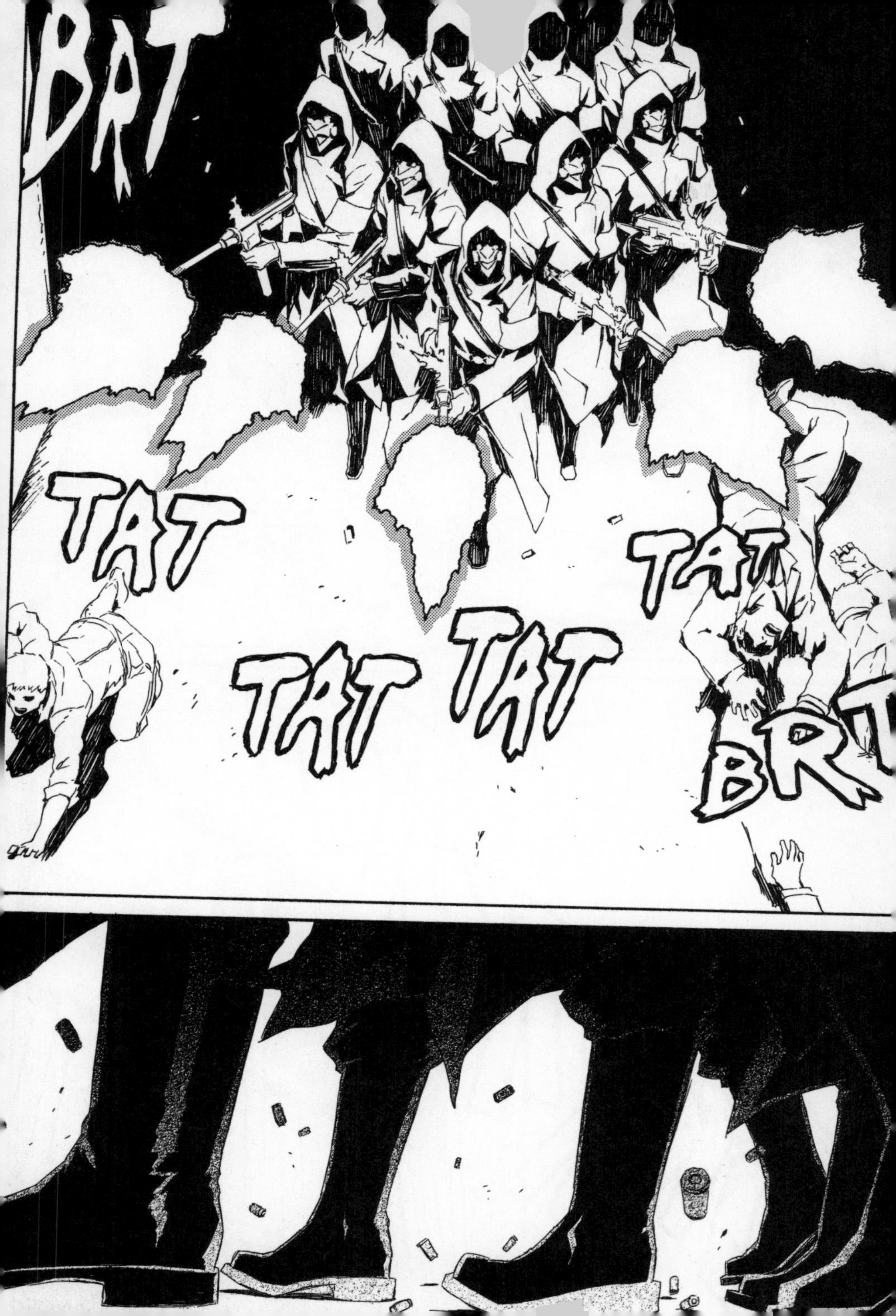
BRT
TAT
TAT
TAT
TAT
BR

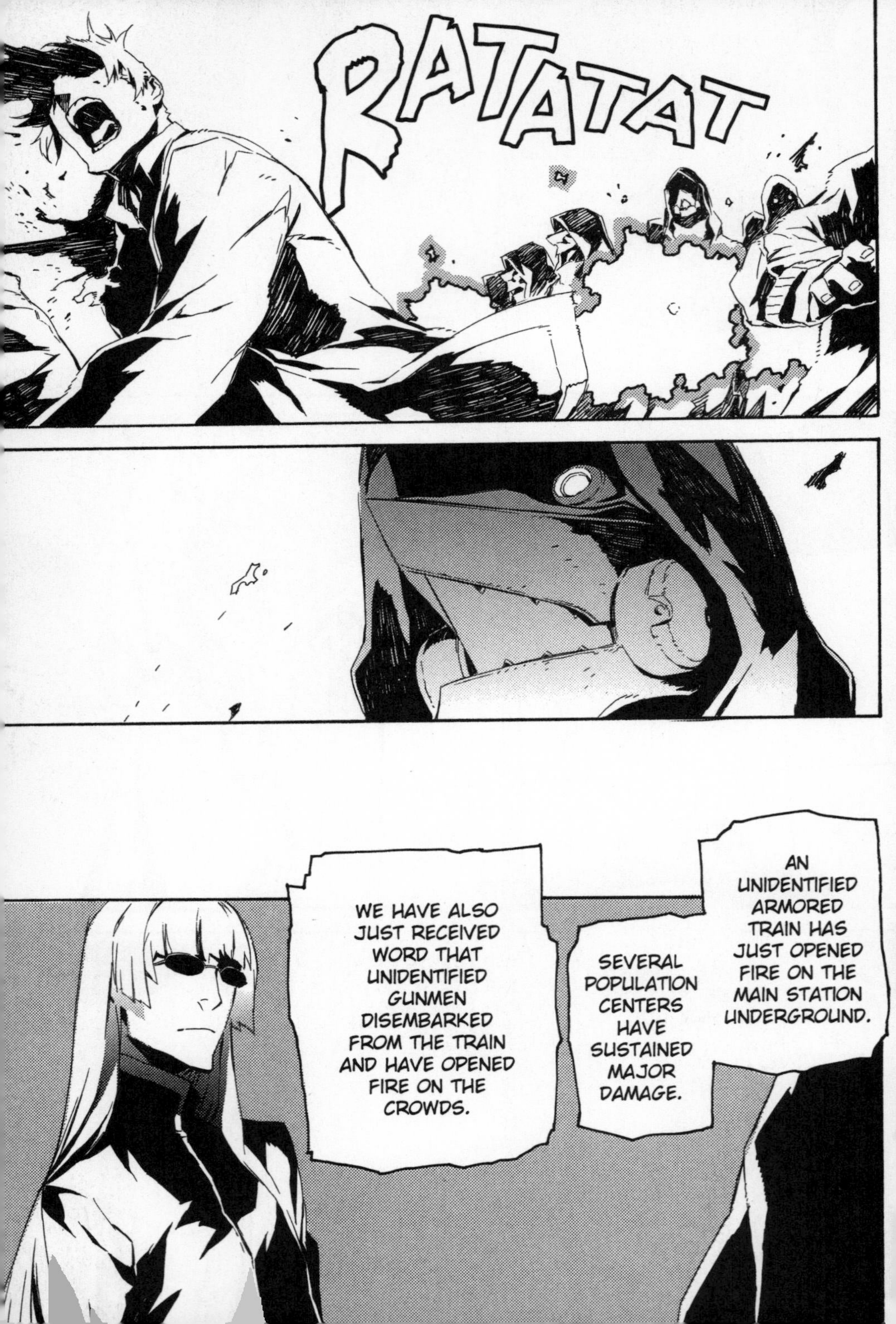
RATATAT
AN UNIDENTIFIED ARMORED TRAIN HAS JUST OPENED FIRE ON THE MAIN STATION UNDERGROUND.
SEVERAL POPULATION CENTERS HAVE SUSTAINED MAJOR DAMAGE.
WE HAVE ALSO JUST RECEIVED WORD THAT UNIDENTIFIED GUNMEN DISEMBARKED FROM THE TRAIN AND HAVE OPENED FIRE ON THE CROWDS.

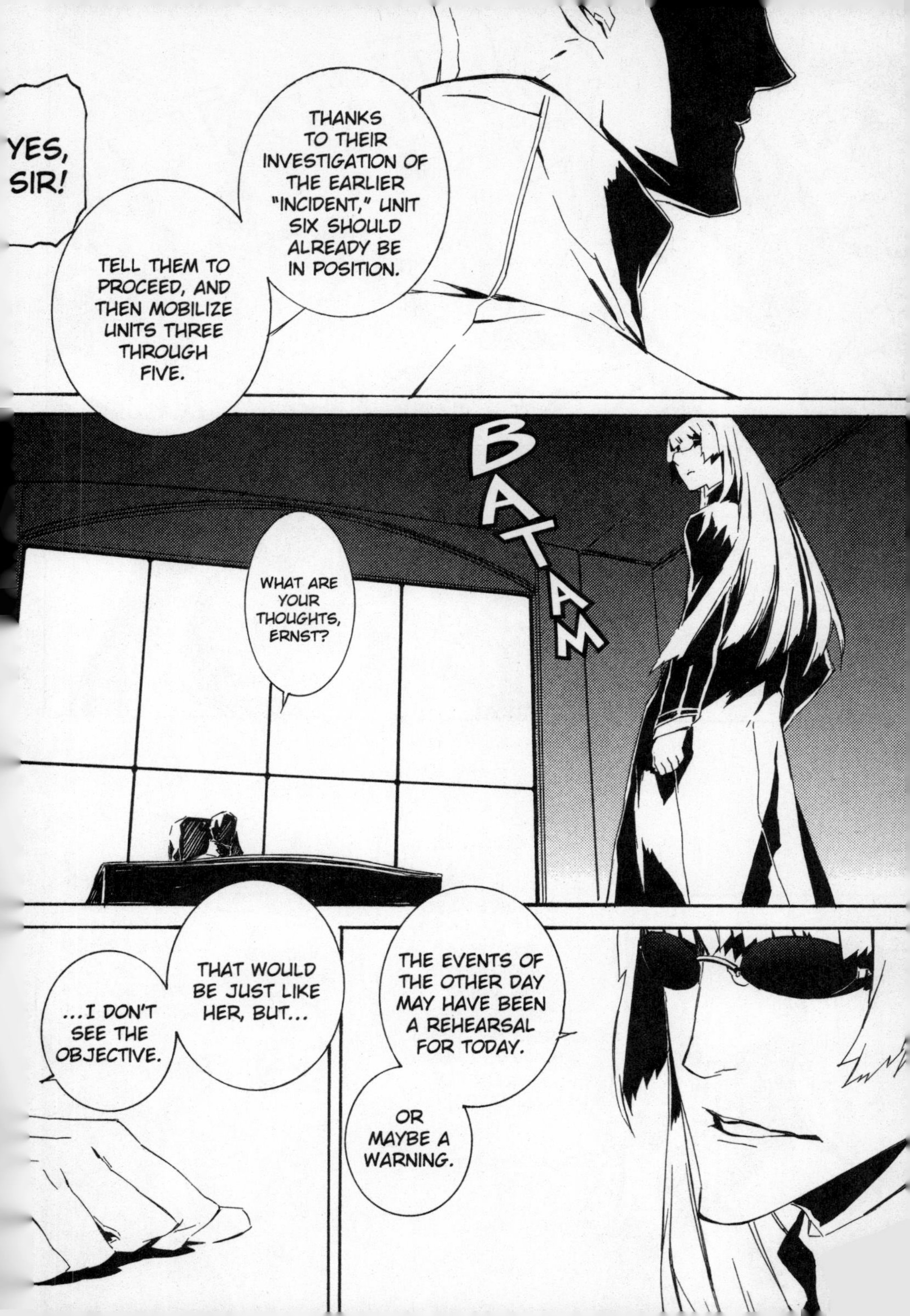
THANKS TO THEIR INVESTIGATION OF THE EARLIER "INCIDENT," UNIT SIX SHOULD ALREADY BE IN POSITION.
TELL THEM TO PROCEED, AND THEN MOBILIZE UNITS THREE THROUGH FIVE.
YES, SIR!
BATAM
WHAT ARE YOUR THOUGHTS, ERNST?
THE EVENTS OF THE OTHER DAY MAY HAVE BEEN A REHEARSAL FOR TODAY.
OR MAYBE A WARNING.
THAT WOULD BE JUST LIKE HER, BUT...
...I DON'T SEE THE OBJECTIVE.

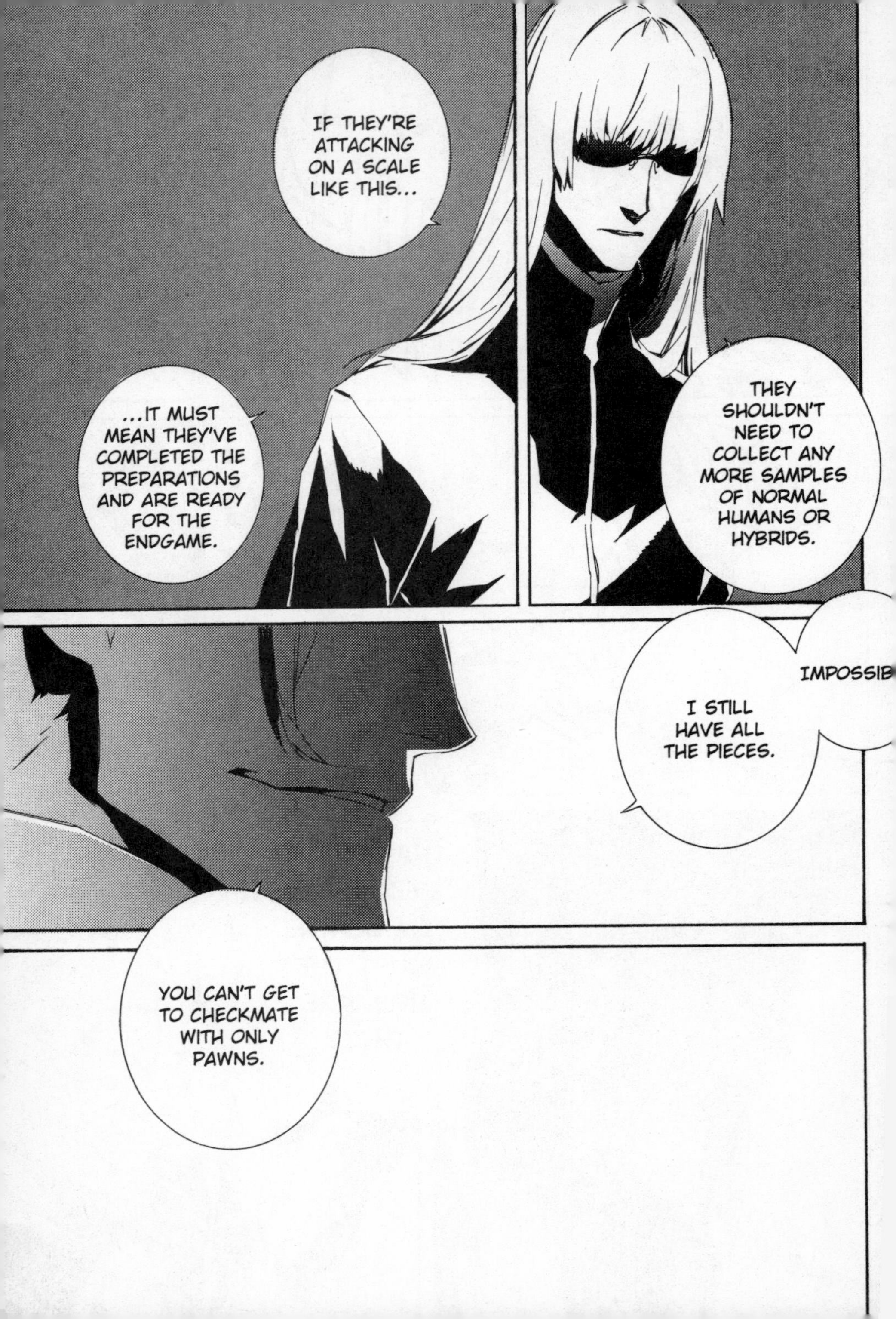
THEY SHOULDN'T NEED TO COLLECT ANY MORE SAMPLES OF NORMAL HUMANS OR HYBRIDS.
IF THEY'RE ATTACKING ON A SCALE LIKE THIS...
...IT MUST MEAN THEY'VE COMPLETED THE PREPARATIONS AND ARE READY FOR THE ENDGAME.
IMPOSSIB
I STILL HAVE ALL THE PIECES.
YOU CAN'T GET TO CHECKMATE WITH ONLY PAWNS.

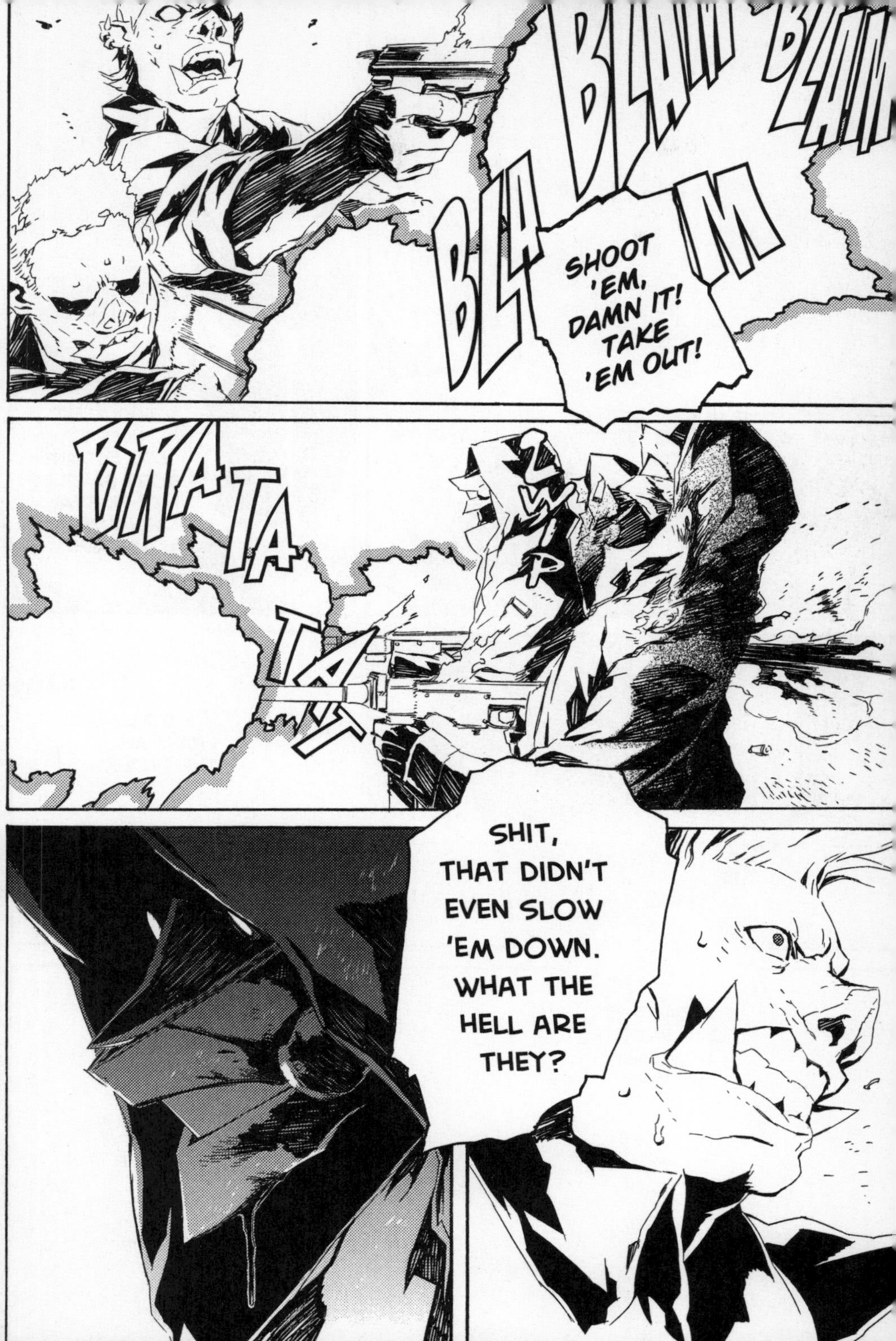
BLAM
BLAM
BLA M
SHOOT 'EM, DAMN IT! TAKE 'EM OUT!
ZWIP
BRATATAT
SHIT, THAT DIDN'T EVEN SLOW 'EM DOWN. WHAT THE HELL ARE THEY?

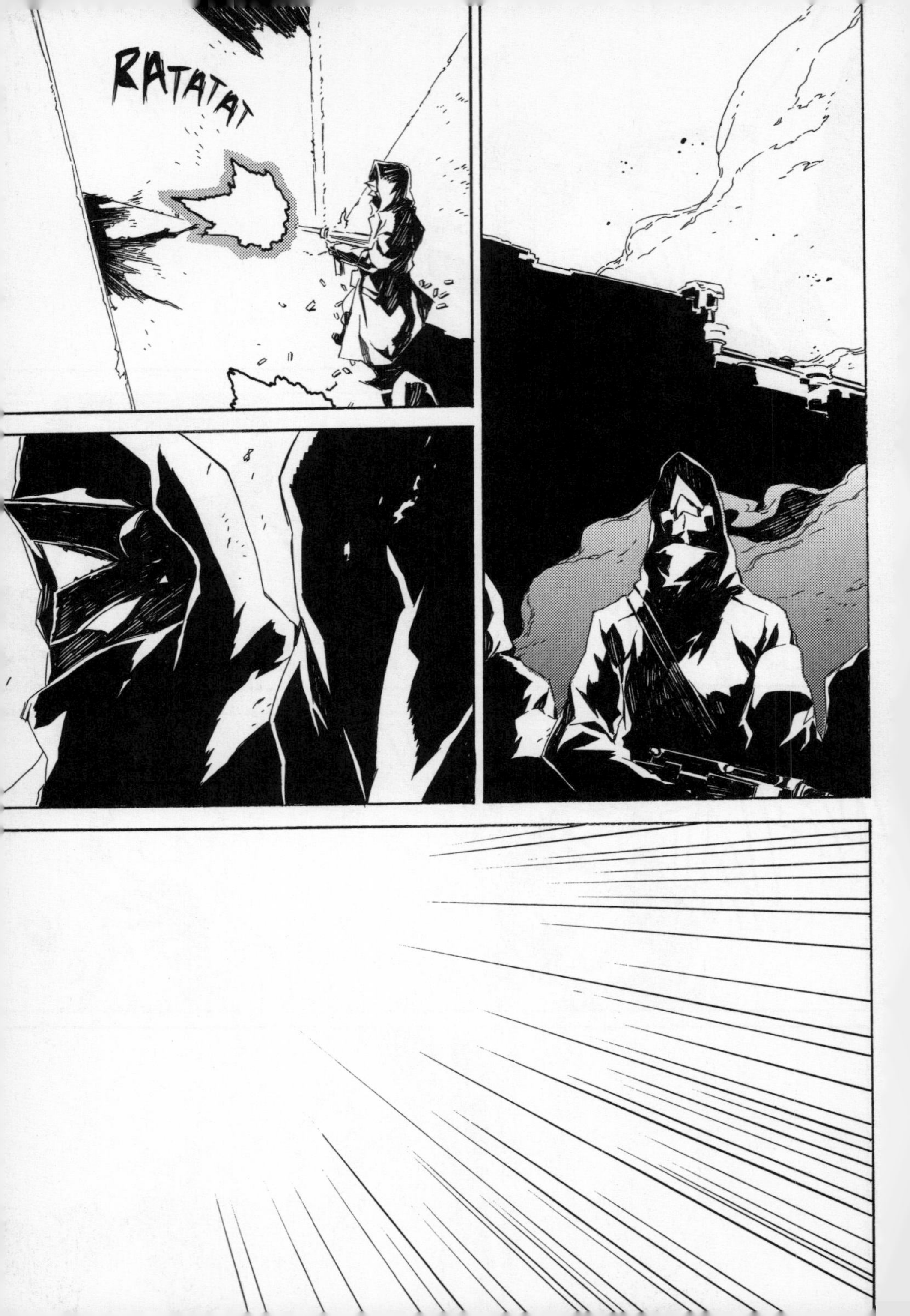
RATATAT

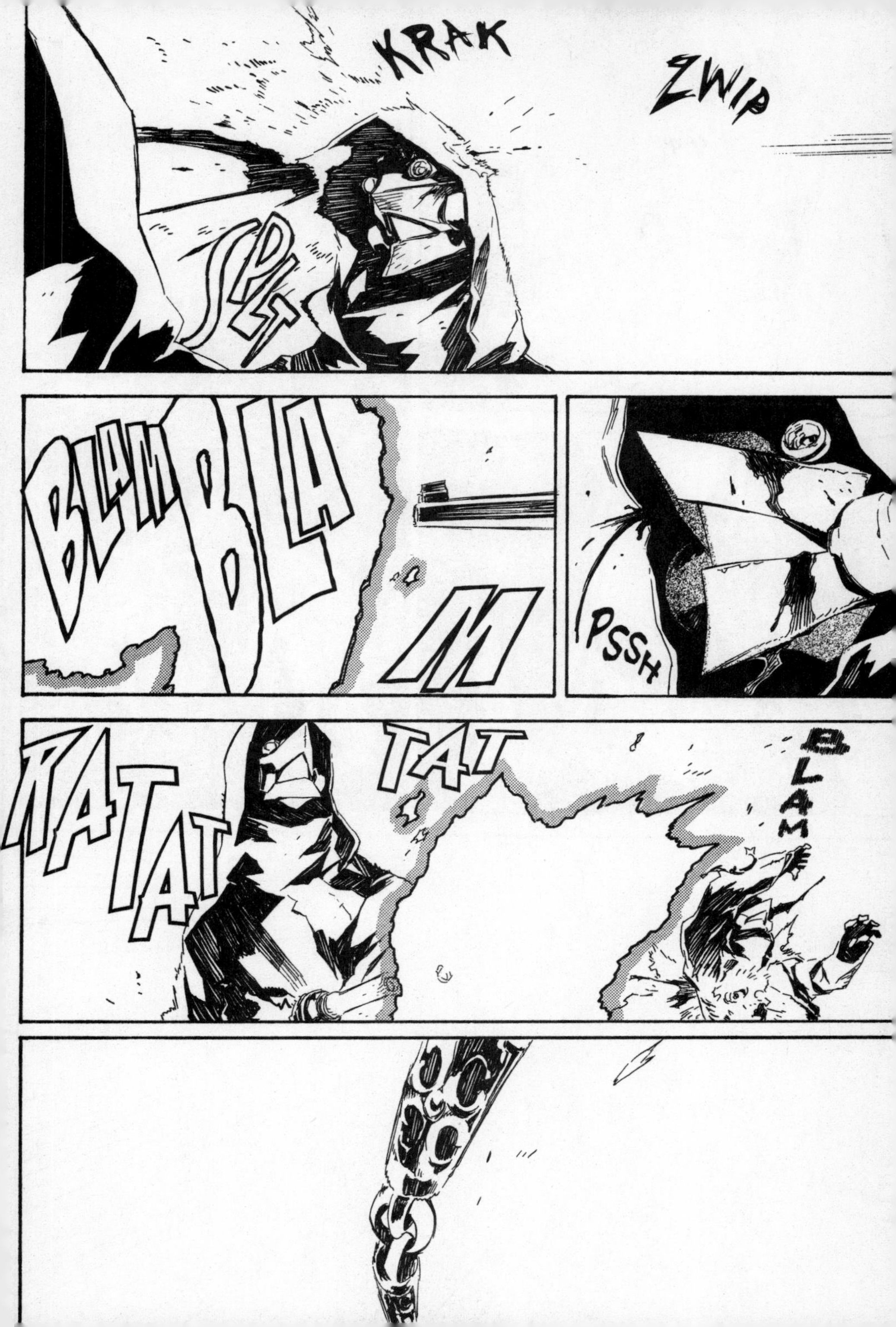
ZWIP
KRAK
SPLT
PSSH
BLAM
BLAM
BLAM
TAT
RATATAT

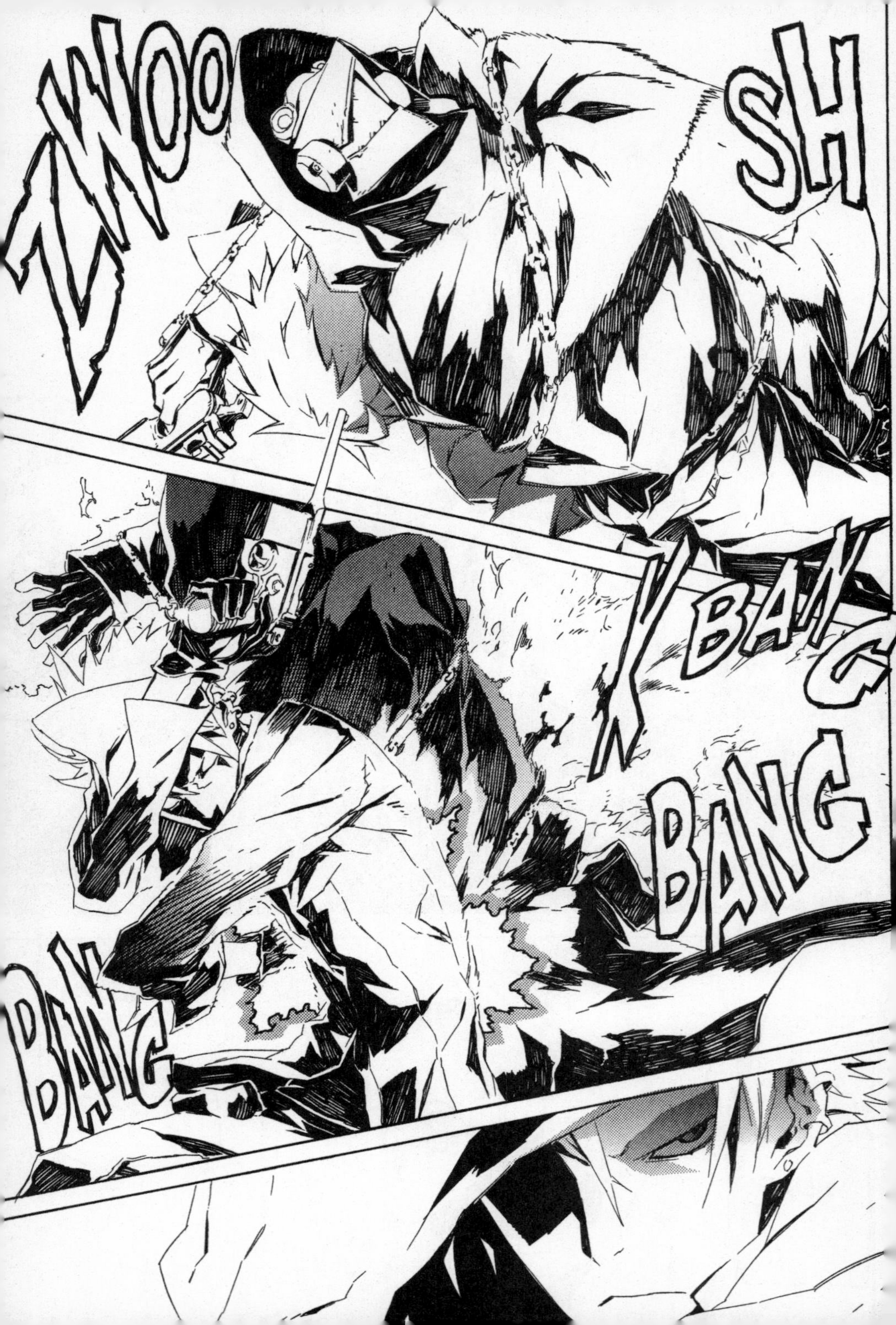
ZWOOSH
BANG
BANG
BANG

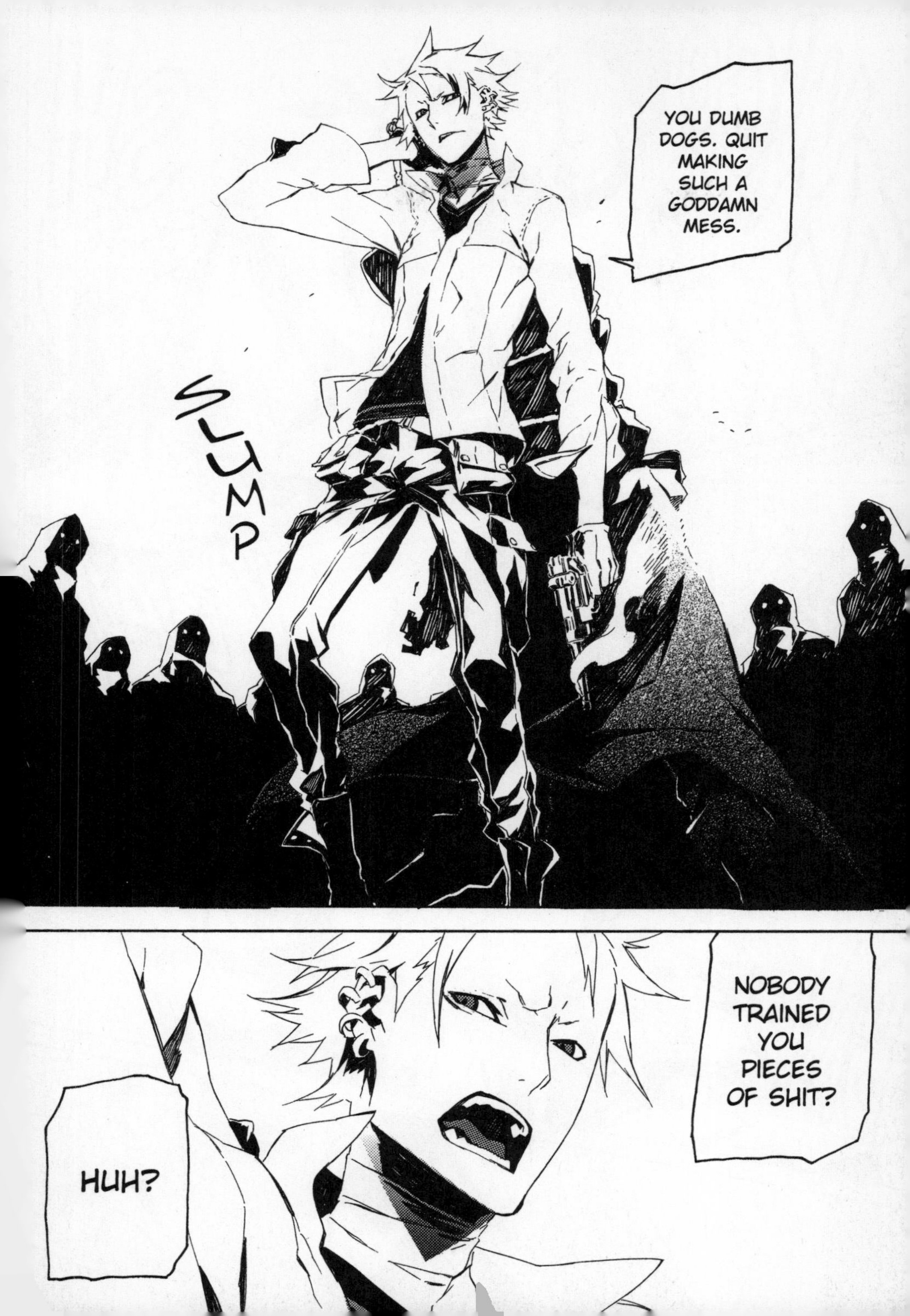
YOU DUMB DOGS. QUIT MAKING SUCH A GODDAMN MESS.
SLUMP
NOBODY TRAINED YOU PIECES OF SHIT?
HUH?

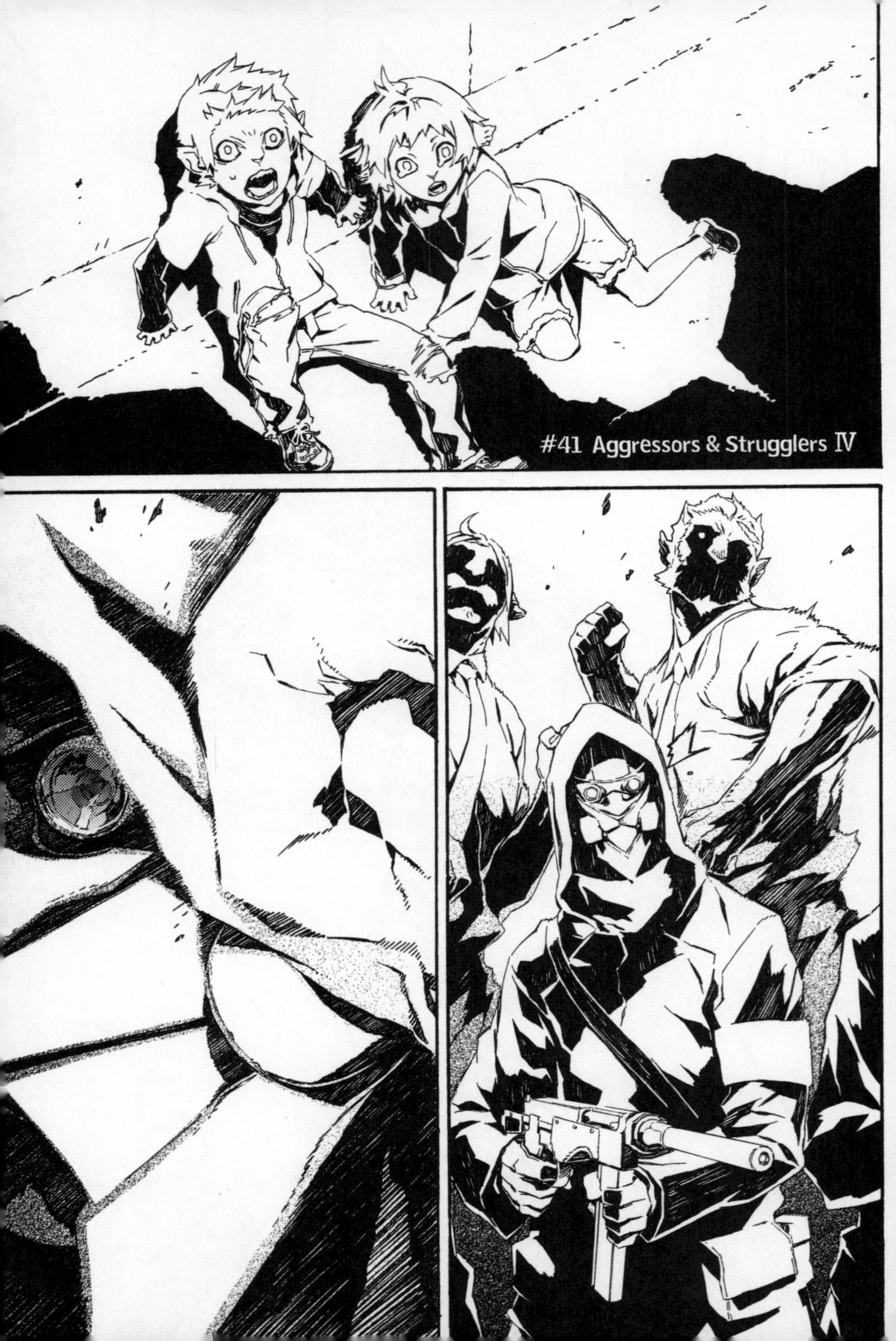
#41 Aggressors & Strugglers IV

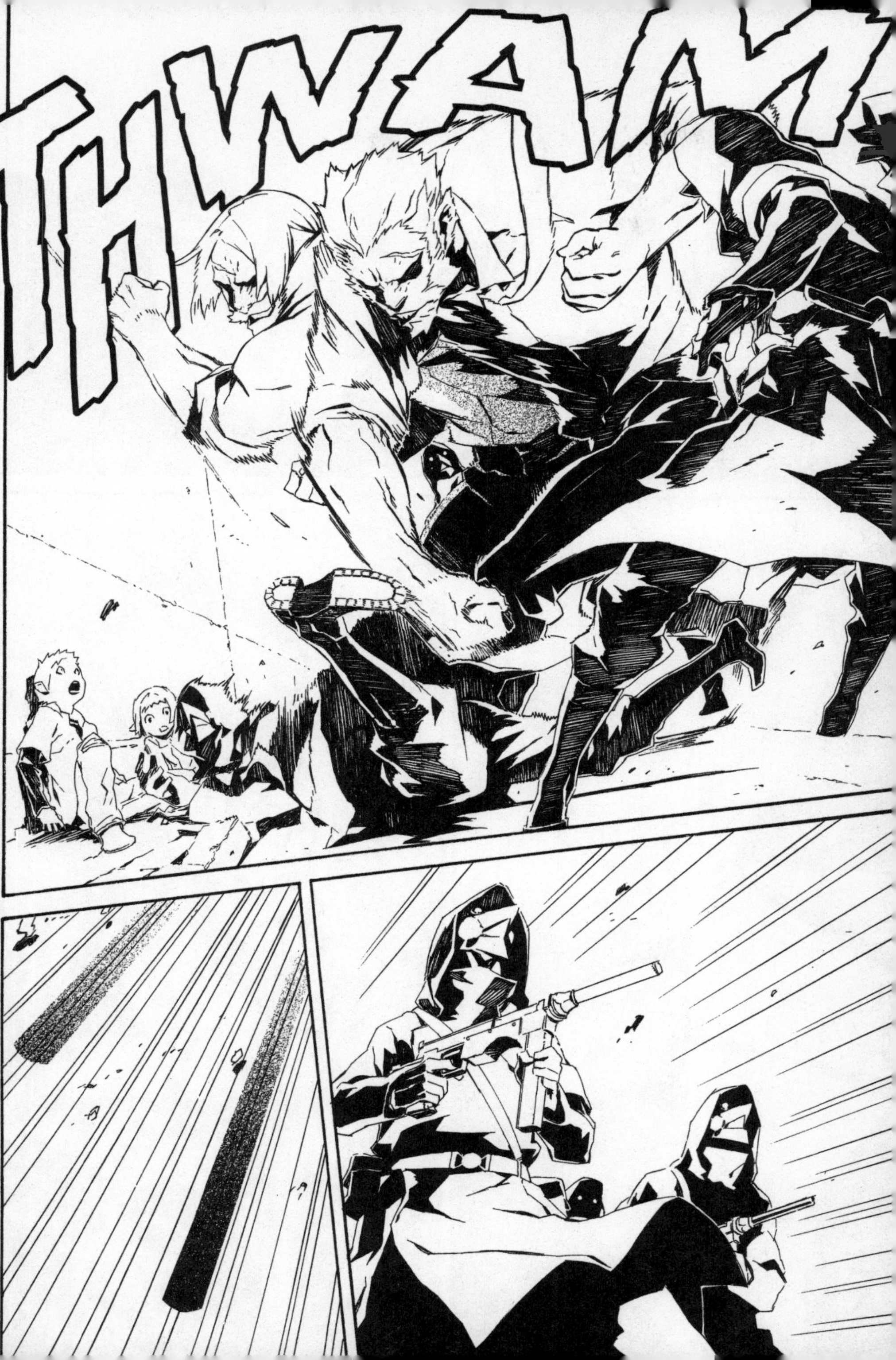
THWAM

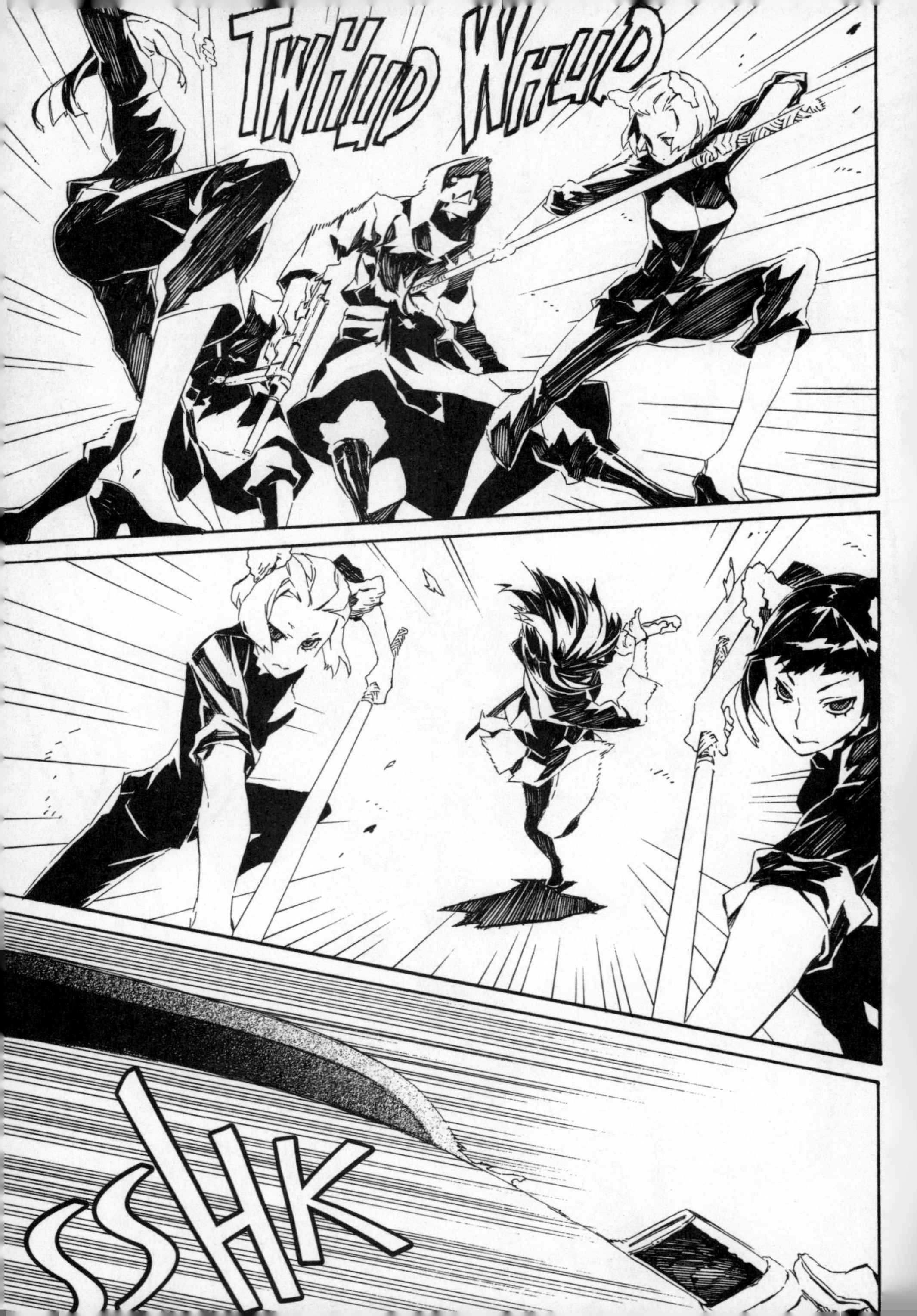
TWHUD WHUD
SSHK

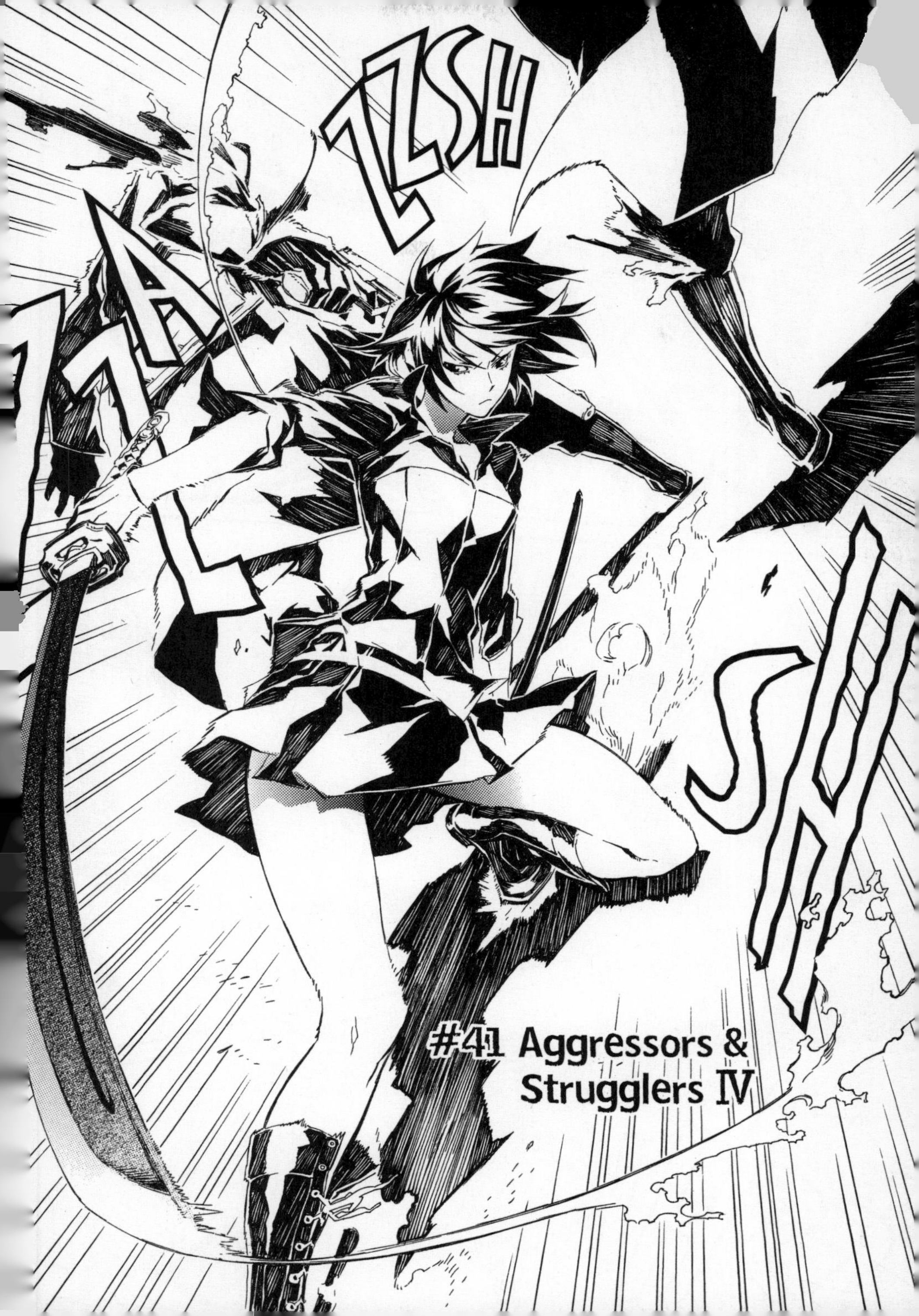
ZZSH
ZA
SH
#41 Aggressors & Strugglers IV

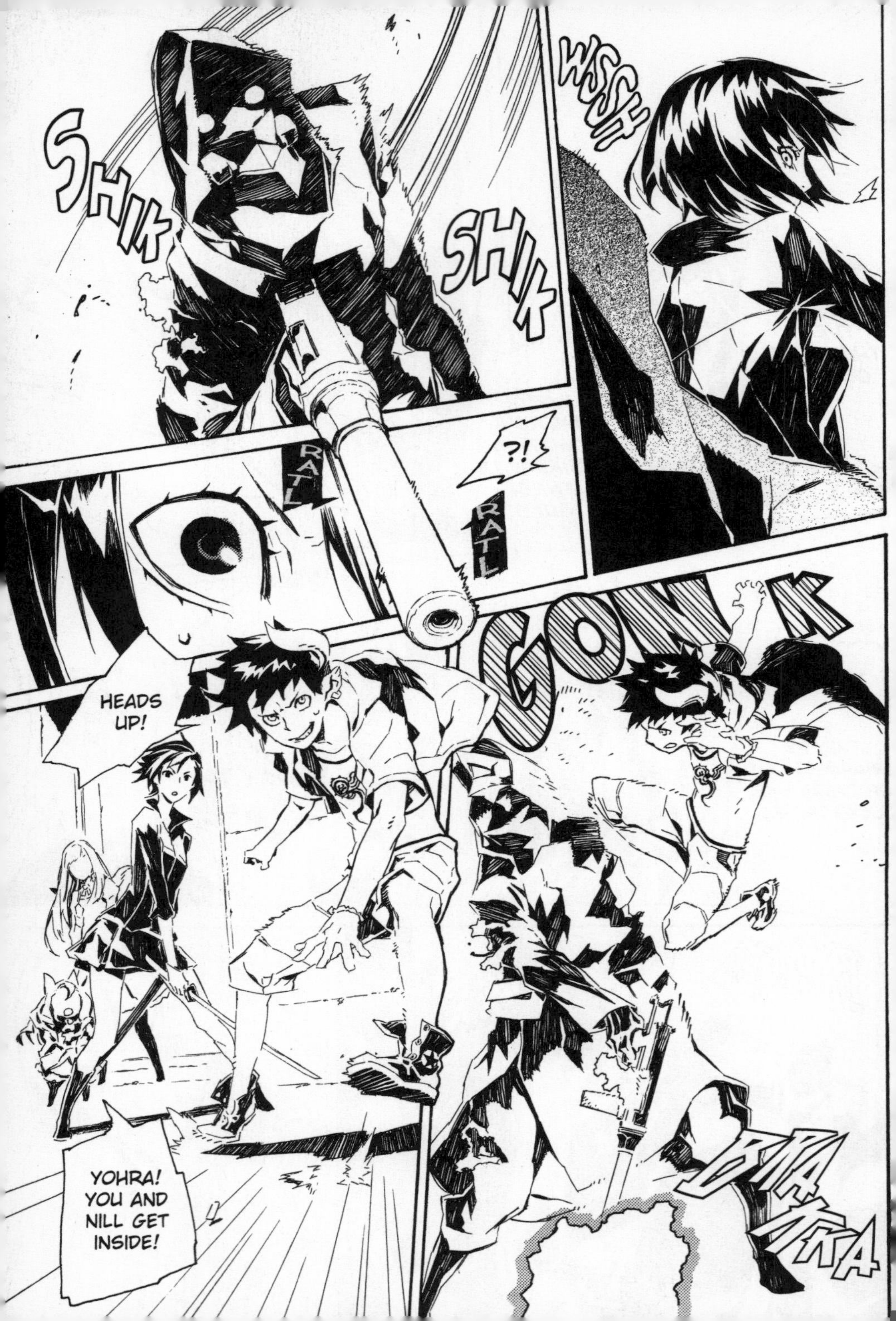
WSSH
SHIK
SHIK
?!
RATL
RATL
GONK
HEADS UP!
YOHRA! YOU AND NILL GET INSIDE!
BRATAKA

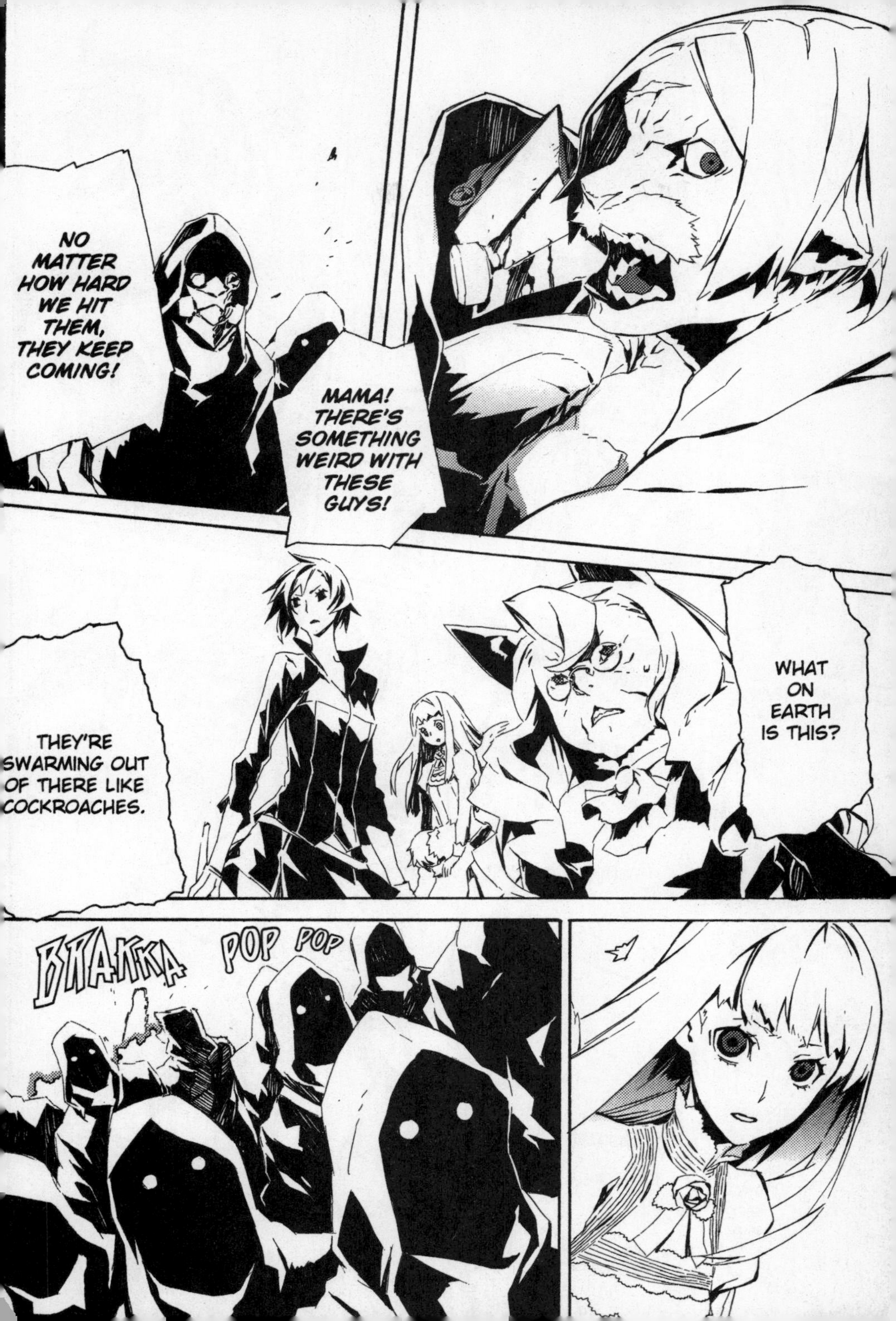
MAMA! THERE'S SOMETHING WEIRD WITH THESE GUYS!
NO MATTER HOW HARD WE HIT THEM, THEY KEEP COMING!
WHAT ON EARTH IS THIS?
THEY'RE SWARMING OUT OF THERE LIKE COCKROACHES.
BRAKKA
POP POP

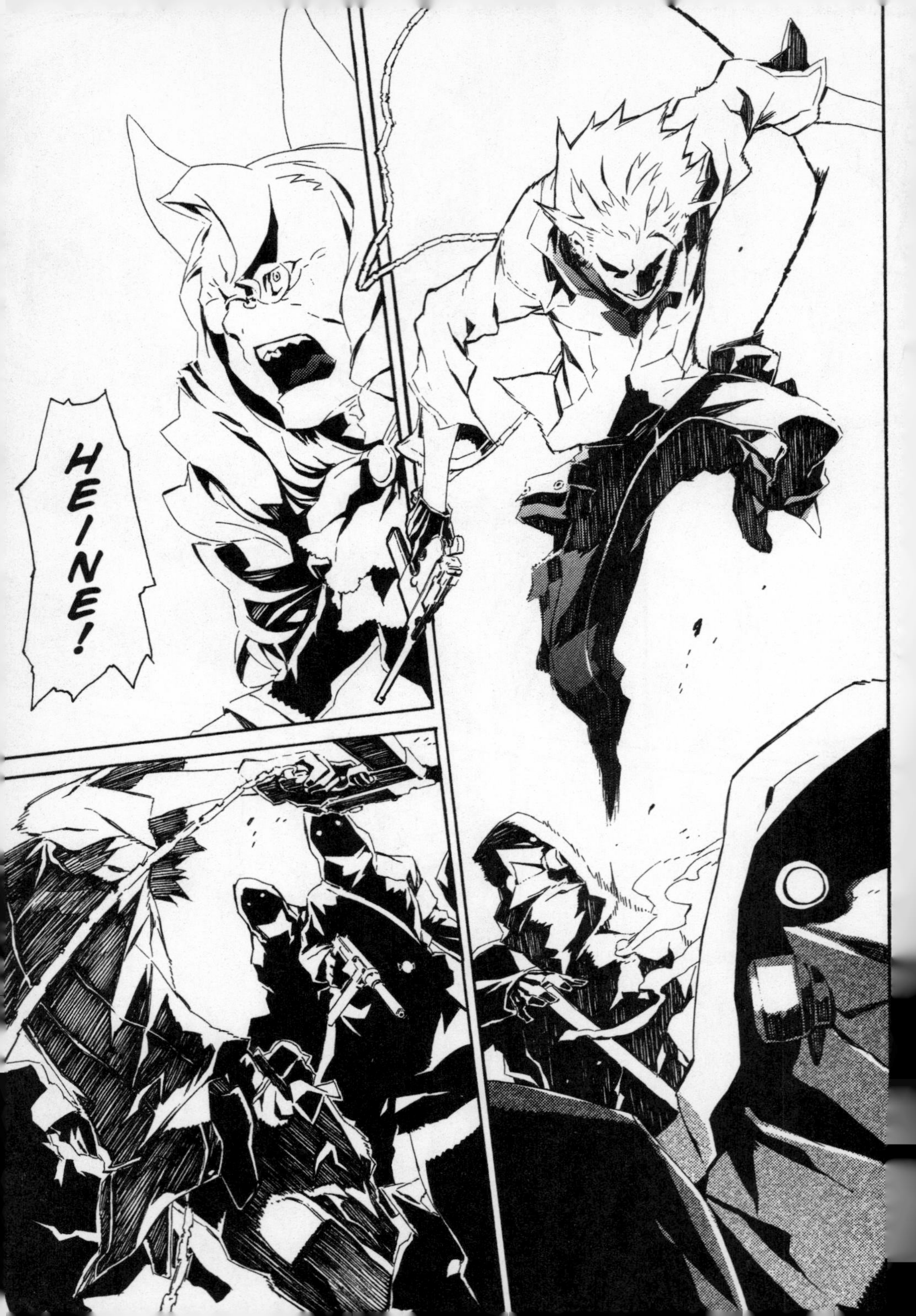
HEINE!

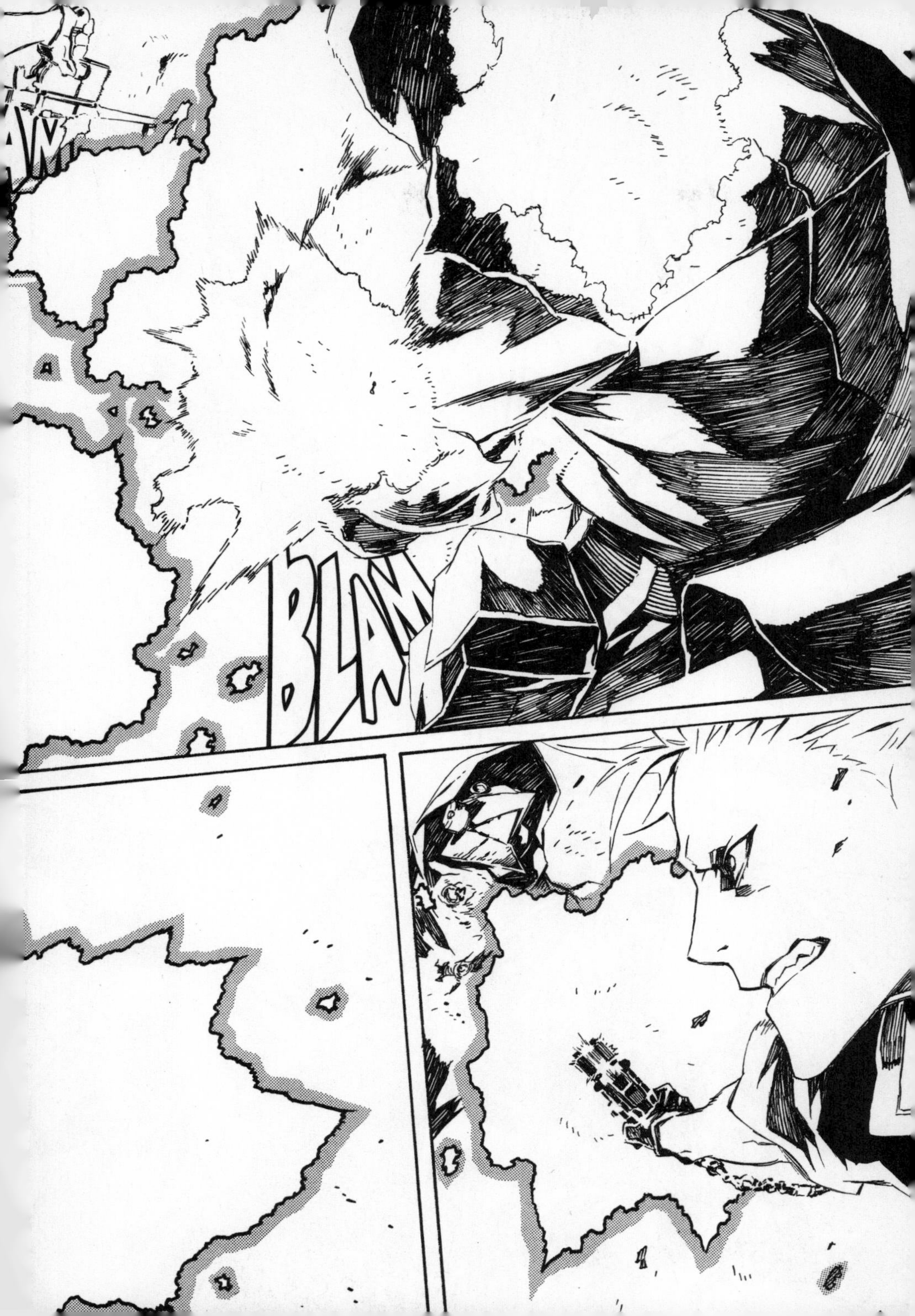
BLAM

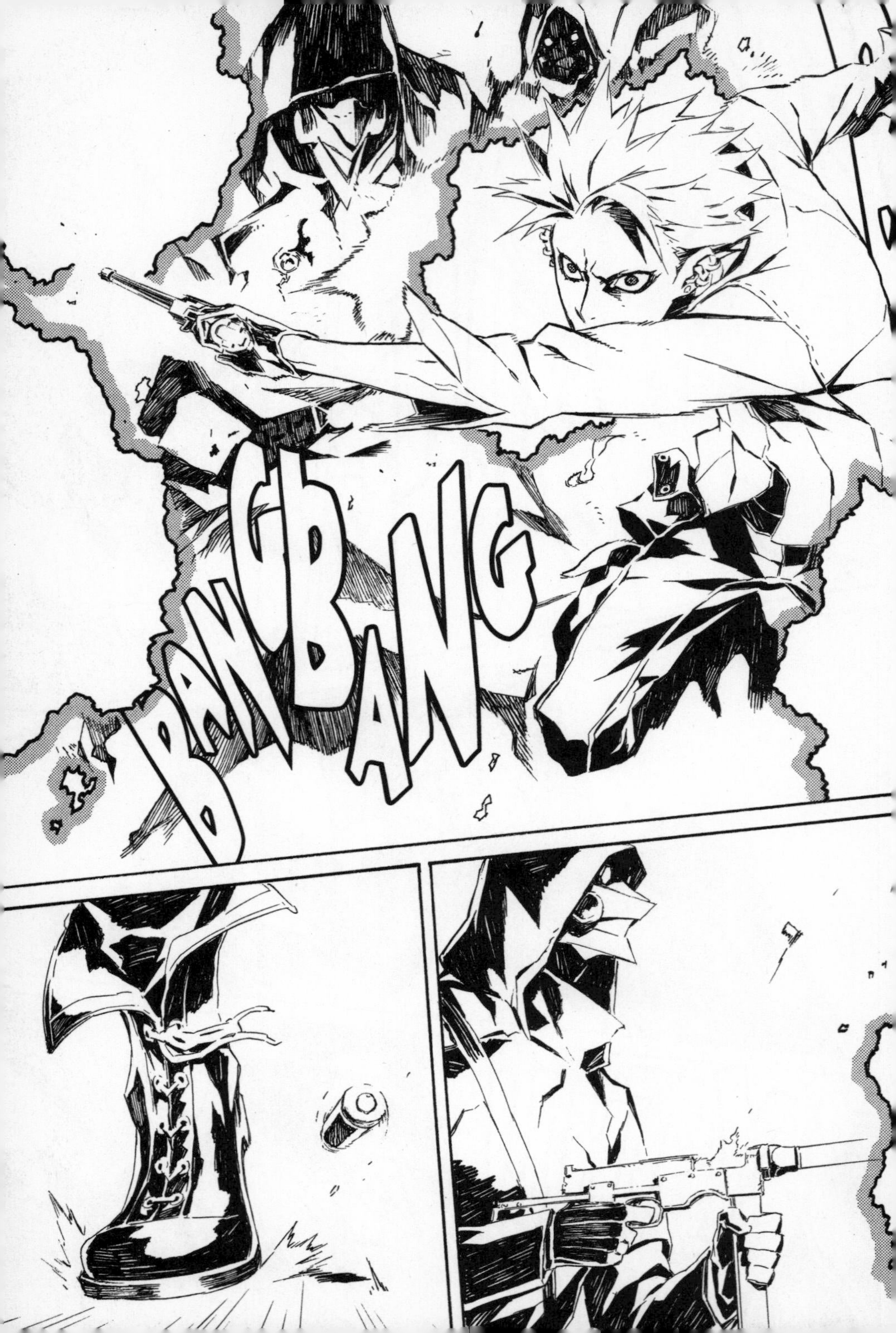
BANG BANG

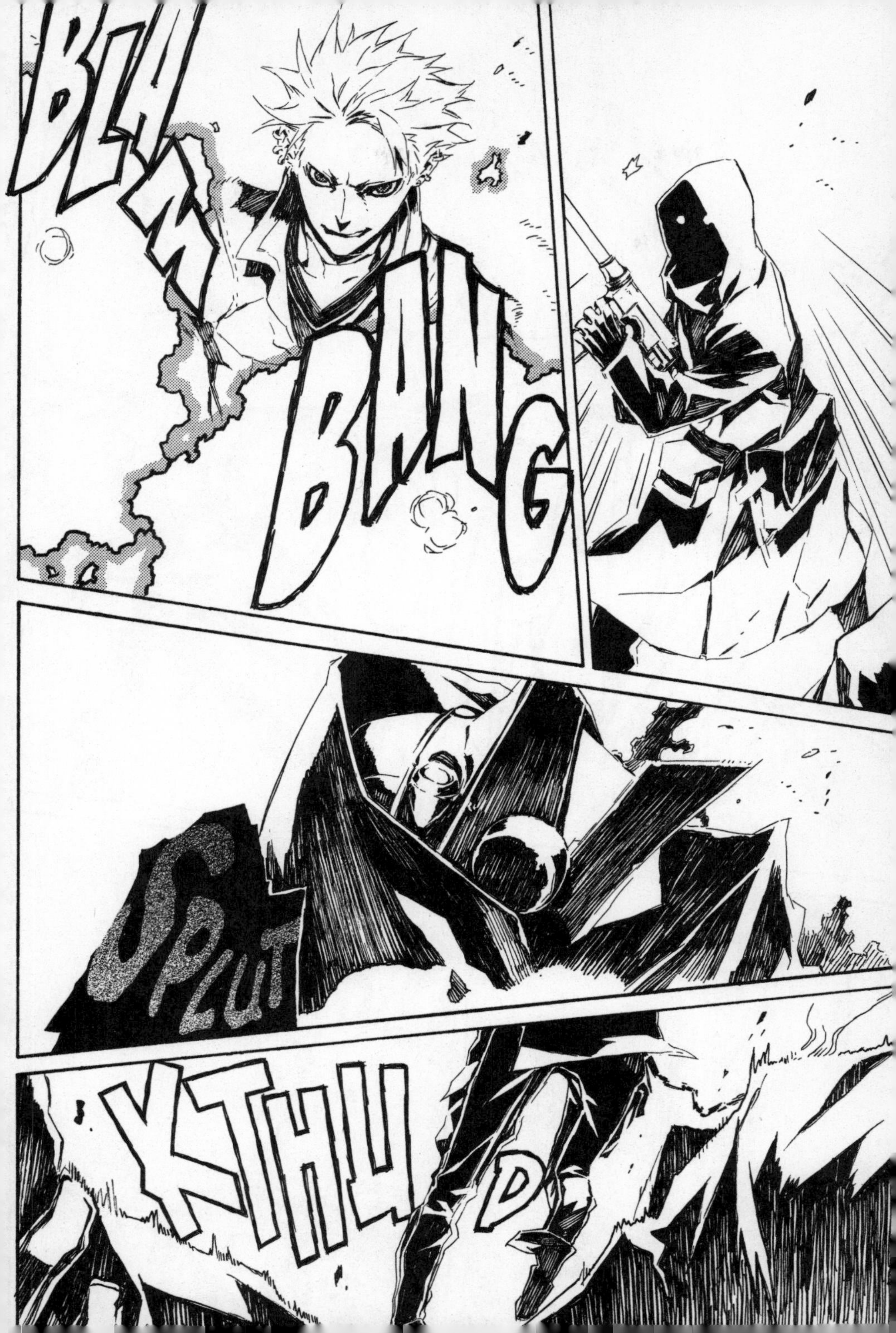
BLAM
BANG
SPLUT
THUD

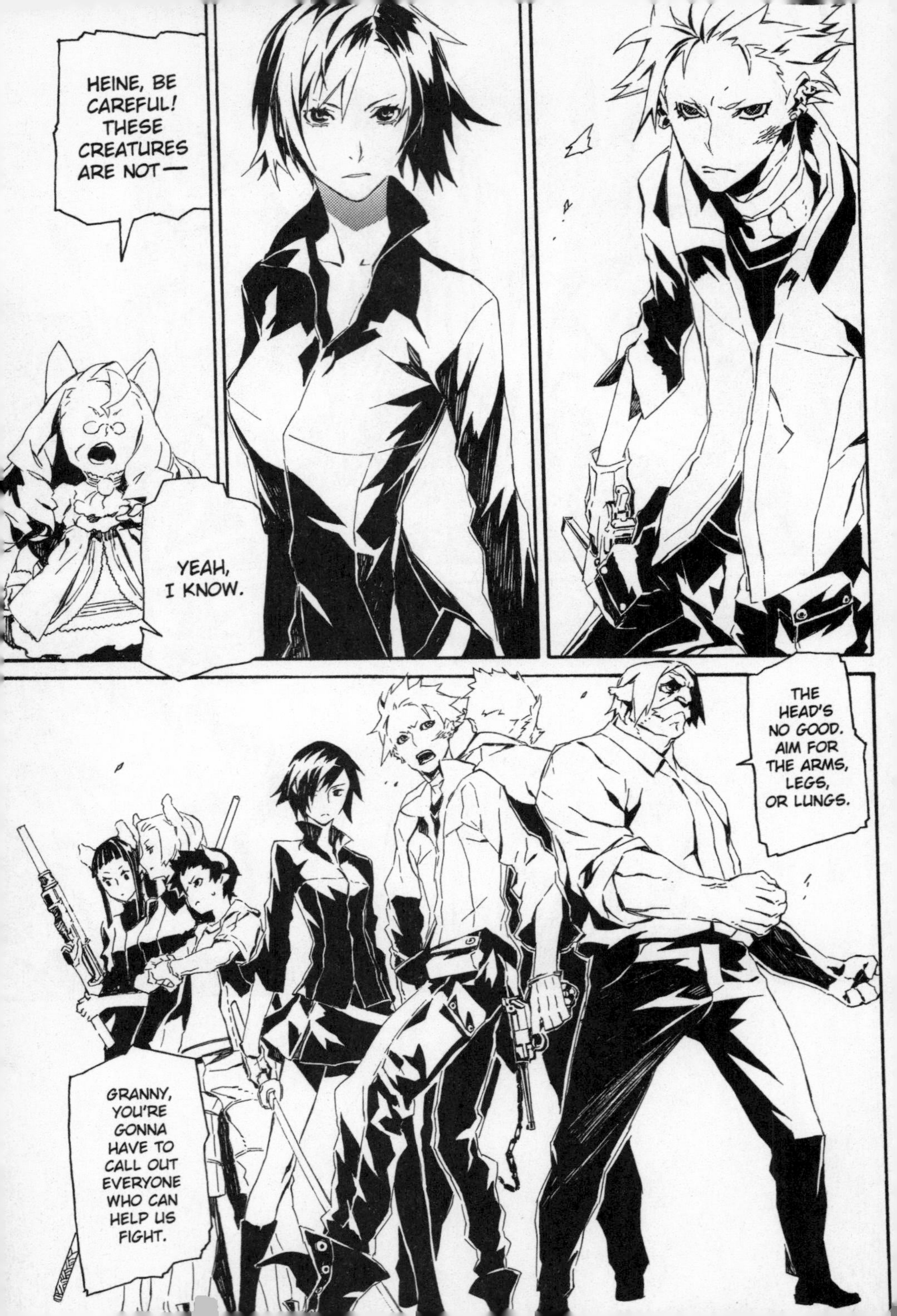
HEINE, BE CAREFUL! THESE CREATURES ARE NOT—
YEAH, I KNOW.
THE HEAD'S NO GOOD. AIM FOR THE ARMS, LEGS, OR LUNGS.
GRANNY, YOU'RE GONNA HAVE TO CALL OUT EVERYONE WHO CAN HELP US FIGHT.

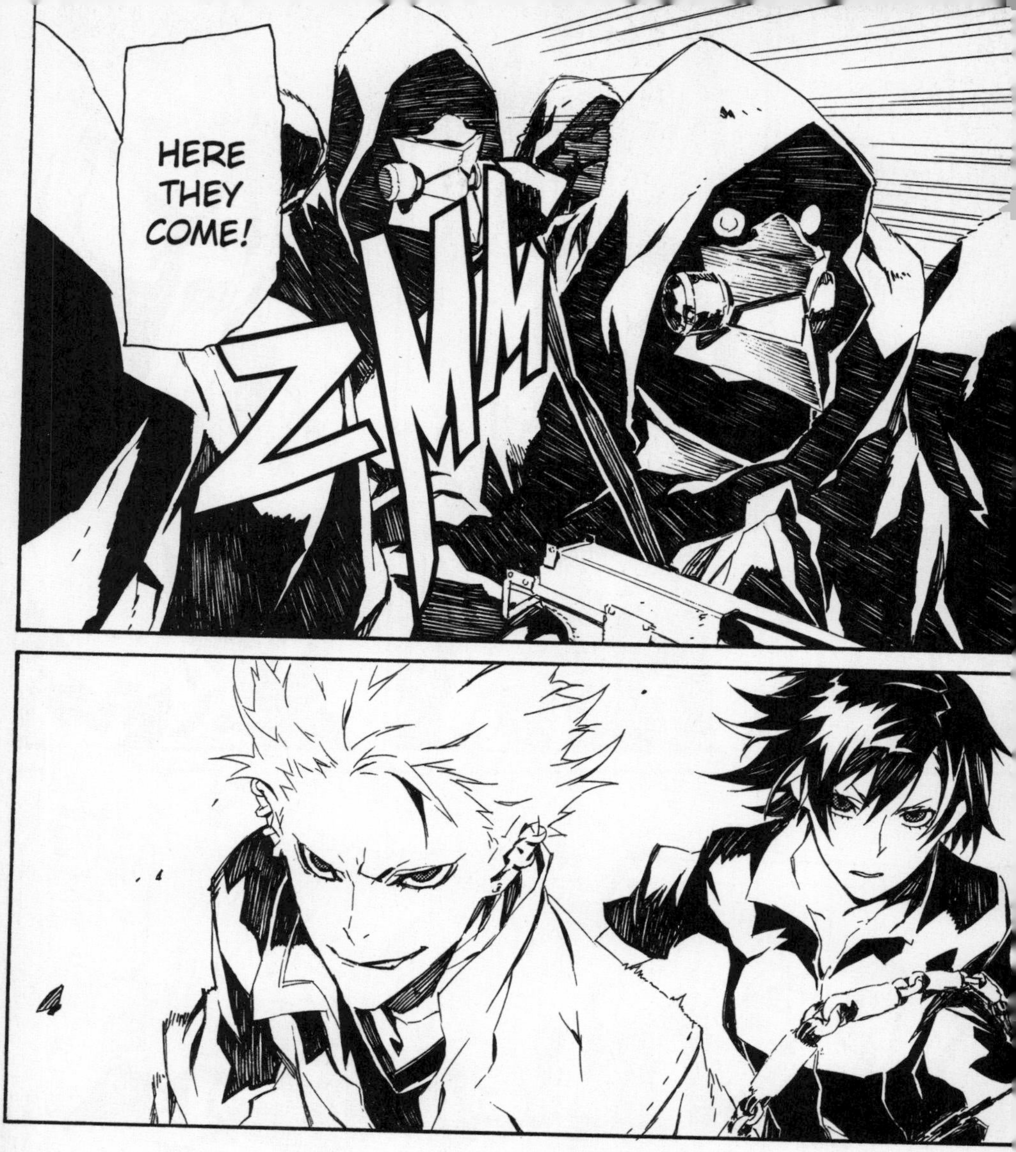
HERE THEY COME!
ZMMM

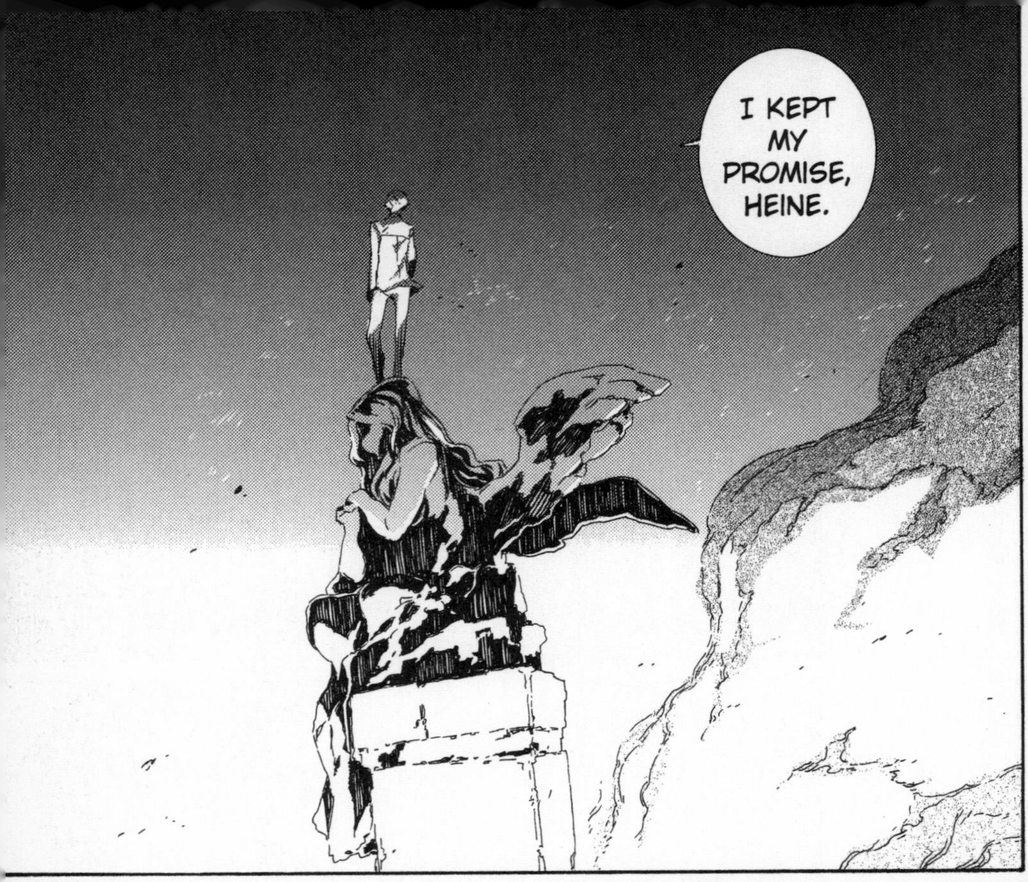
I KEPT MY PROMISE, HEINE.

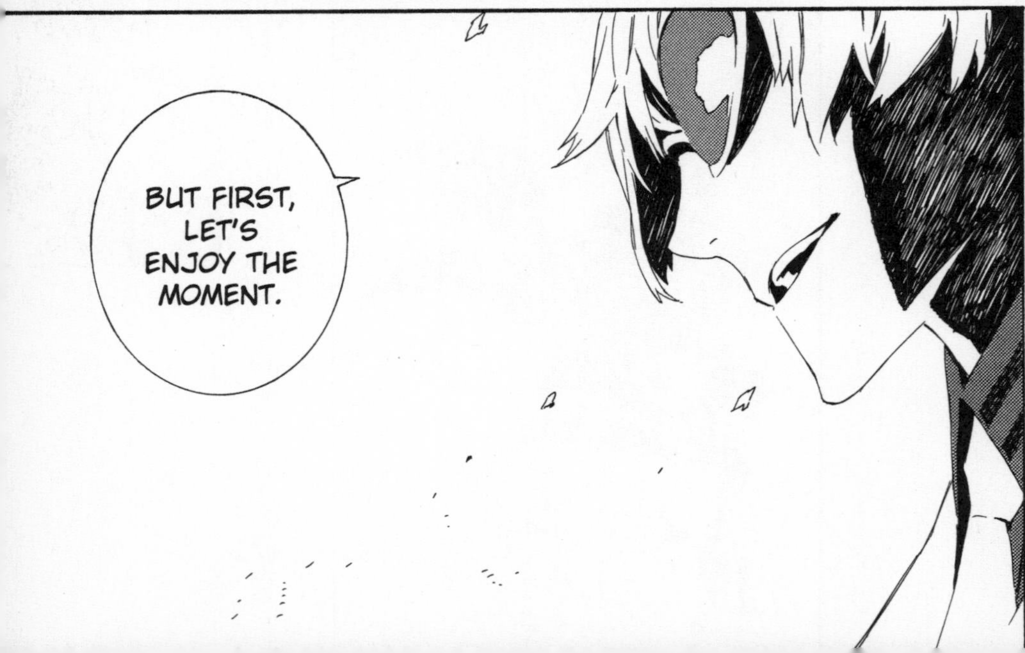
BUT FIRST, LET'S ENJOY THE MOMENT.

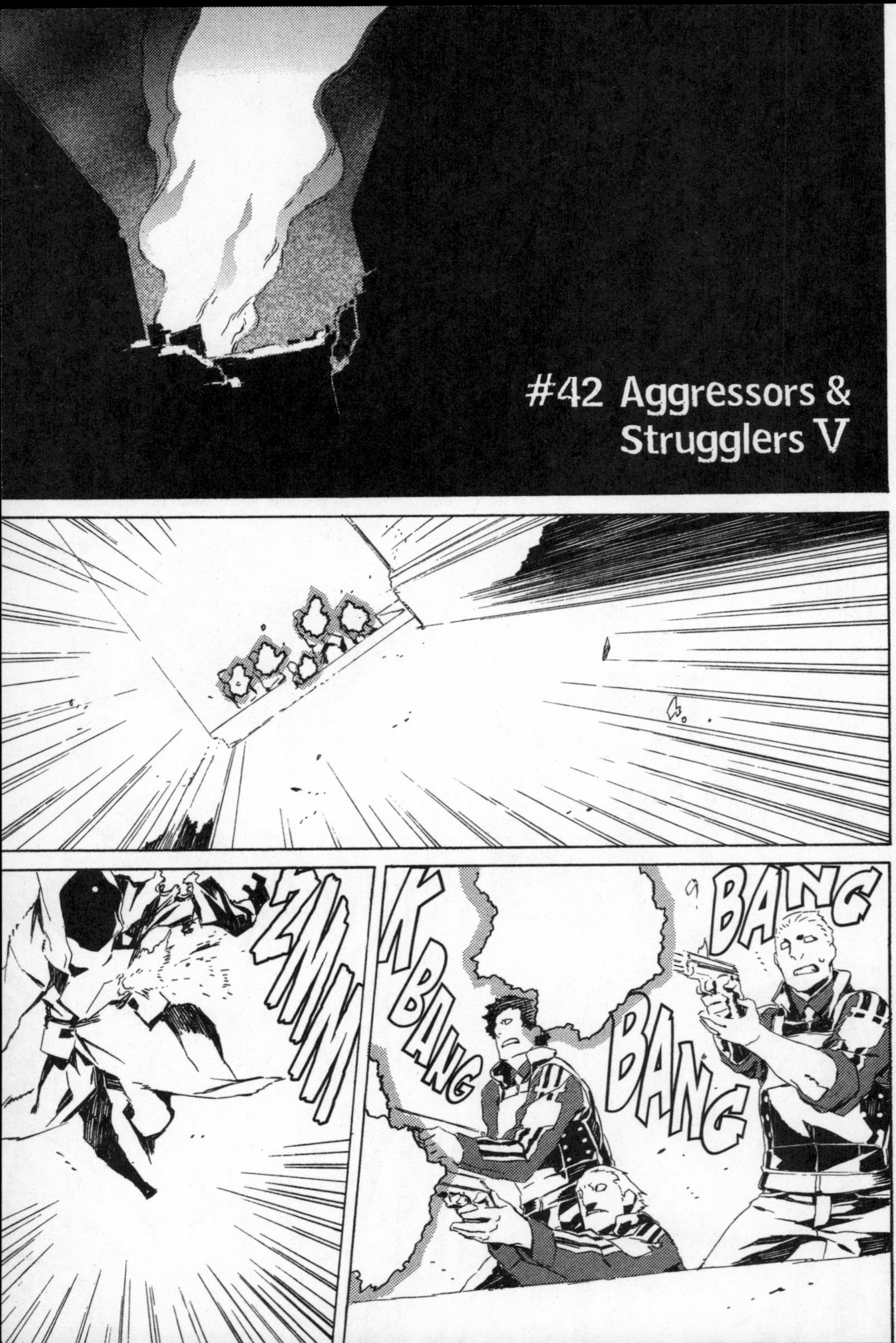
#42 Aggressors & Strugglers V
BANG
BANG
BANG
BANG
ZMMM

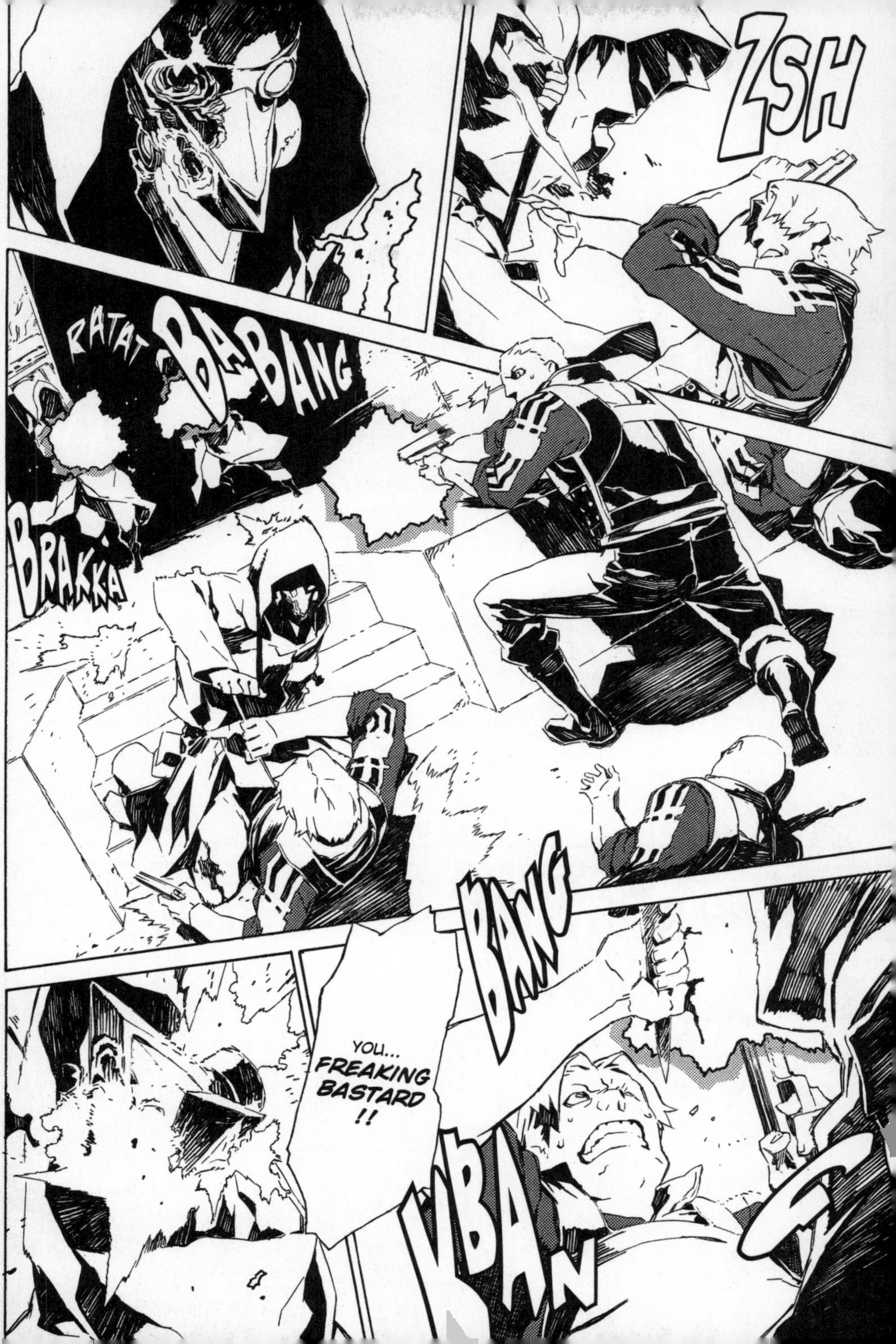
ZSH
RATAT
BABANG
BRAKKA
BANG
YOU... FREAKING BASTARD!!
BAN

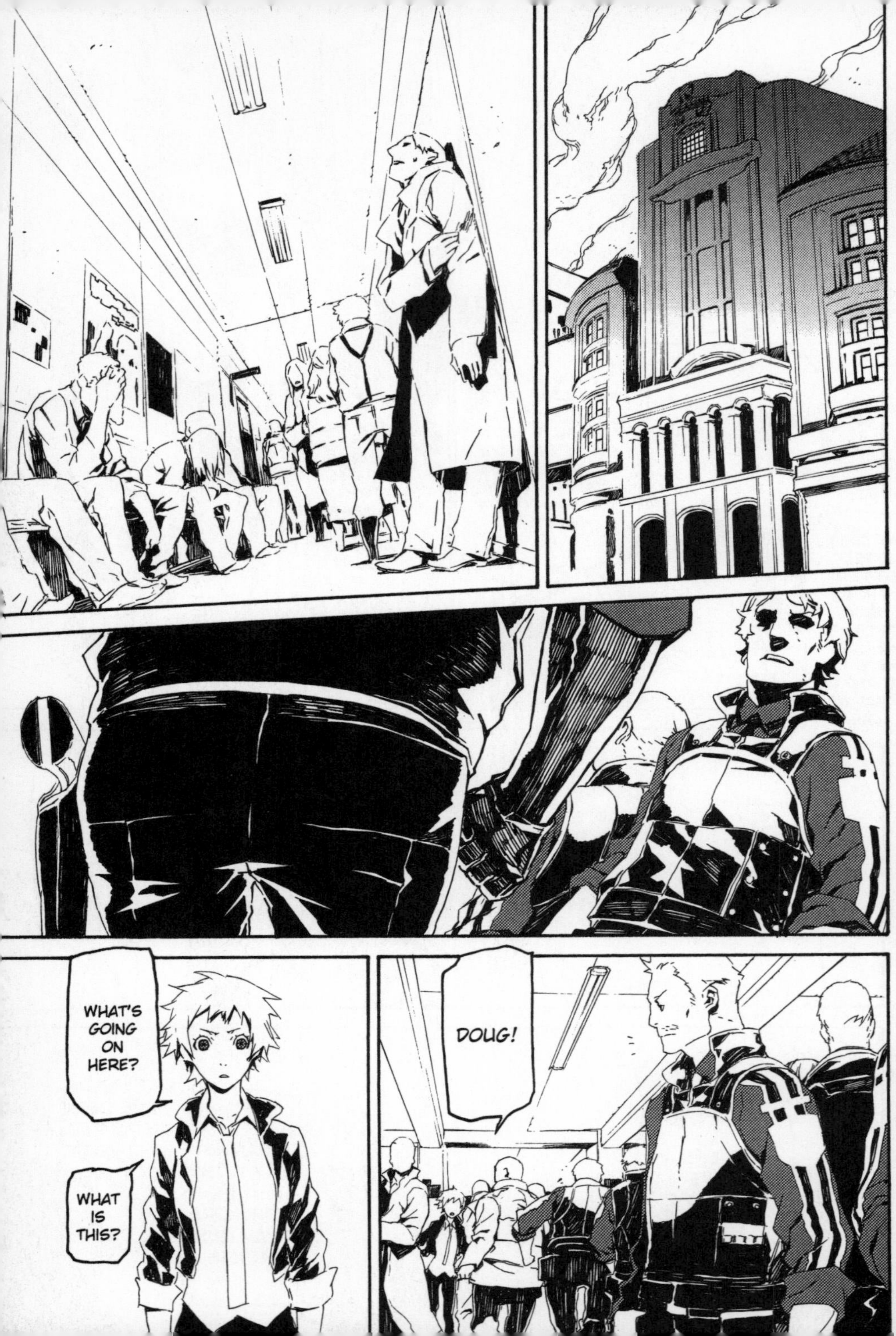
DOUG!
WHAT'S GOING ON HERE?
WHAT IS THIS?

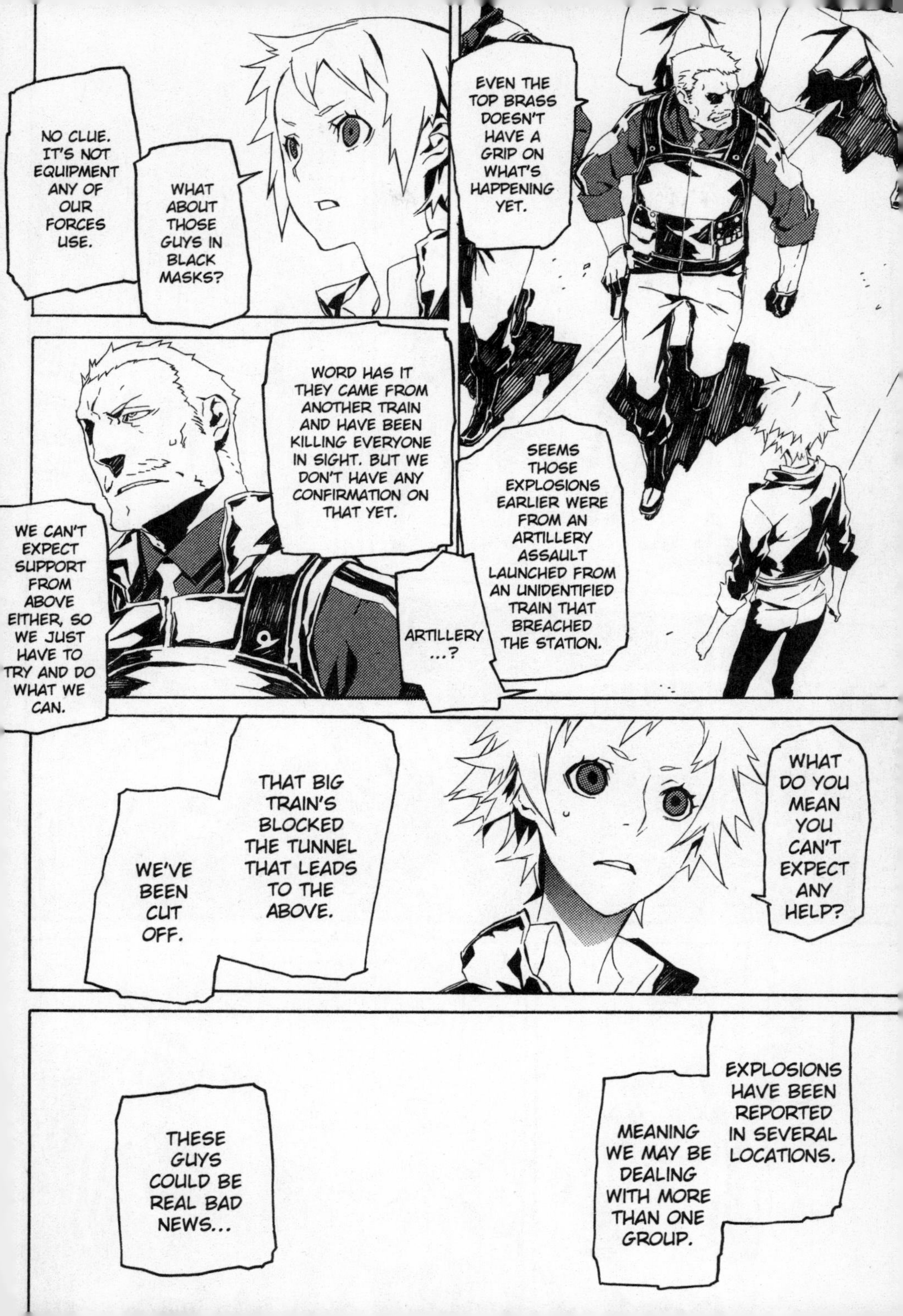
EVEN THE TOP BRASS DOESN'T HAVE A GRIP ON WHAT'S HAPPENING YET.
SEEMS THOSE EXPLOSIONS EARLIER WERE FROM AN ARTILLERY ASSAULT LAUNCHED FROM AN UNIDENTIFIED TRAIN THAT BREACHED THE STATION.
WHAT ABOUT THOSE GUYS IN BLACK MASKS?
NO CLUE. IT'S NOT EQUIPMENT ANY OF OUR FORCES USE.
ARTILLERY ...?
WORD HAS IT THEY CAME FROM ANOTHER TRAIN AND HAVE BEEN KILLING EVERYONE IN SIGHT. BUT WE DON'T HAVE ANY CONFIRMATION ON THAT YET.
WE CAN'T EXPECT SUPPORT FROM ABOVE EITHER, SO WE JUST HAVE TO TRY AND DO WHAT WE CAN.
WHAT DO YOU MEAN YOU CAN'T EXPECT ANY HELP?
THAT BIG TRAIN'S BLOCKED THE TUNNEL THAT LEADS TO THE ABOVE.
WE'VE BEEN CUT OFF.
EXPLOSIONS HAVE BEEN REPORTED IN SEVERAL LOCATIONS.
MEANING WE MAY BE DEALING WITH MORE THAN ONE GROUP.
THESE GUYS COULD BE REAL BAD NEWS...

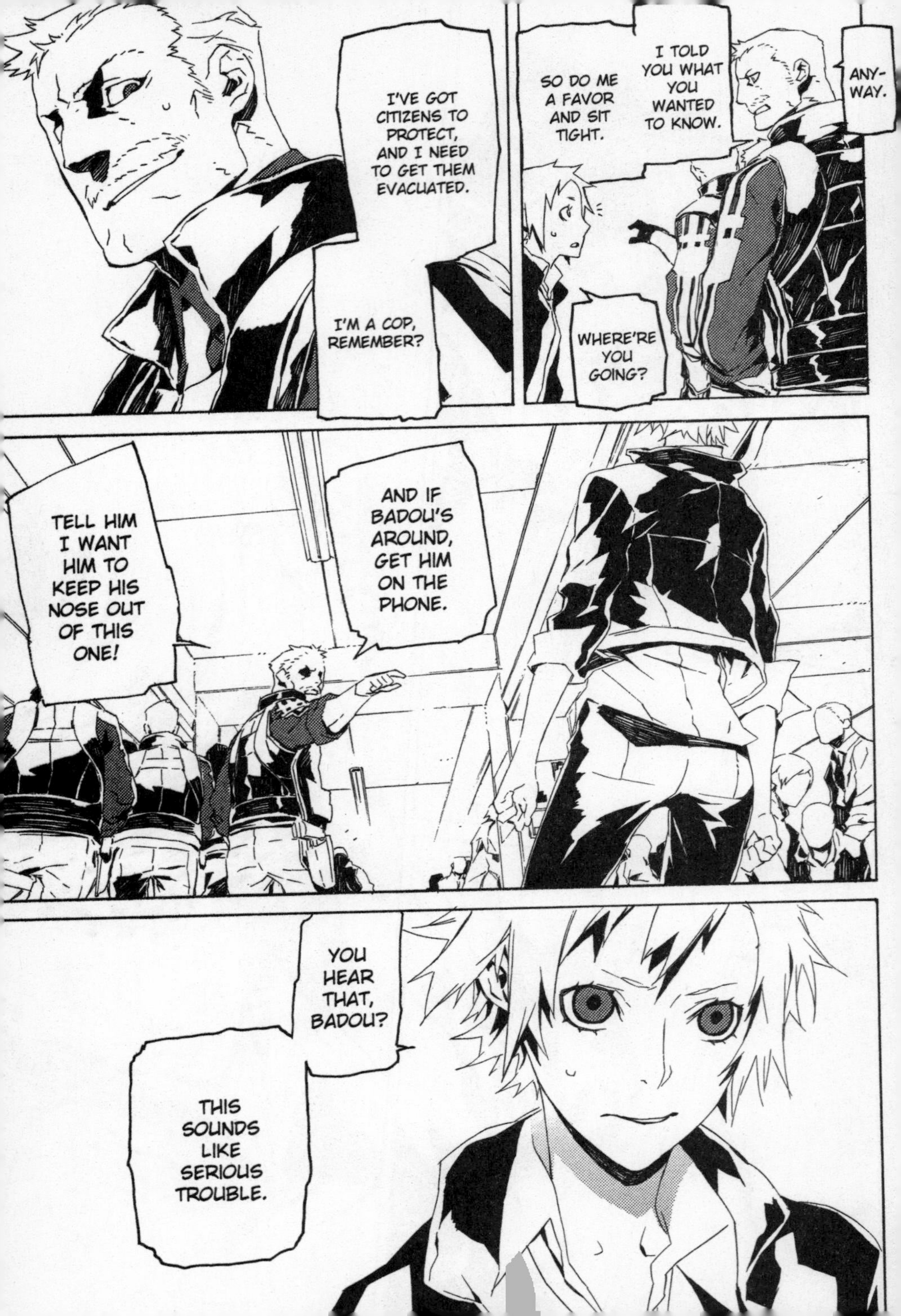
ANY-WAY.
I TOLD YOU WHAT YOU WANTED TO KNOW.
SO DO ME A FAVOR AND SIT TIGHT.
WHERE'RE YOU GOING?
I'VE GOT CITIZENS TO PROTECT, AND I NEED TO GET THEM EVACUATED.
I'M A COP, REMEMBER?
AND IF BADOU'S AROUND, GET HIM ON THE PHONE.
TELL HIM I WANT HIM TO KEEP HIS NOSE OUT OF THIS ONE!
YOU HEAR THAT, BADOU?
THIS SOUNDS LIKE SERIOUS TROUBLE.

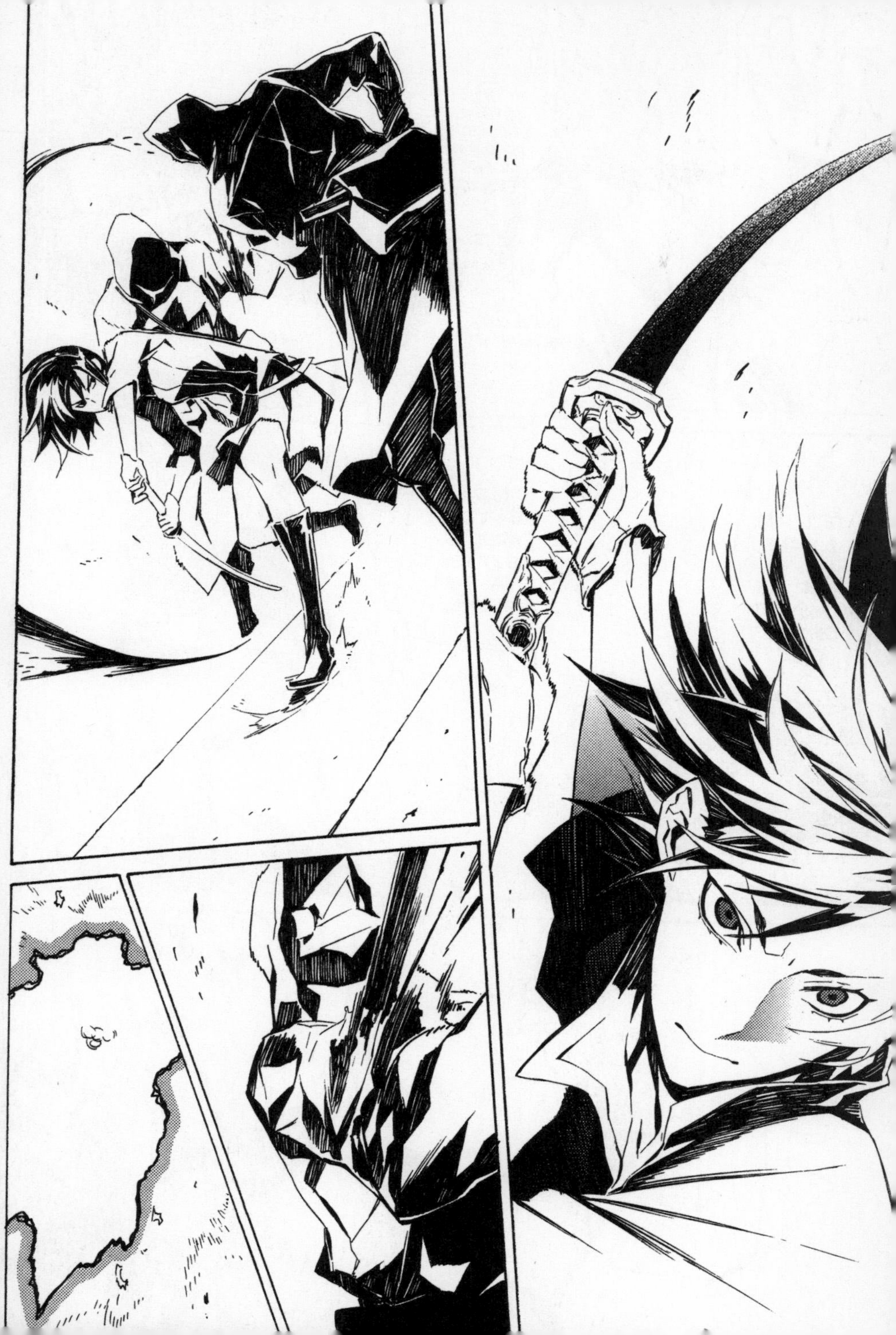

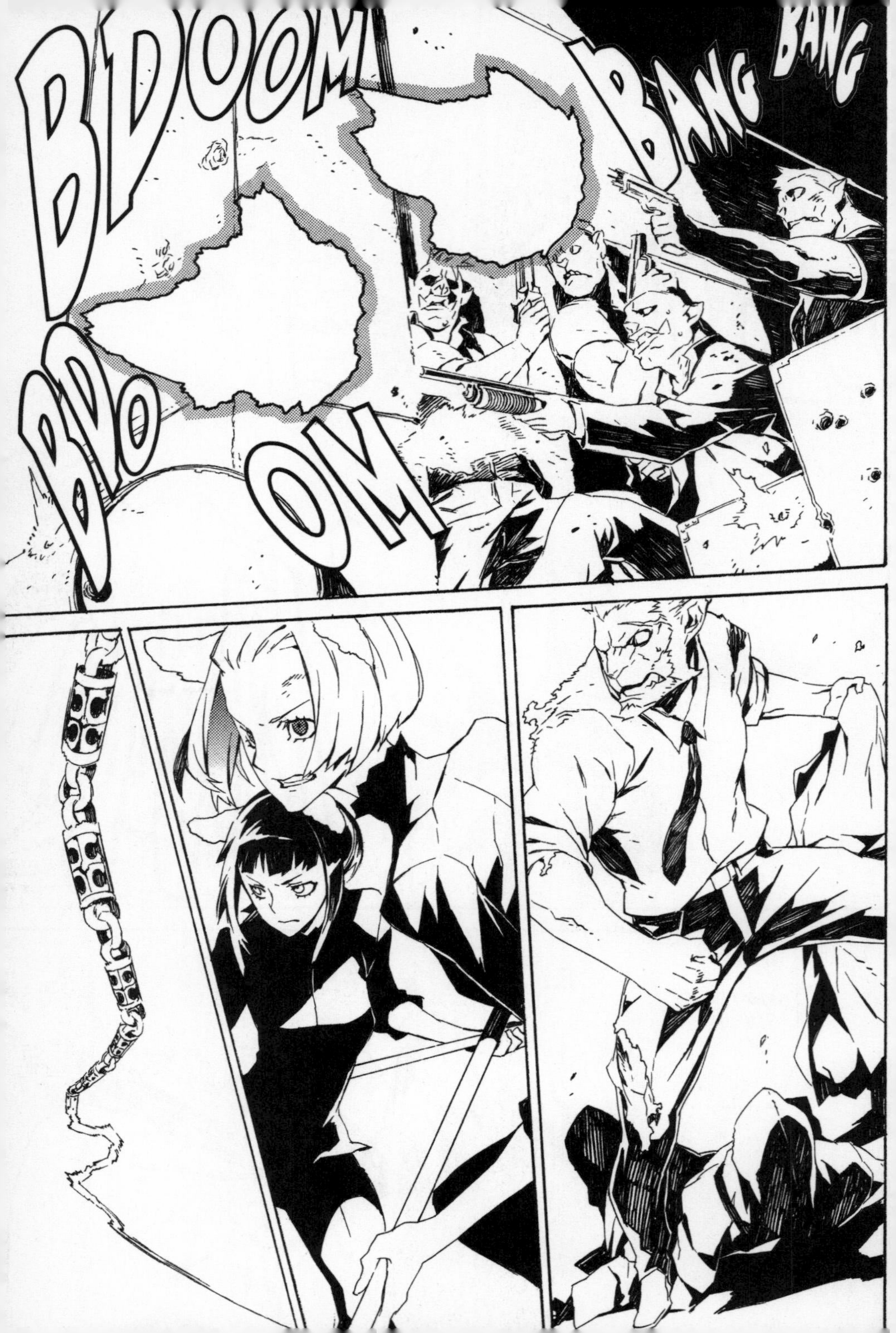
BANG BANG
BDOOM
BDOOM

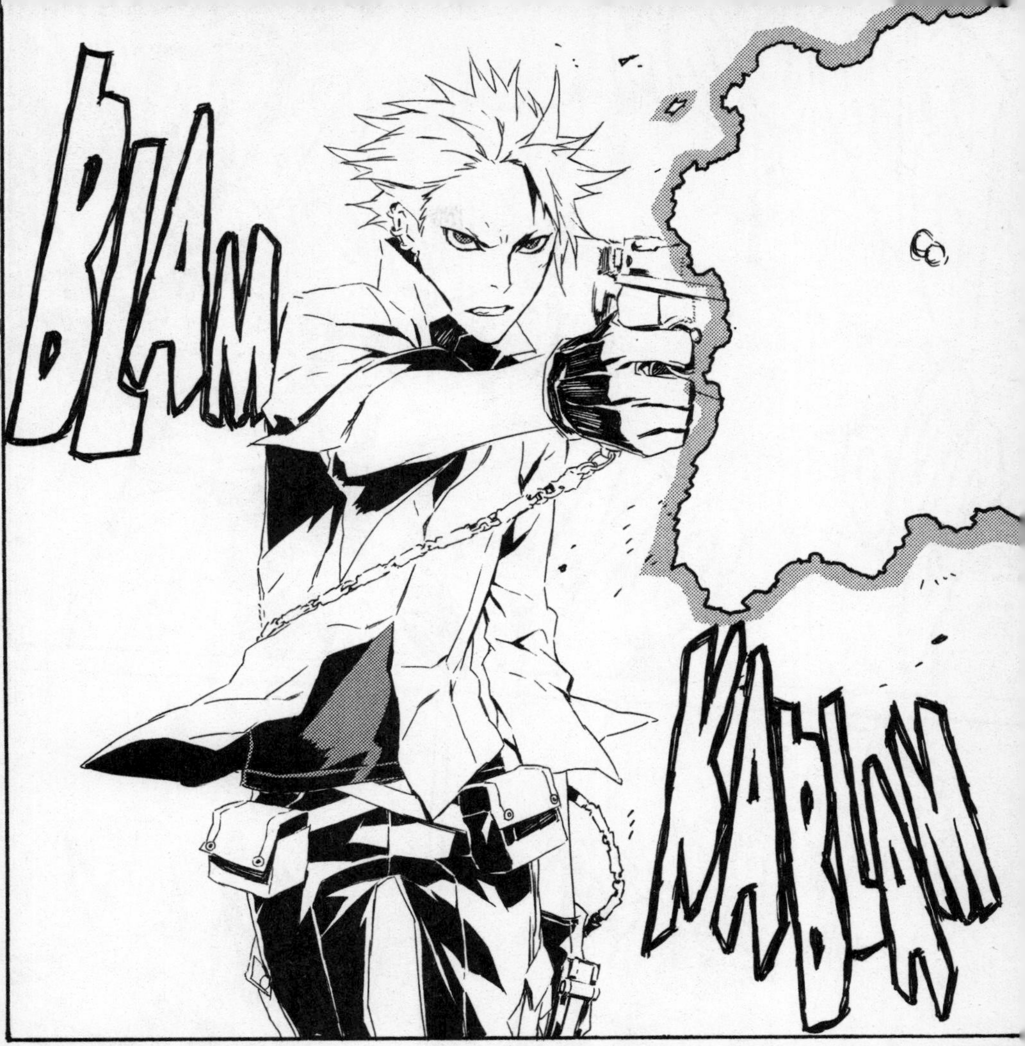
BLAM
KABLAM
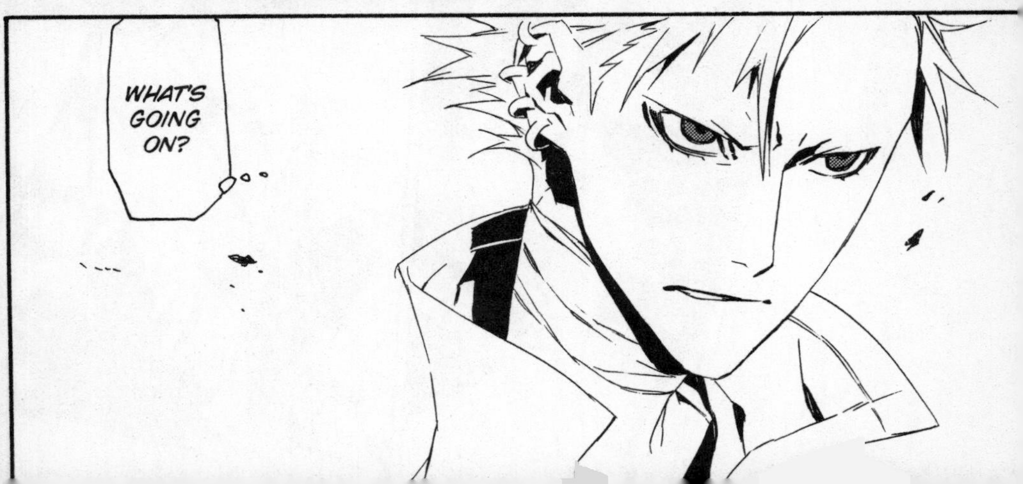
WHAT'S GOING ON?

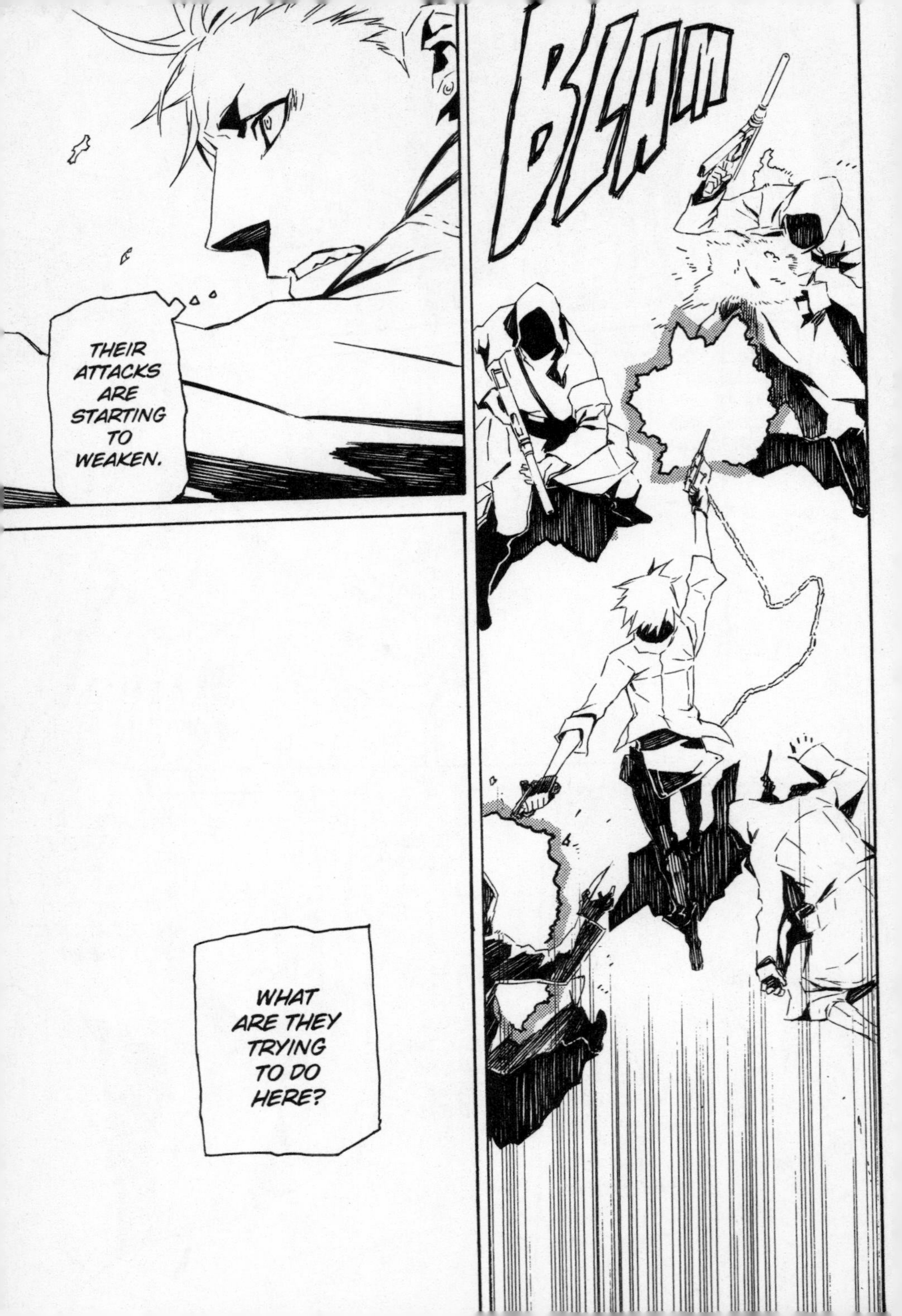
BLAM
THEIR ATTACKS ARE STARTING TO WEAKEN.
WHAT ARE THEY TRYING TO DO HERE?

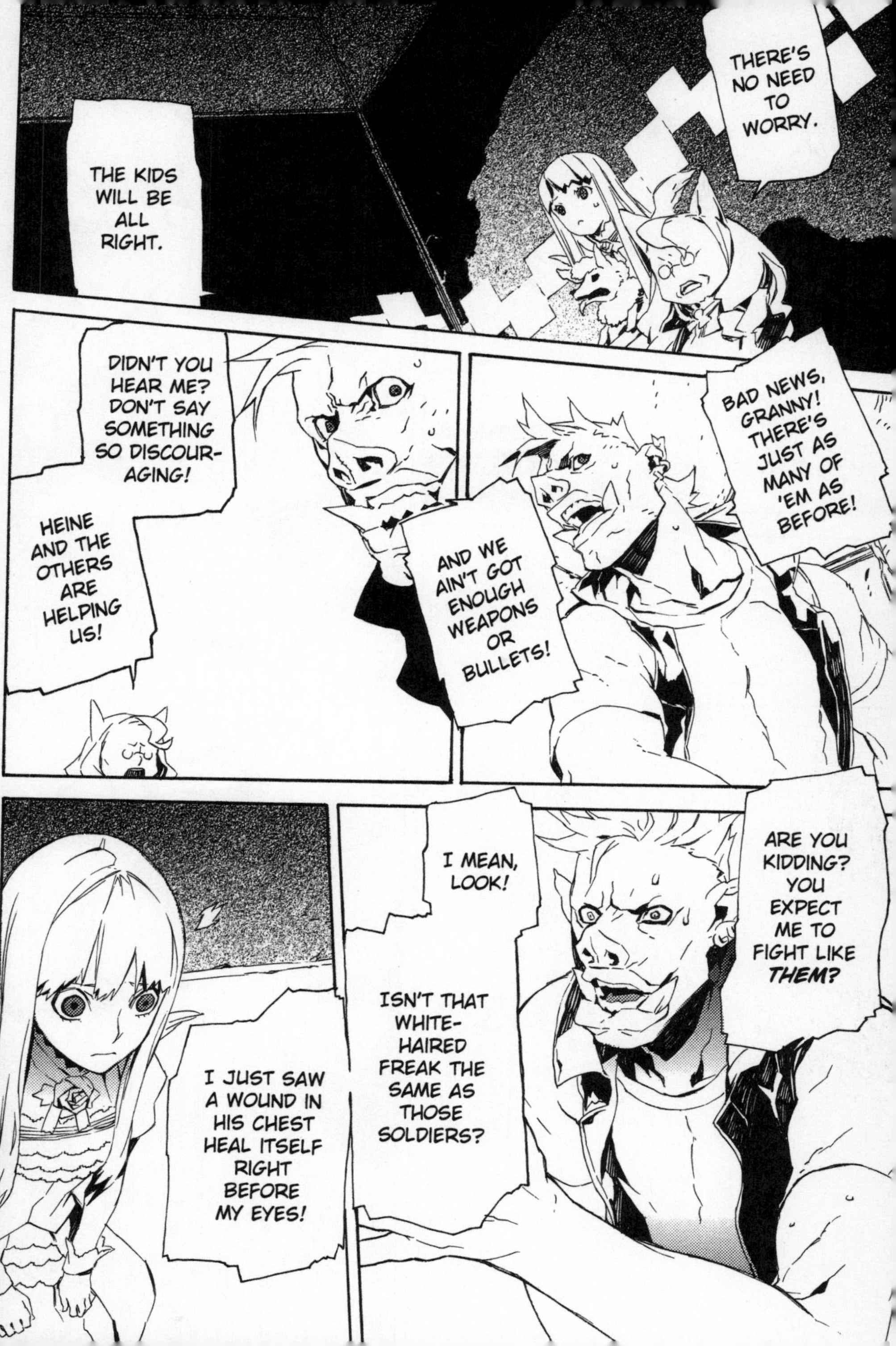
THERE'S NO NEED TO WORRY.
THE KIDS WILL BE ALL RIGHT.
BAD NEWS, GRANNY! THERE'S JUST AS MANY OF 'EM AS BEFORE!
AND WE AIN'T GOT ENOUGH WEAPONS OR BULLETS!
DIDN'T YOU HEAR ME? DON'T SAY SOMETHING SO DISCOURAGING!
HEINE AND THE OTHERS ARE HELPING US!
ARE YOU KIDDING? YOU EXPECT ME TO FIGHT LIKE *THEM?*
I MEAN, LOOK!
ISN'T THAT WHITE-HAIRED FREAK THE SAME AS THOSE SOLDIERS?
I JUST SAW A WOUND IN HIS CHEST HEAL ITSELF RIGHT BEFORE MY EYES!

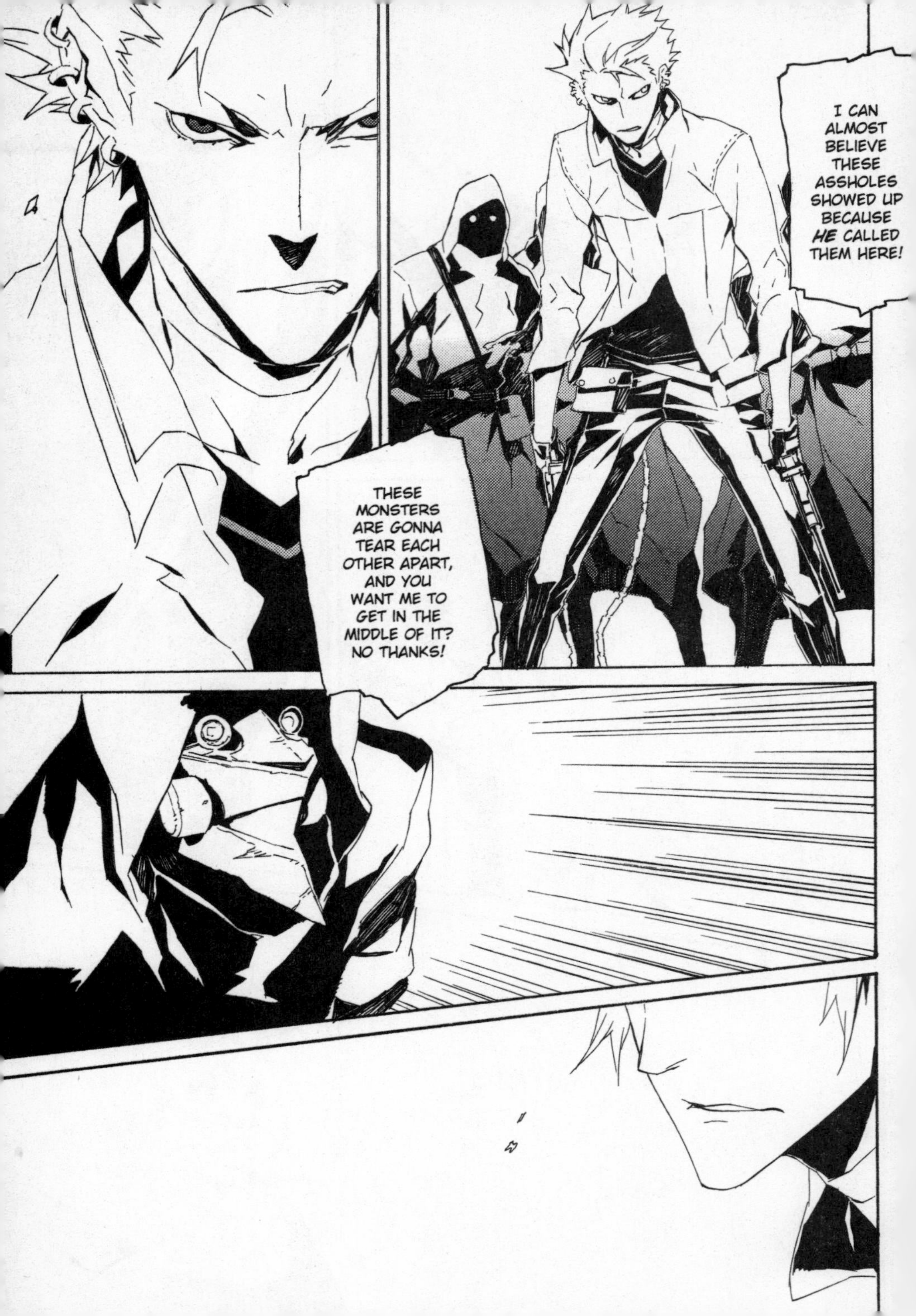
I CAN ALMOST BELIEVE THESE ASSHOLES SHOWED UP BECAUSE *HE* CALLED THEM HERE!
THESE MONSTERS ARE GONNA TEAR EACH OTHER APART, AND YOU WANT ME TO GET IN THE MIDDLE OF IT? NO THANKS!

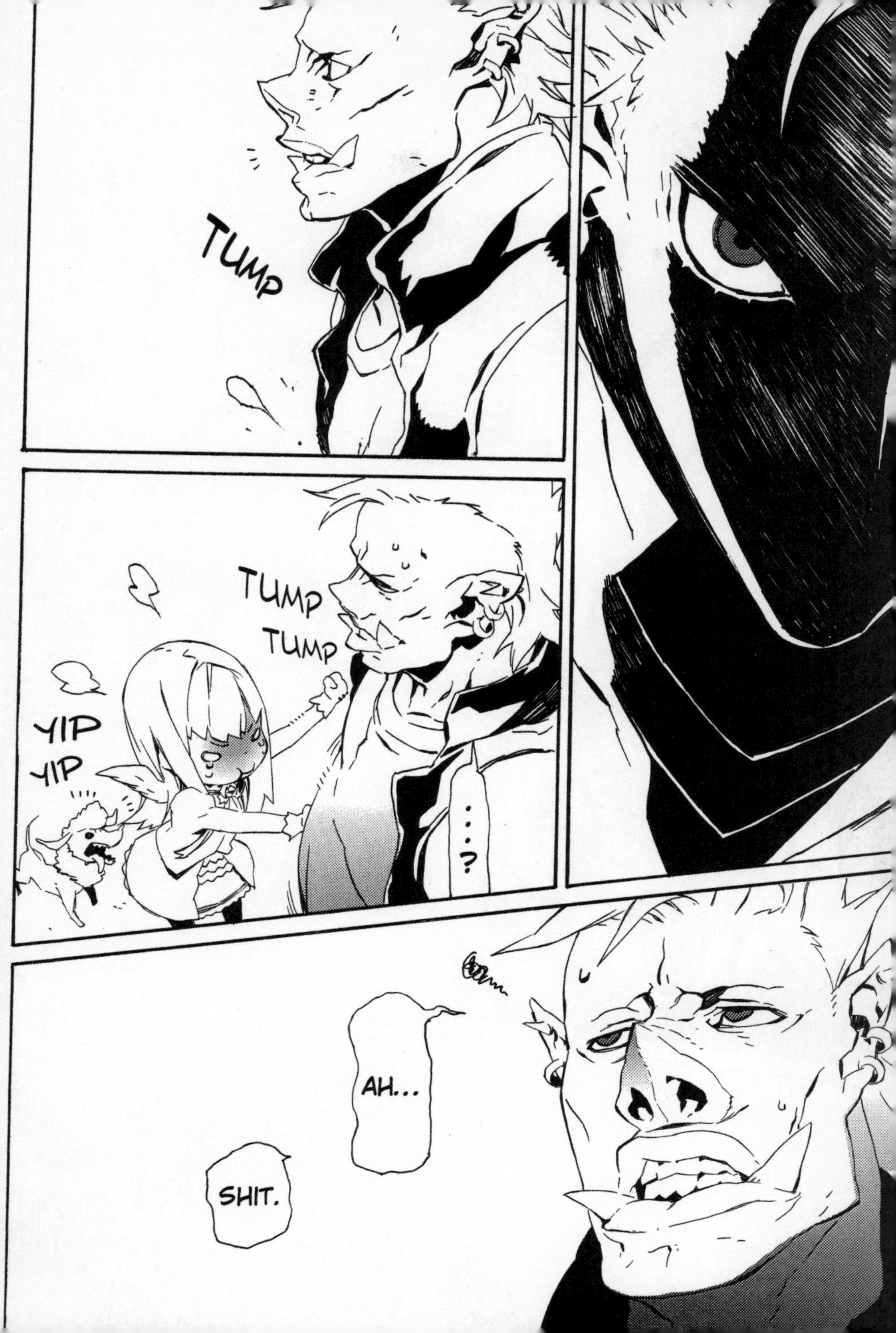
TUMP
TUMP
TUMP
YIP
YIP
...?
AH...
SHIT.

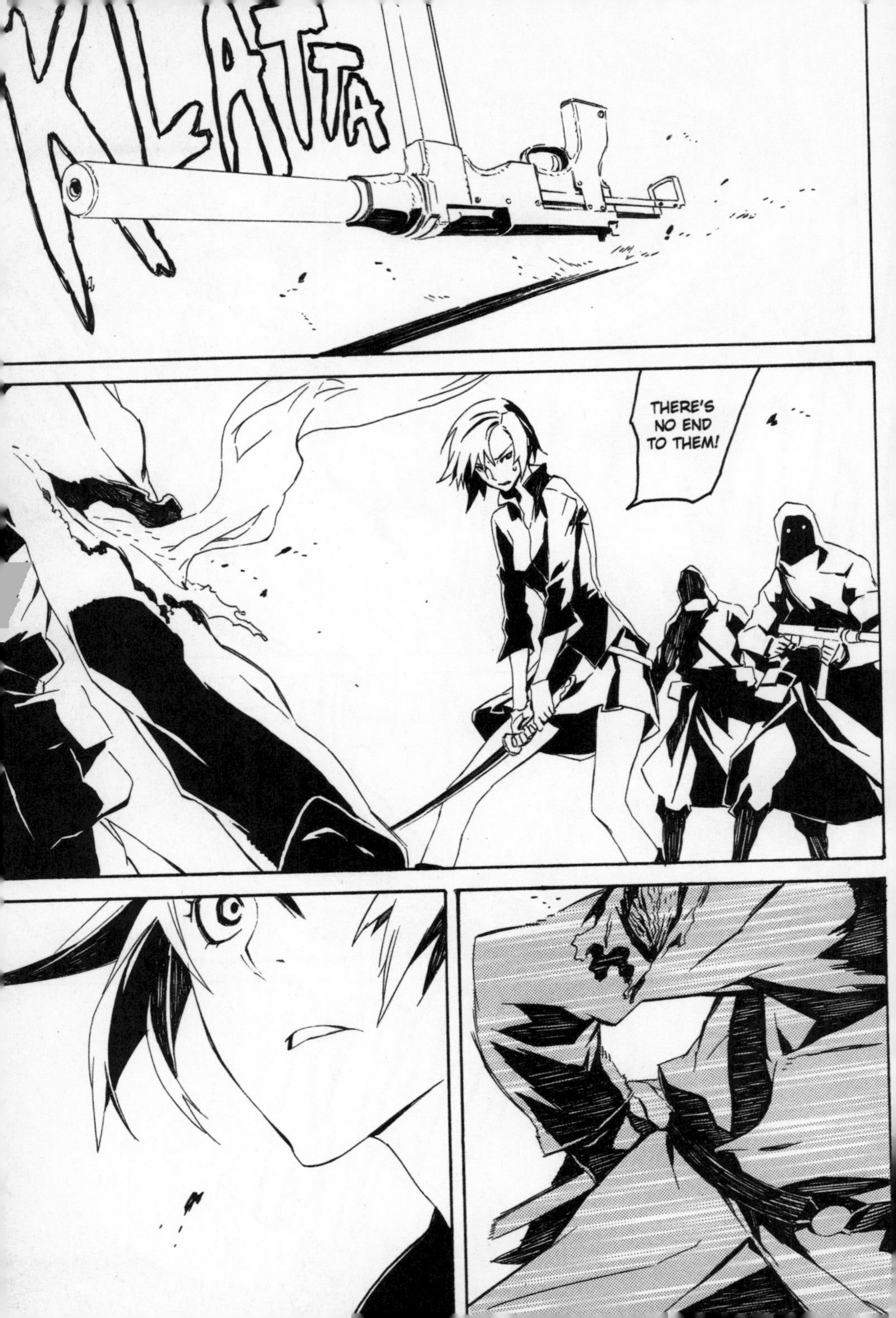
KLATTA
THERE'S NO END TO THEM!

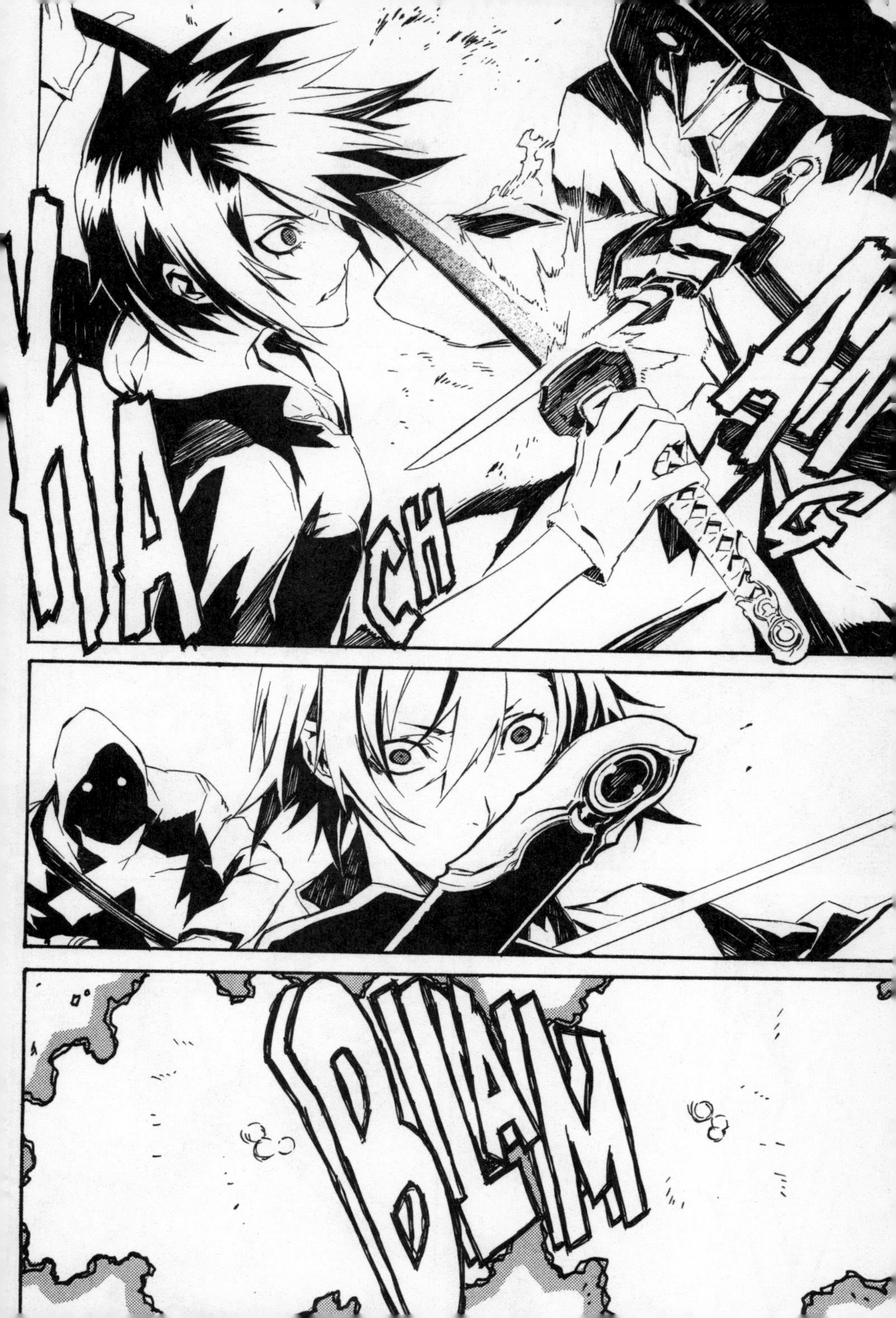
SHACHING
BLAM

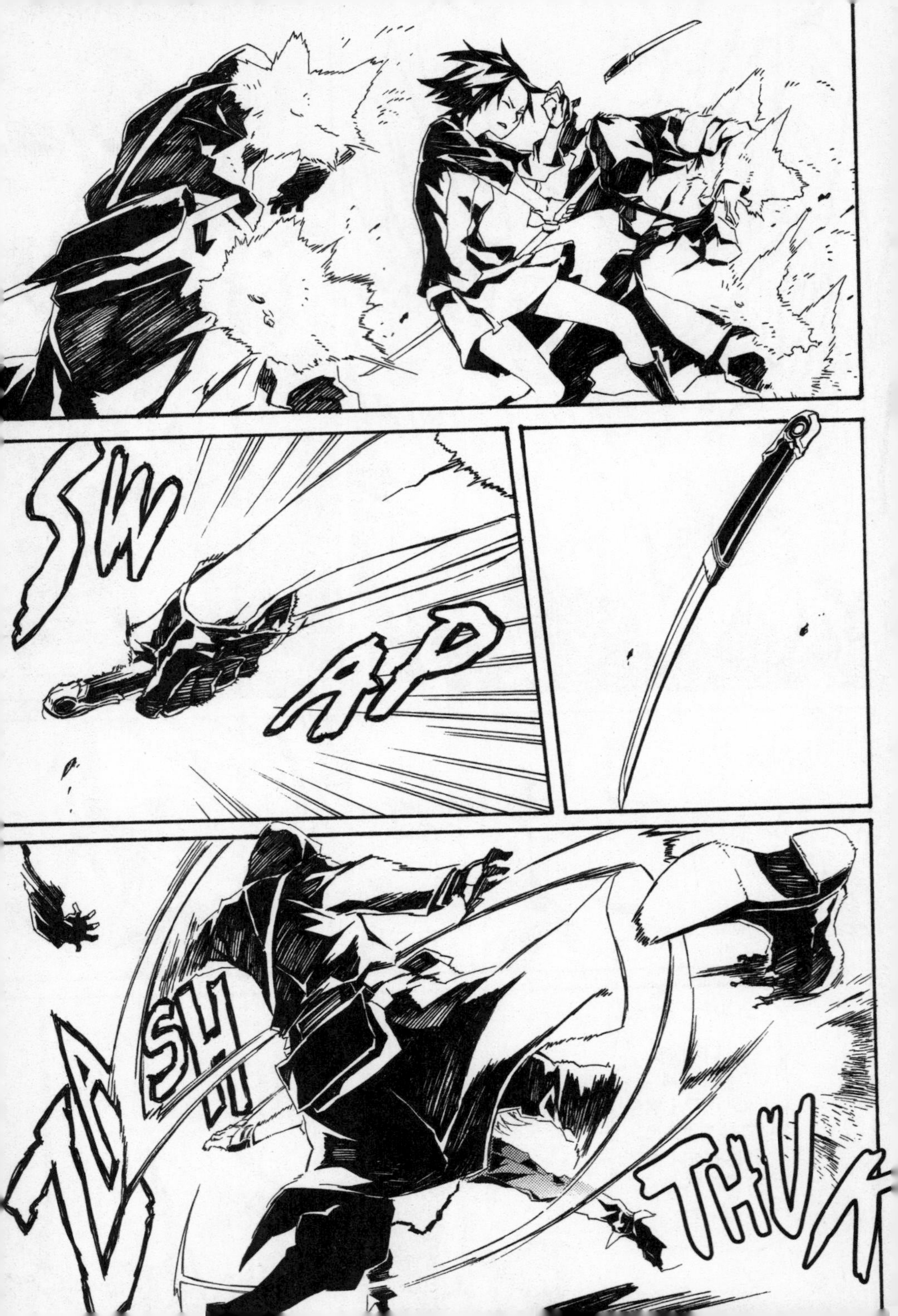
SWAP
THU
ZASHH

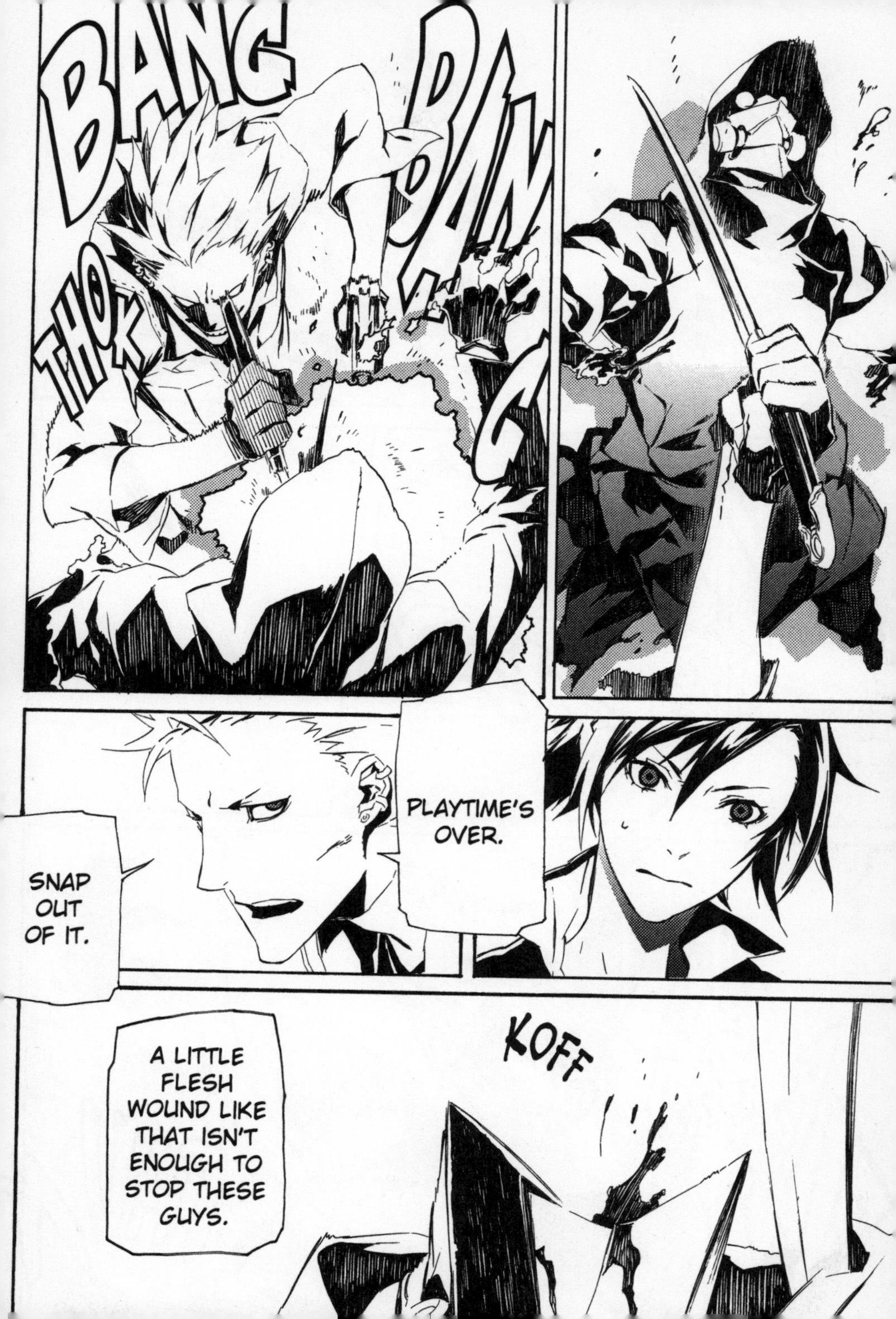
BAM
BANG
THOK
PLAYTIME'S OVER.
SNAP OUT OF IT.
KOFF
A LITTLE FLESH WOUND LIKE THAT ISN'T ENOUGH TO STOP THESE GUYS.

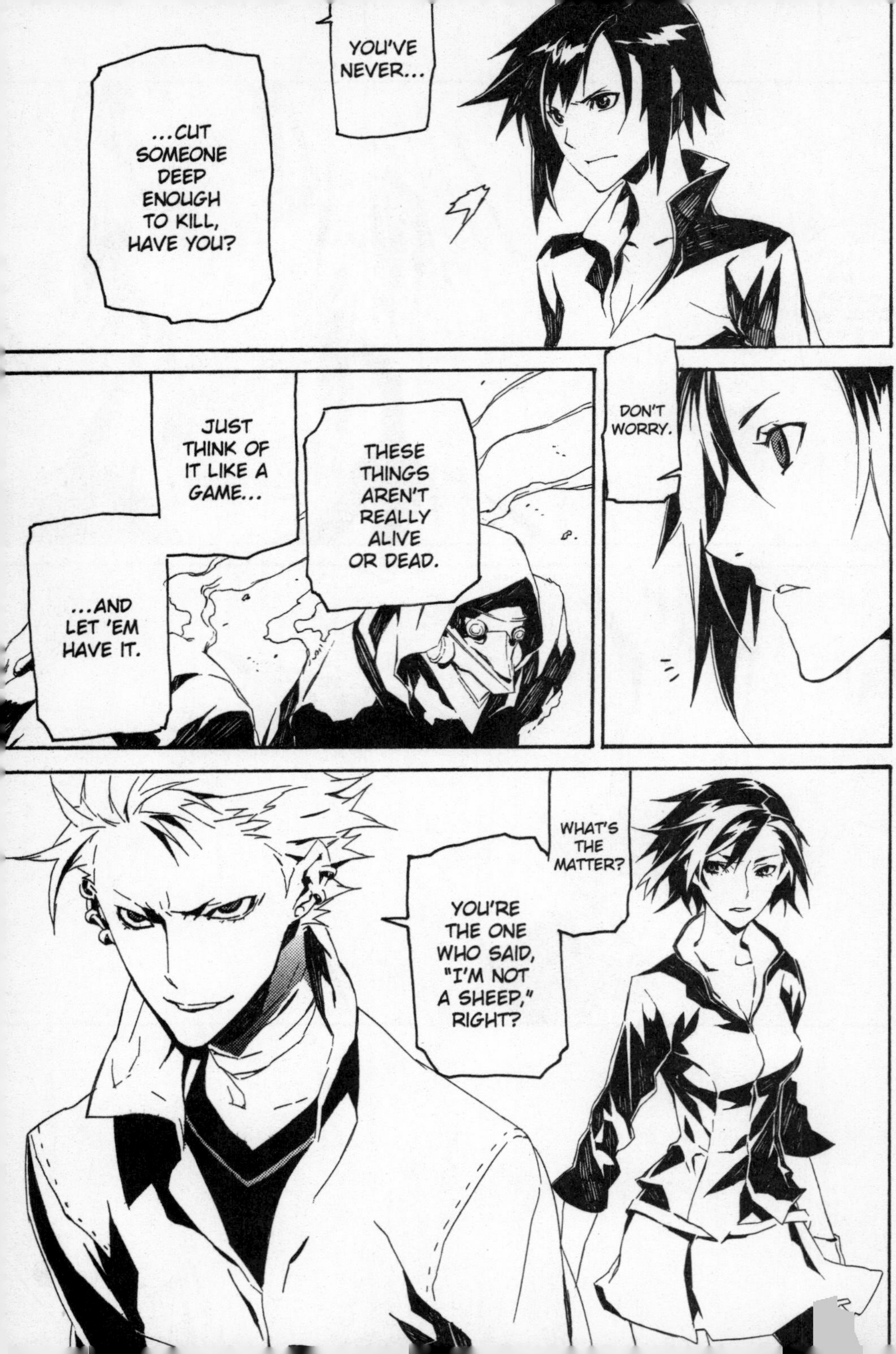
YOU'VE NEVER...
...CUT SOMEONE DEEP ENOUGH TO KILL, HAVE YOU?
DON'T WORRY.
THESE THINGS AREN'T REALLY ALIVE OR DEAD.
JUST THINK OF IT LIKE A GAME...
...AND LET 'EM HAVE IT.
WHAT'S THE MATTER?
YOU'RE THE ONE WHO SAID, "I'M NOT A SHEEP," RIGHT?

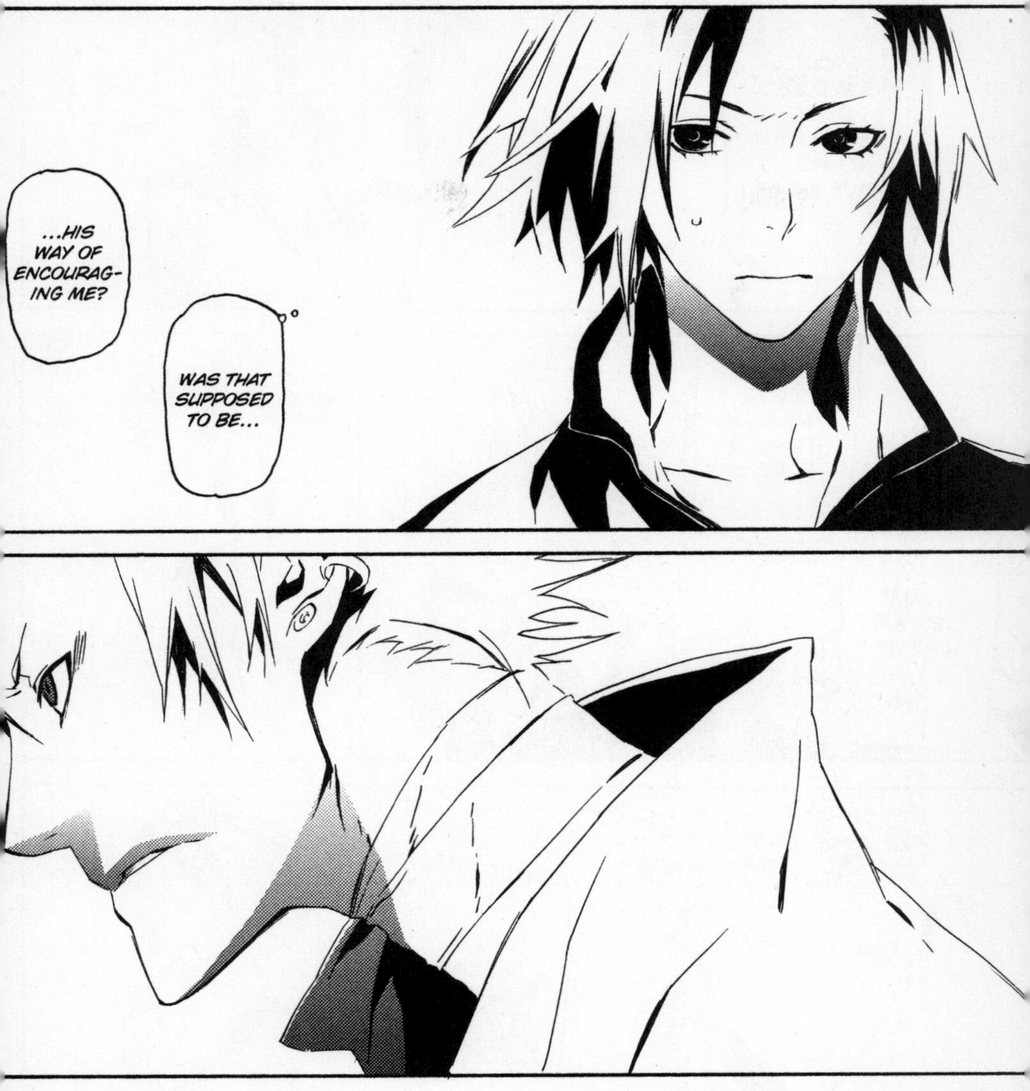
WAS THAT SUPPOSED TO BE...
...HIS WAY OF ENCOURAG-ING ME?

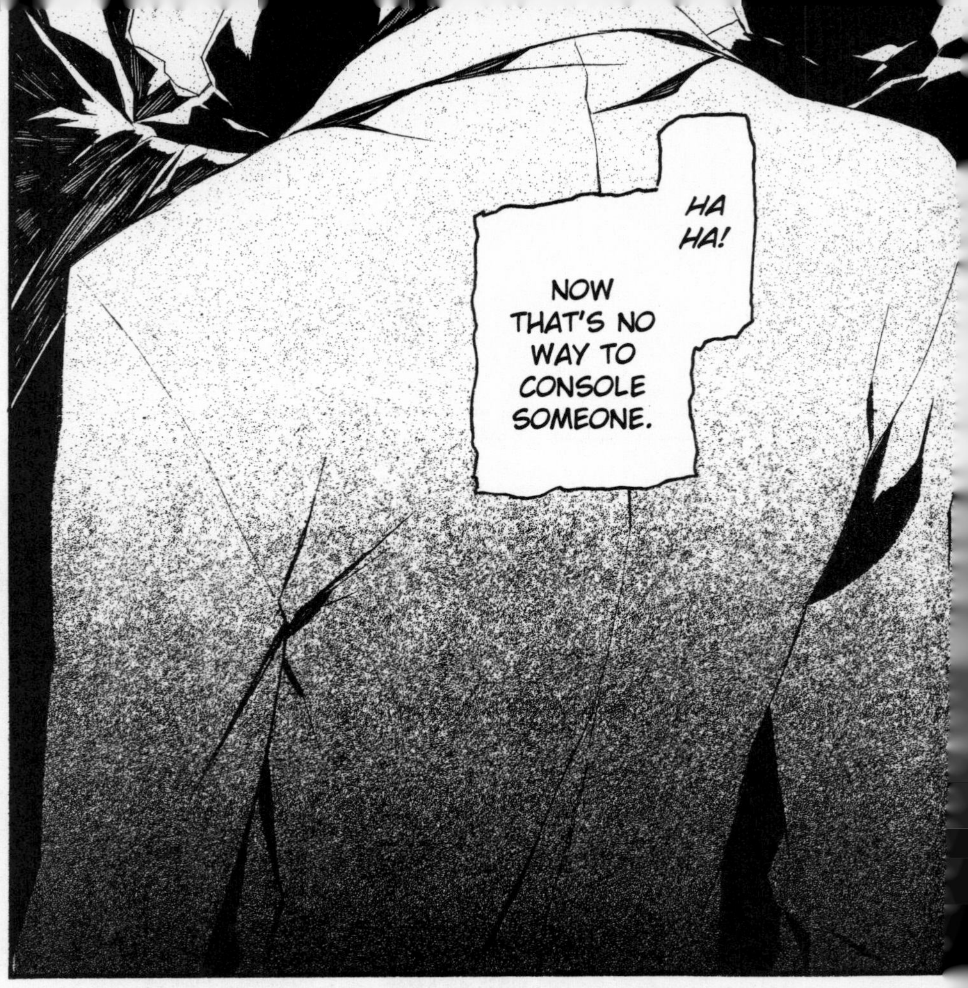
HA HA!
NOW THAT'S NO WAY TO CONSOLE SOMEONE.
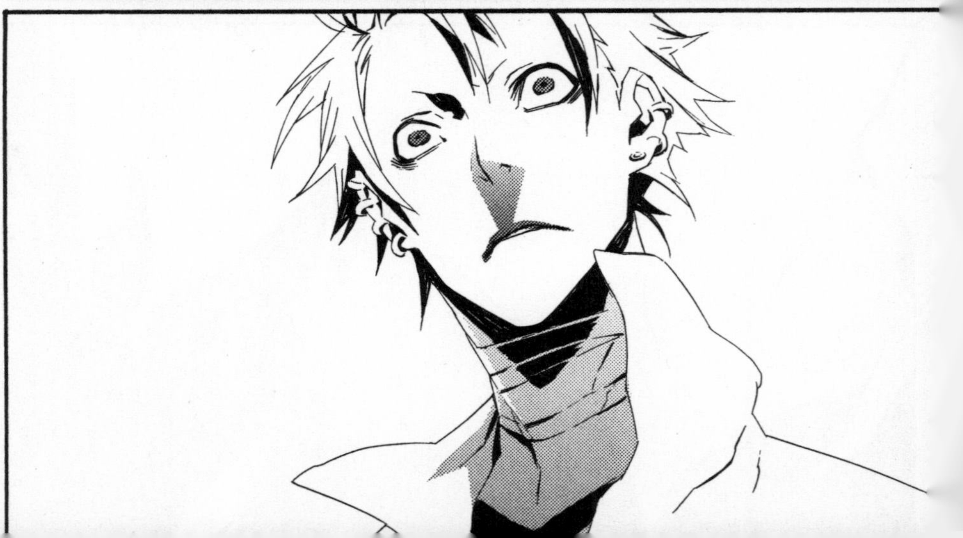

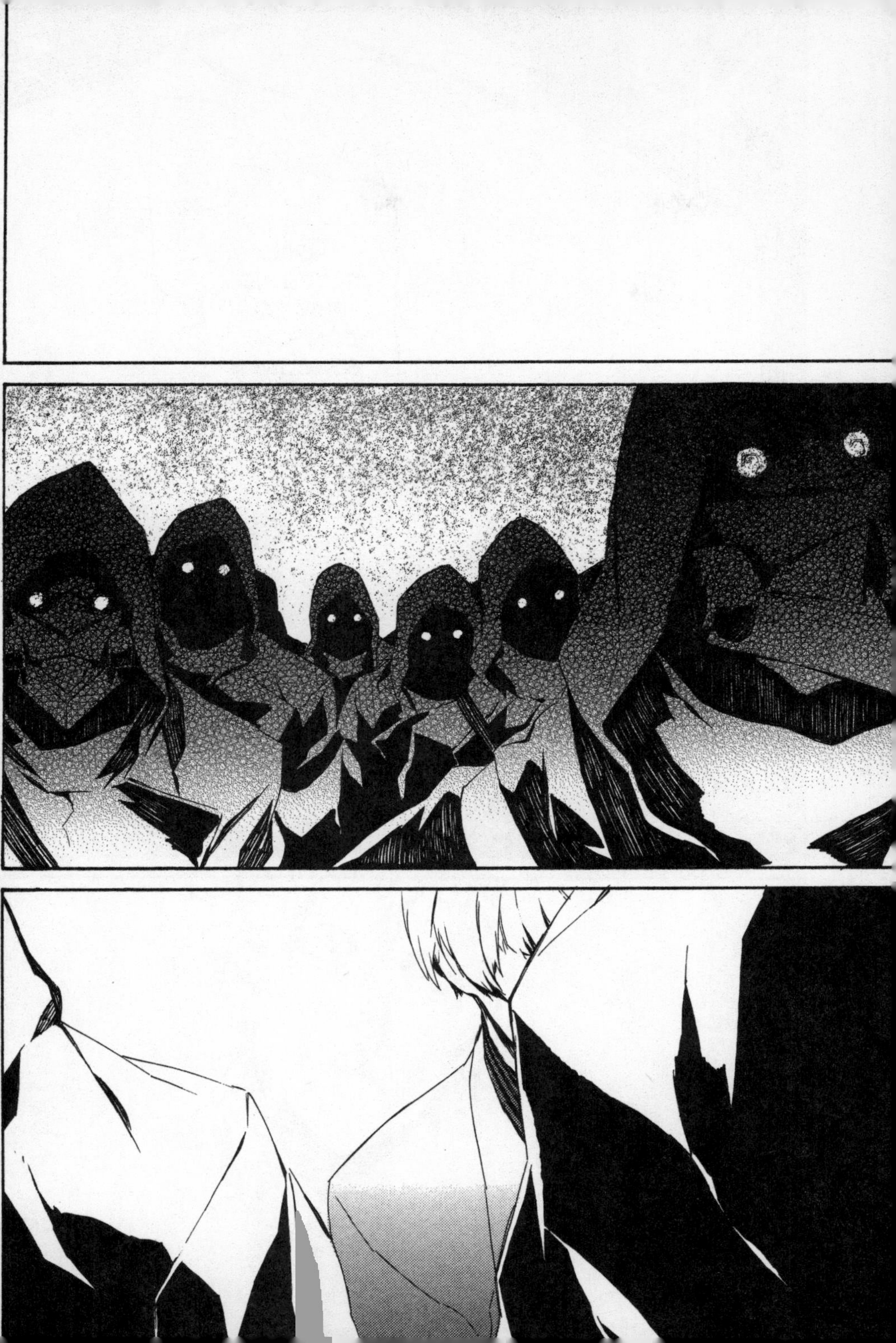

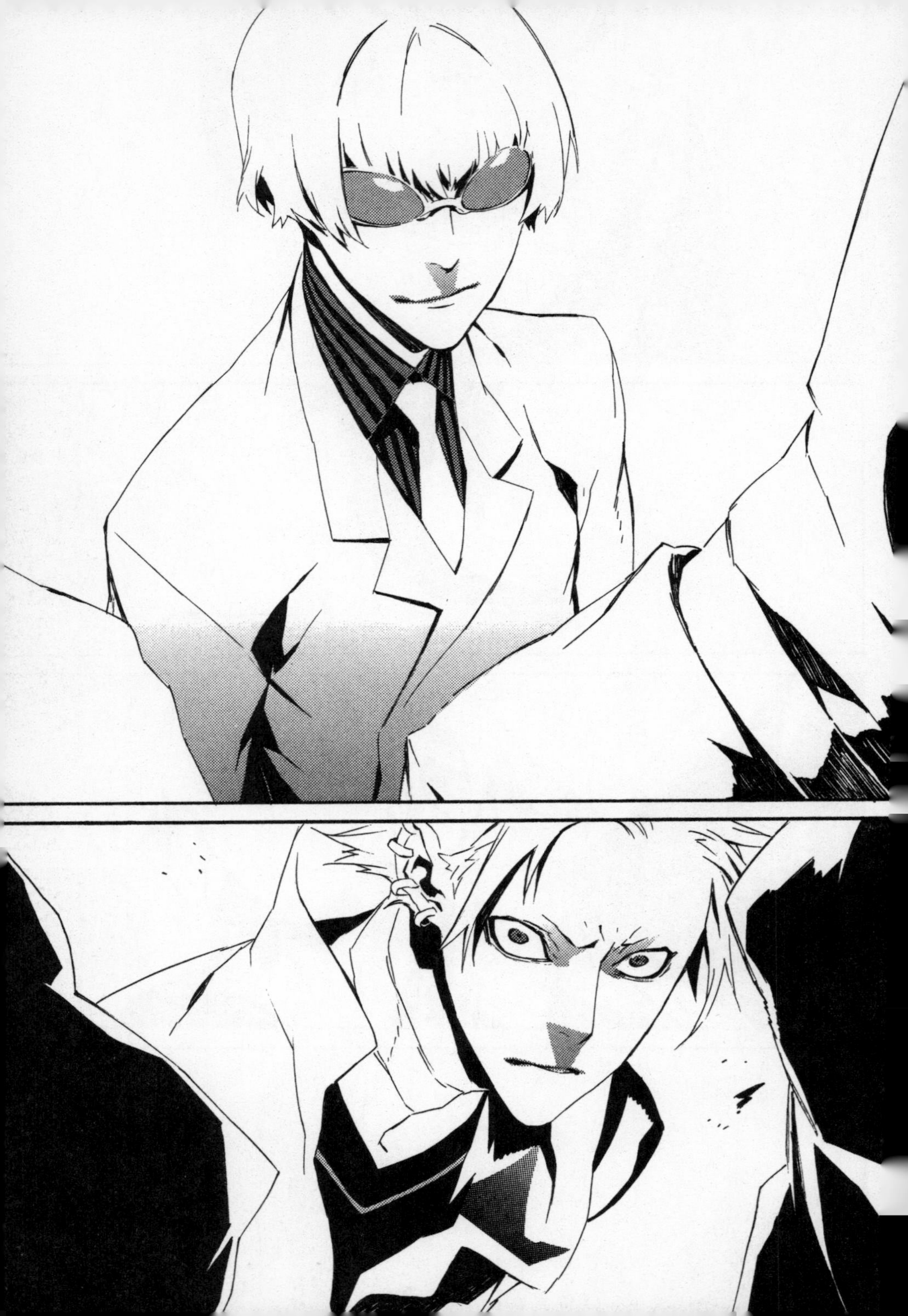

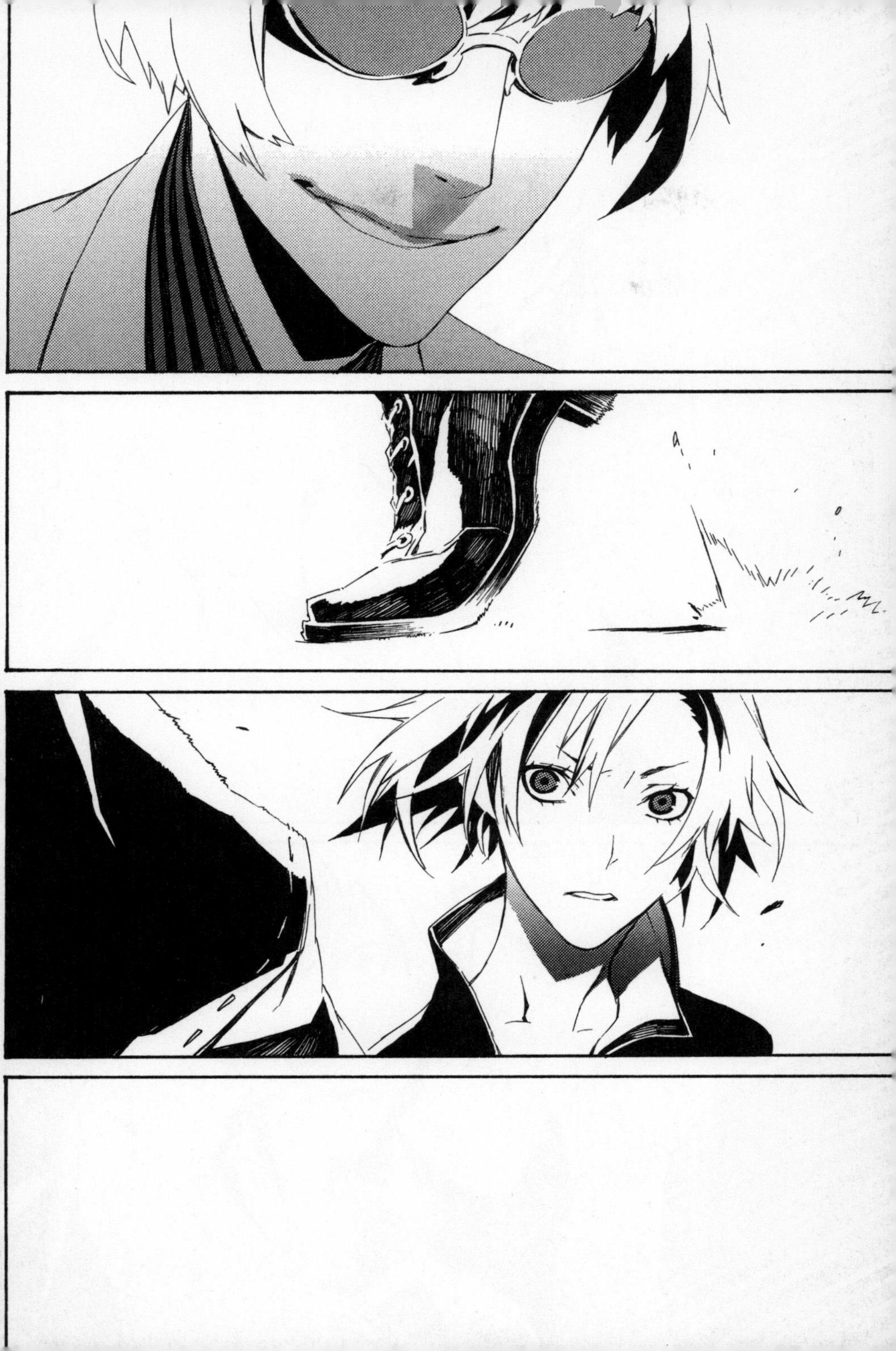

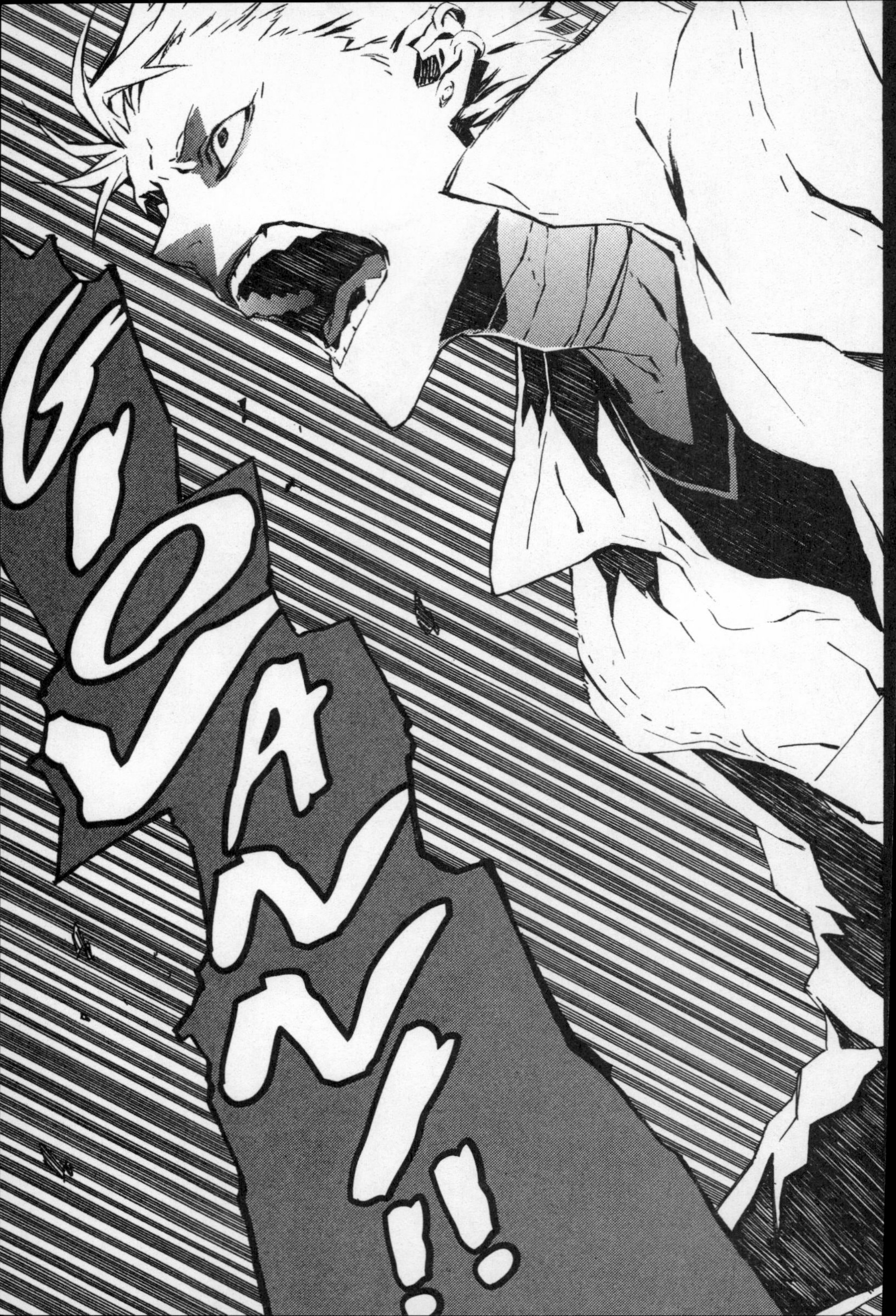
GOSANN!!

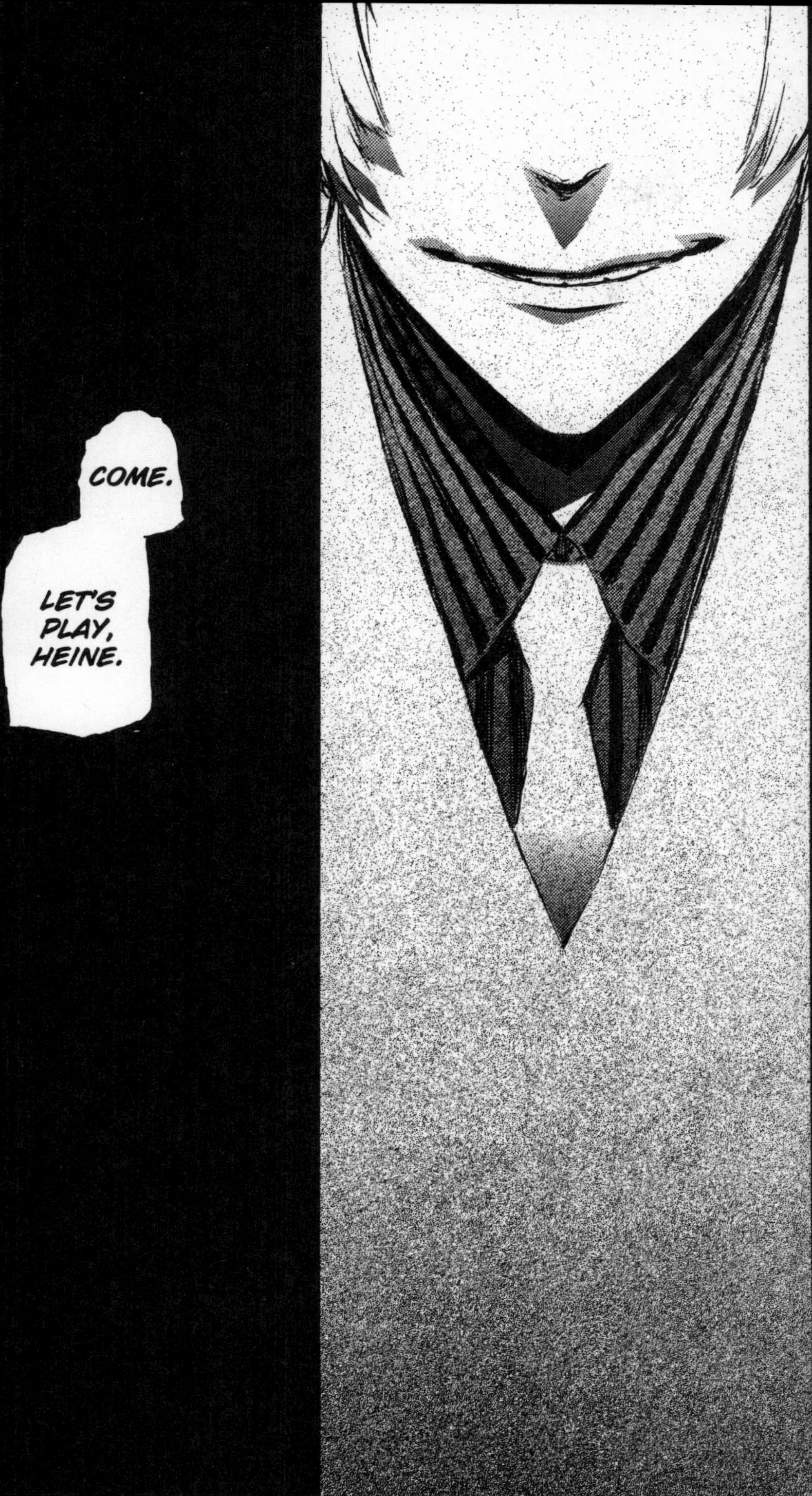
COME.
LET'S PLAY, HEINE.

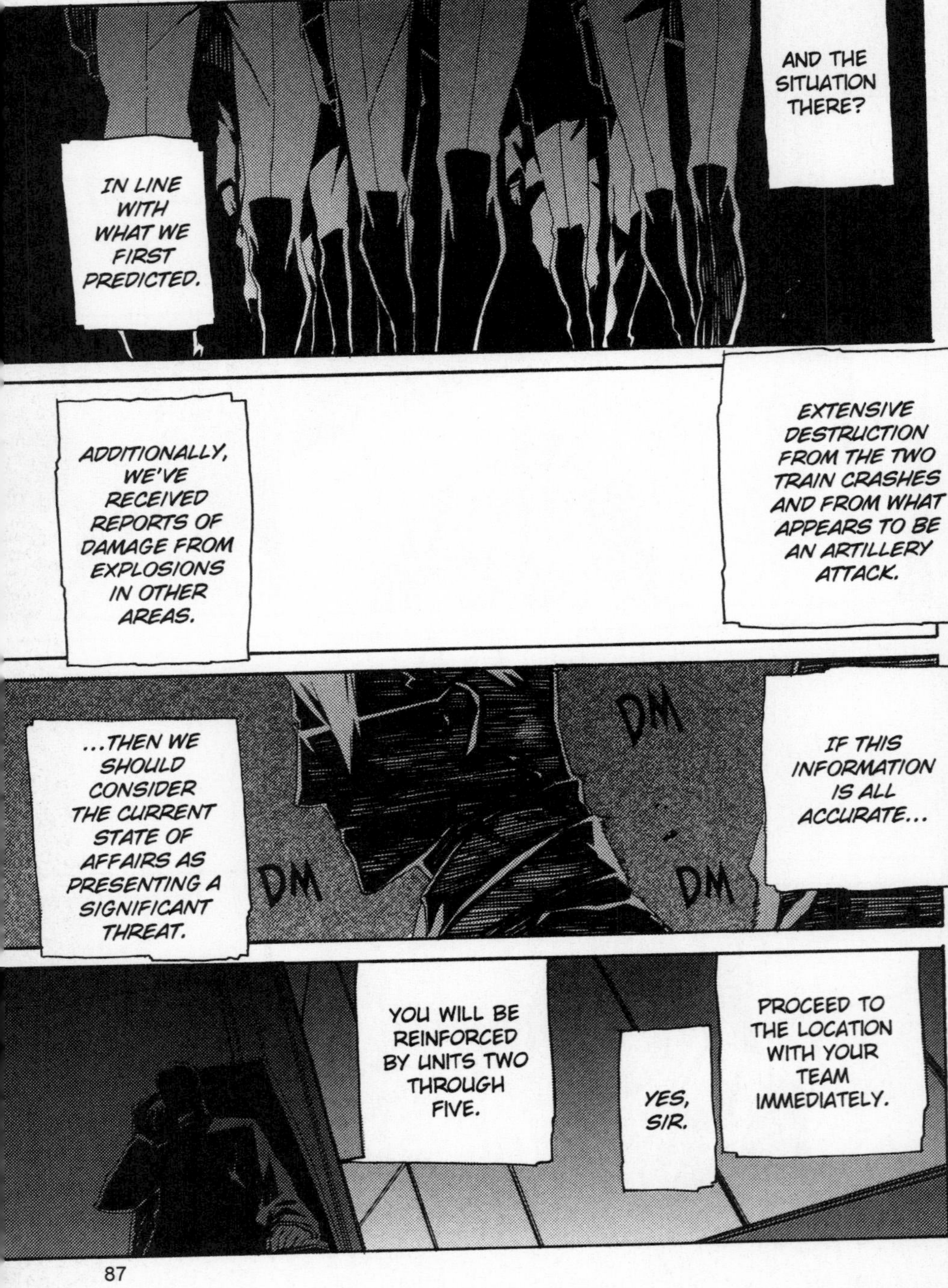
AND THE SITUATION THERE?
IN LINE WITH WHAT WE FIRST PREDICTED.
EXTENSIVE DESTRUCTION FROM THE TWO TRAIN CRASHES AND FROM WHAT APPEARS TO BE AN ARTILLERY ATTACK.
ADDITIONALLY, WE'VE RECEIVED REPORTS OF DAMAGE FROM EXPLOSIONS IN OTHER AREAS.
IF THIS INFORMATION IS ALL ACCURATE...
DM
DM
DM
...THEN WE SHOULD CONSIDER THE CURRENT STATE OF AFFAIRS AS PRESENTING A SIGNIFICANT THREAT.
PROCEED TO THE LOCATION WITH YOUR TEAM IMMEDIATELY.
YES, SIR.
YOU WILL BE REINFORCED BY UNITS TWO THROUGH FIVE.

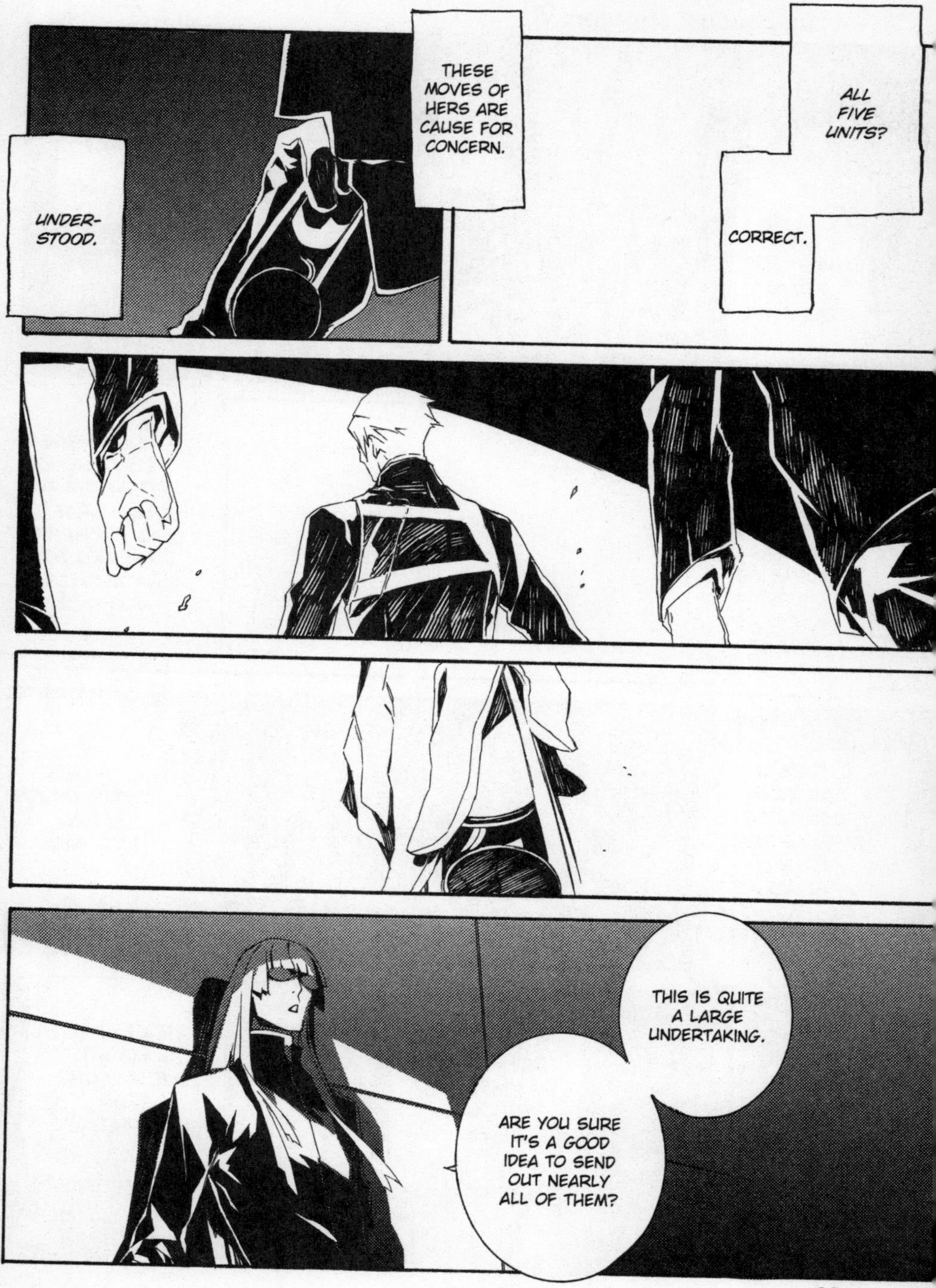
ALL FIVE UNITS?
CORRECT.
THESE MOVES OF HERS ARE CAUSE FOR CONCERN.
UNDERSTOOD.
THIS IS QUITE A LARGE UNDERTAKING.
ARE YOU SURE IT'S A GOOD IDEA TO SEND OUT NEARLY ALL OF THEM?

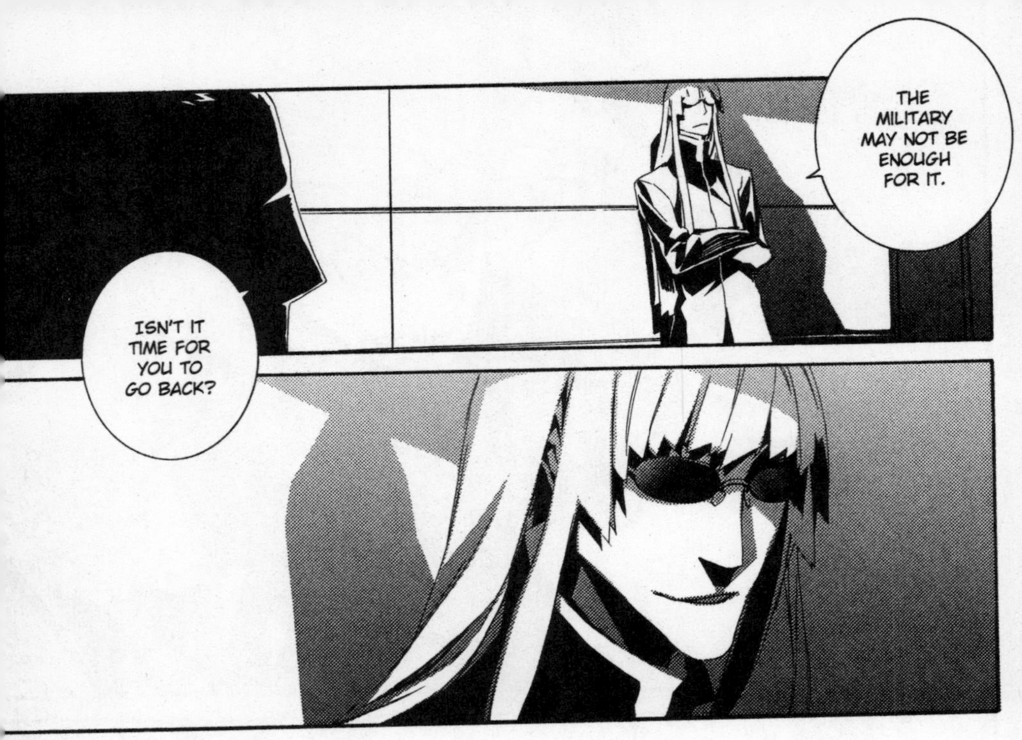
THE MILITARY MAY NOT BE ENOUGH FOR IT.
ISN'T IT TIME FOR YOU TO GO BACK?

#43 Aggressors & Strugglers VI

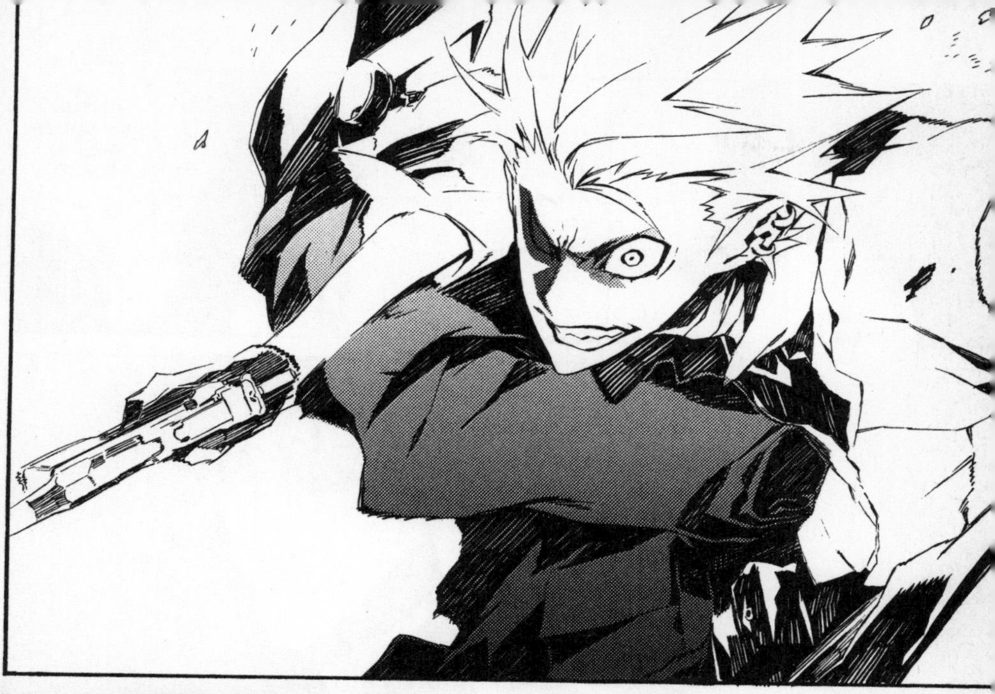
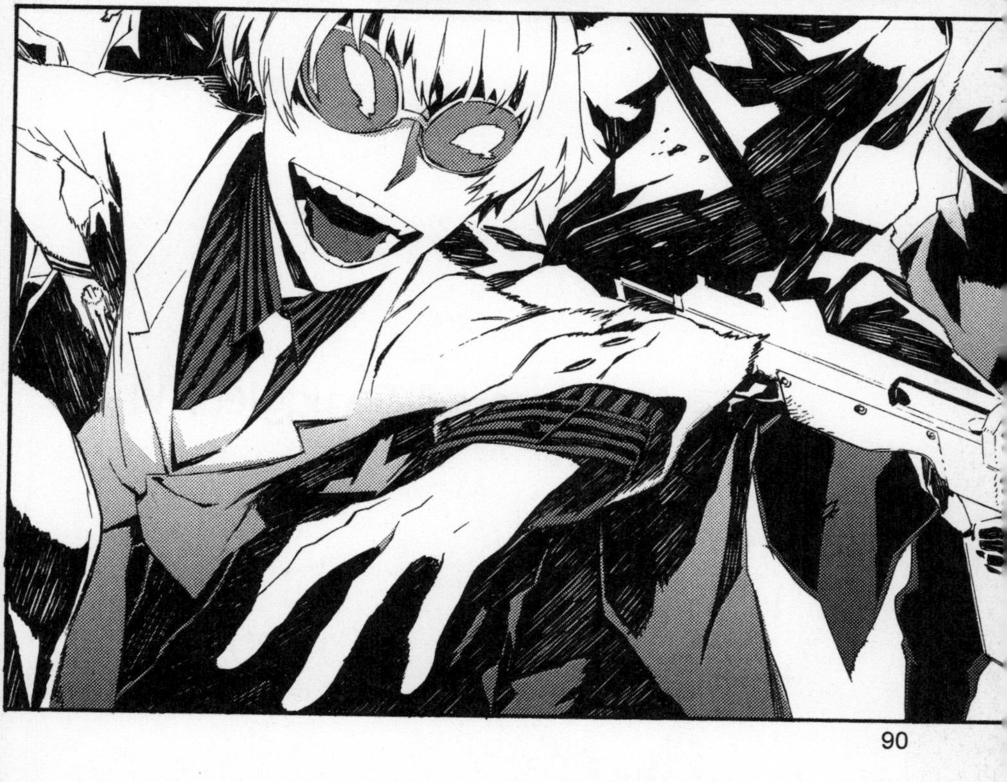

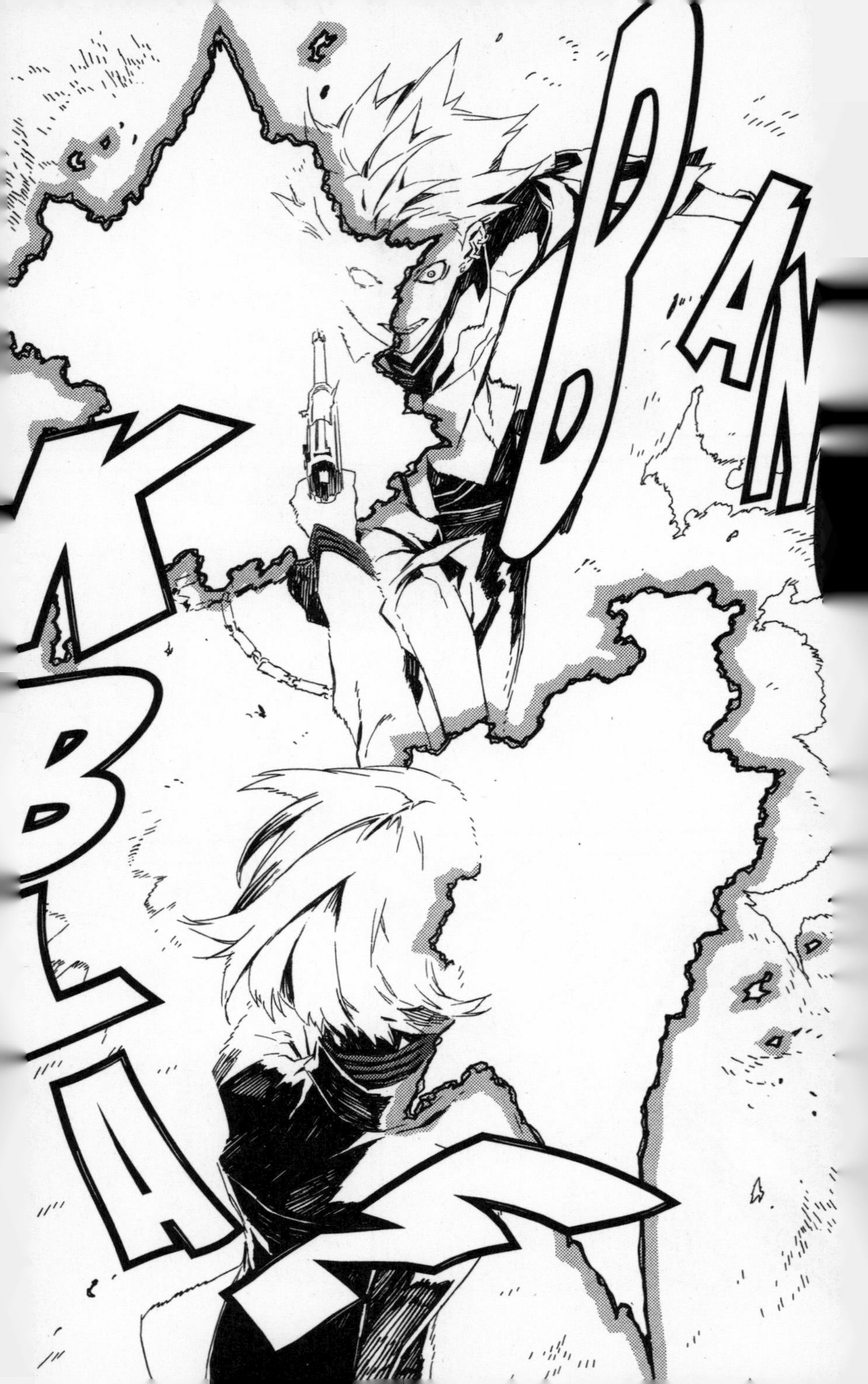
BAM
KABLAM

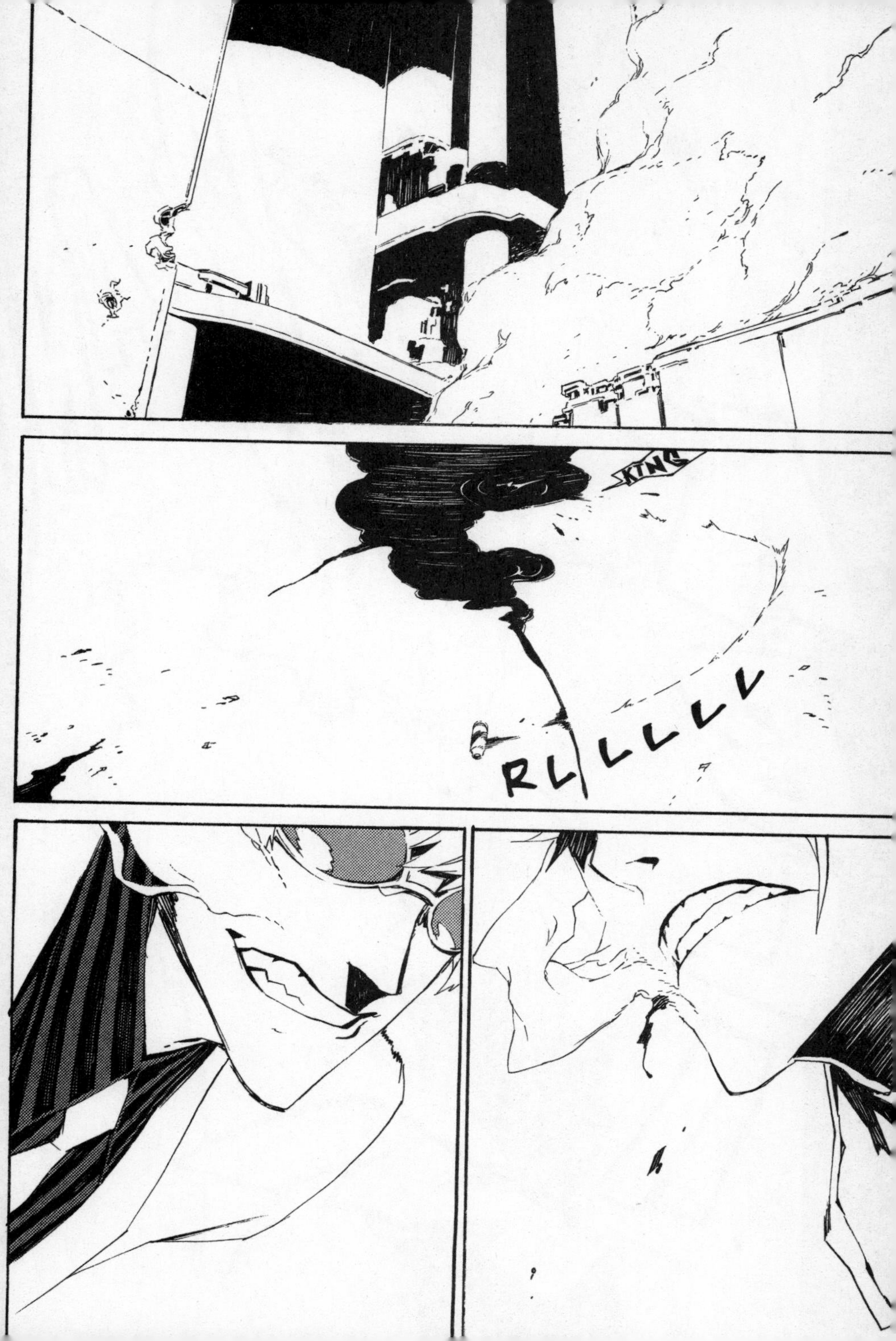
KTNG
RLLLLLL

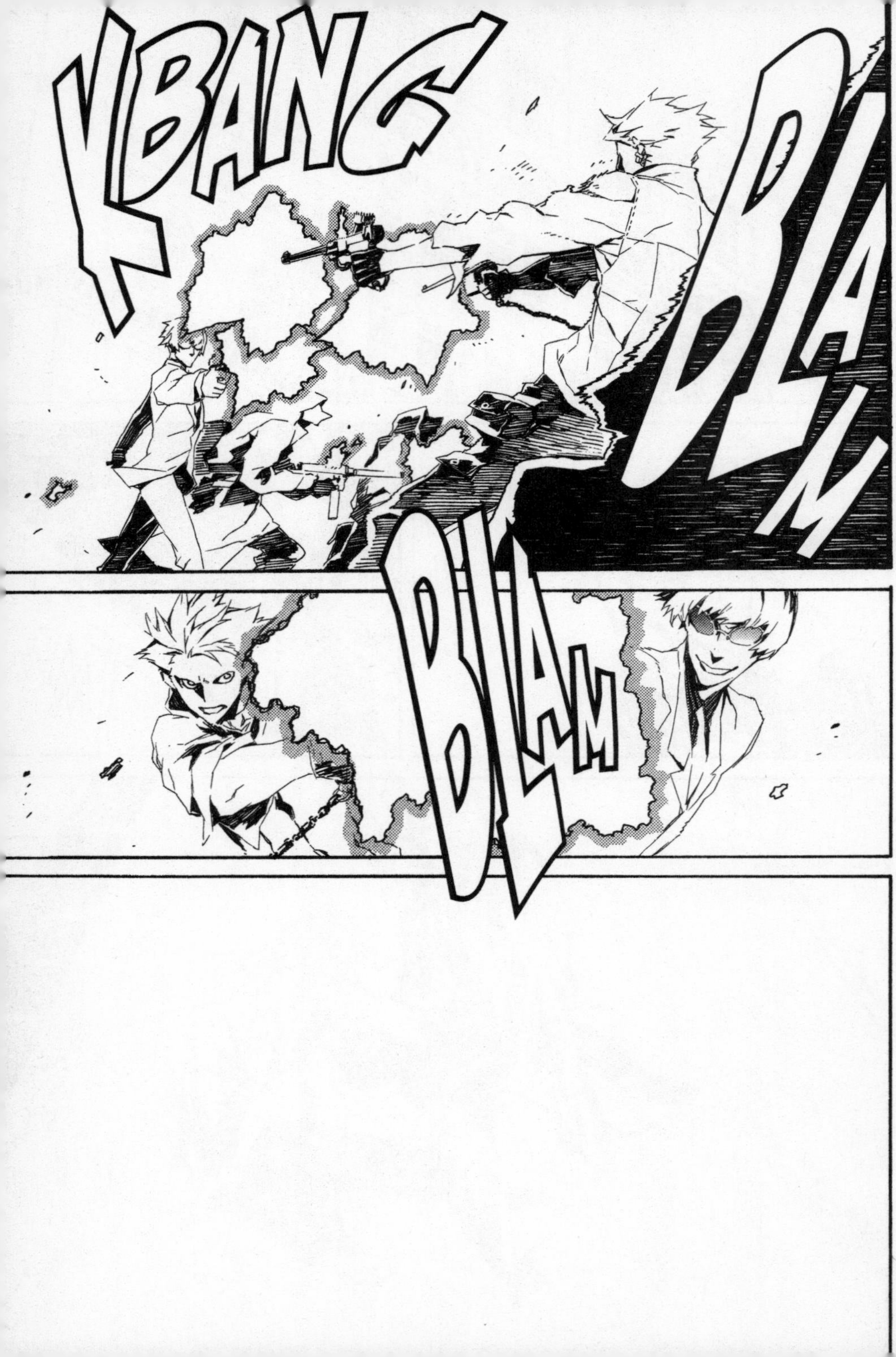
BLAM
KBANG
BLAM

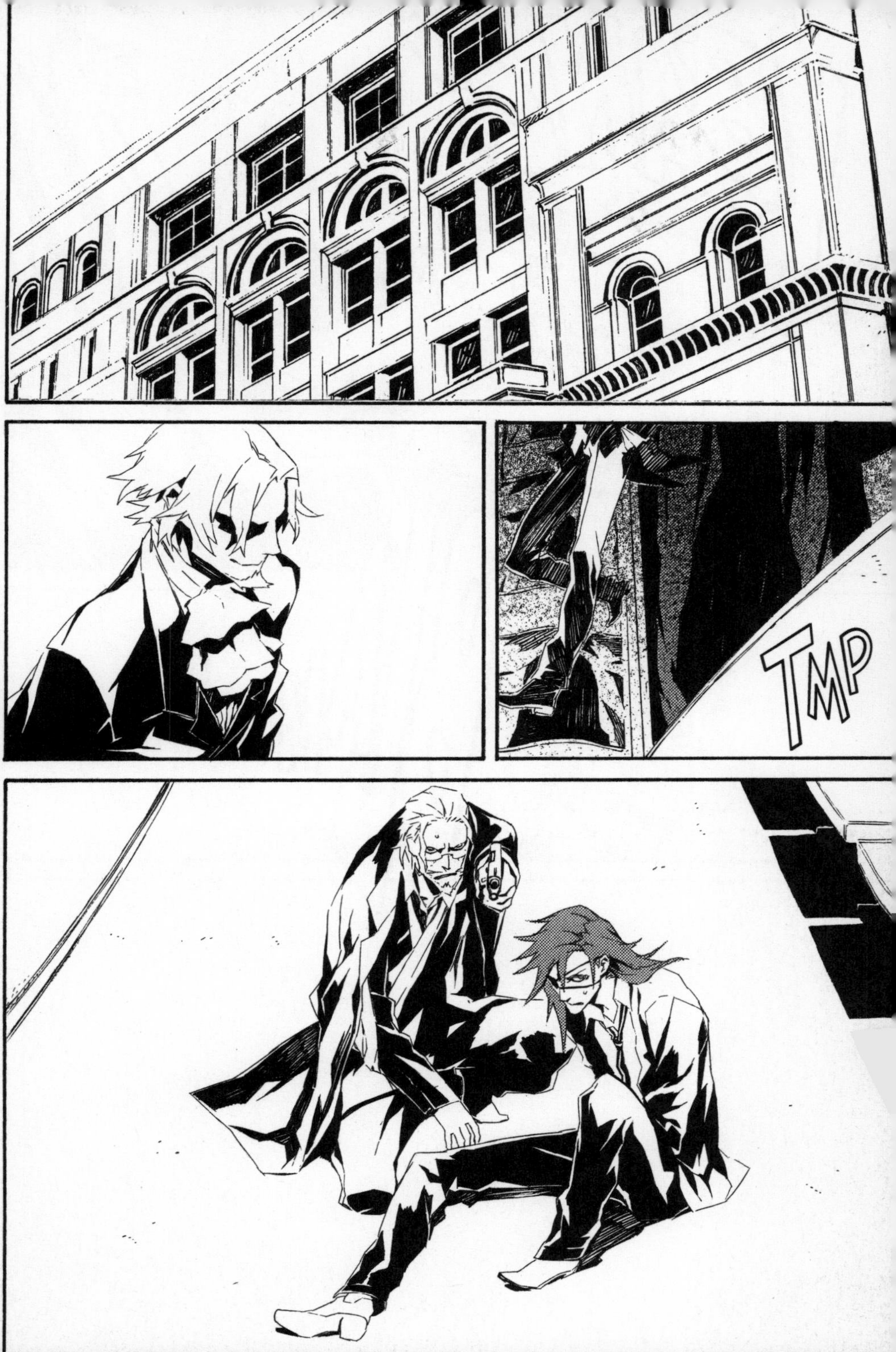
TMP

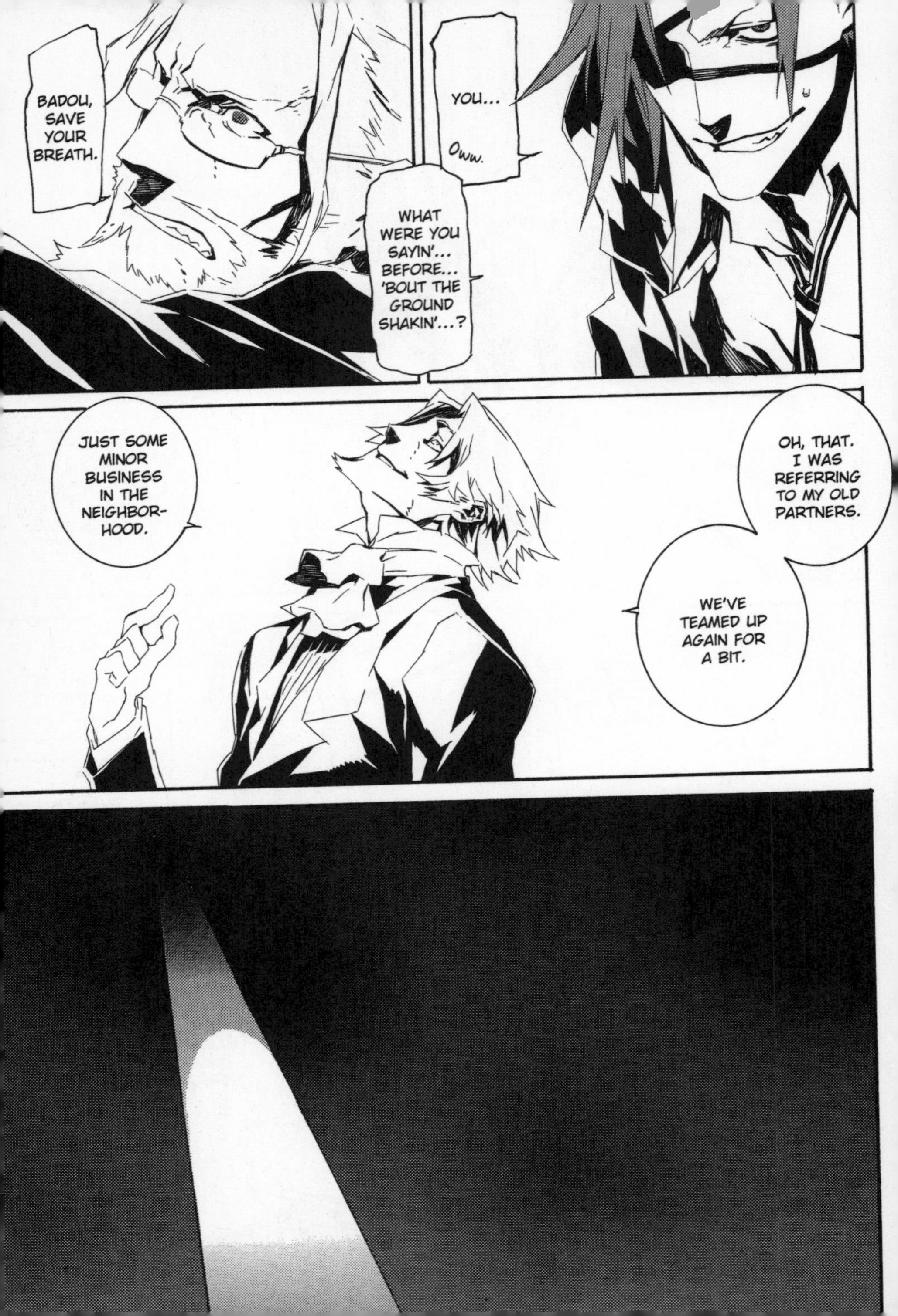
YOU...
Oww.
WHAT WERE YOU SAYIN'... BEFORE... 'BOUT THE GROUND SHAKIN'...?
BADOU, SAVE YOUR BREATH.
OH, THAT. I WAS REFERRING TO MY OLD PARTNERS.
WE'VE TEAMED UP AGAIN FOR A BIT.
JUST SOME MINOR BUSINESS IN THE NEIGHBOR-HOOD.

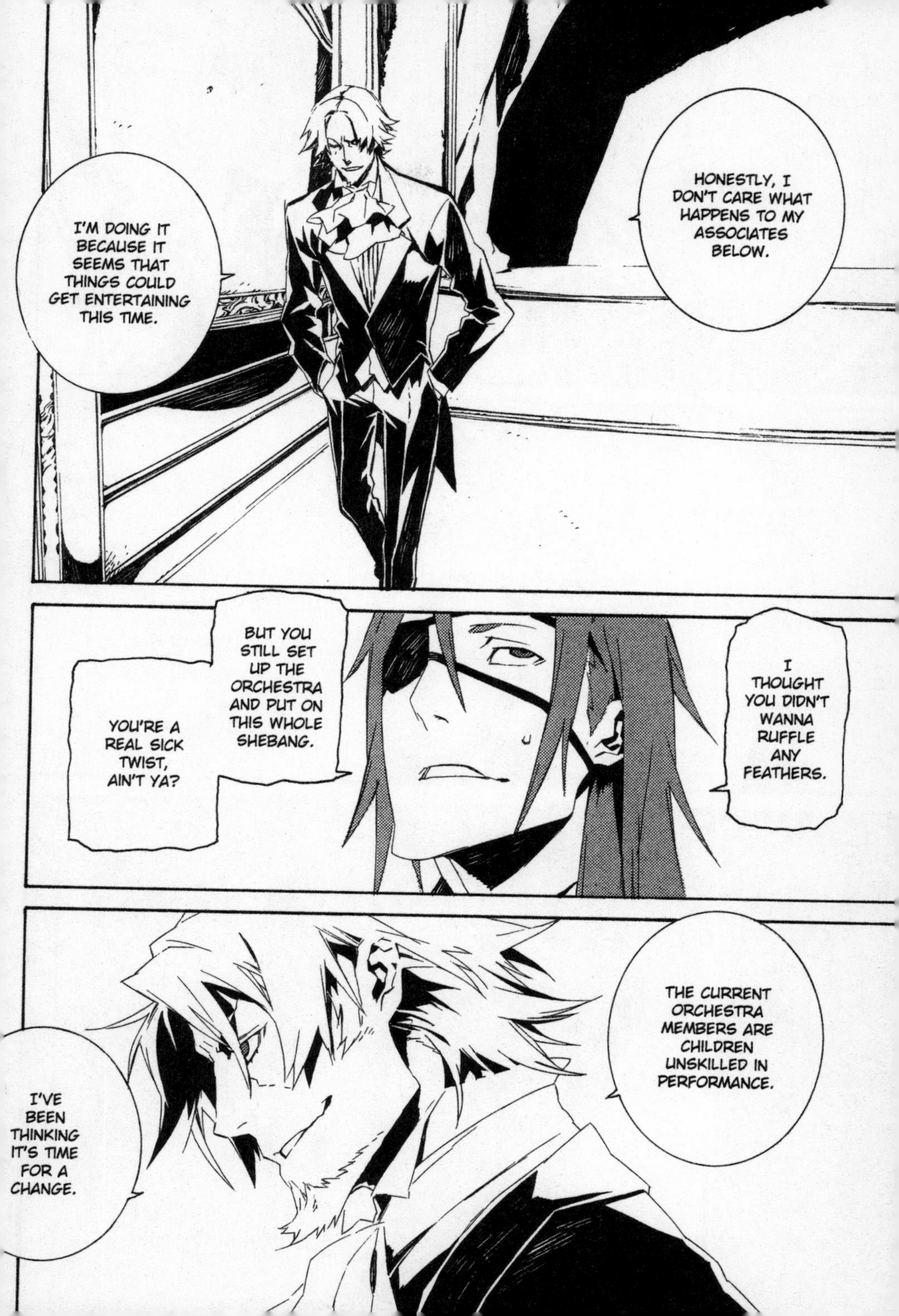

HONESTLY, I DON'T CARE WHAT HAPPENS TO MY ASSOCIATES BELOW.
I'M DOING IT BECAUSE IT SEEMS THAT THINGS COULD GET ENTERTAINING THIS TIME.
I THOUGHT YOU DIDN'T WANNA RUFFLE ANY FEATHERS.
BUT YOU STILL SET UP THE ORCHESTRA AND PUT ON THIS WHOLE SHEBANG.
YOU'RE A REAL SICK TWIST, AIN'T YA?
THE CURRENT ORCHESTRA MEMBERS ARE CHILDREN UNSKILLED IN PERFORMANCE.
I'VE BEEN THINKING IT'S TIME FOR A CHANGE.

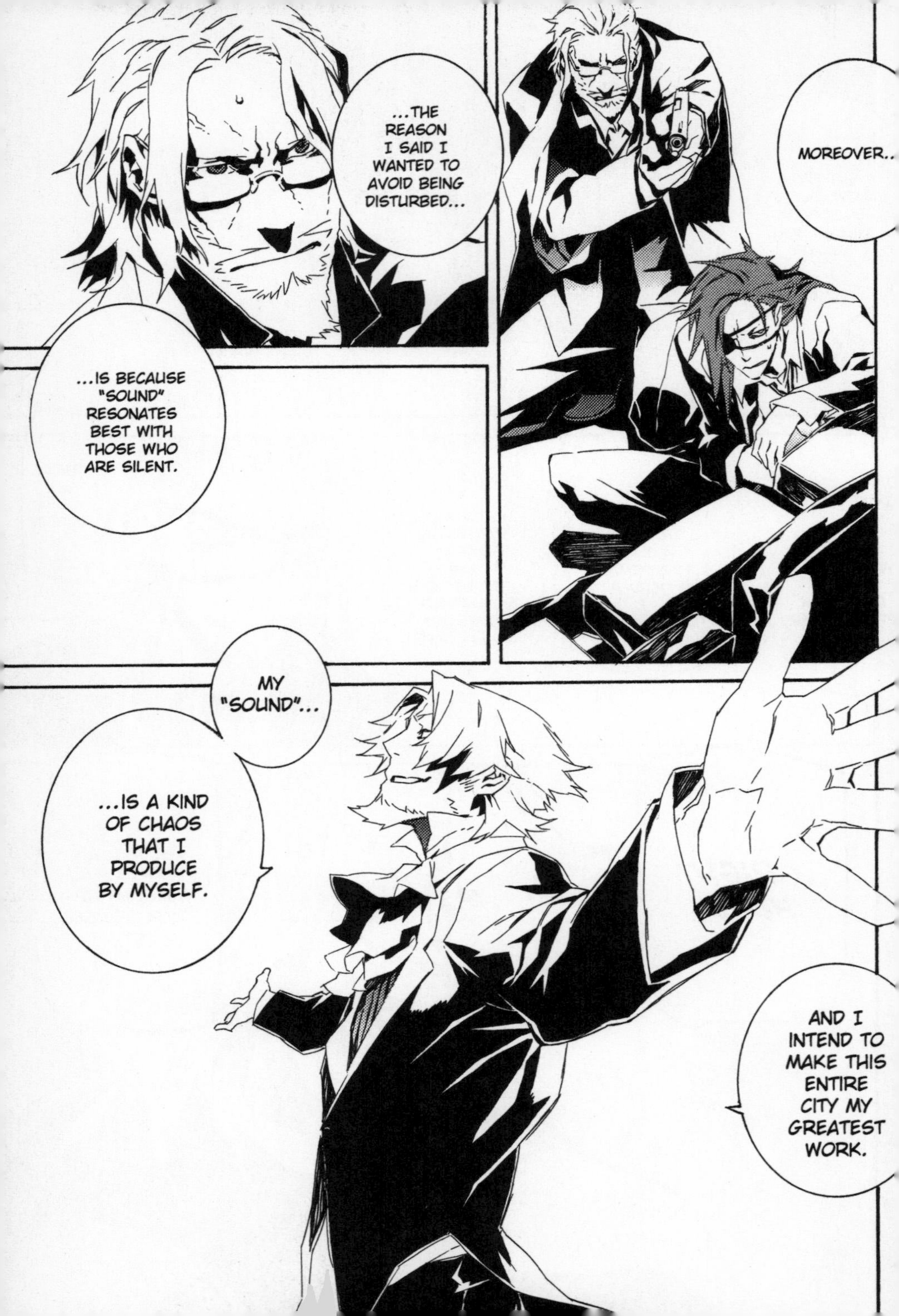
MOREOVER..
...THE REASON I SAID I WANTED TO AVOID BEING DISTURBED...
...IS BECAUSE "SOUND" RESONATES BEST WITH THOSE WHO ARE SILENT.
MY "SOUND"...
...IS A KIND OF CHAOS THAT I PRODUCE BY MYSELF.
AND I INTEND TO MAKE THIS ENTIRE CITY MY GREATEST WORK.

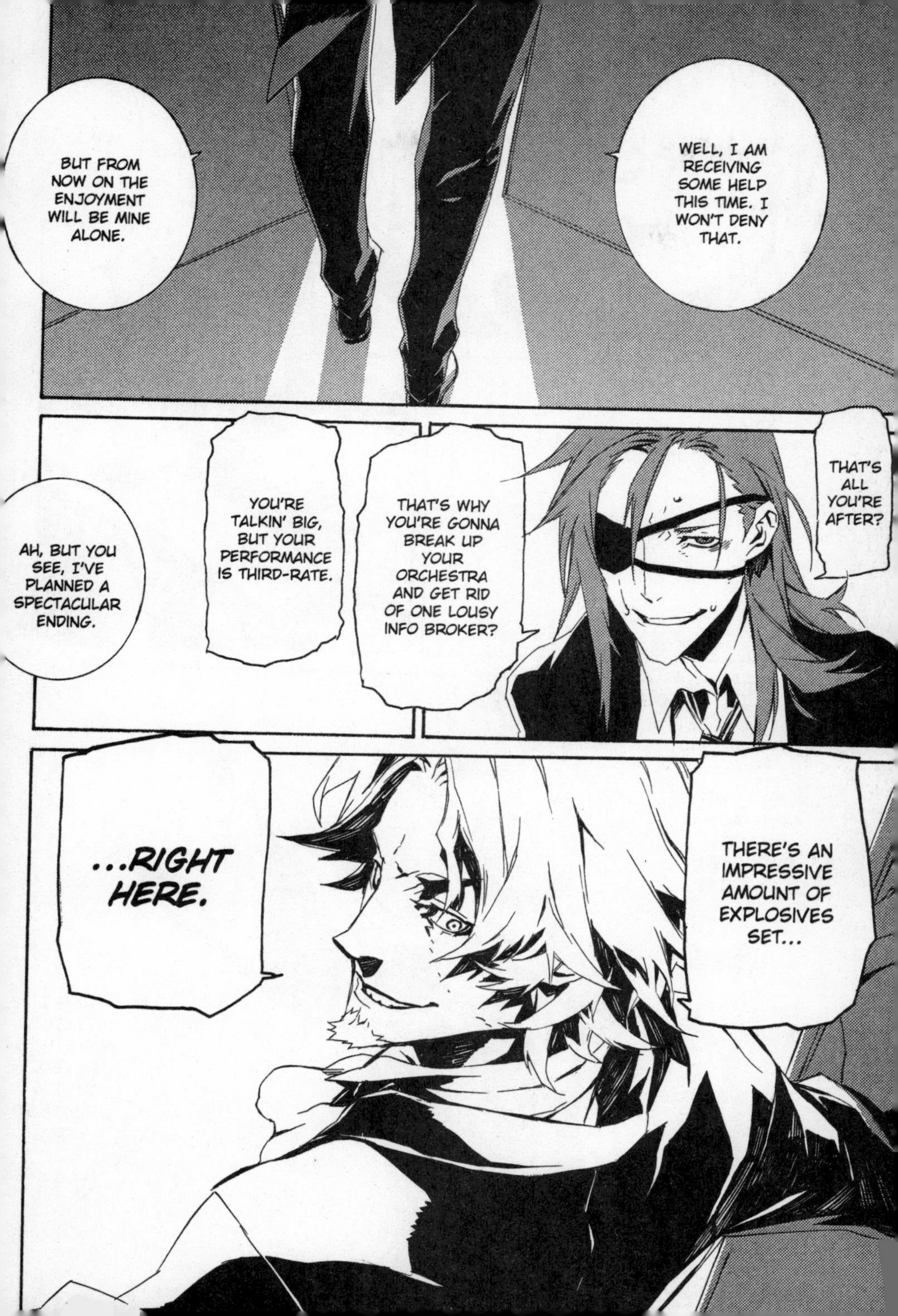
WELL, I AM RECEIVING SOME HELP THIS TIME. I WON'T DENY THAT.
BUT FROM NOW ON THE ENJOYMENT WILL BE MINE ALONE.
THAT'S ALL YOU'RE AFTER?
THAT'S WHY YOU'RE GONNA BREAK UP YOUR ORCHESTRA AND GET RID OF ONE LOUSY INFO BROKER?
YOU'RE TALKIN' BIG, BUT YOUR PERFORMANCE IS THIRD-RATE.
AH, BUT YOU SEE, I'VE PLANNED A SPECTACULAR ENDING.
THERE'S AN IMPRESSIVE AMOUNT OF EXPLOSIVES SET...
...RIGHT HERE.

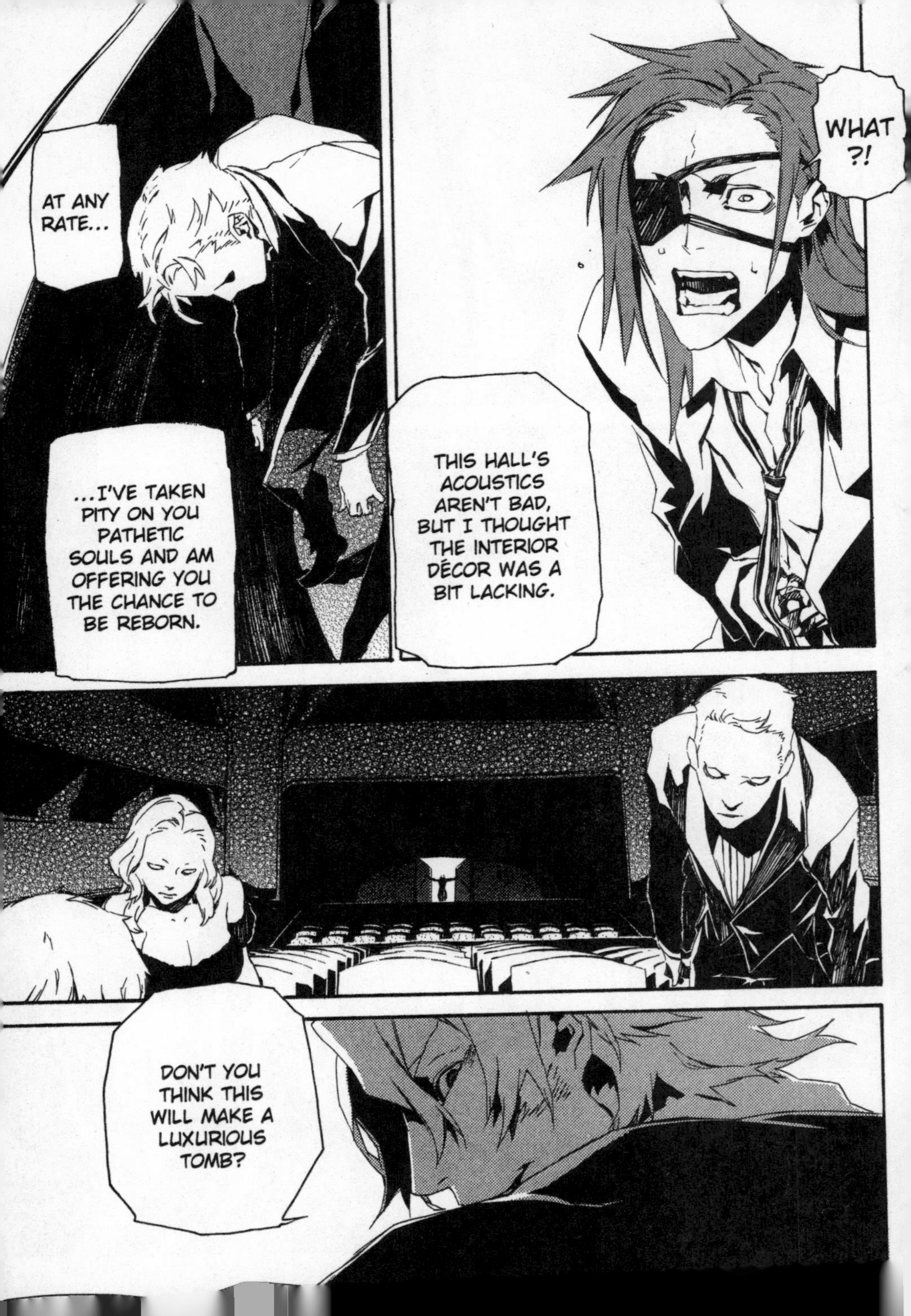
WHAT ?!
THIS HALL'S ACOUSTICS AREN'T BAD, BUT I THOUGHT THE INTERIOR DÉCOR WAS A BIT LACKING.
AT ANY RATE...
...I'VE TAKEN PITY ON YOU PATHETIC SOULS AND AM OFFERING YOU THE CHANCE TO BE REBORN.
DON'T YOU THINK THIS WILL MAKE A LUXURIOUS TOMB?

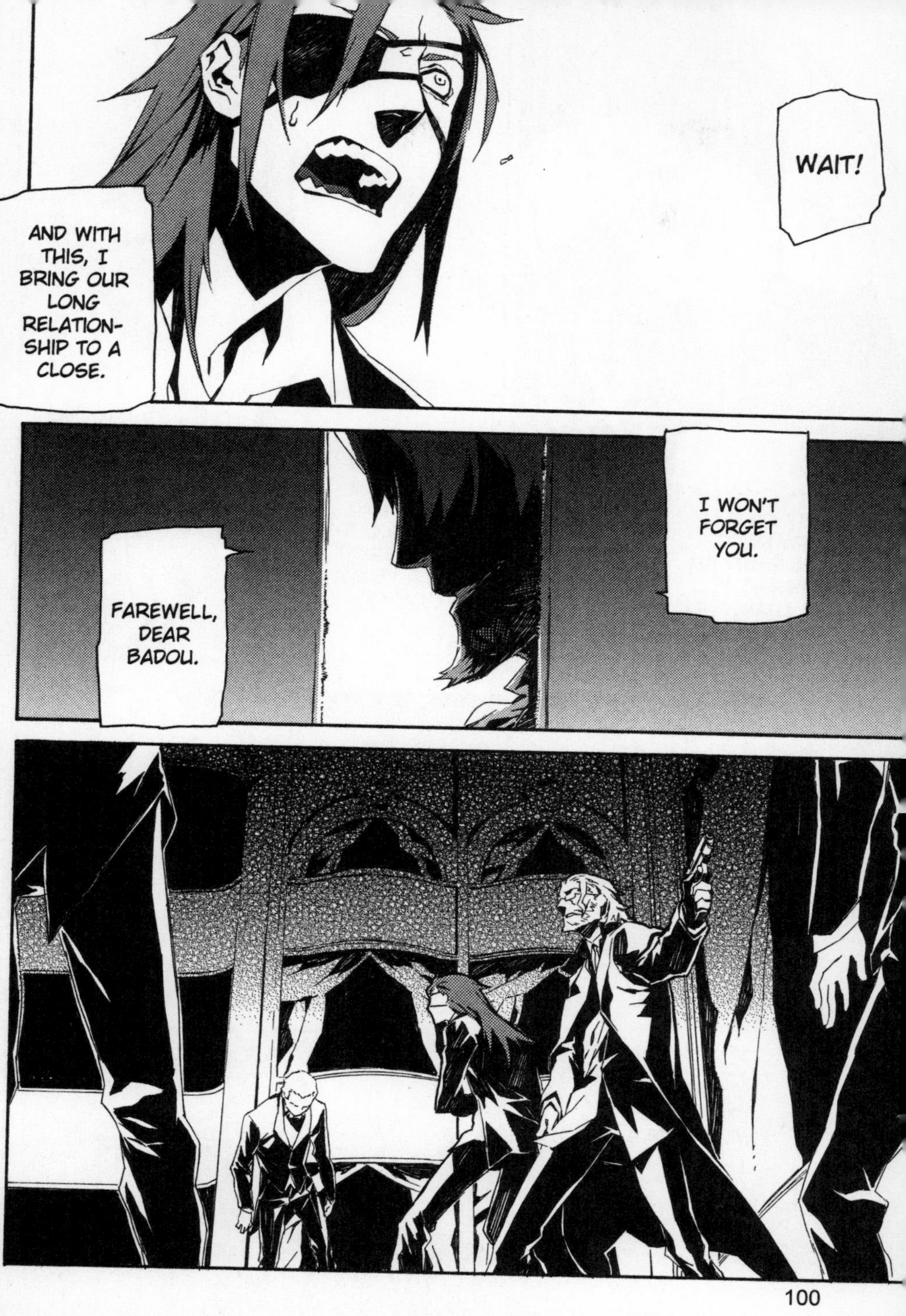
WAIT!
AND WITH THIS, I BRING OUR LONG RELATION-SHIP TO A CLOSE.
I WON'T FORGET YOU.
FAREWELL, DEAR BADOU.

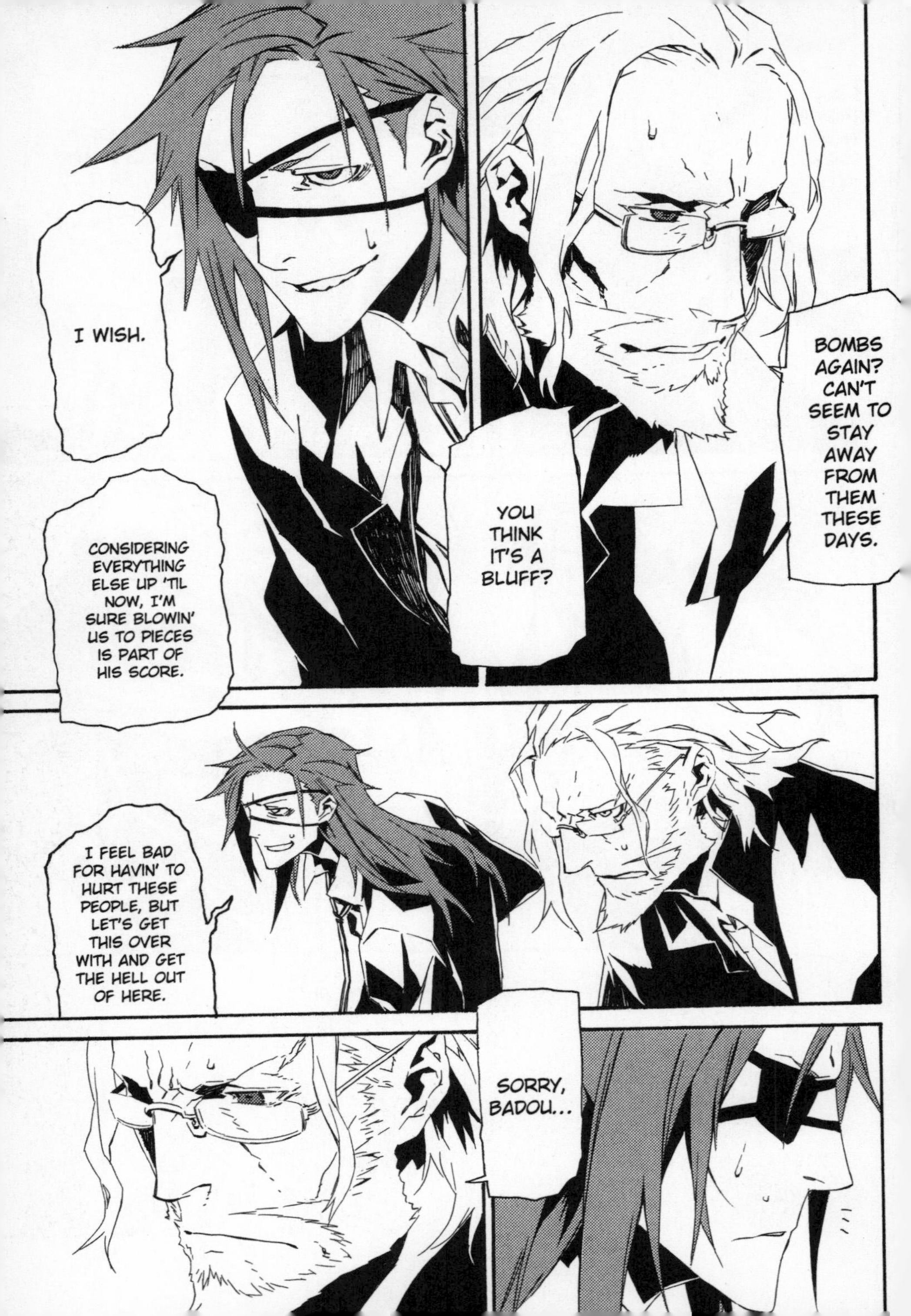
BOMBS AGAIN? CAN'T SEEM TO STAY AWAY FROM THEM THESE DAYS.
YOU THINK IT'S A BLUFF?
I WISH.
CONSIDERING EVERYTHING ELSE UP 'TIL NOW, I'M SURE BLOWIN' US TO PIECES IS PART OF HIS SCORE.
I FEEL BAD FOR HAVIN' TO HURT THESE PEOPLE, BUT LET'S GET THIS OVER WITH AND GET THE HELL OUT OF HERE.
SORRY, BADOU...

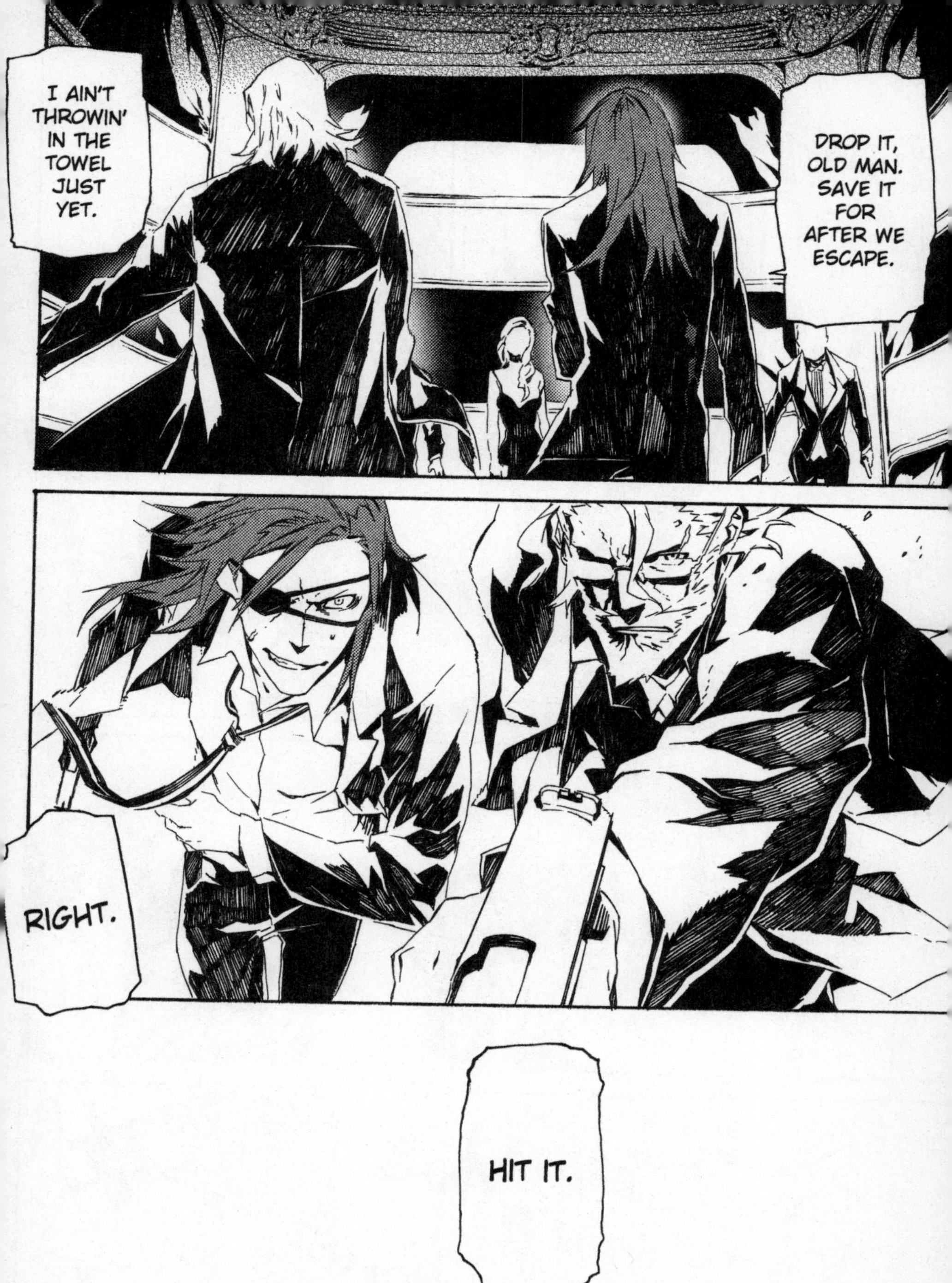
DROP IT, OLD MAN. SAVE IT FOR AFTER WE ESCAPE.
I AIN'T THROWIN' IN THE TOWEL JUST YET.
RIGHT.
HIT IT.

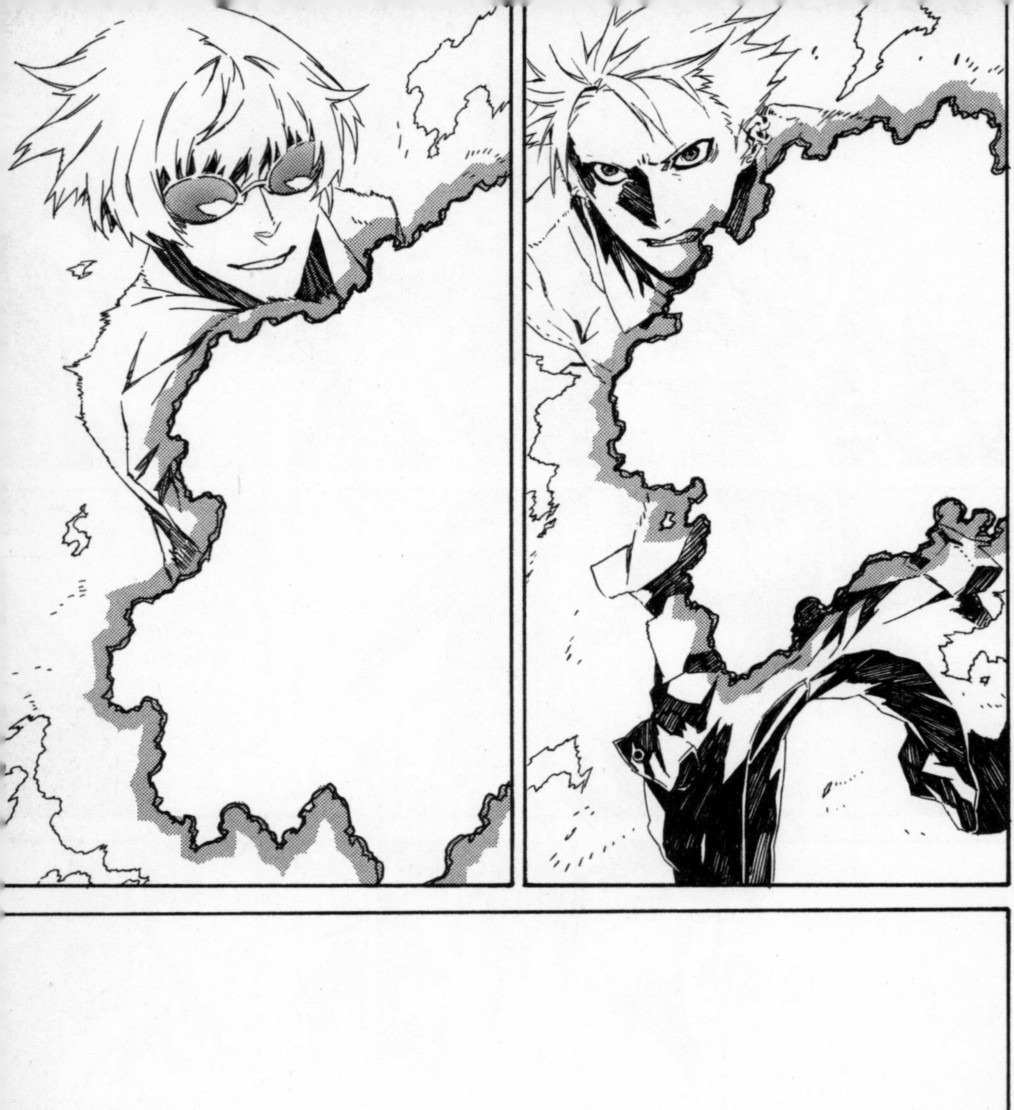

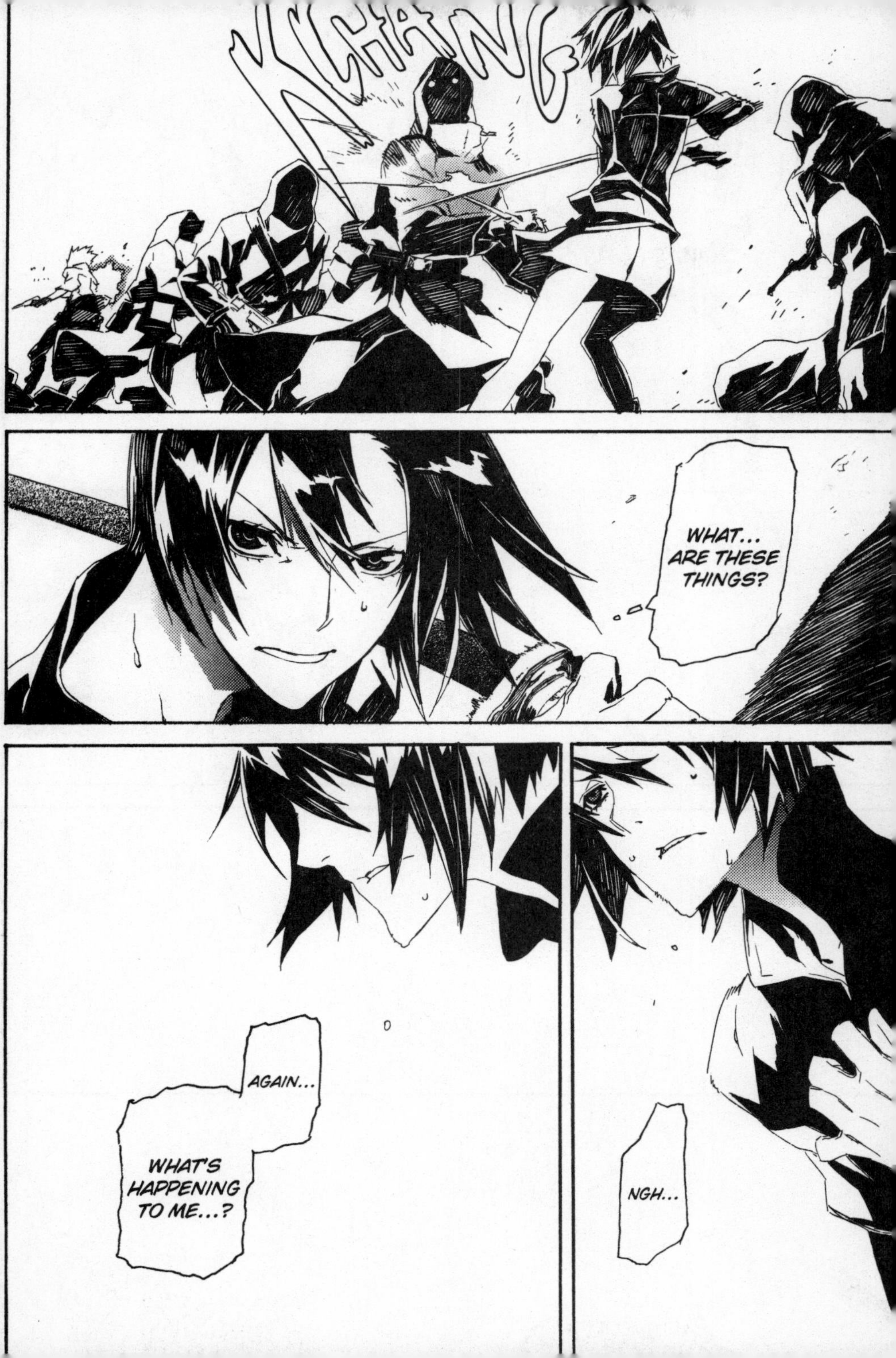
WHAT... ARE THESE THINGS?
NGH...
AGAIN...
WHAT'S HAPPENING TO ME...?

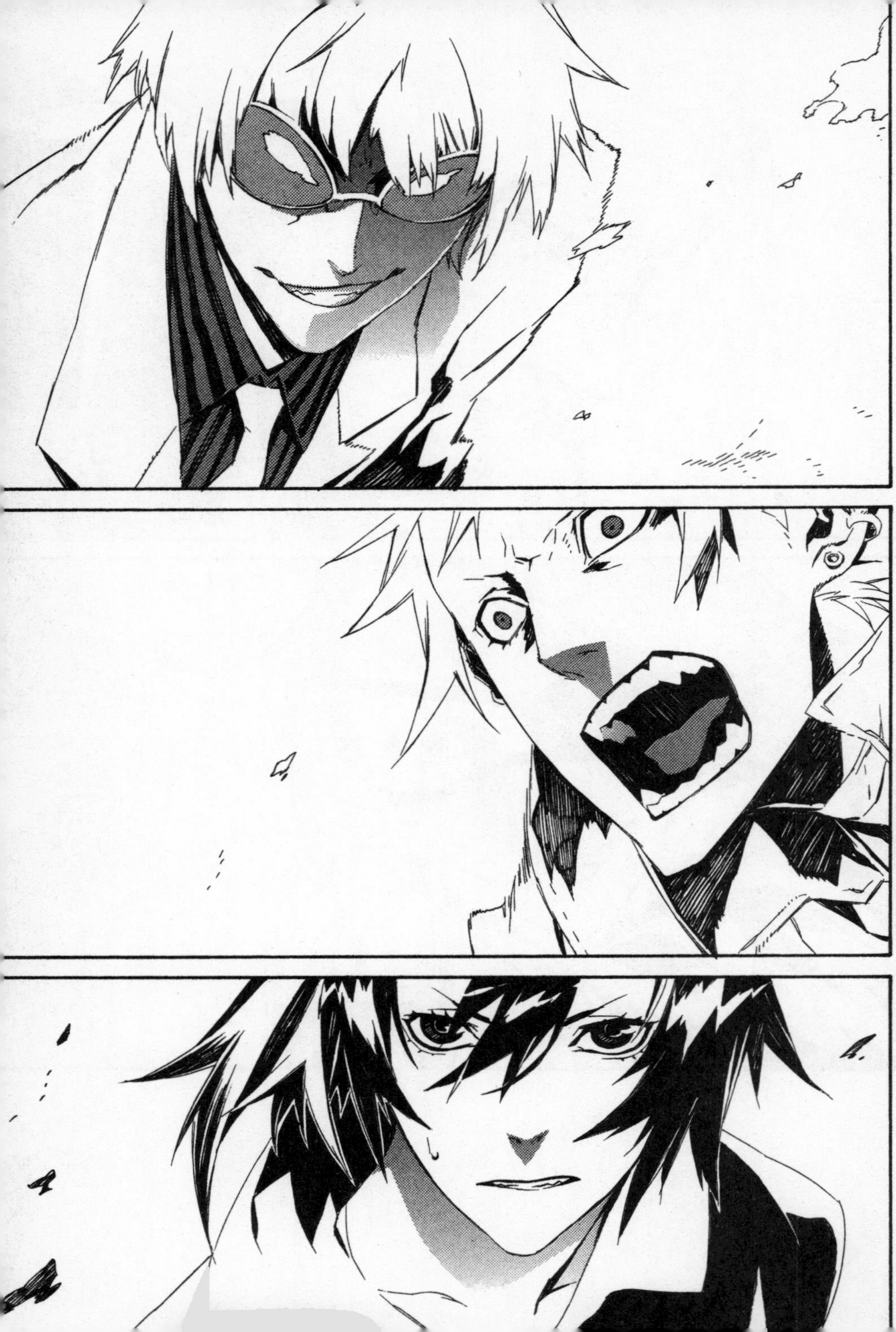

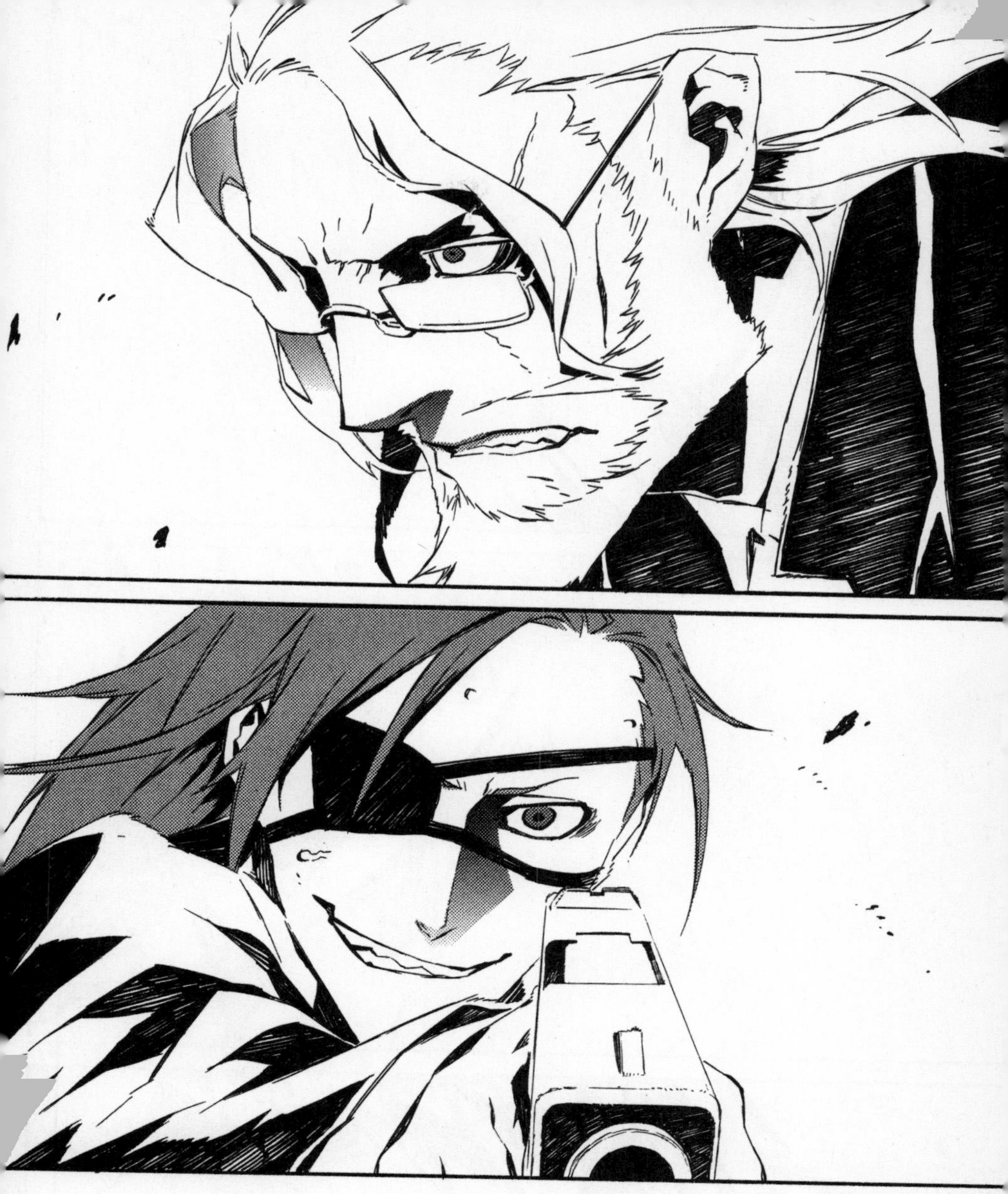

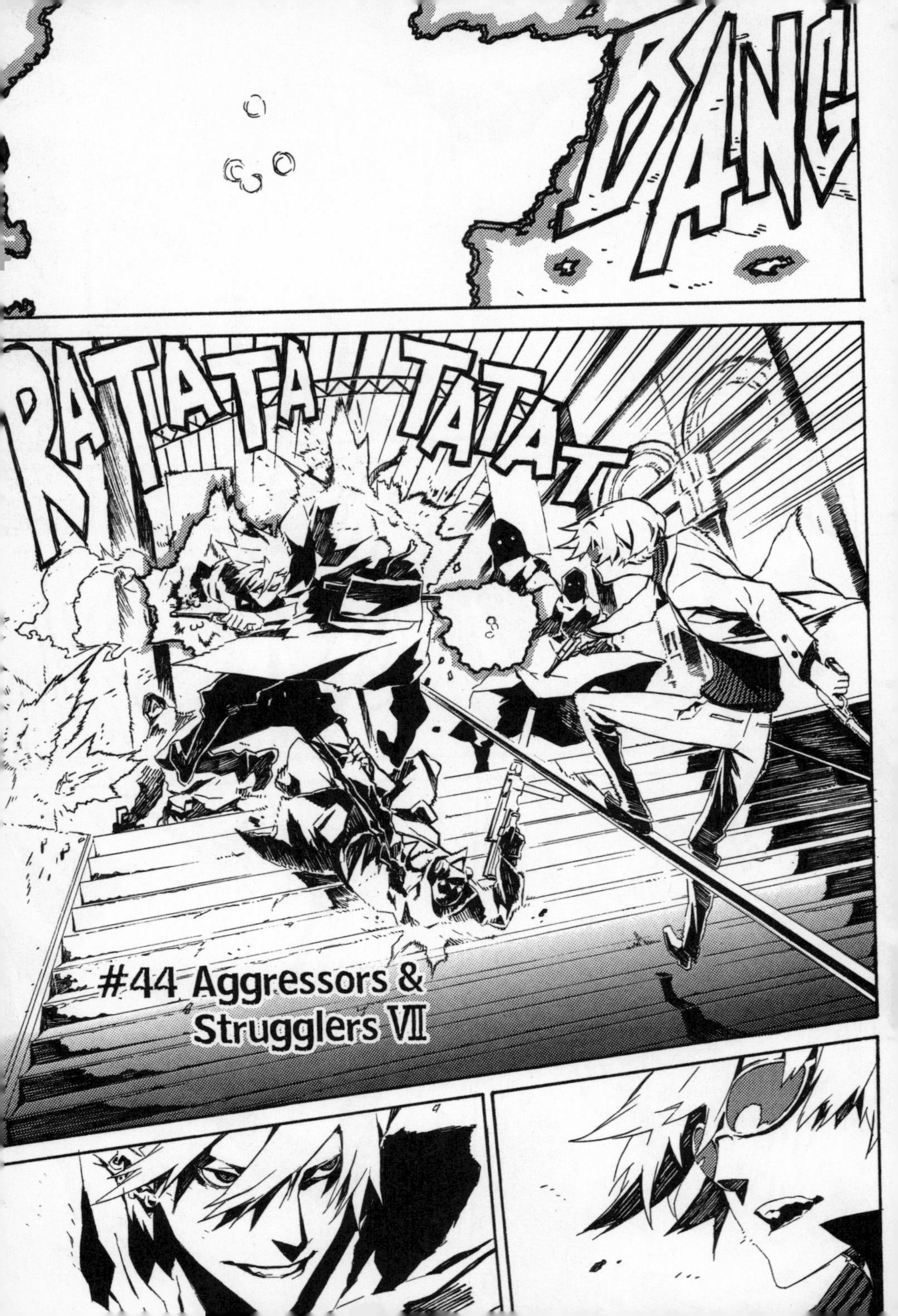
BANG
RATATATA
TATAT
#44 Aggressors & Strugglers VII

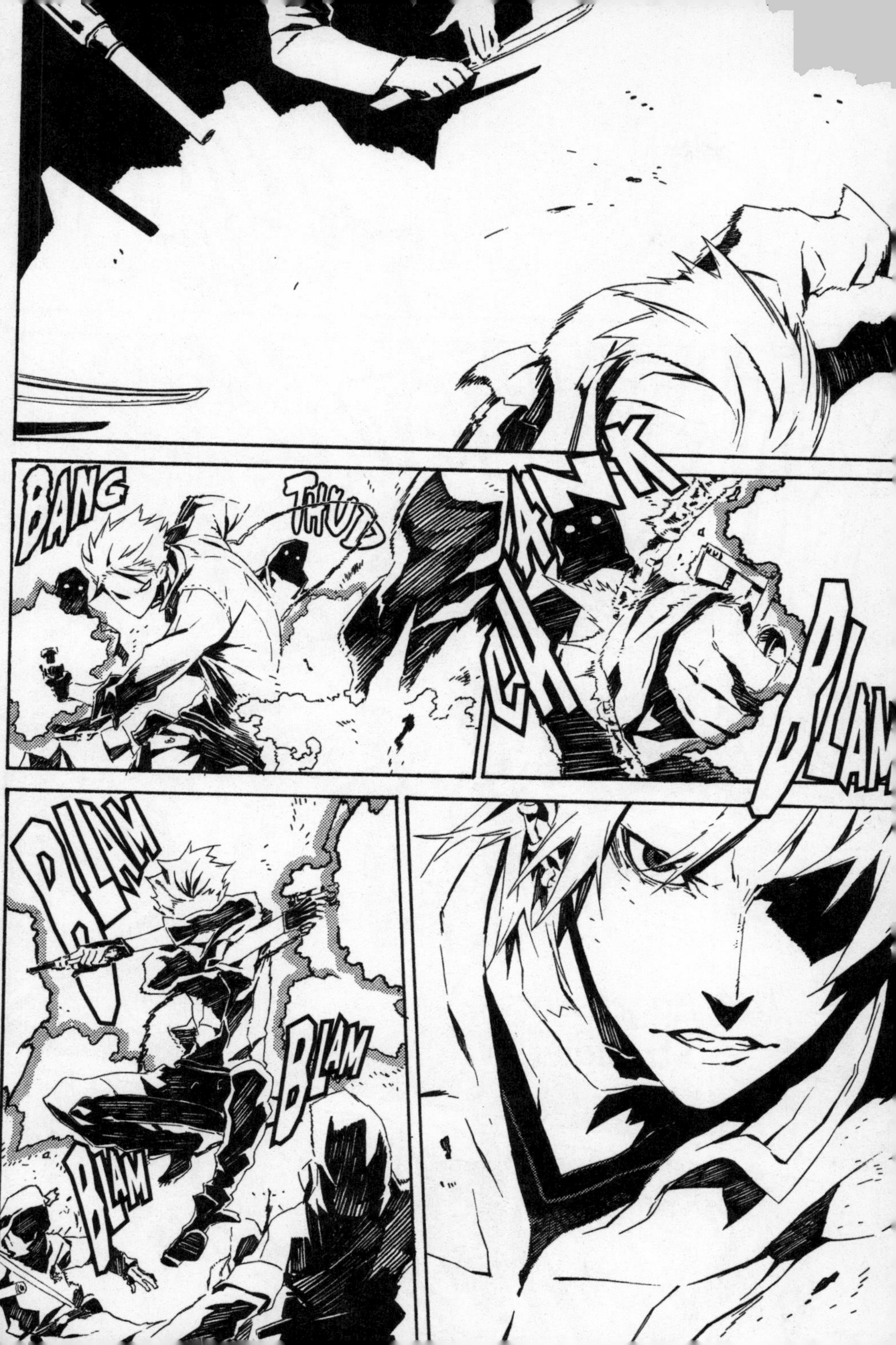
CHANK
BLAM
THUD
BANG
BLAM
BLAM
BLAM

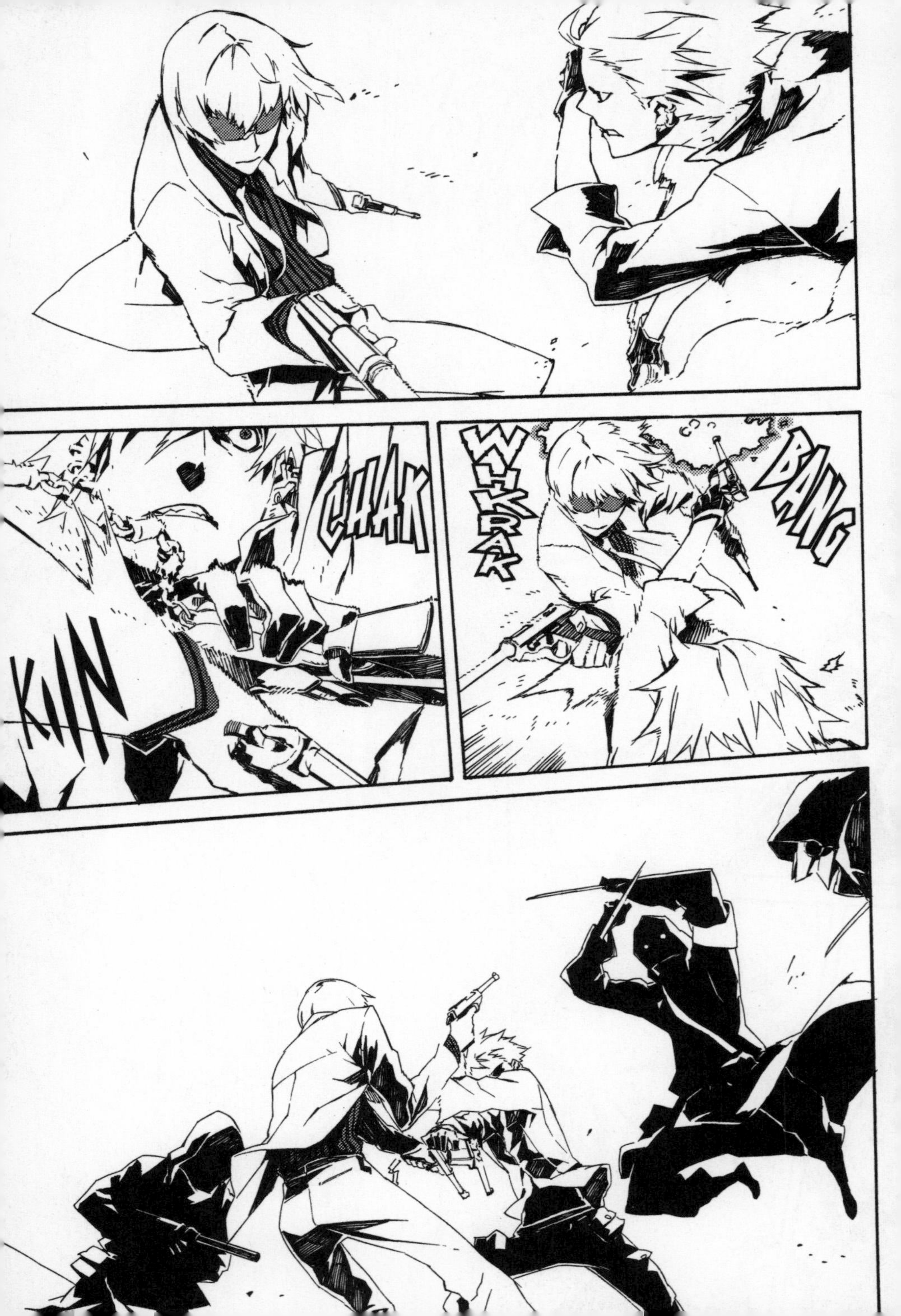
BANG
WYKRAK
CHAK
KIIN

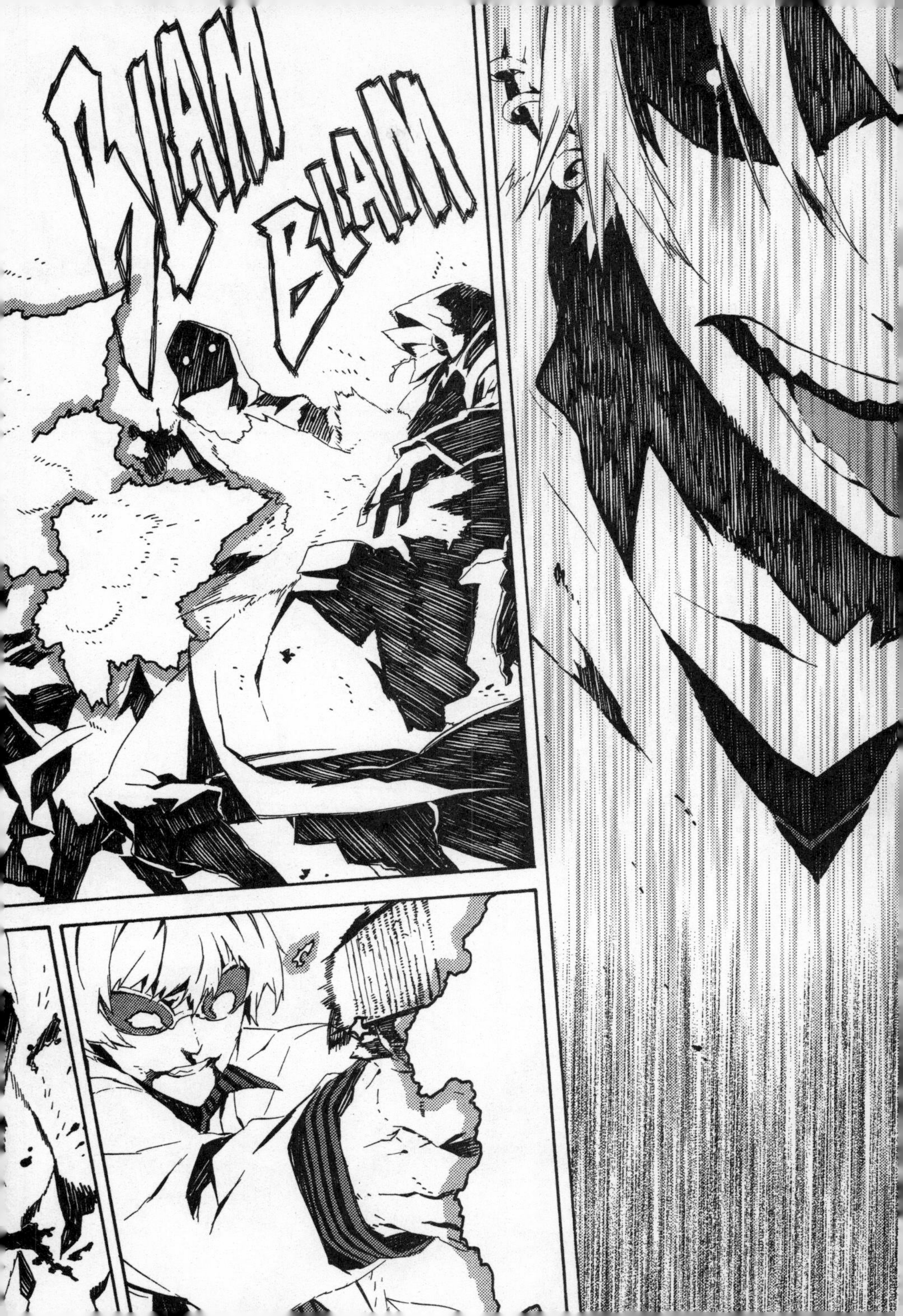
BLAM
BLAM

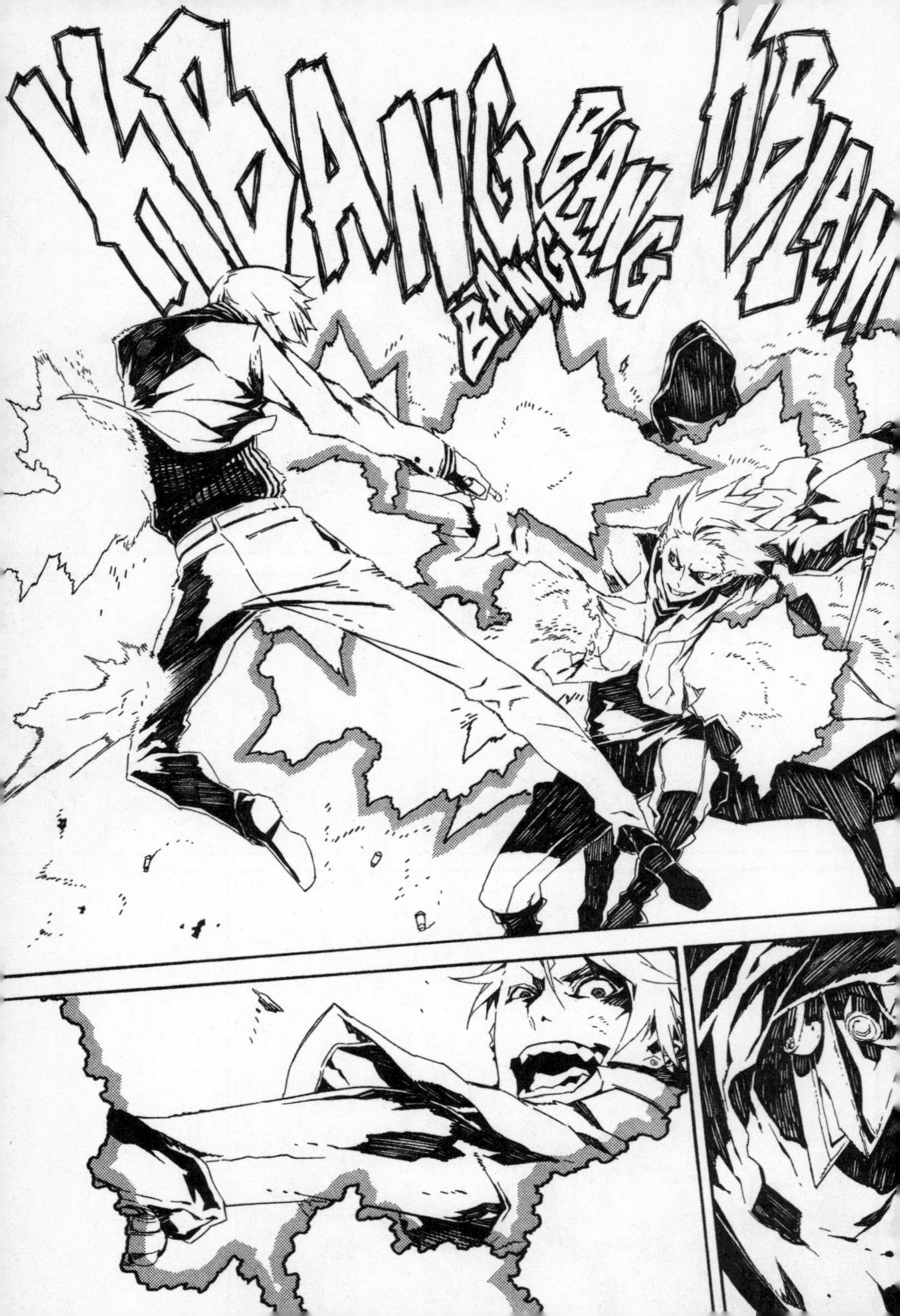
BANG
BANG
KBANG

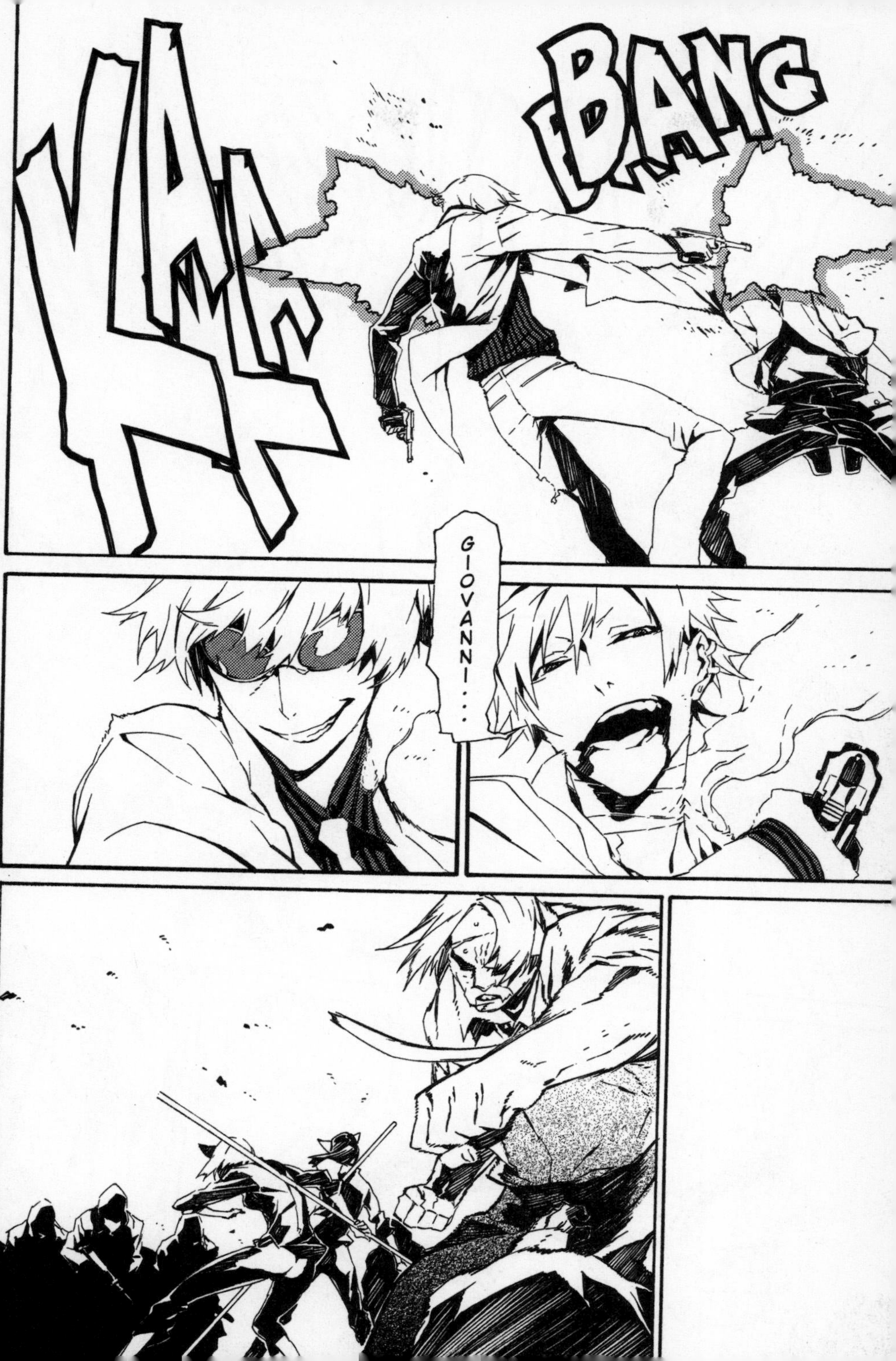
BANG
GIOVANNI...

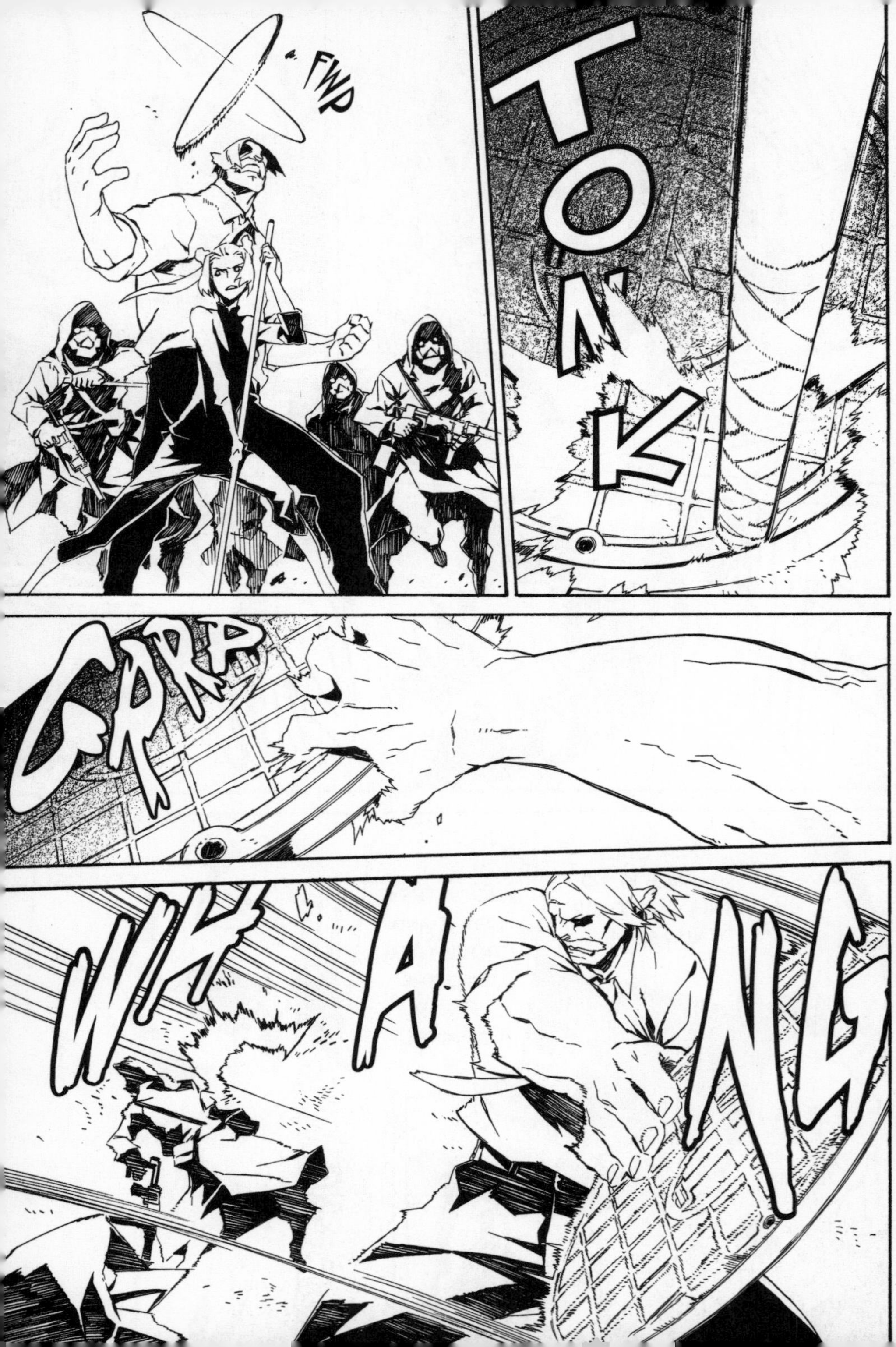
TONK
FWP
GRRP
WHANG

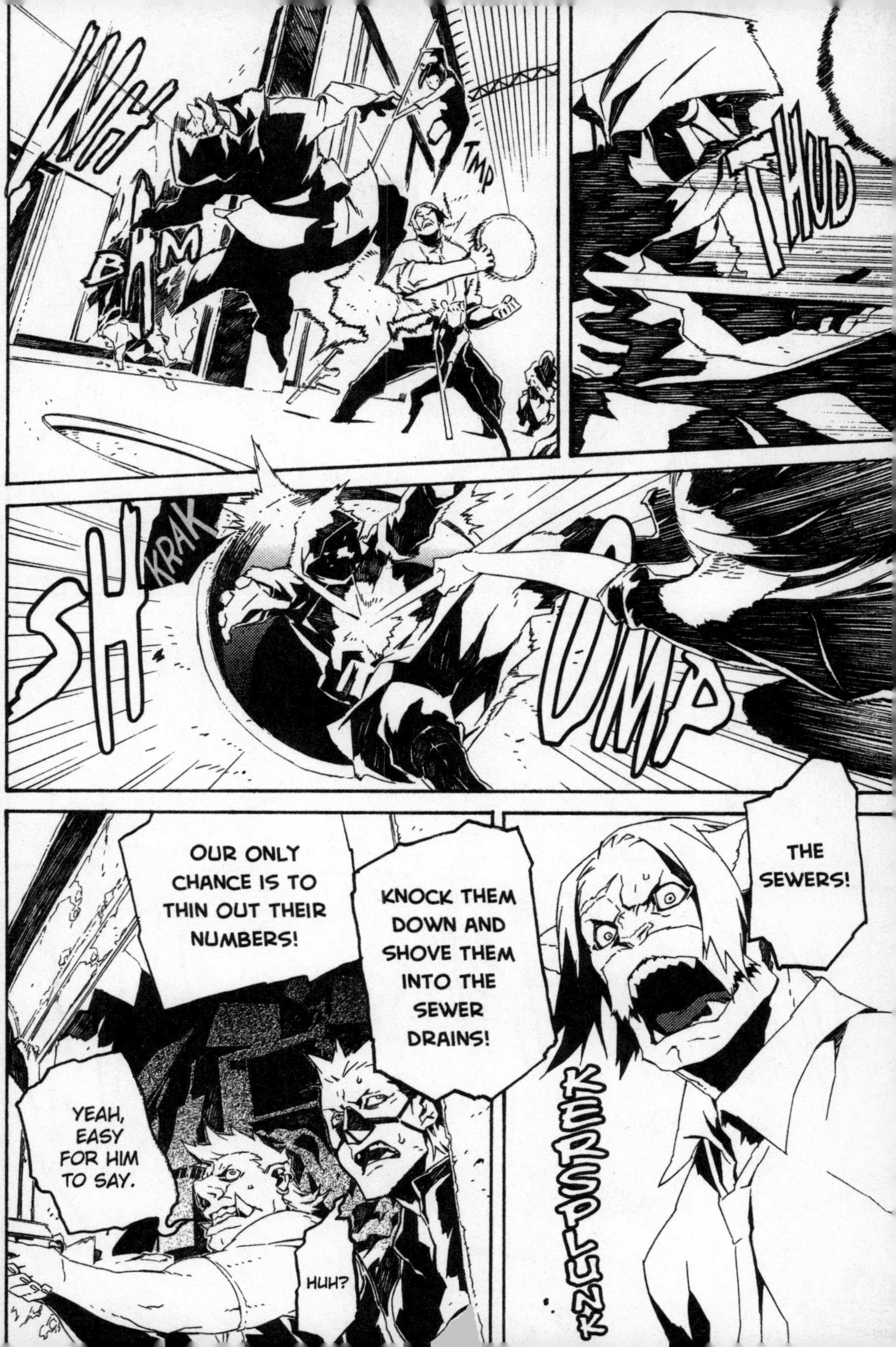
THUD
TMP
KRAK
THE SEWERS!
KERSPLUNK
OUR ONLY CHANCE IS TO THIN OUT THEIR NUMBERS!
KNOCK THEM DOWN AND SHOVE THEM INTO THE SEWER DRAINS!
YEAH, EASY FOR HIM TO SAY.
HUH?

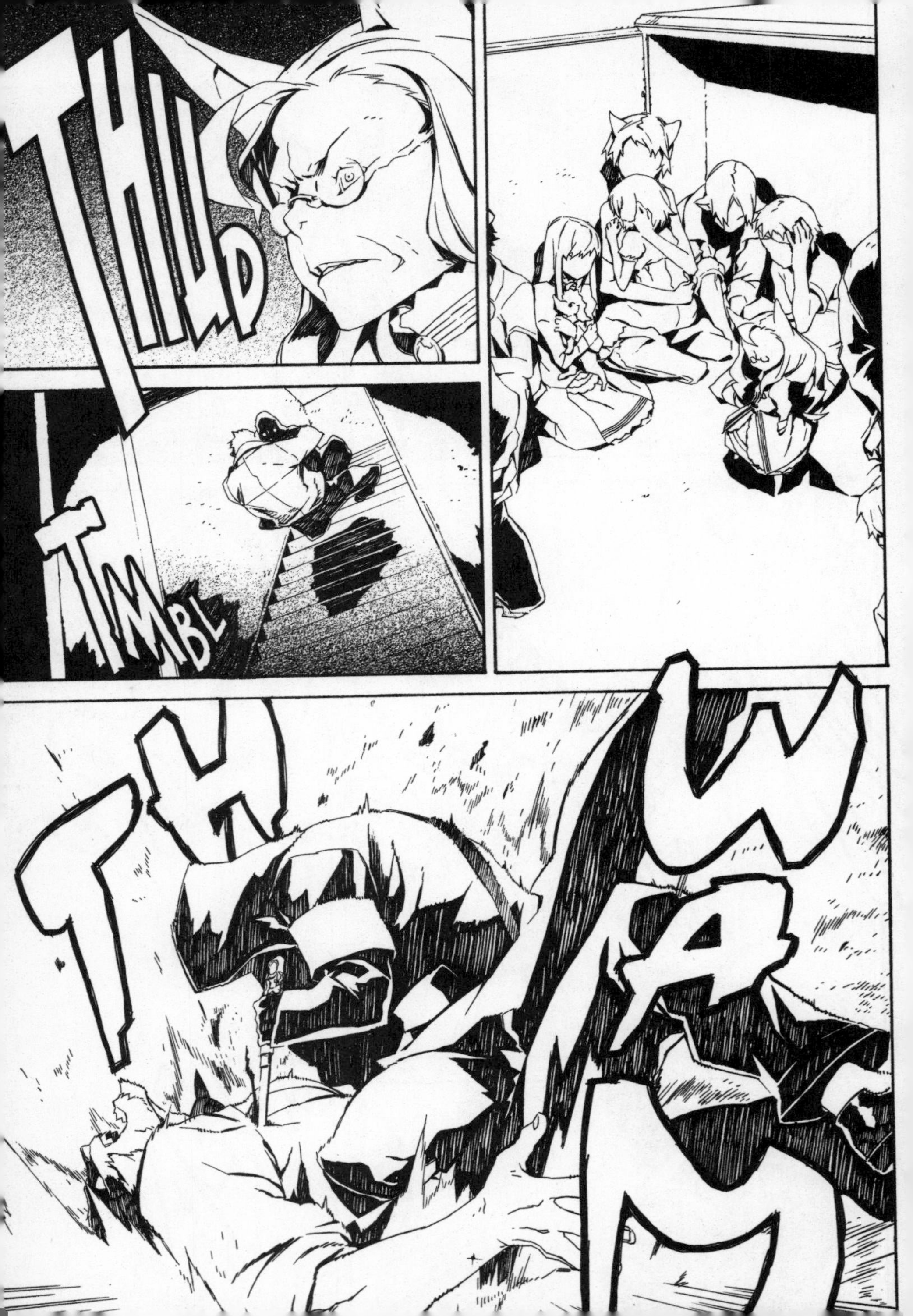
THUD
TMBL
THWAM

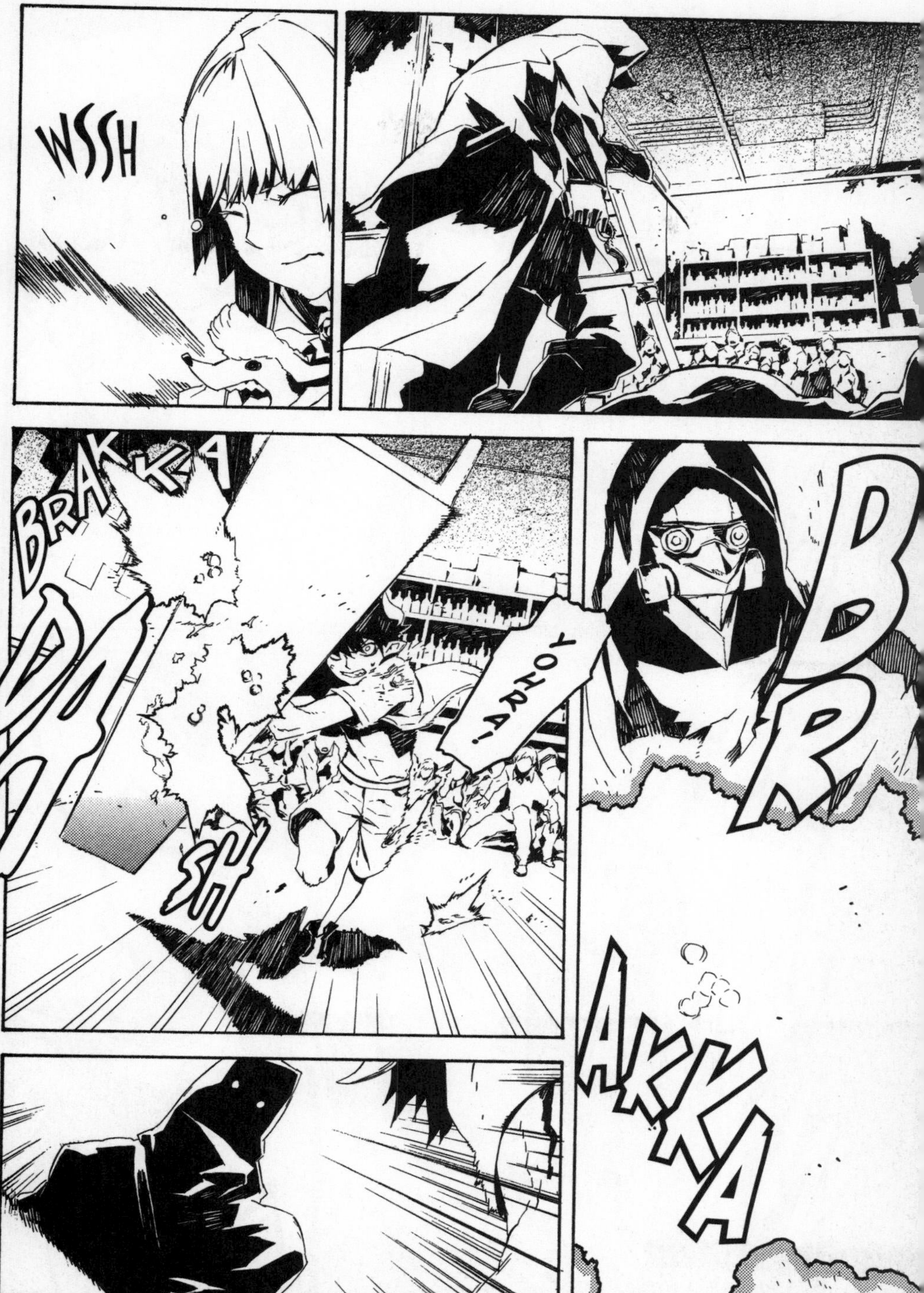

WSSH
BRAKKA
BRAKKA
YOHRA!
DASH

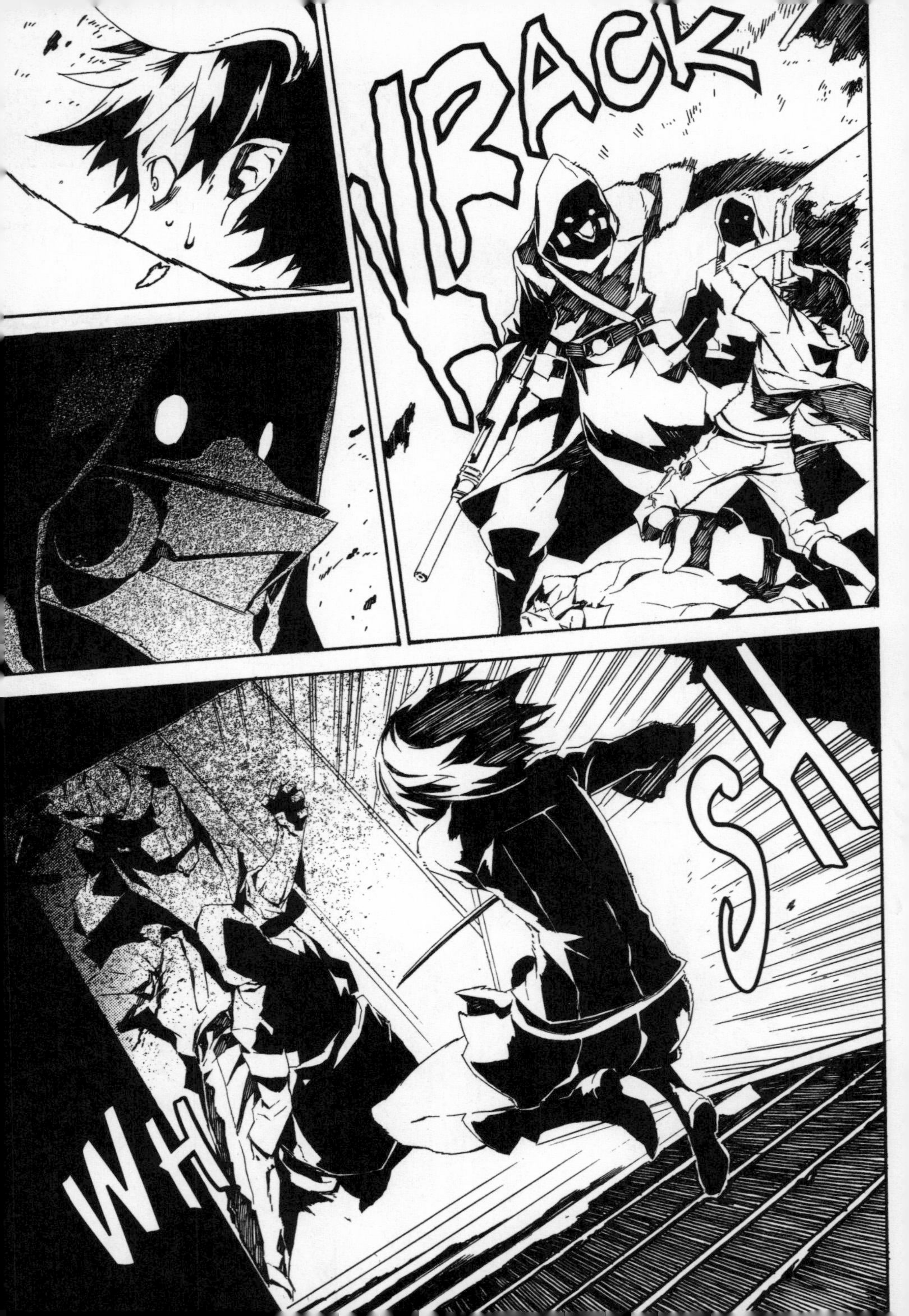
WRACK
SH
WH

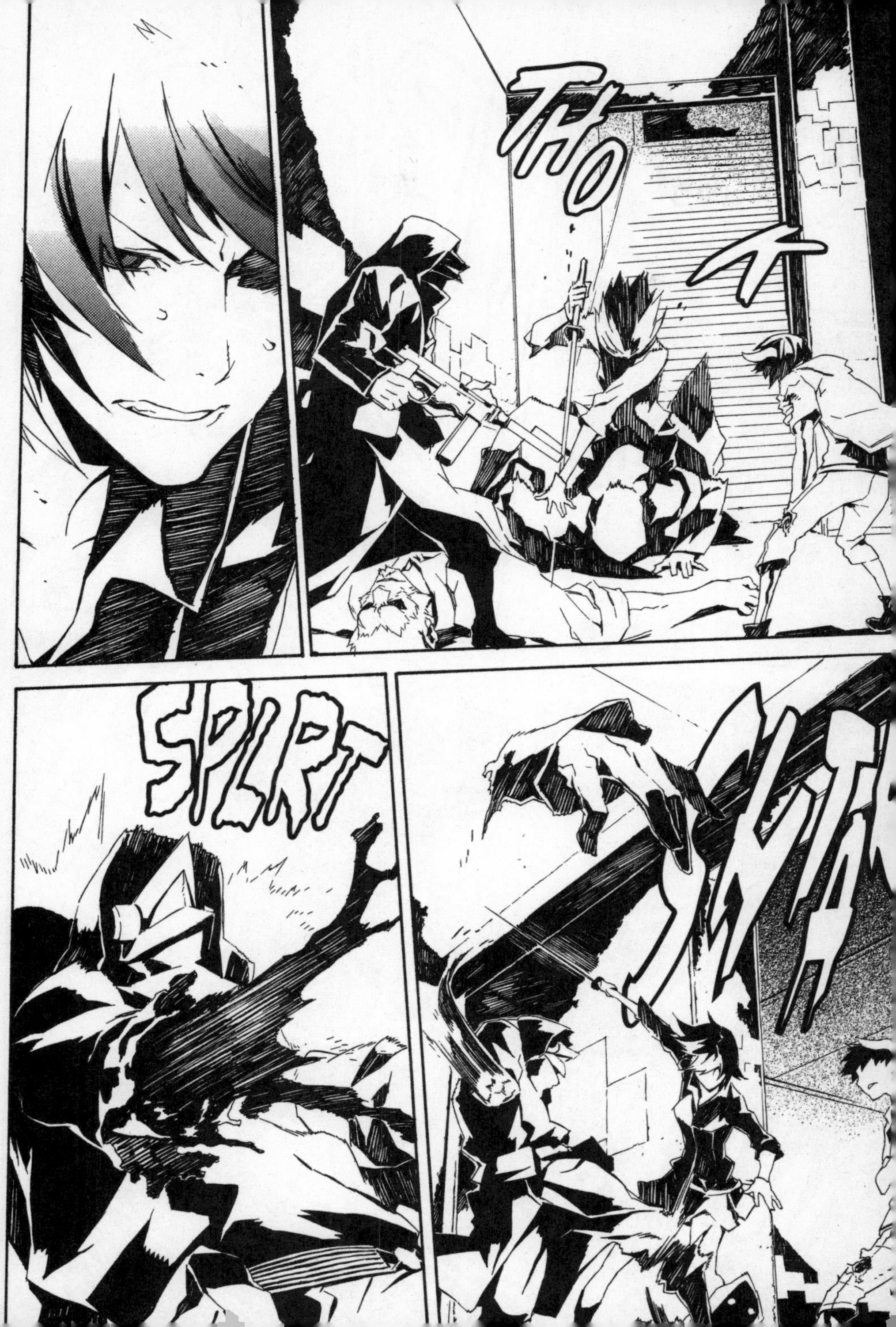
THOK
SPLRT

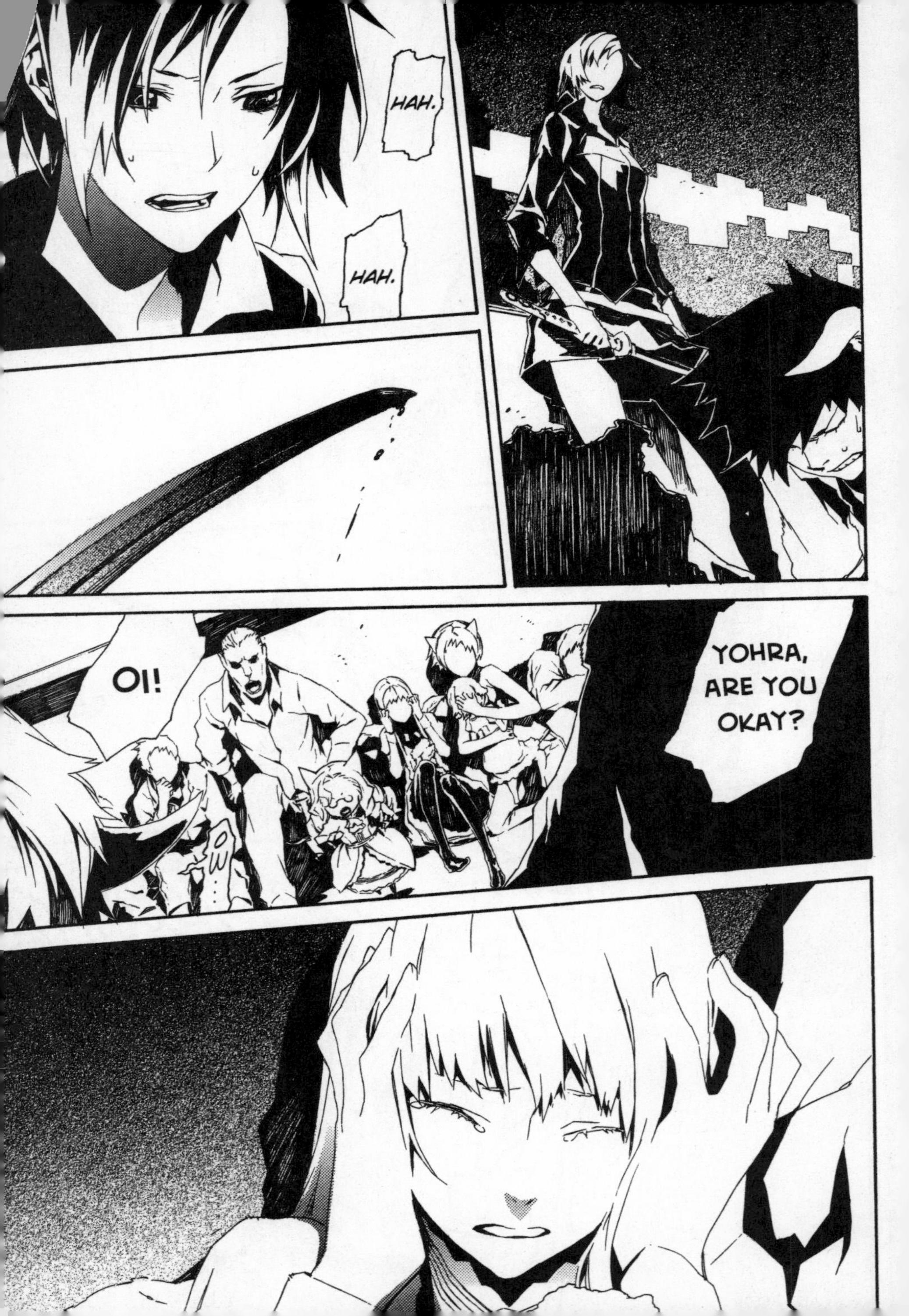
HAH.
HAH.
YOHRA, ARE YOU OKAY?
OI!
OW...

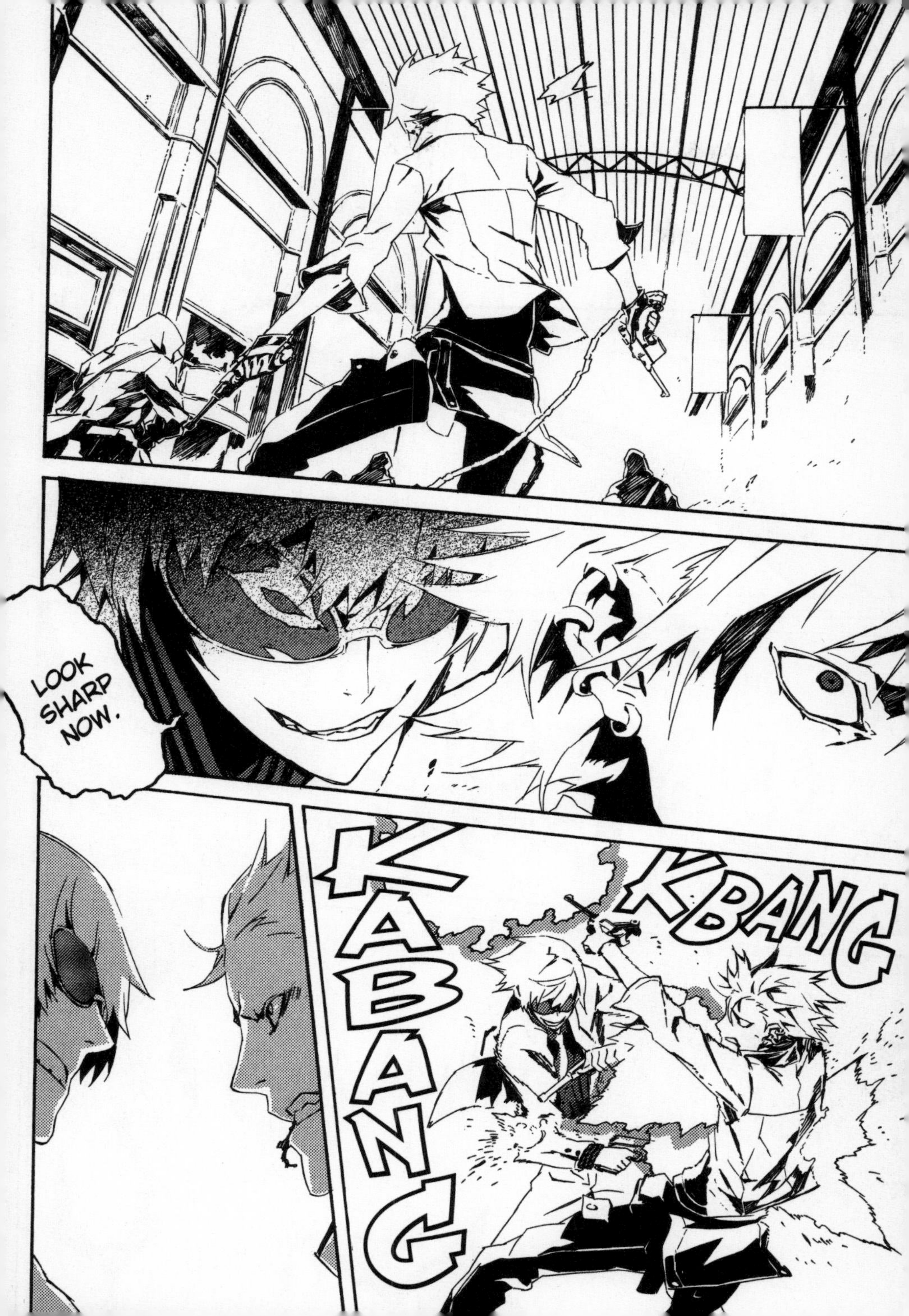
LOOK SHARP NOW.
KBANG
KABANG

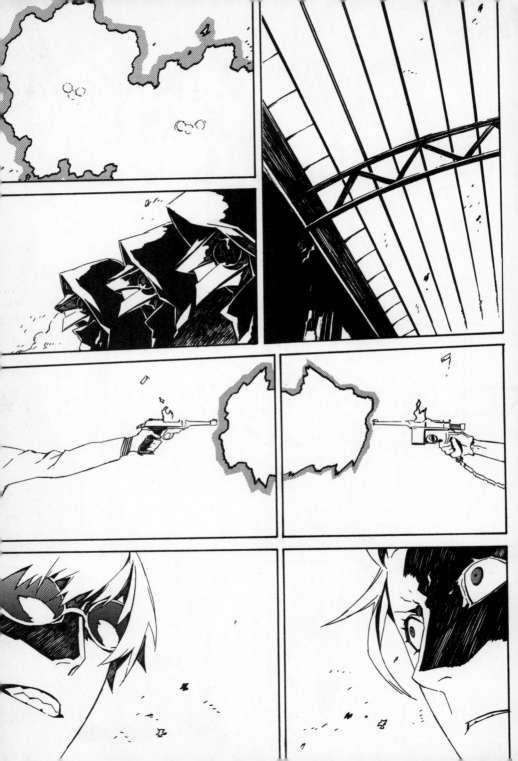

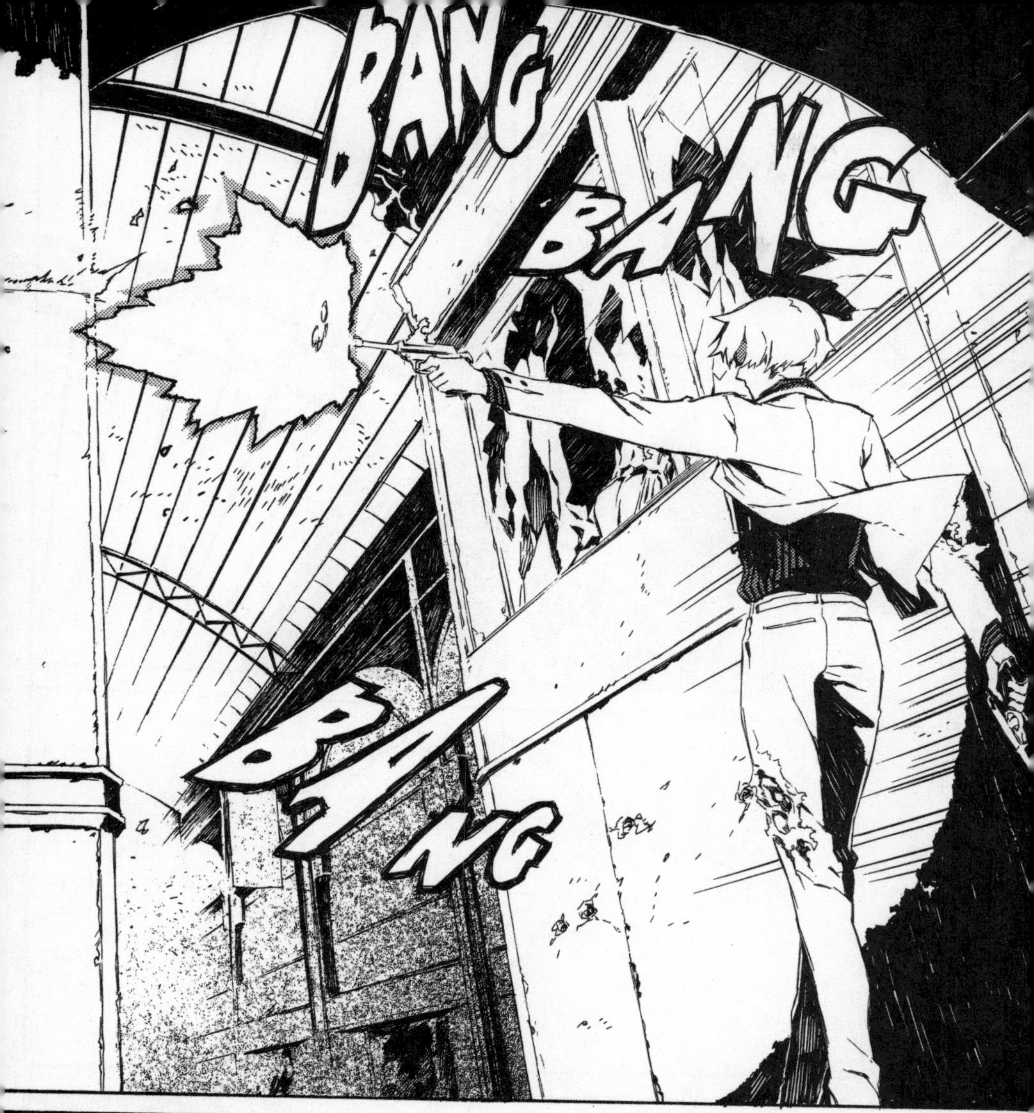
BANG
BANG
BANG
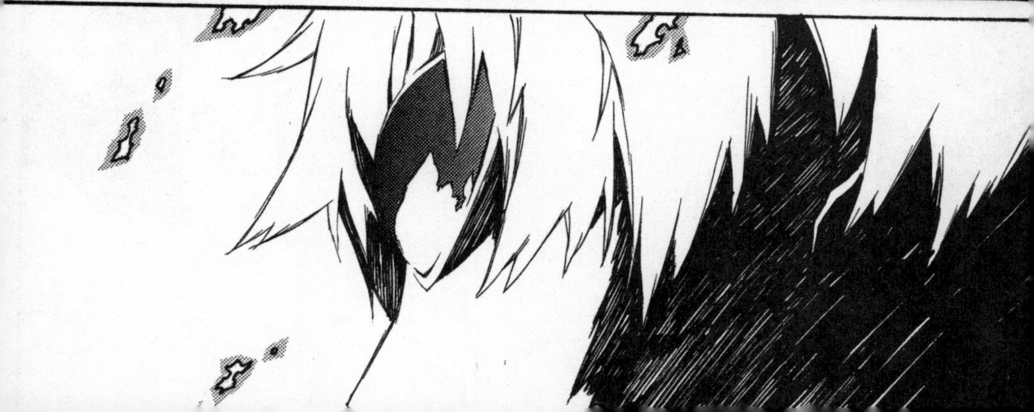

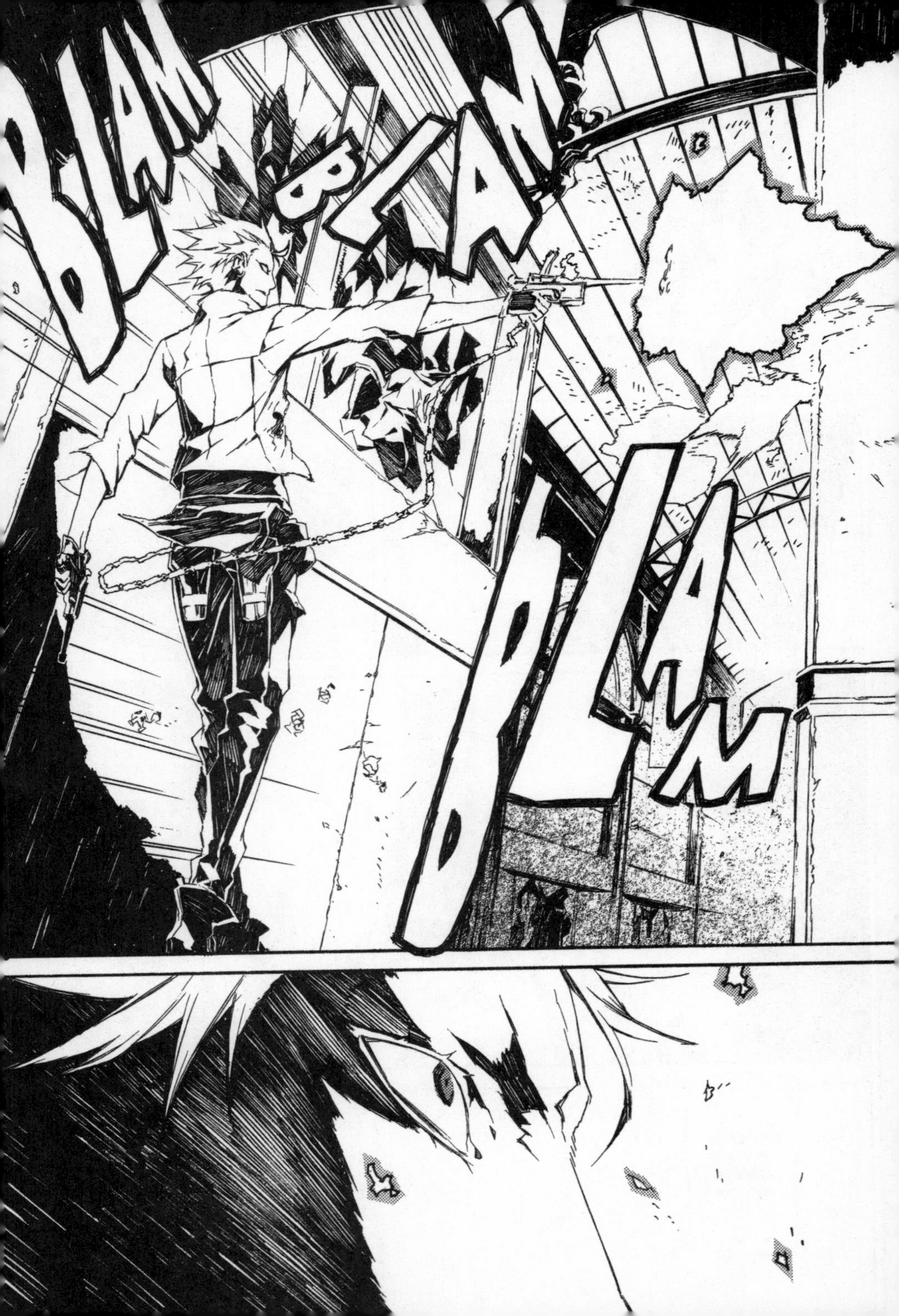
BLAM
BLAM
BLAM

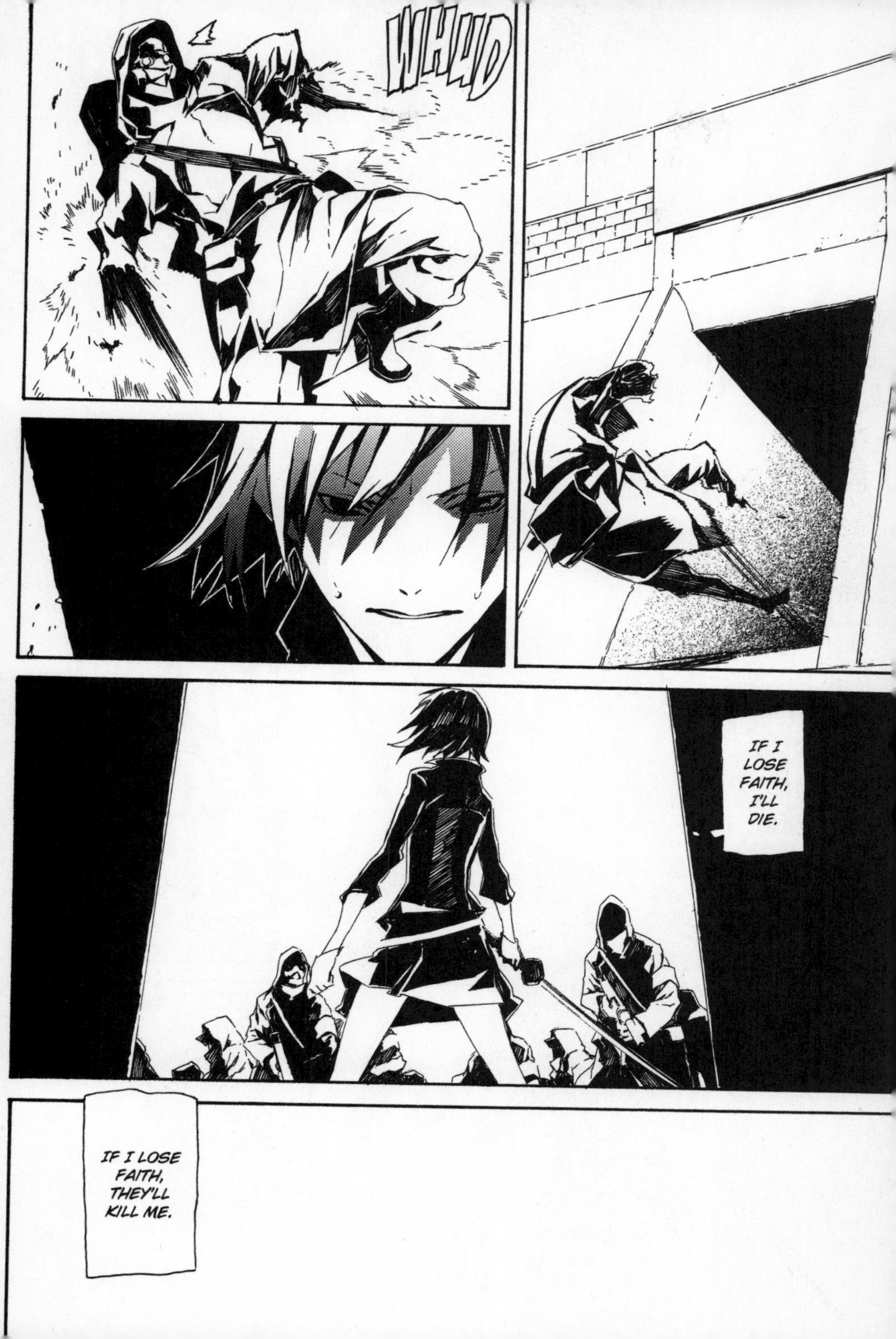
WHUD
IF I LOSE FAITH, I'LL DIE.
IF I LOSE FAITH, THEY'LL KILL ME.

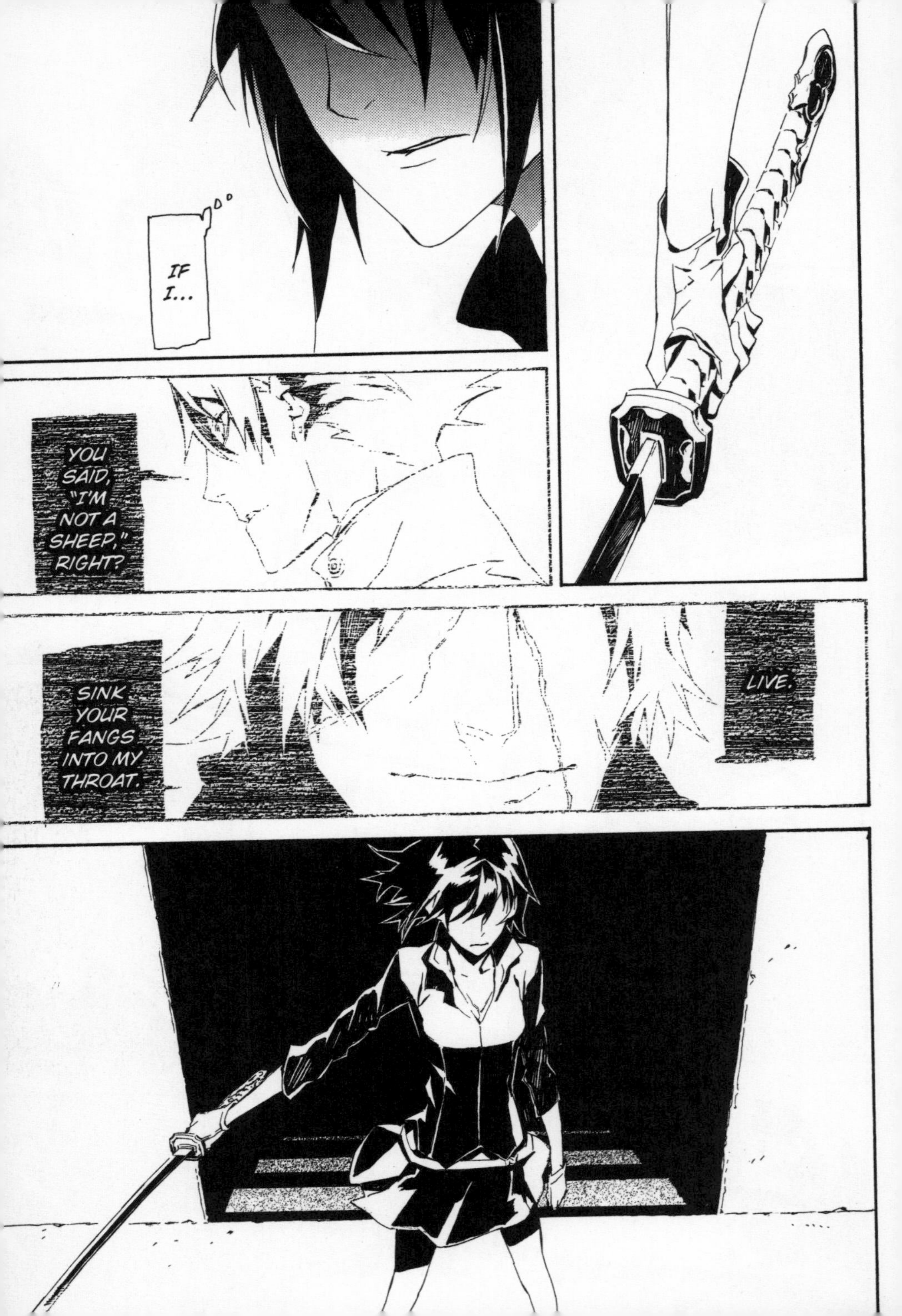
IF I...
YOU SAID, "I'M NOT A SHEEP," RIGHT?
LIVE.
SINK YOUR FANGS INTO MY THROAT.

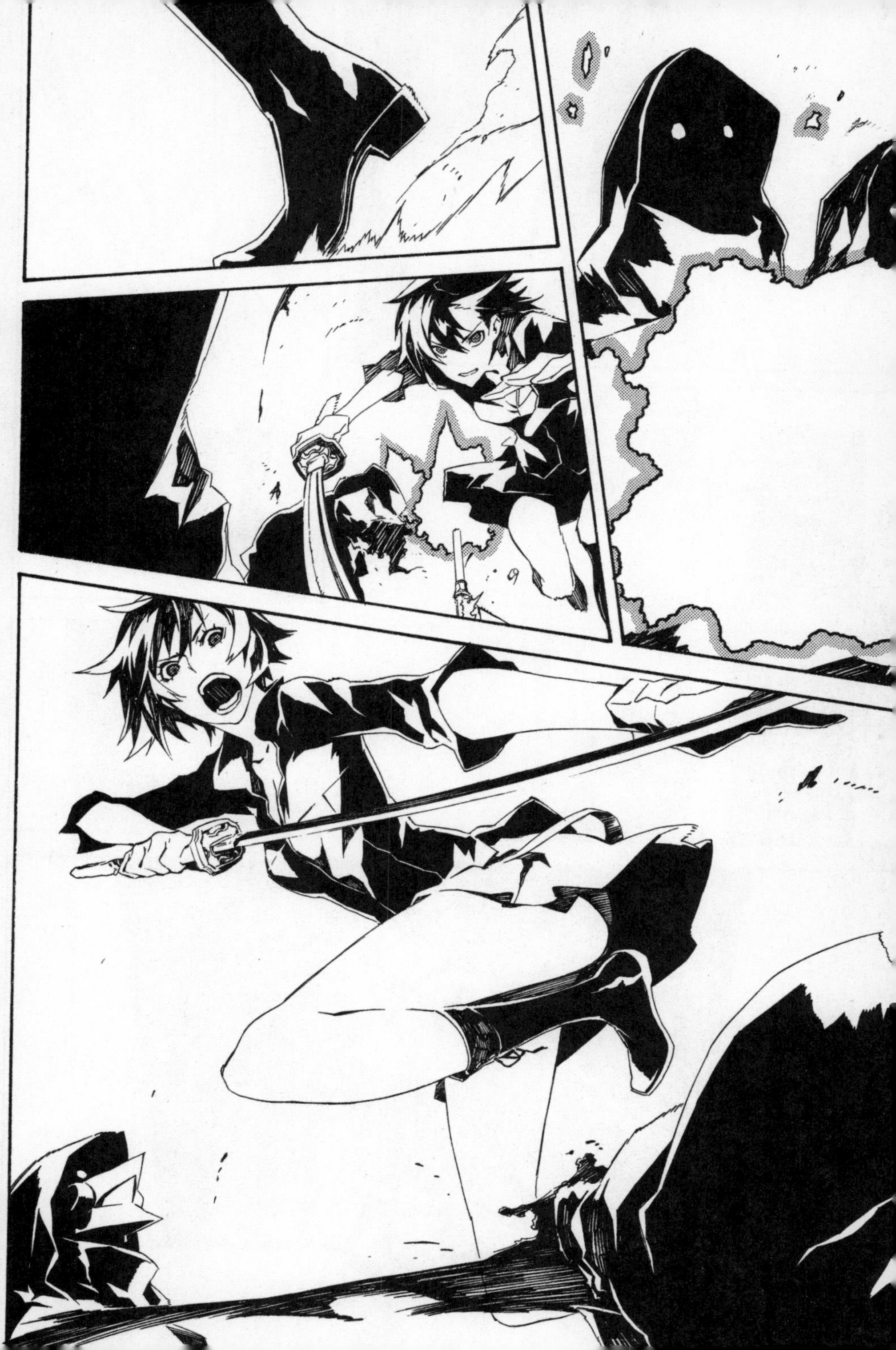

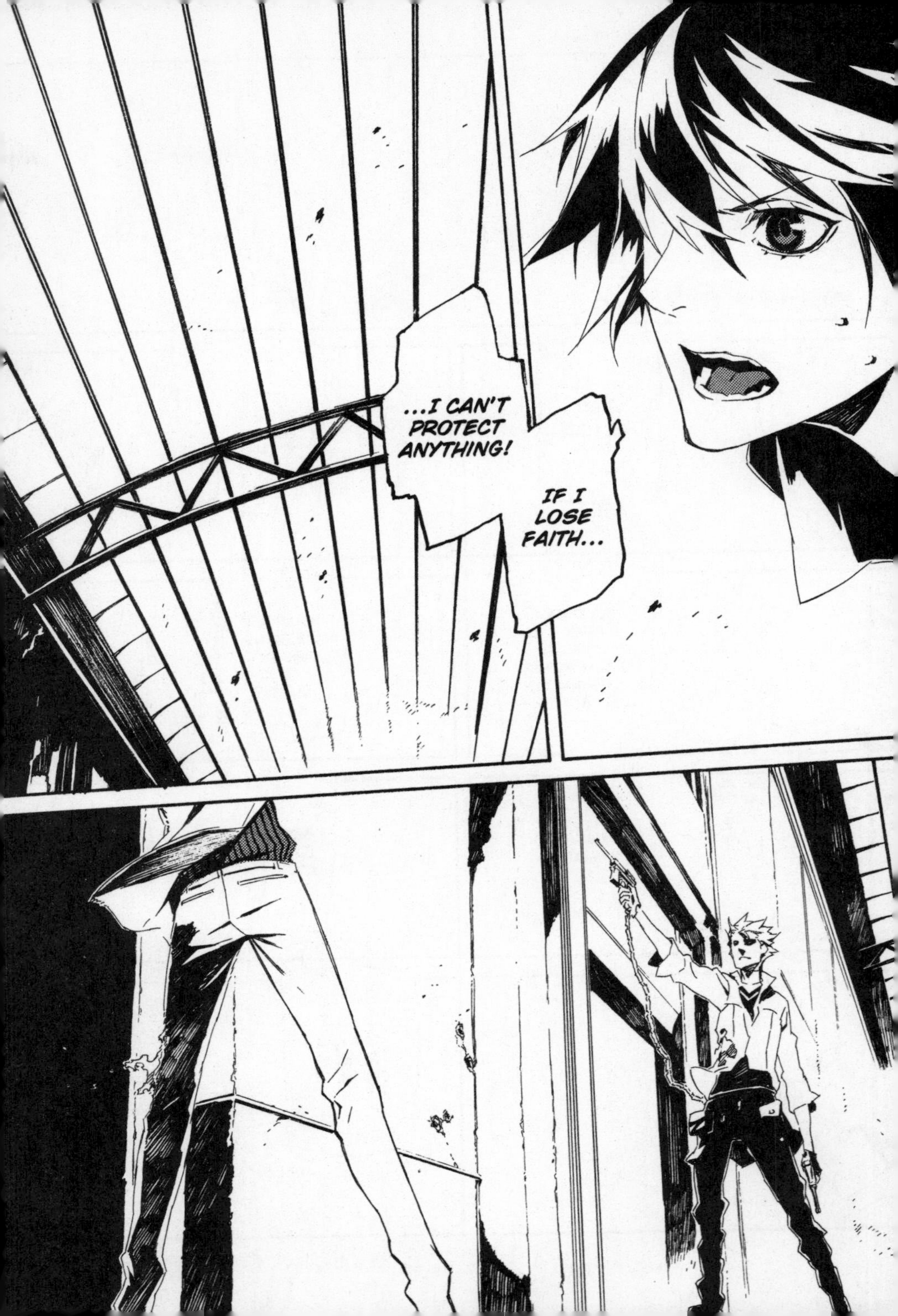
IF I LOSE FAITH...
...I CAN'T PROTECT ANYTHING!

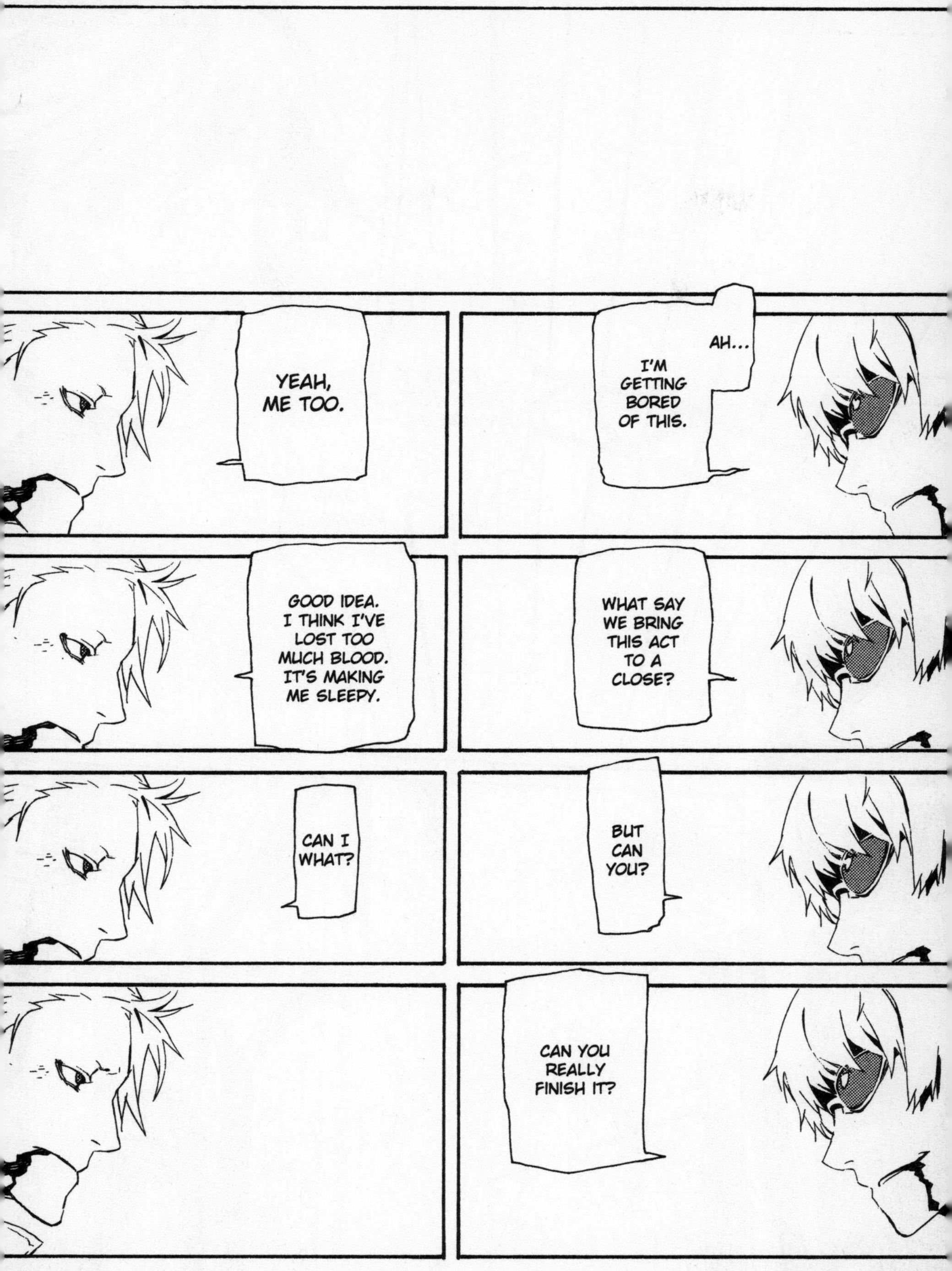
AH... I'M GETTING BORED OF THIS.
YEAH, ME TOO.
WHAT SAY WE BRING THIS ACT TO A CLOSE?
GOOD IDEA. I THINK I'VE LOST TOO MUCH BLOOD. IT'S MAKING ME SLEEPY.
BUT CAN YOU?
CAN I WHAT?
CAN YOU REALLY FINISH IT?

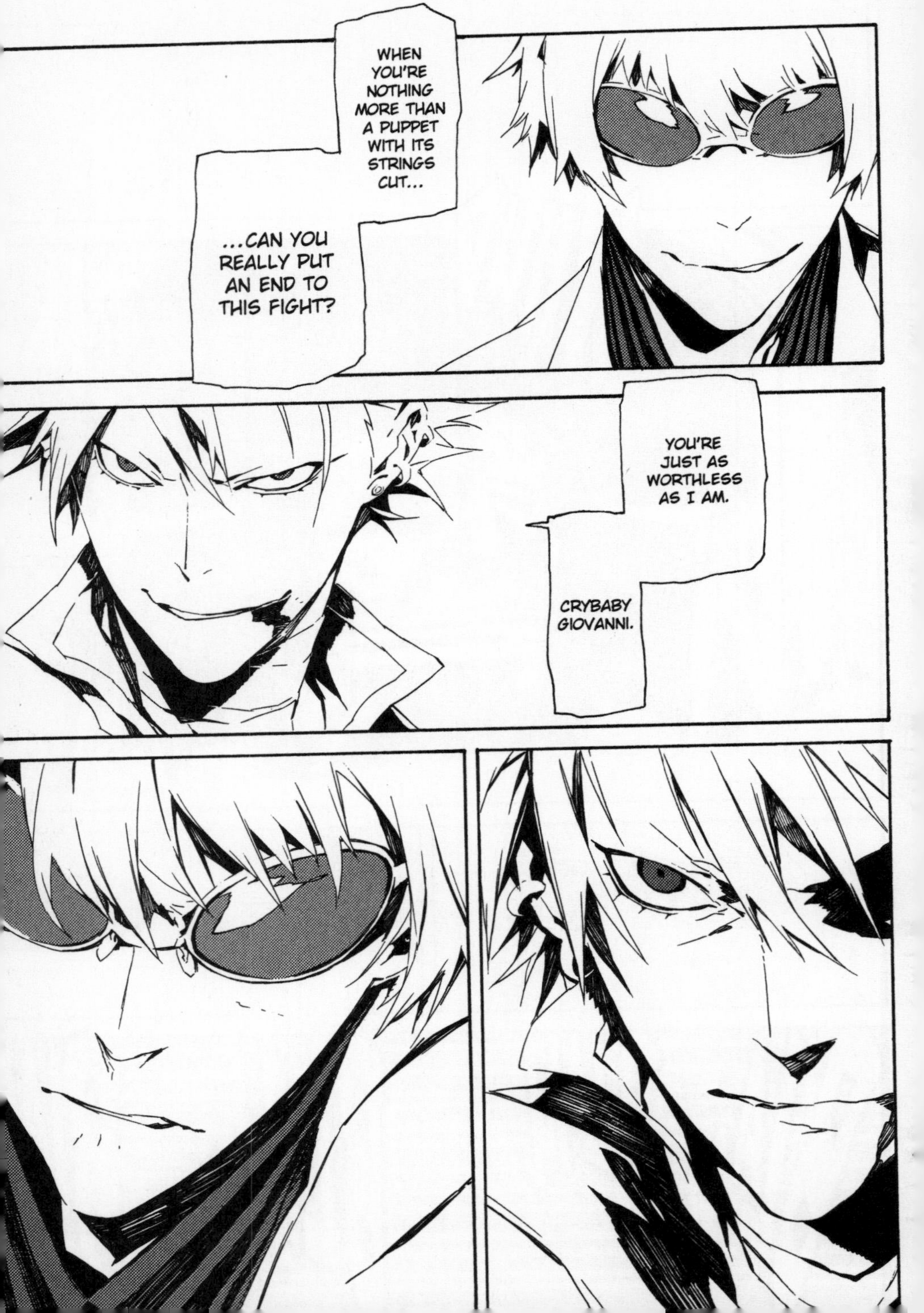
WHEN YOU'RE NOTHING MORE THAN A PUPPET WITH ITS STRINGS CUT...
...CAN YOU REALLY PUT AN END TO THIS FIGHT?
YOU'RE JUST AS WORTHLESS AS I AM.
CRYBABY GIOVANNI.

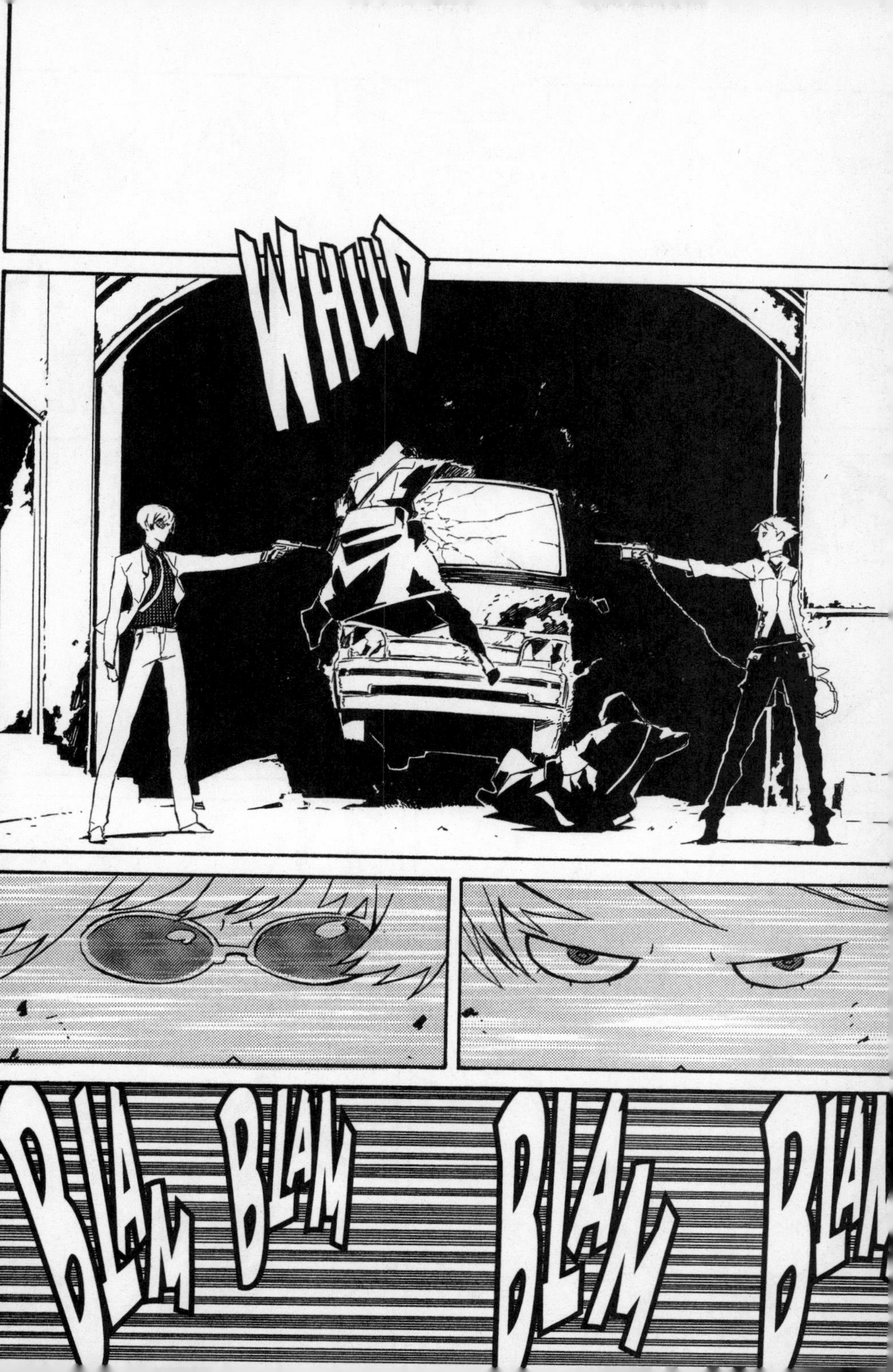
WHUD
BLA
BLAM
BLAM
BLAM

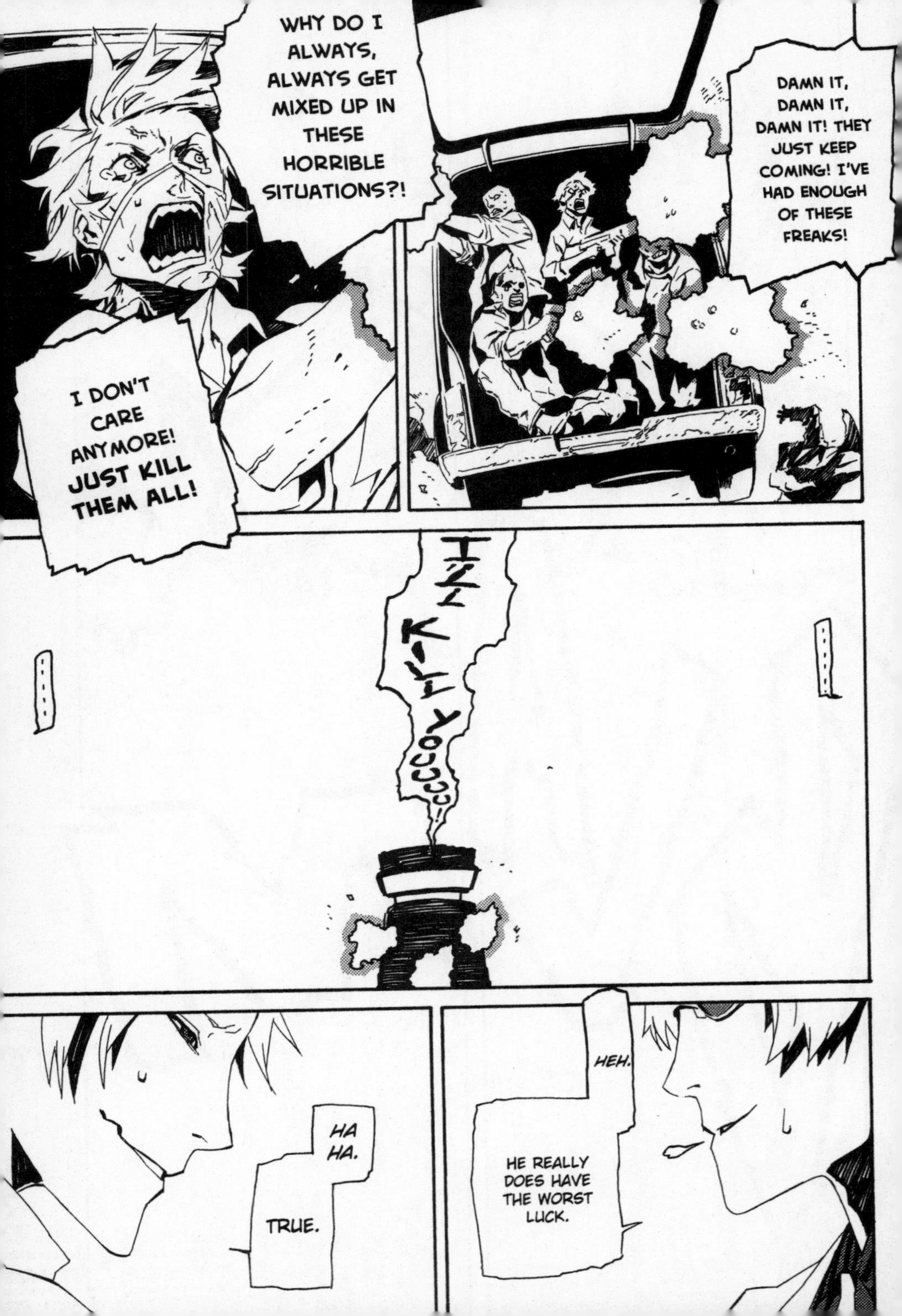
DAMN IT, DAMN IT, DAMN IT! THEY JUST KEEP COMING! I'VE HAD ENOUGH OF THESE FREAKS!
WHY DO I ALWAYS, ALWAYS GET MIXED UP IN THESE HORRIBLE SITUATIONS?!
I DON'T CARE ANYMORE! JUST KILL THEM ALL!
......
I'LL KILL YOUUUUU!!
......
HEH.
HE REALLY DOES HAVE THE WORST LUCK.
HA HA.
TRUE.

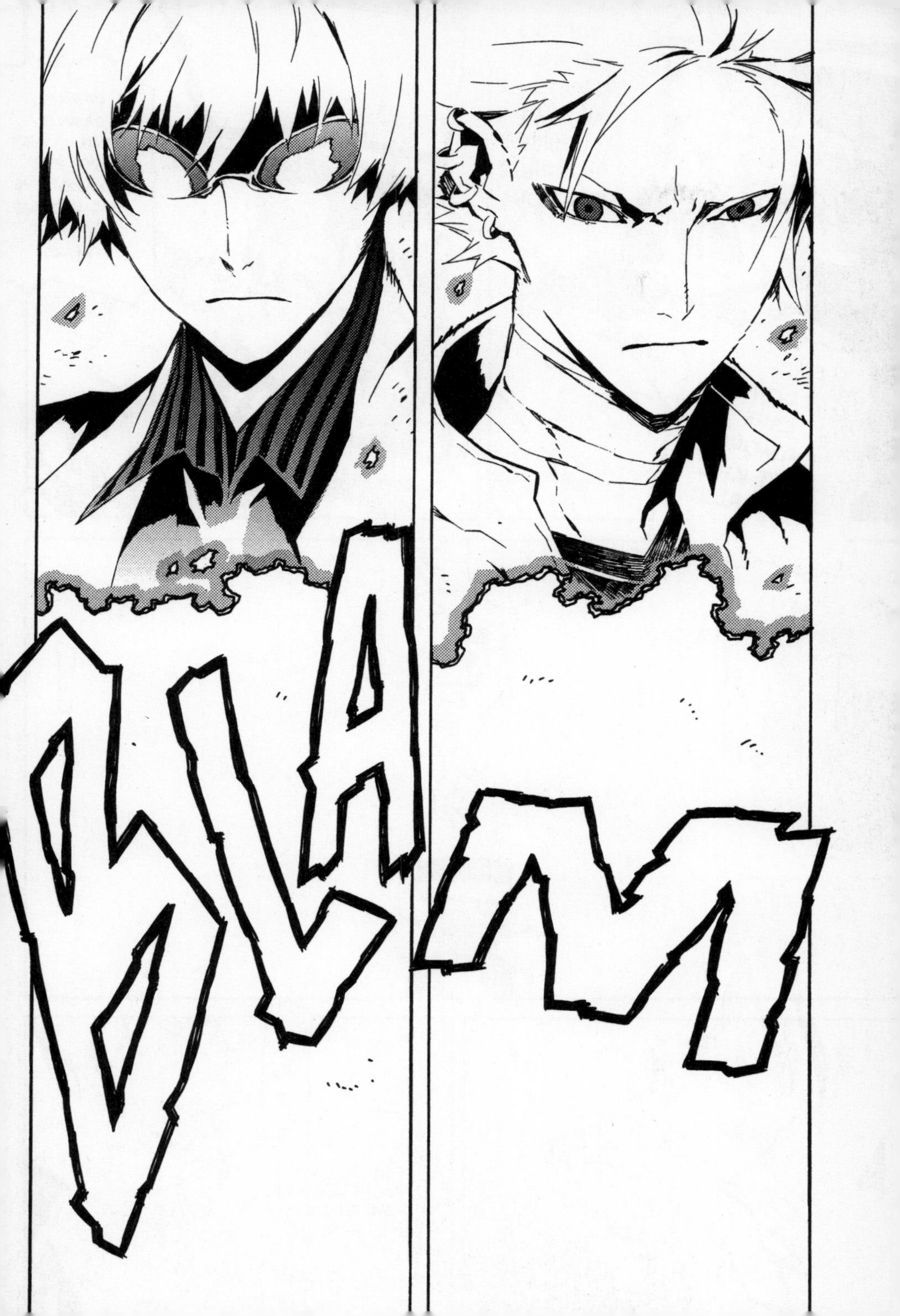
SLAM

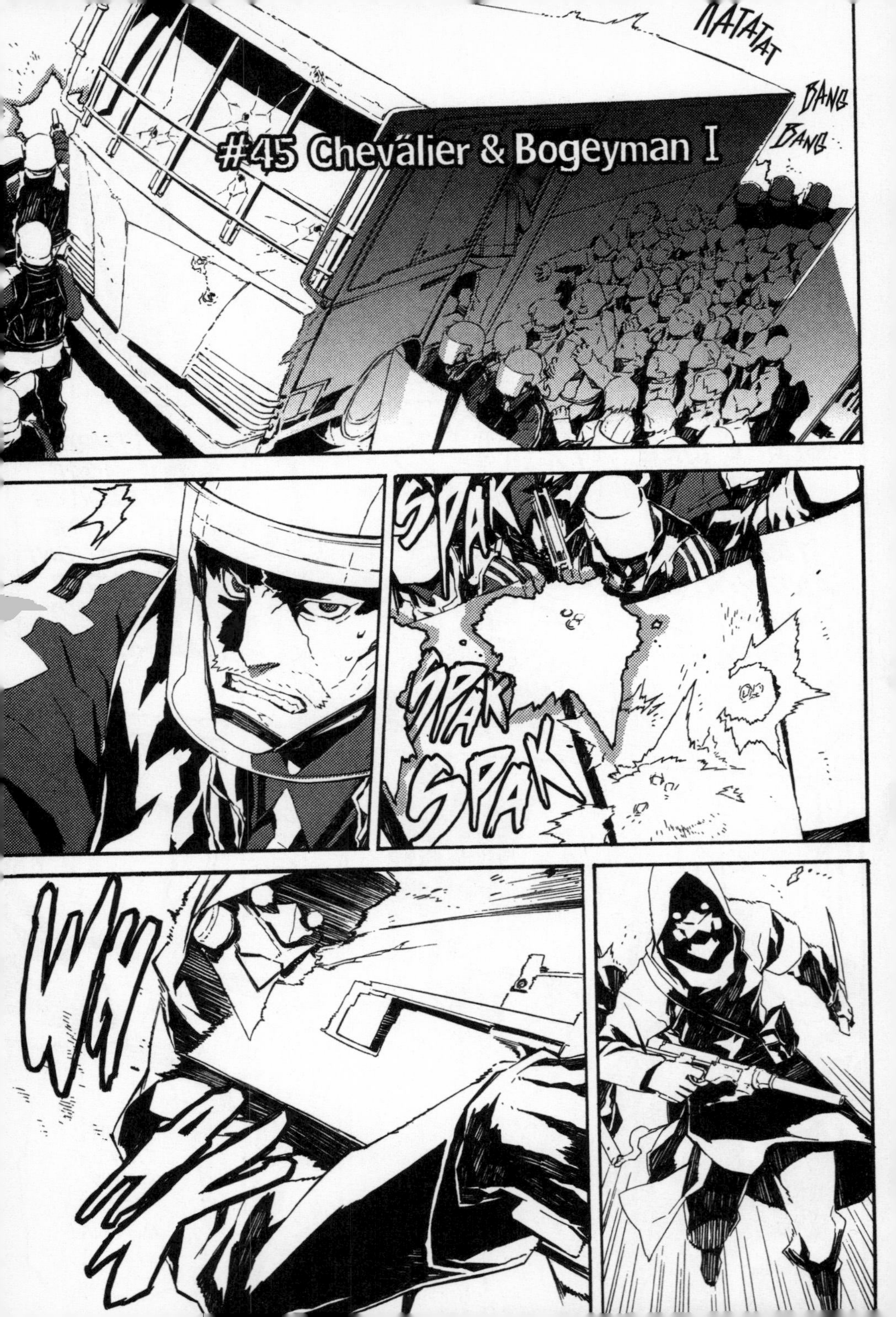
#45 Chevälier & Bogeyman I
NATATAT
BANG
BANG
SPAK
SPAK
SPAK
WHY

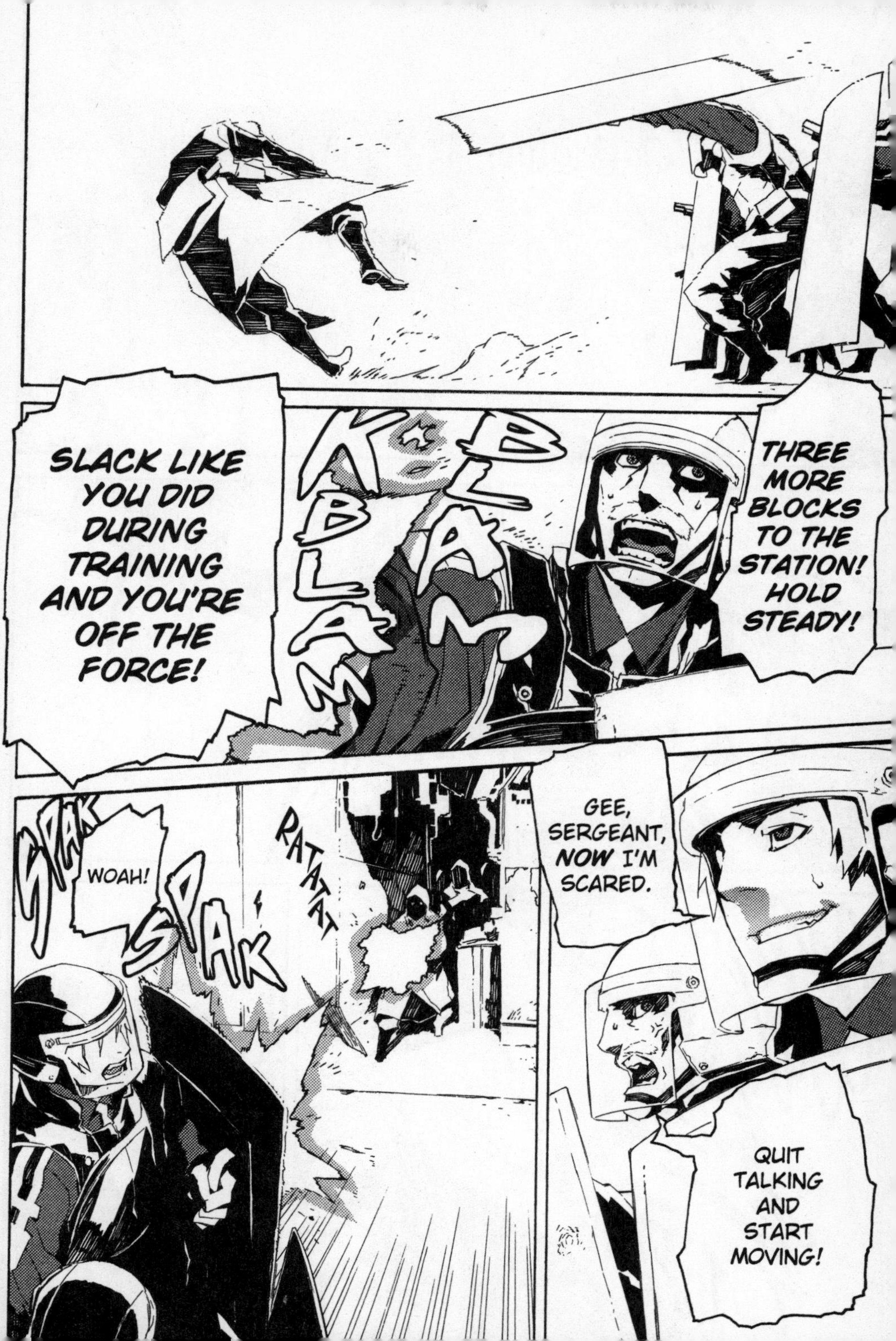
THREE MORE BLOCKS TO THE STATION! HOLD STEADY!
KABLAM
KABLAM
SLACK LIKE YOU DID DURING TRAINING AND YOU'RE OFF THE FORCE!
GEE, SERGEANT, *NOW* I'M SCARED.
QUIT TALKING AND START MOVING!
RATATATAT
SPAK
SPAK
WOAH!

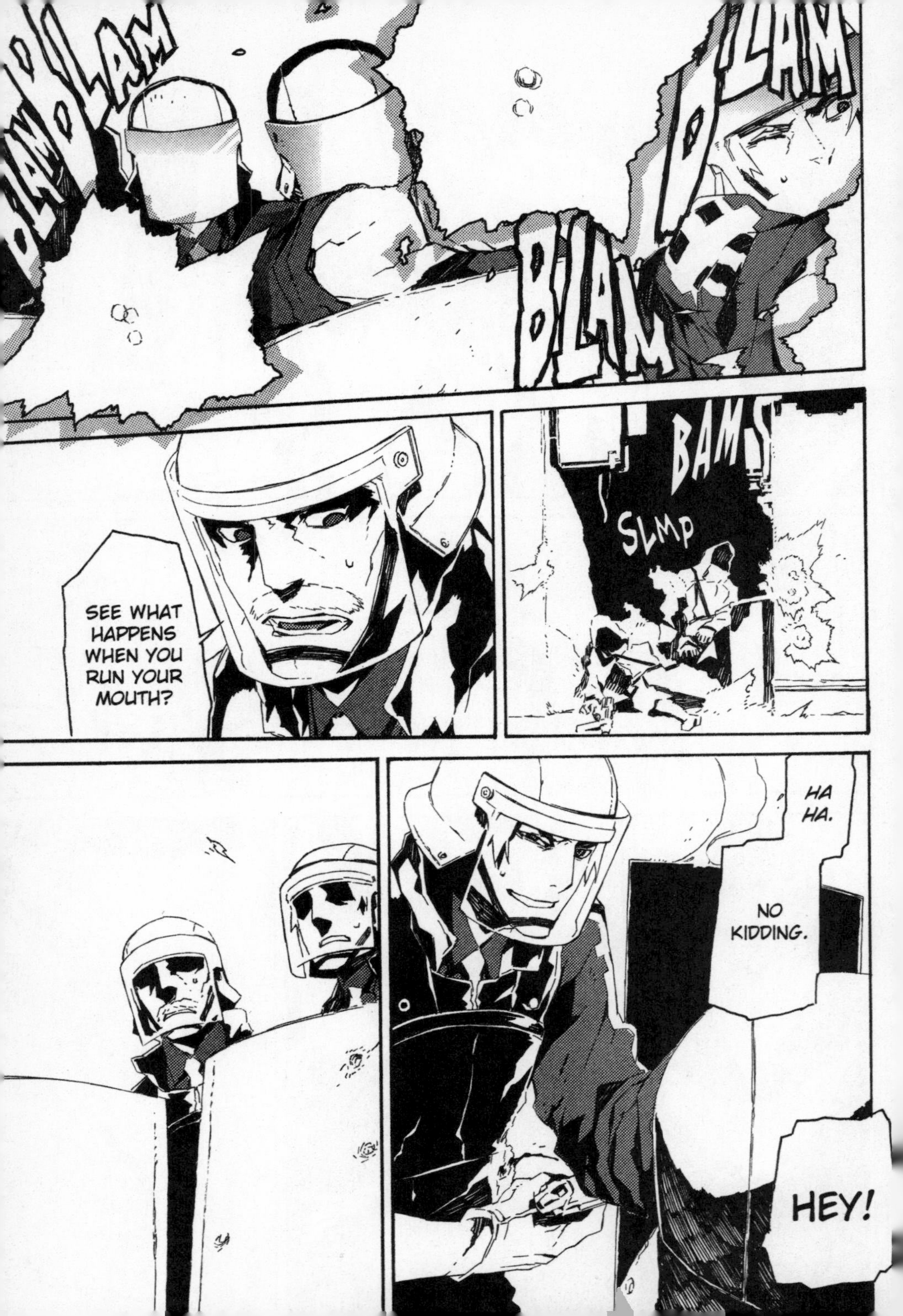
BLAM
BLAM
BLAM
BLAM
BAM
SLMP
SEE WHAT HAPPENS WHEN YOU RUN YOUR MOUTH?
HA HA.
NO KIDDING.
HEY!

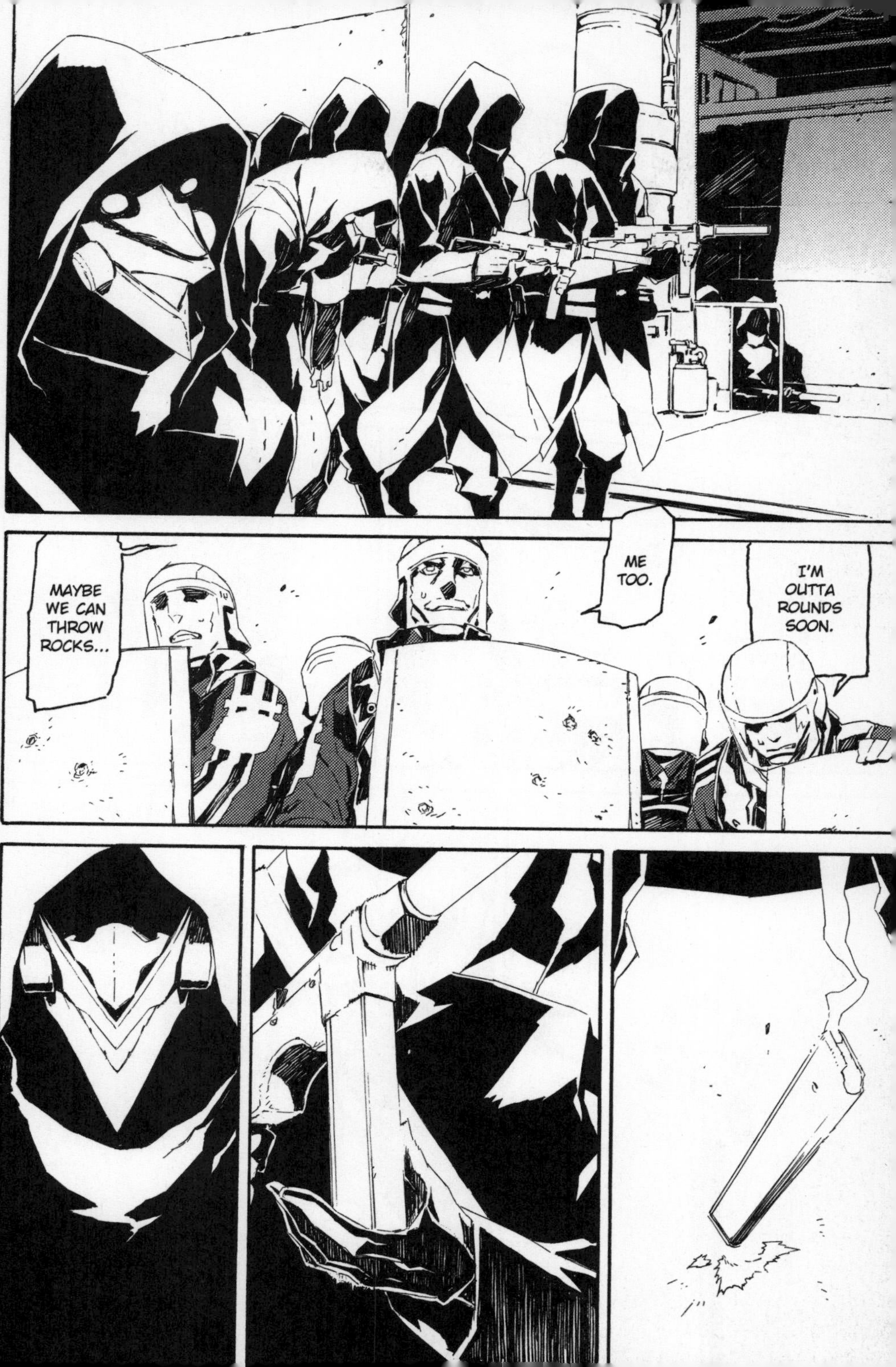
I'M OUTTA ROUNDS SOON.
ME TOO.
MAYBE WE CAN THROW ROCKS...

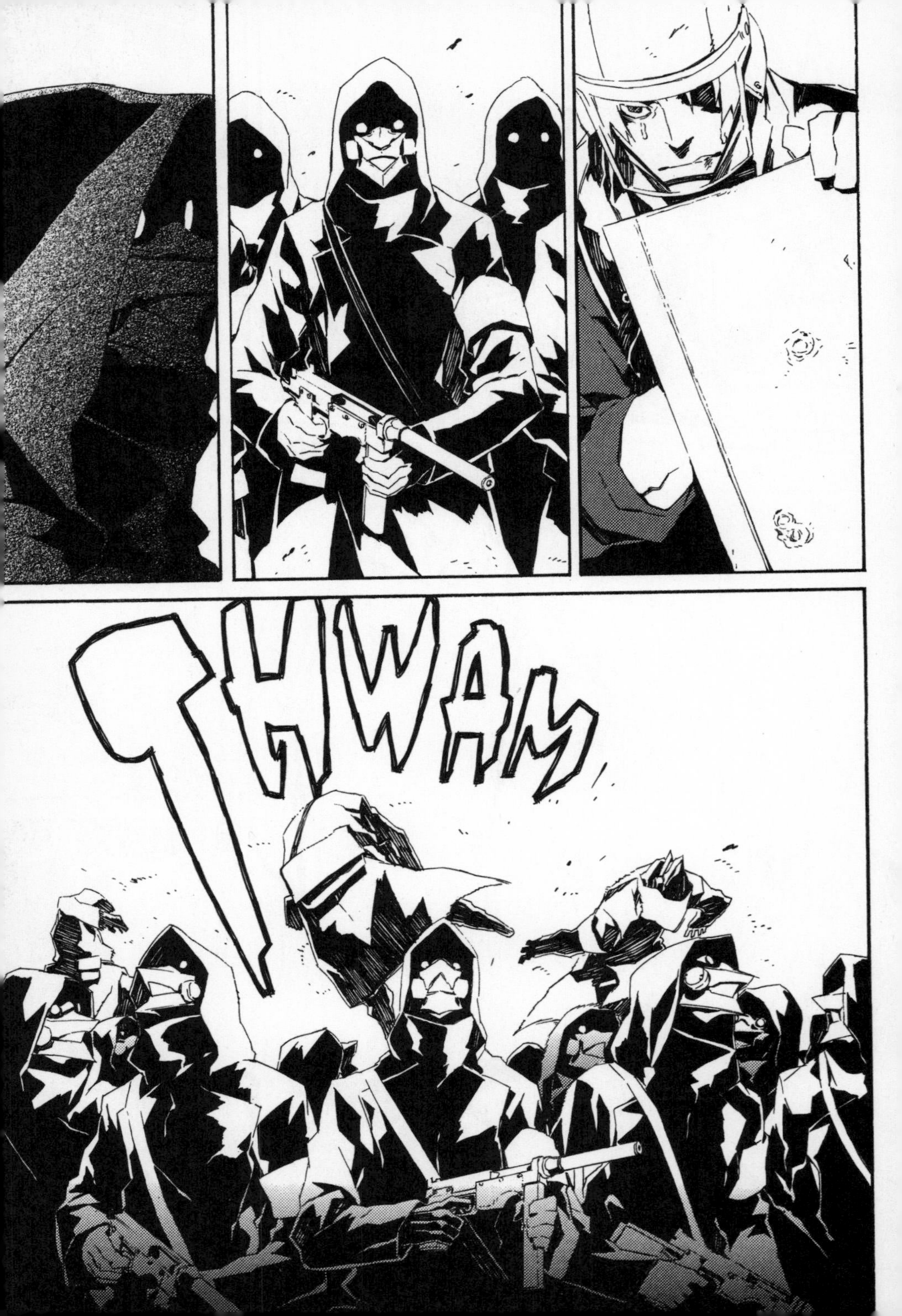
THWAM

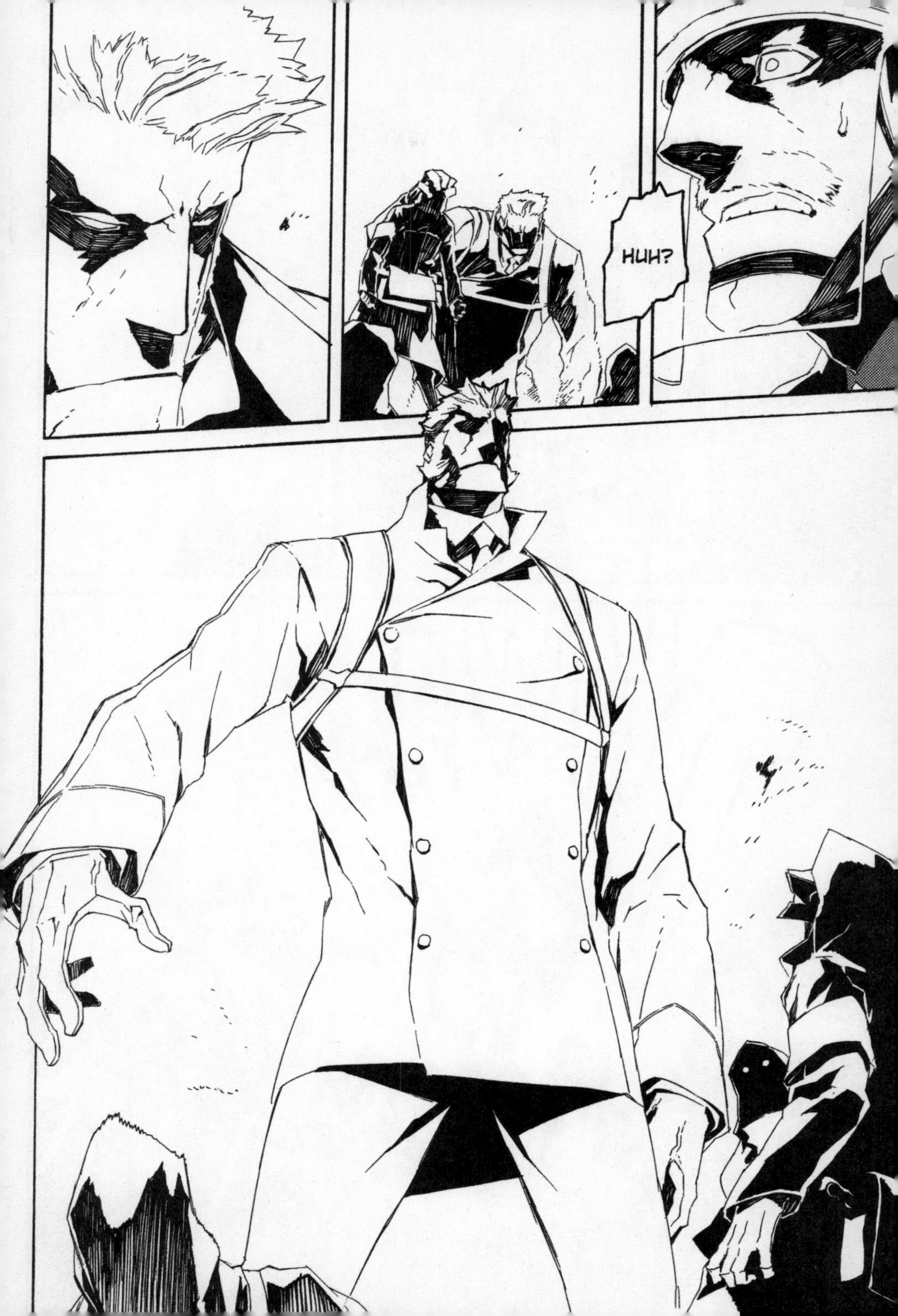
HUH?

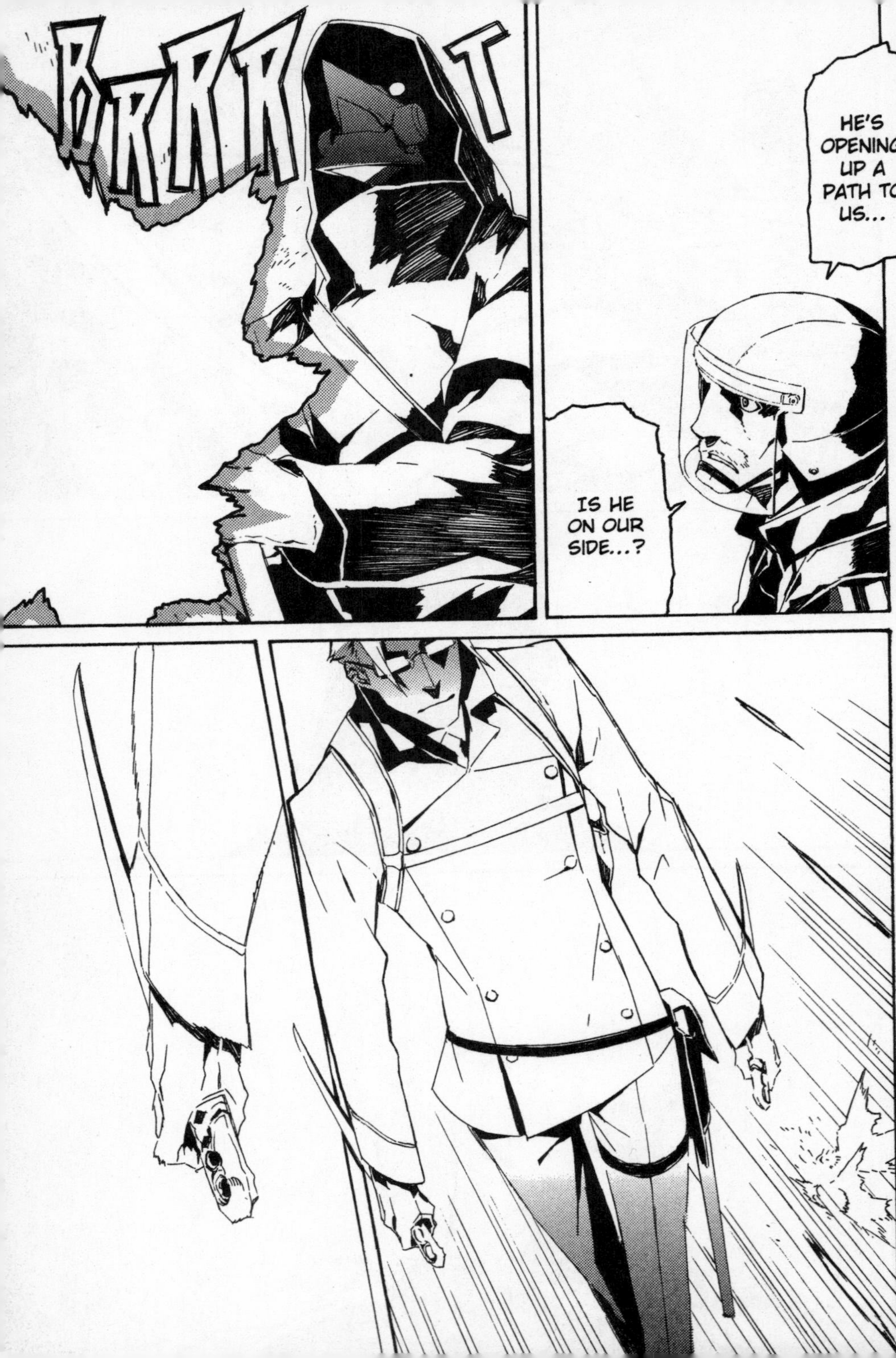
HE'S OPENING UP A PATH TO US...
IS HE ON OUR SIDE...?
BRRRAT

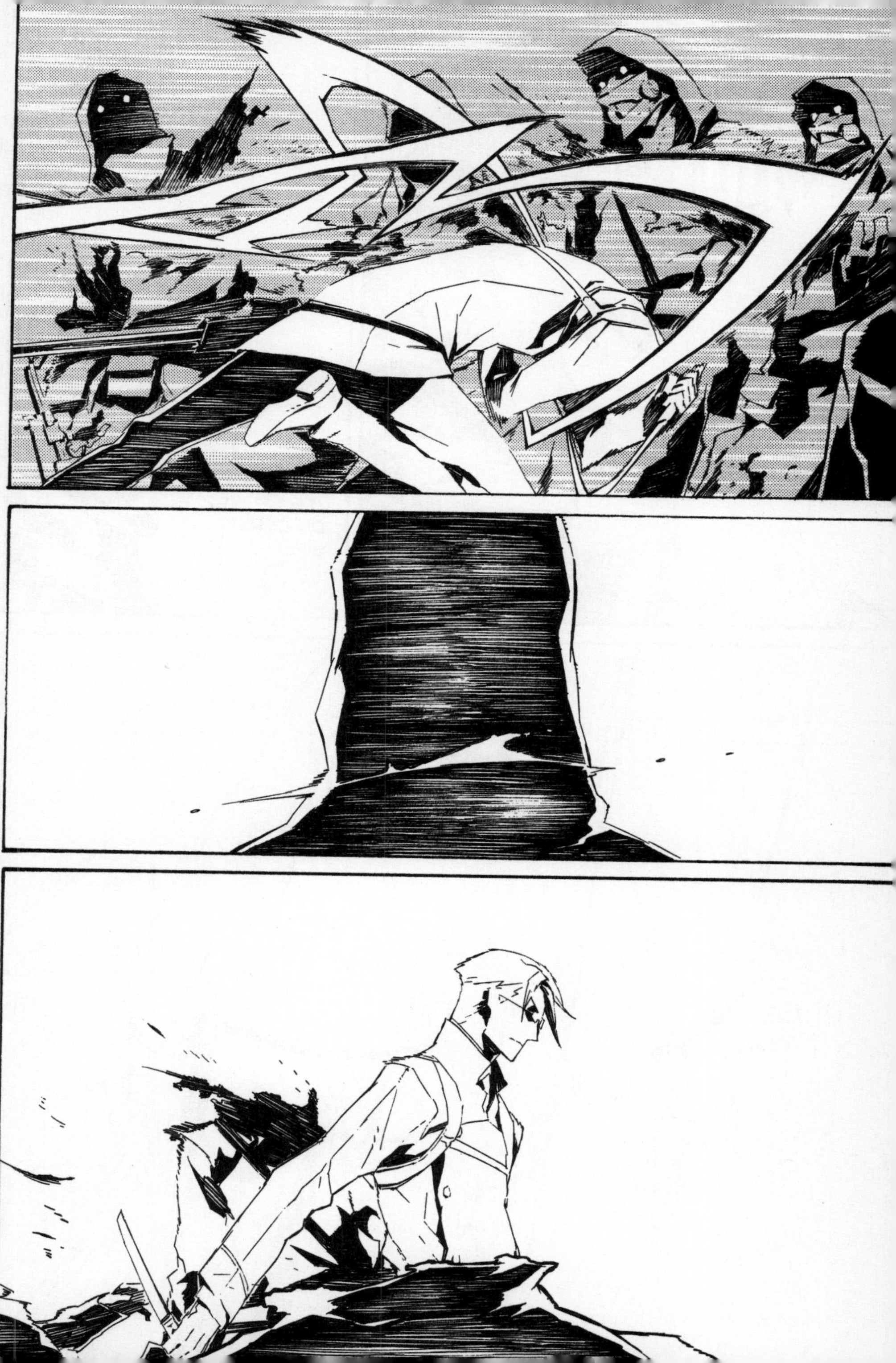

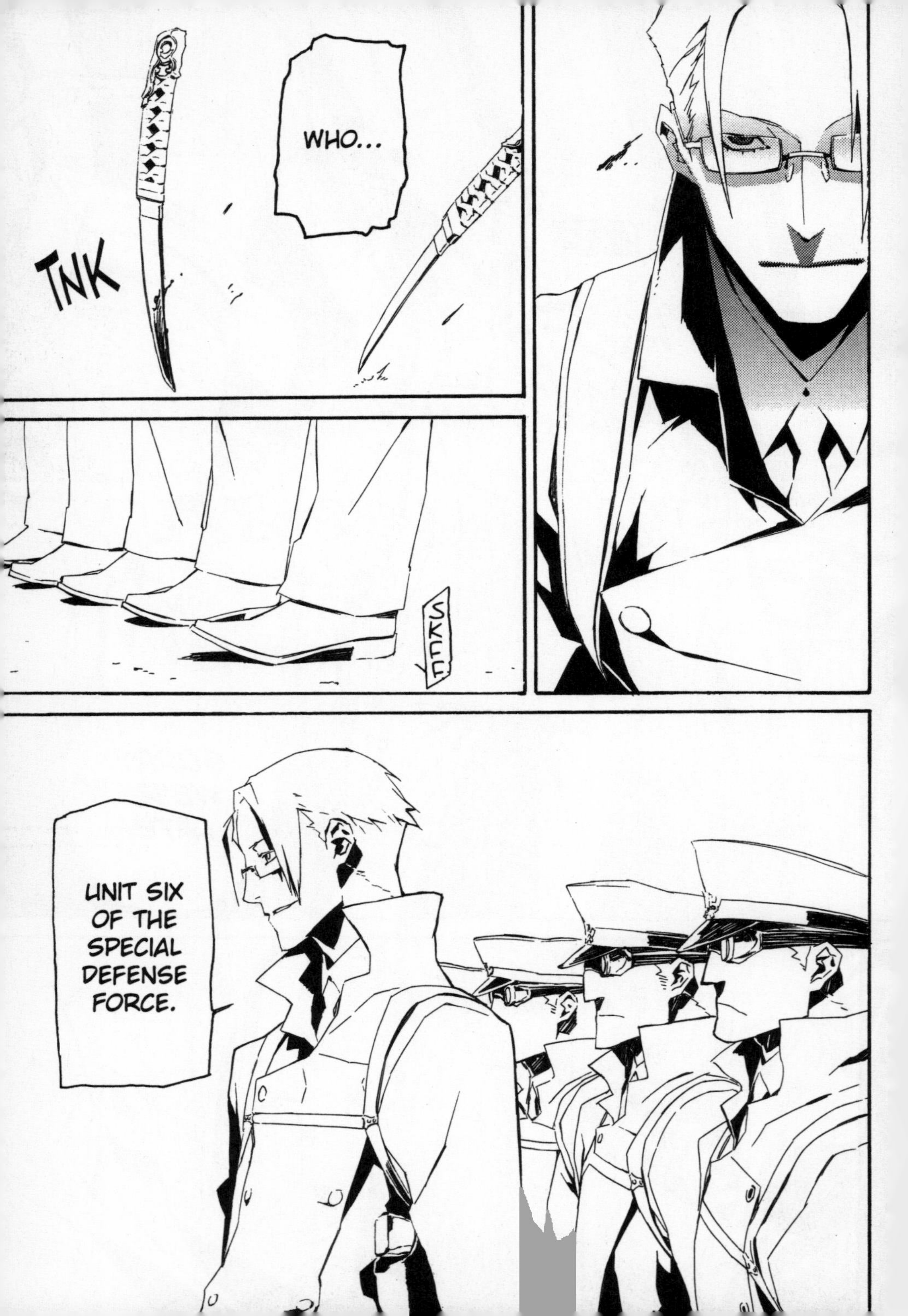
WHO...
TNK
SKFF
UNIT SIX OF THE SPECIAL DEFENSE FORCE.

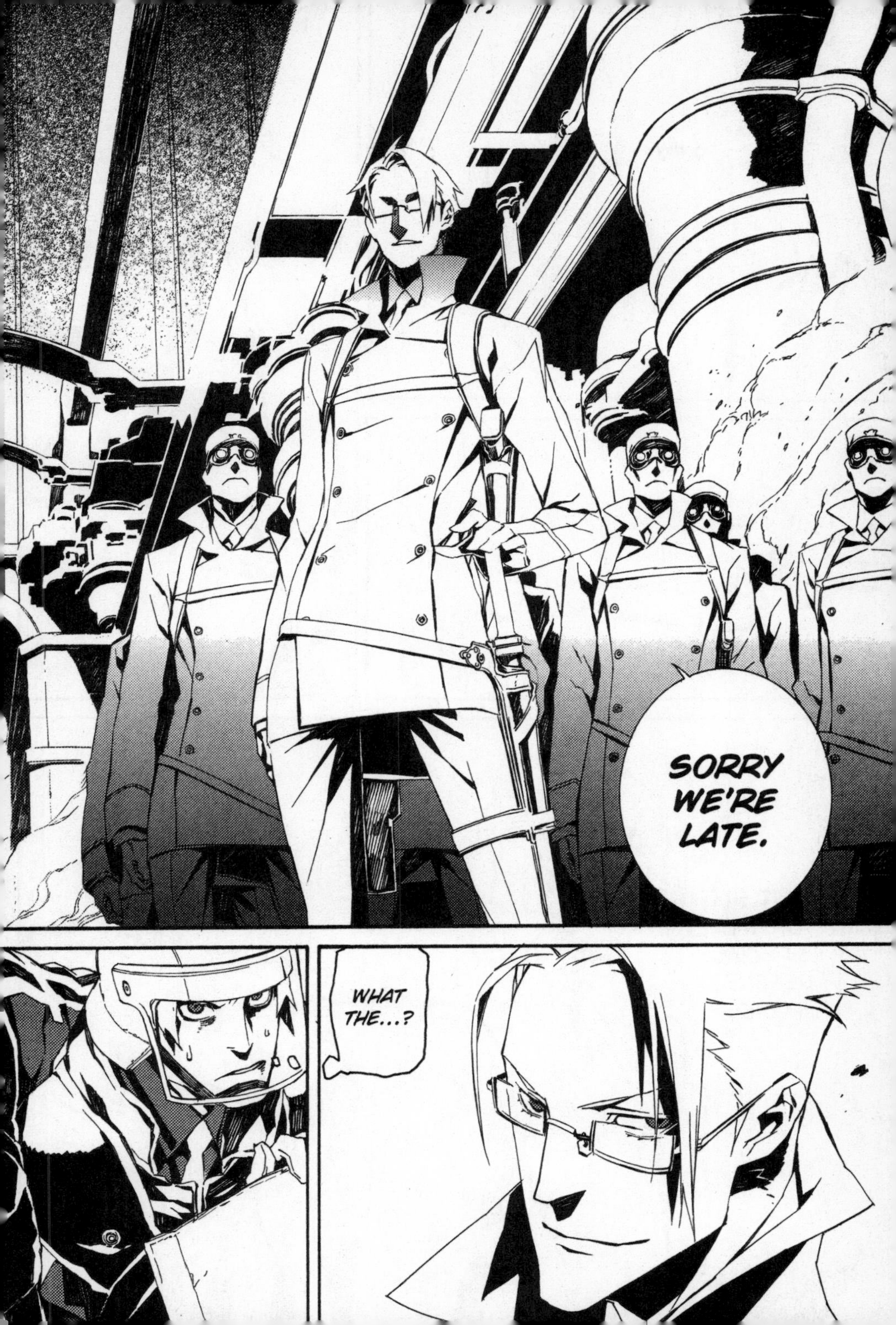
SORRY WE'RE LATE.
WHAT THE...?

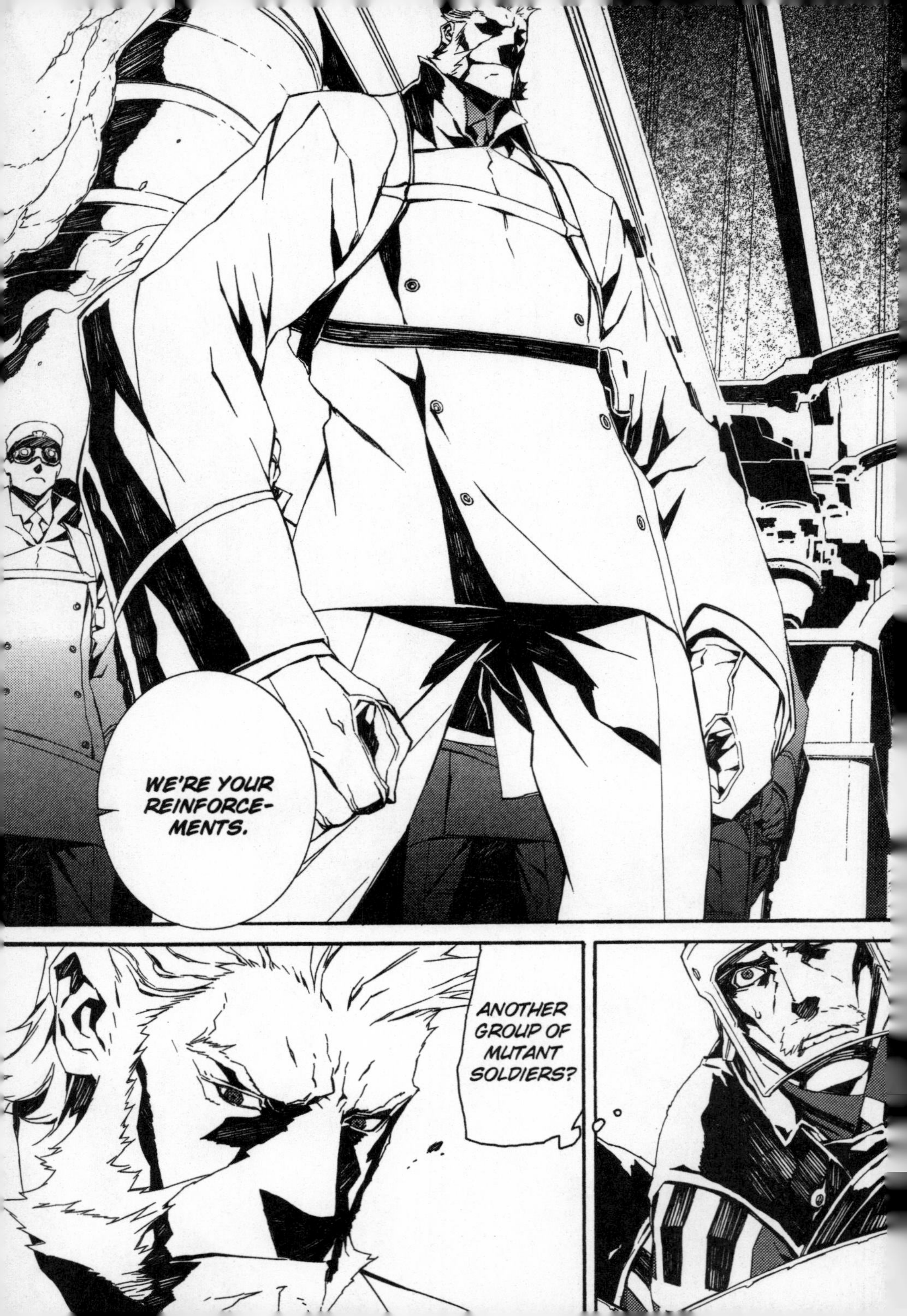
WE'RE YOUR REINFORCE-MENTS.
ANOTHER GROUP OF MUTANT SOLDIERS?

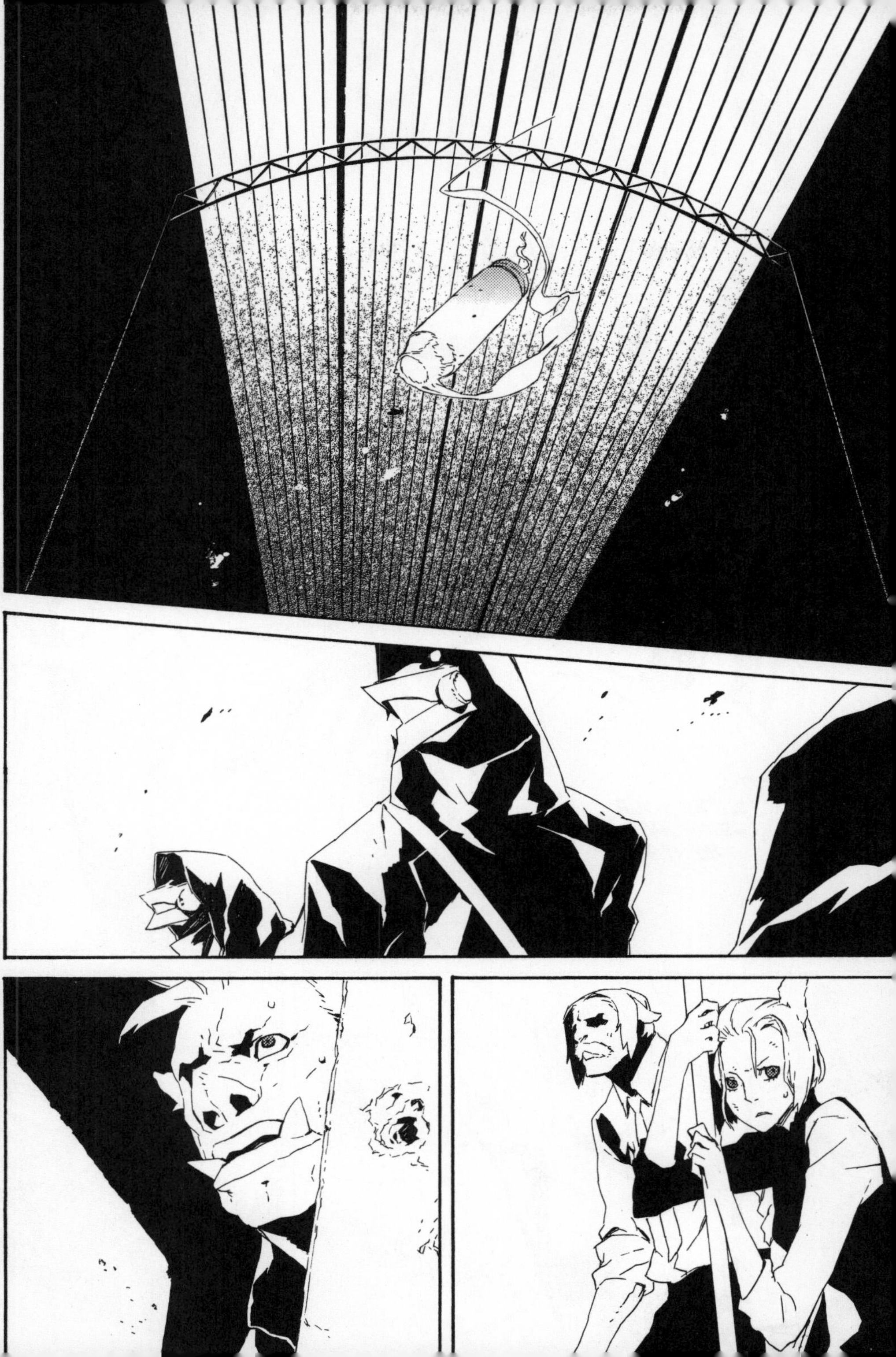

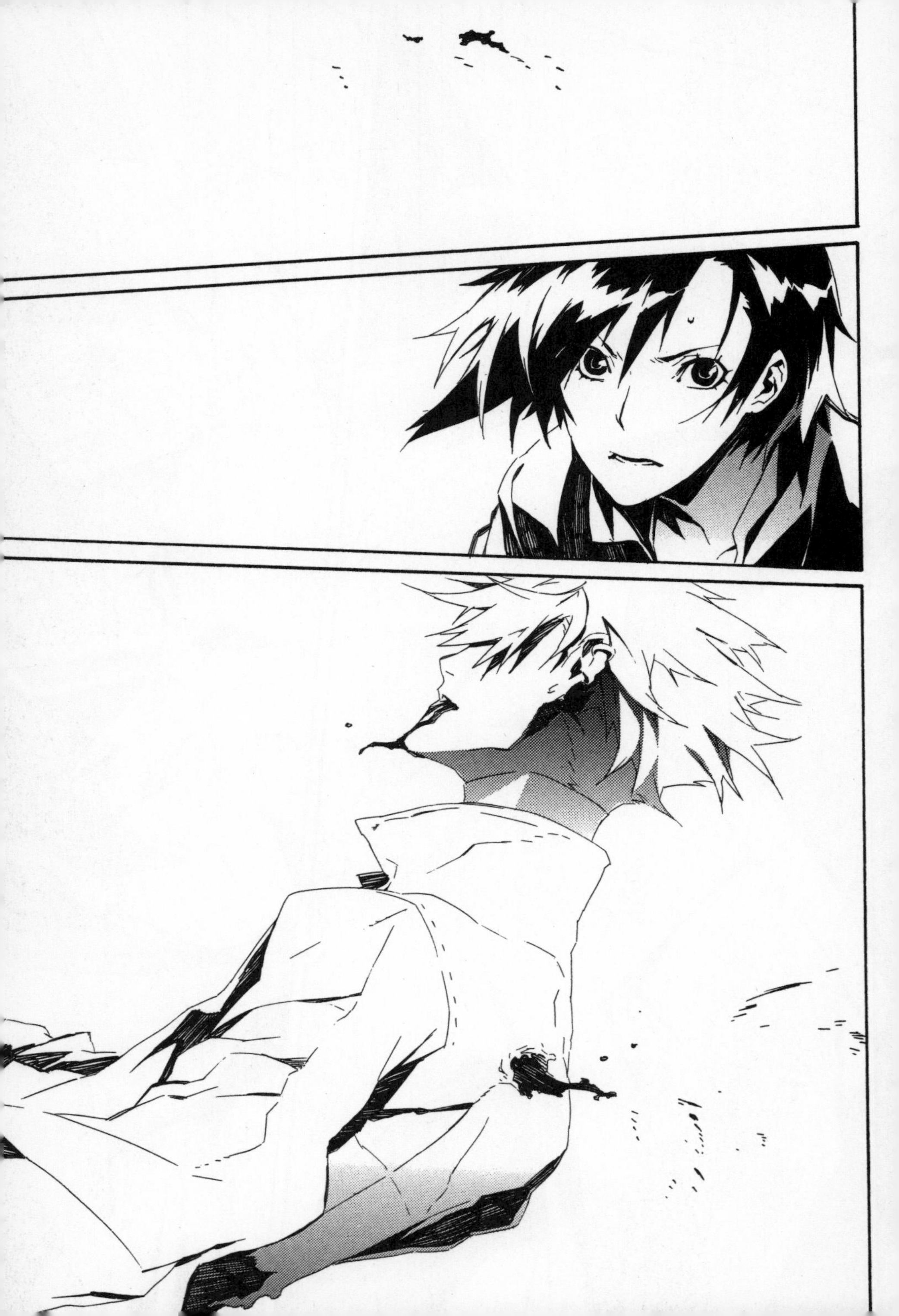

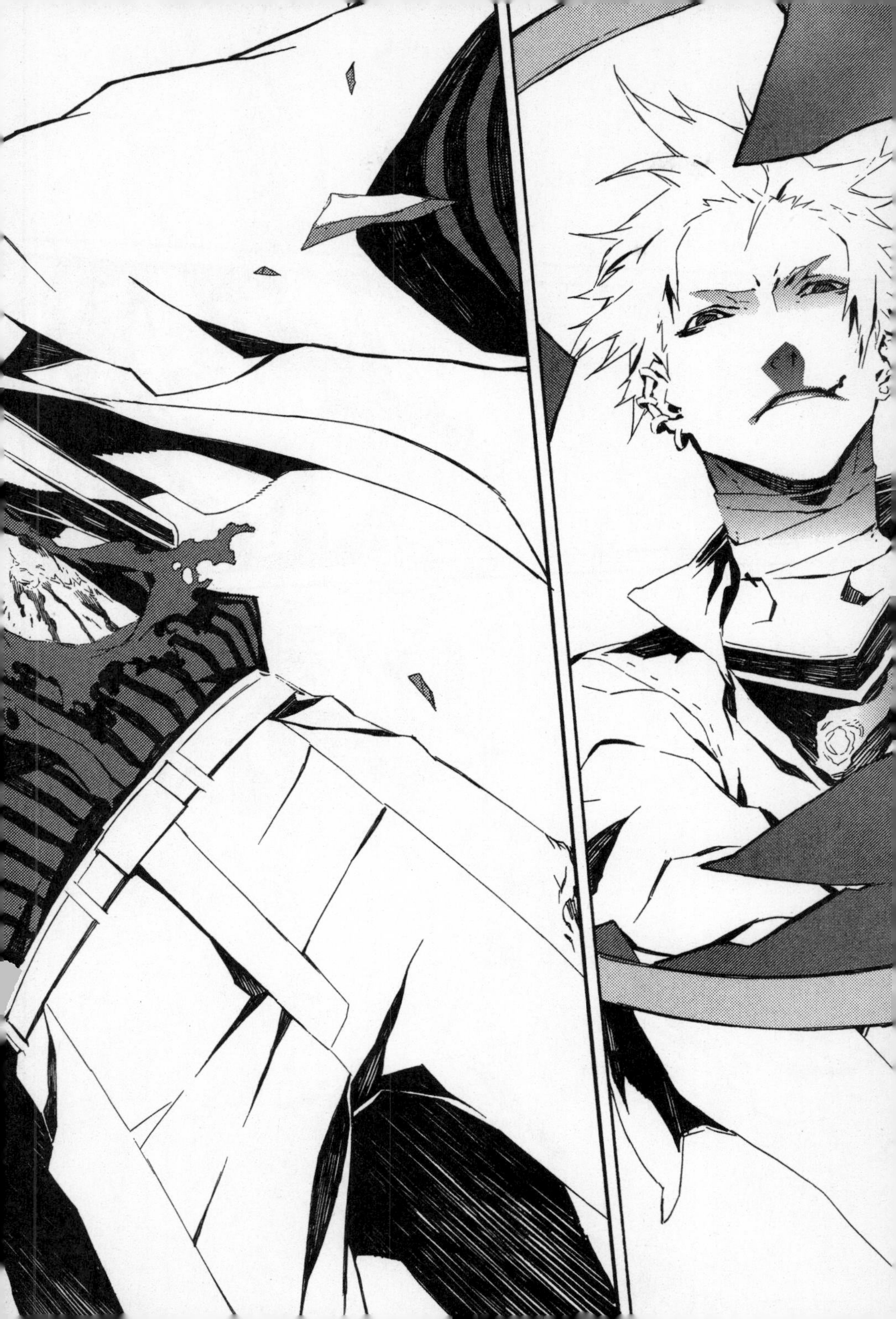

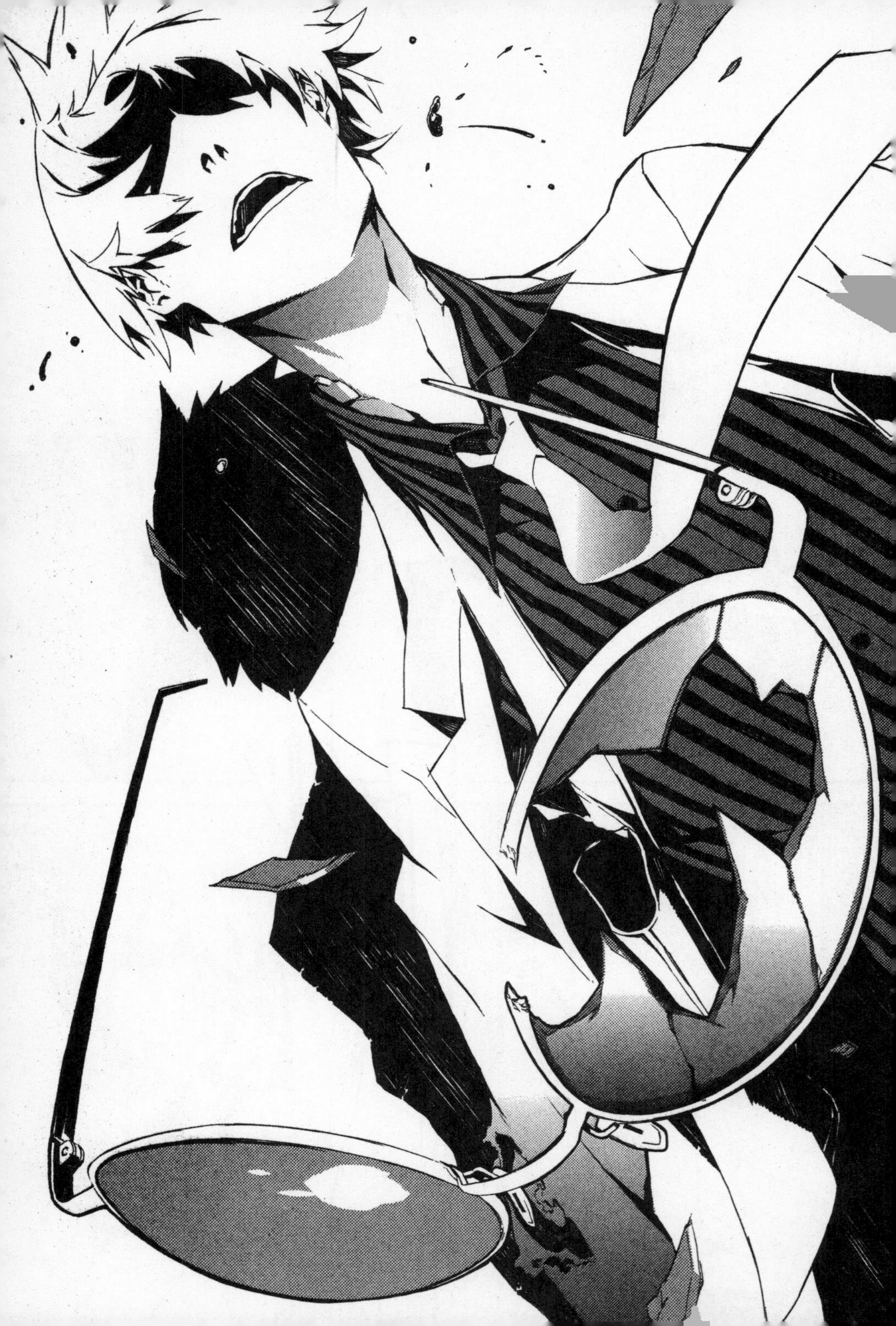

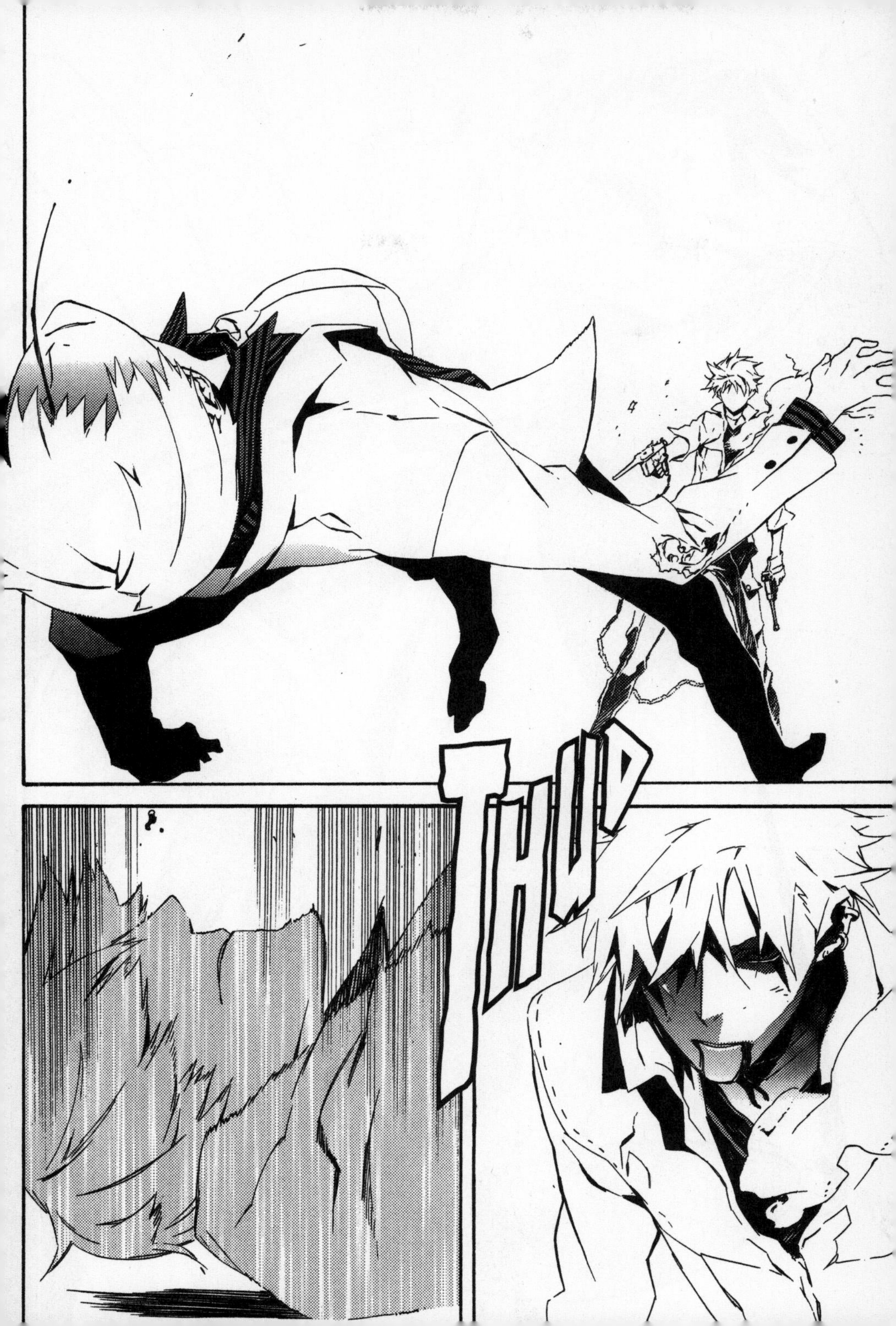
THUD

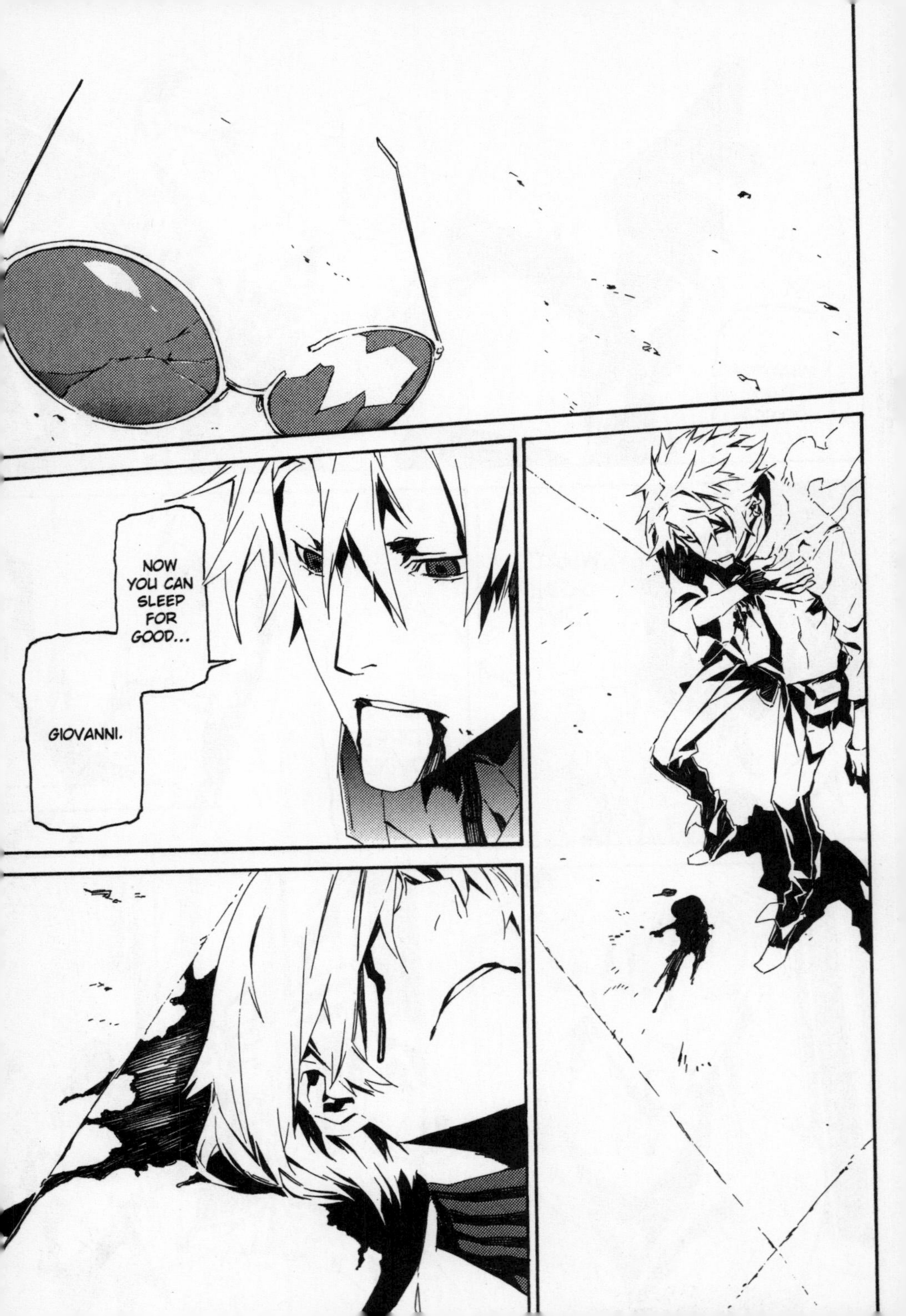
NOW YOU CAN SLEEP FOR GOOD...
GIOVANNI.

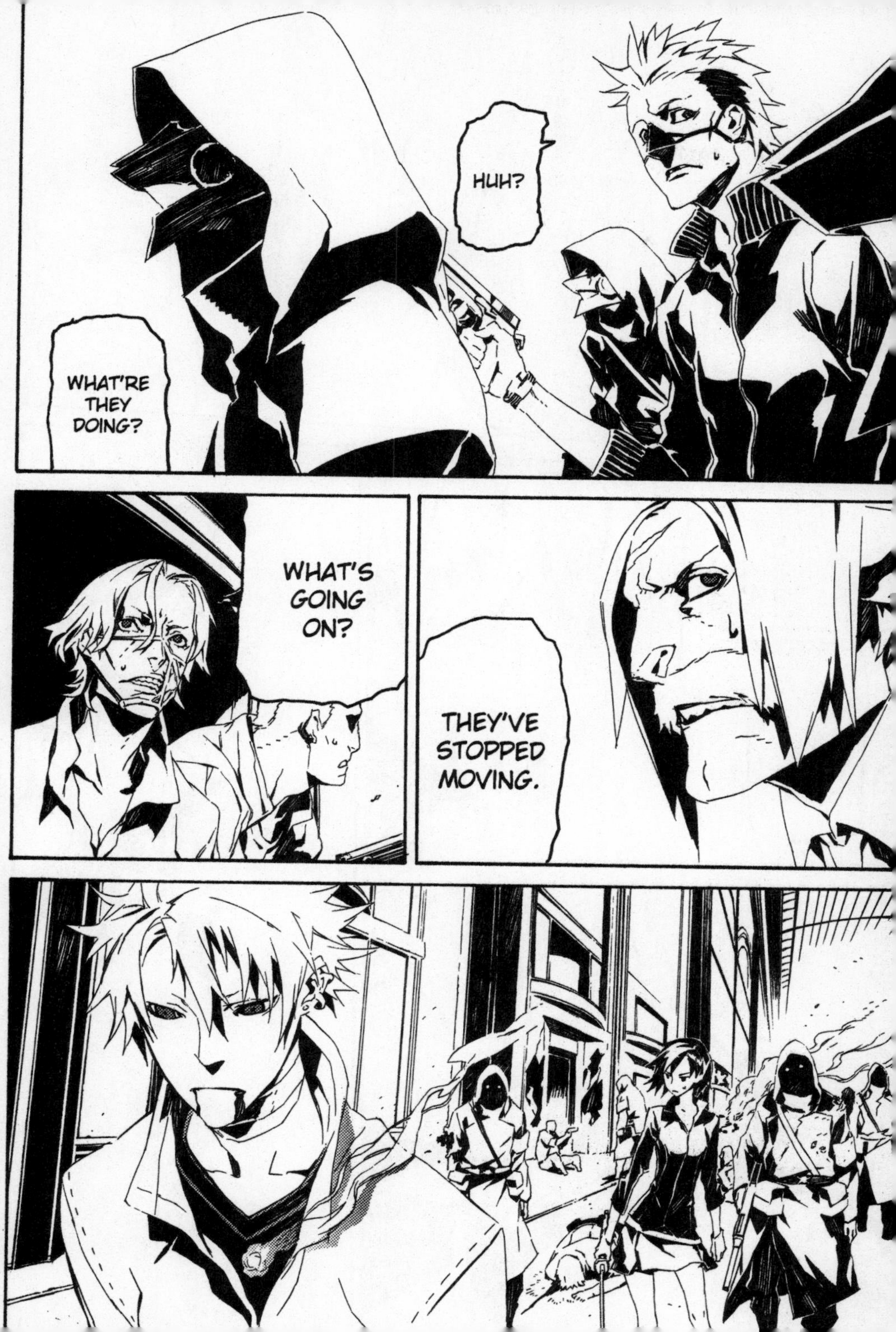
HUH?
WHAT'RE THEY DOING?
THEY'VE STOPPED MOVING.
WHAT'S GOING ON?

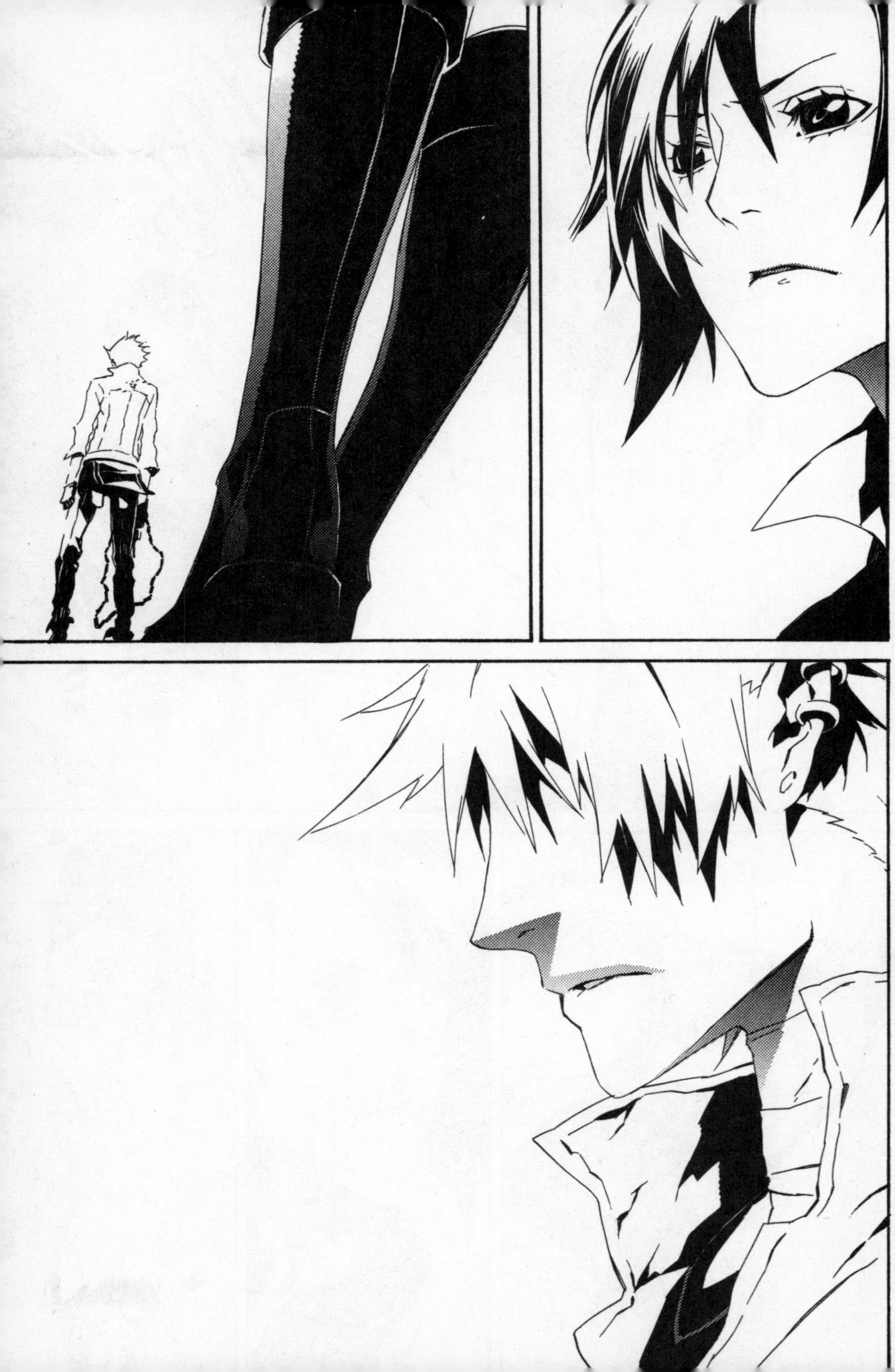

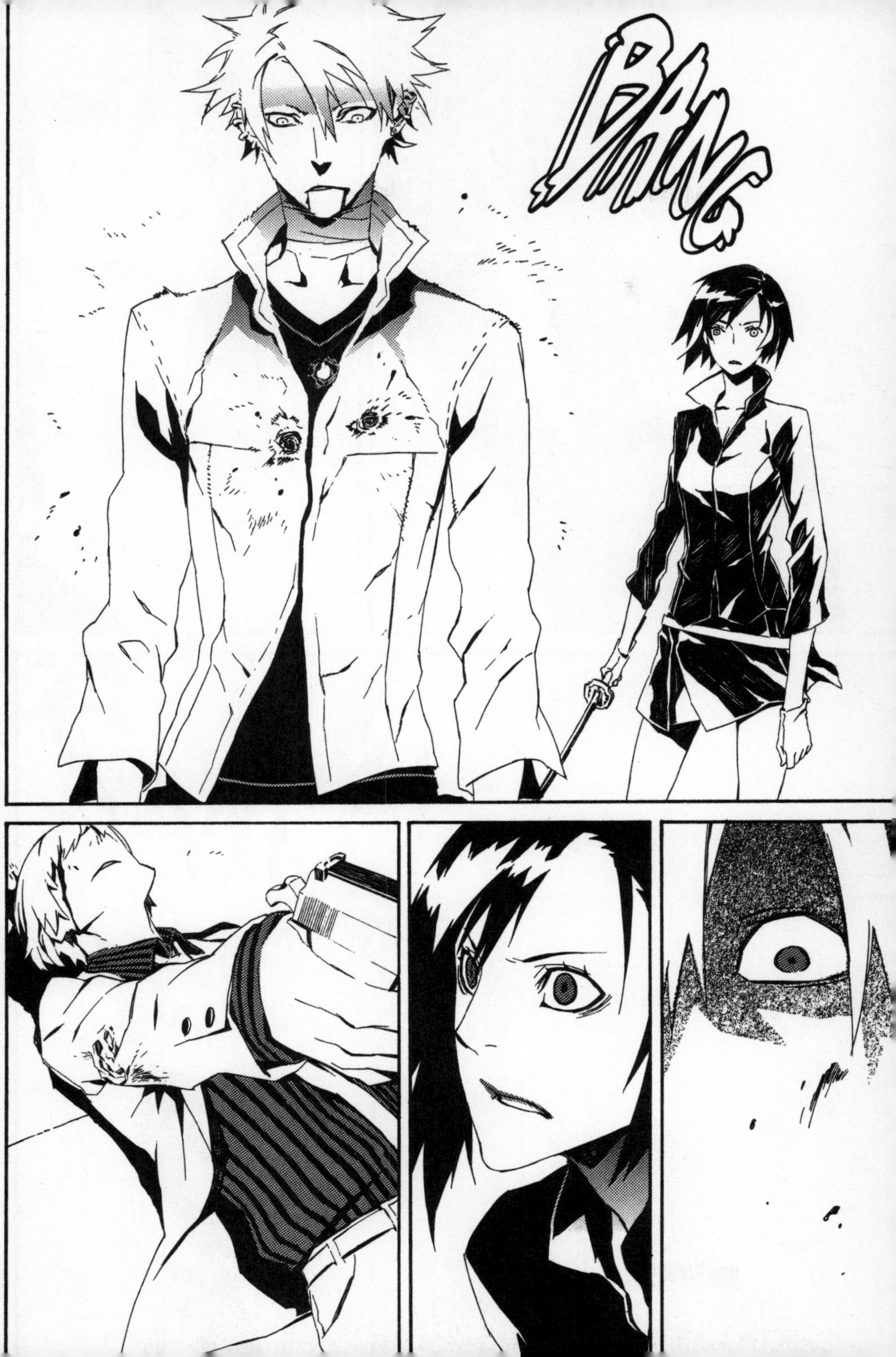
BLAM

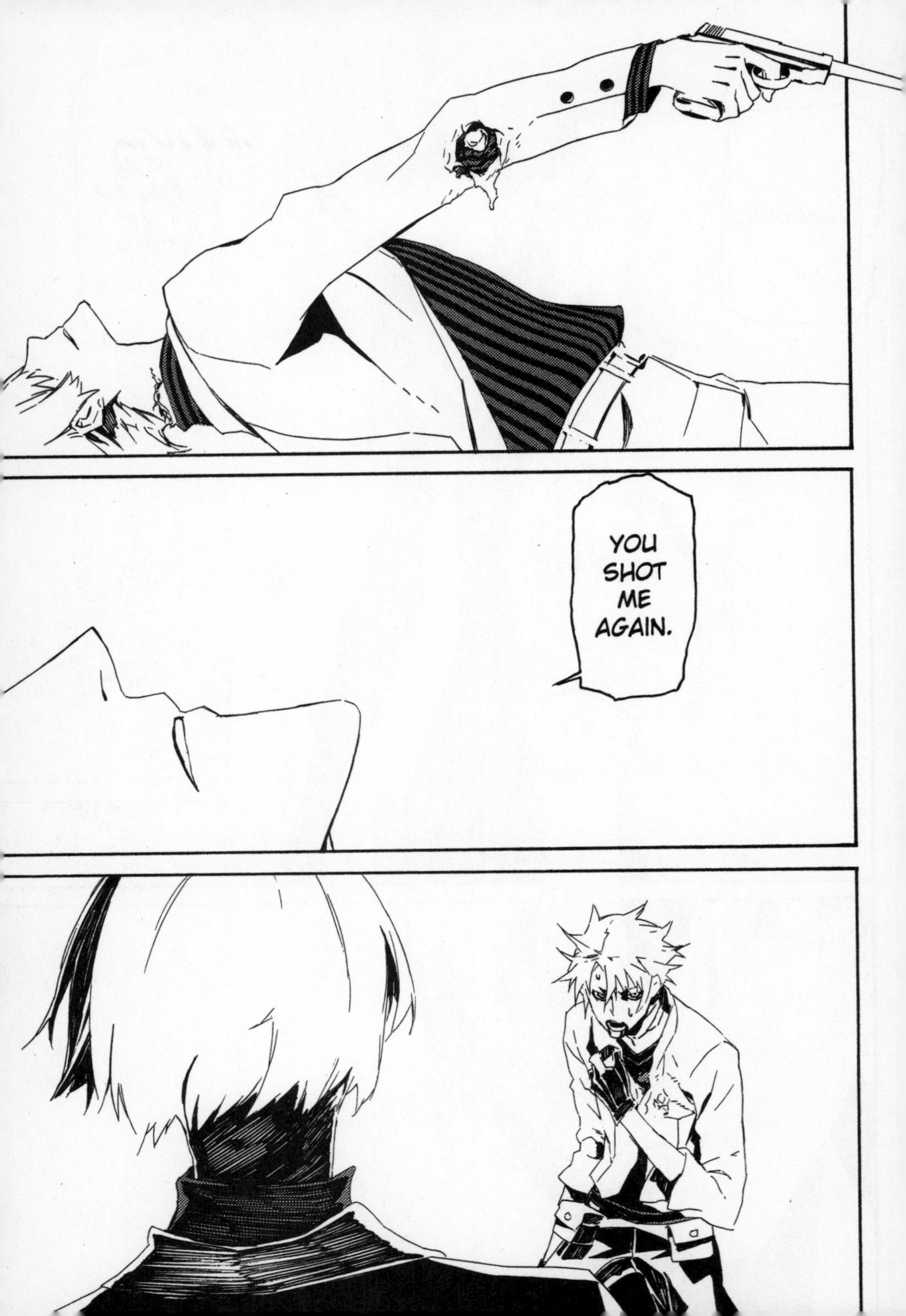
YOU SHOT ME AGAIN.

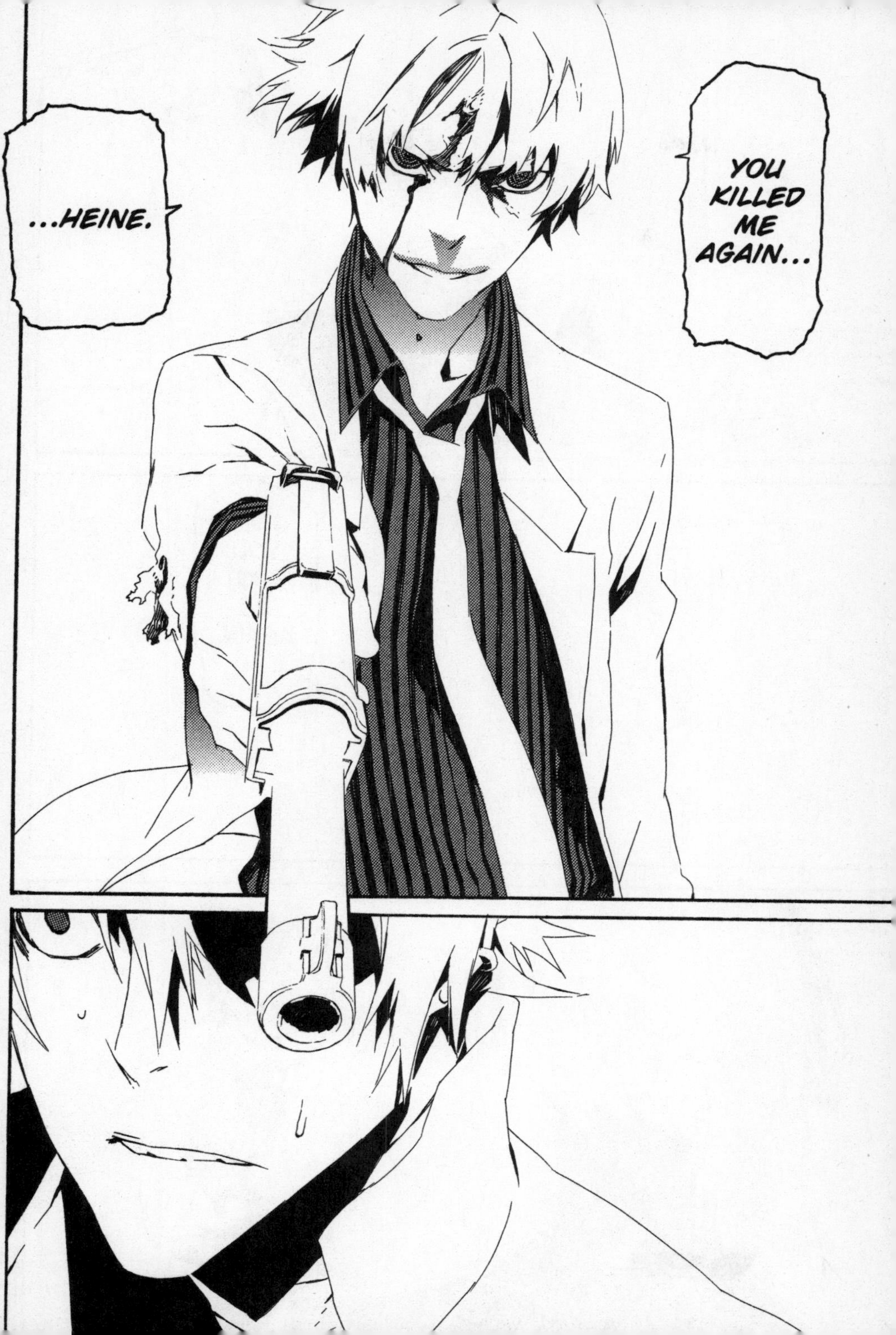
YOU KILLED ME AGAIN...
...HEINE.

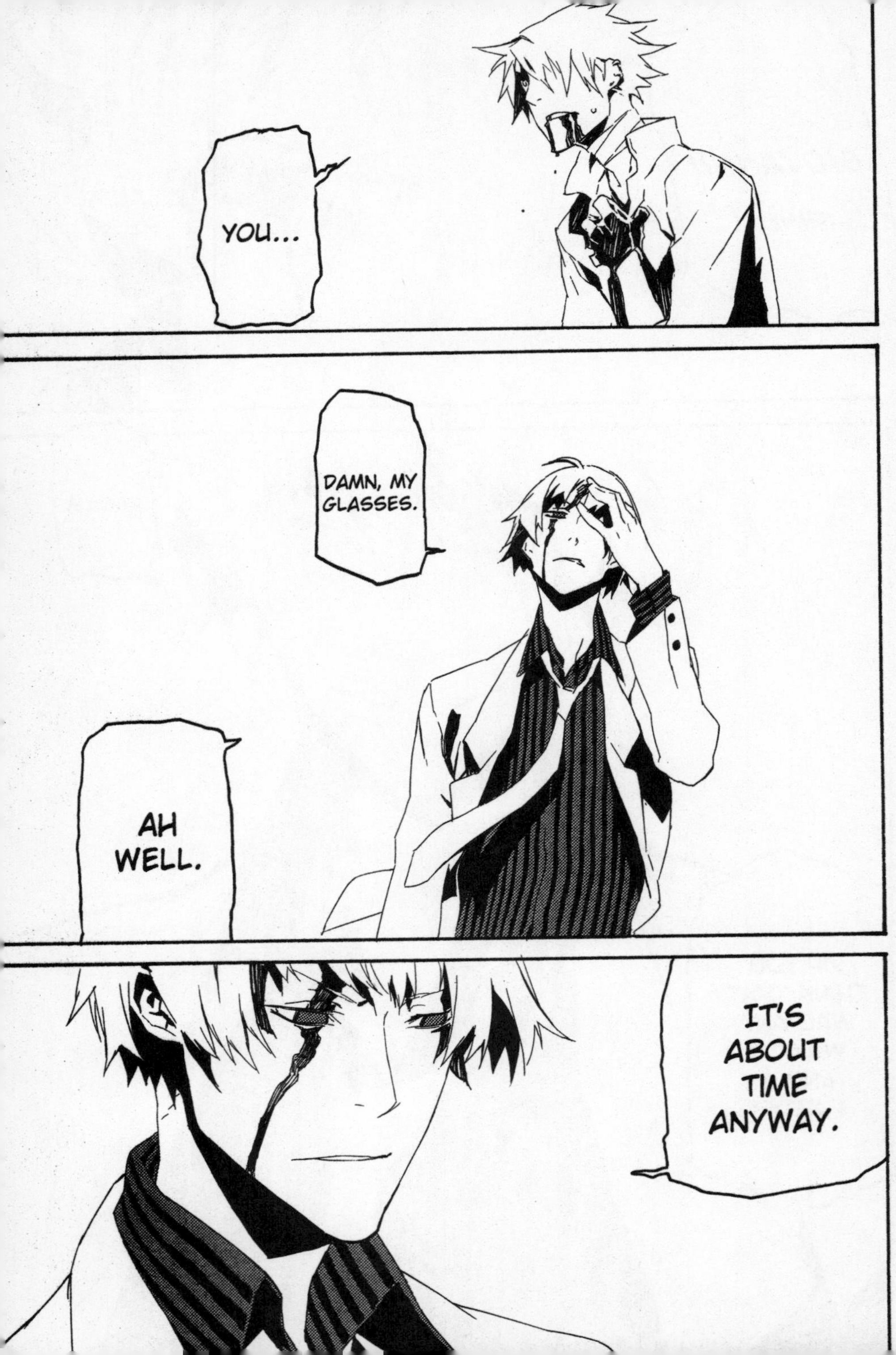
YOU...
DAMN, MY GLASSES.
AH WELL.
IT'S ABOUT TIME ANYWAY.

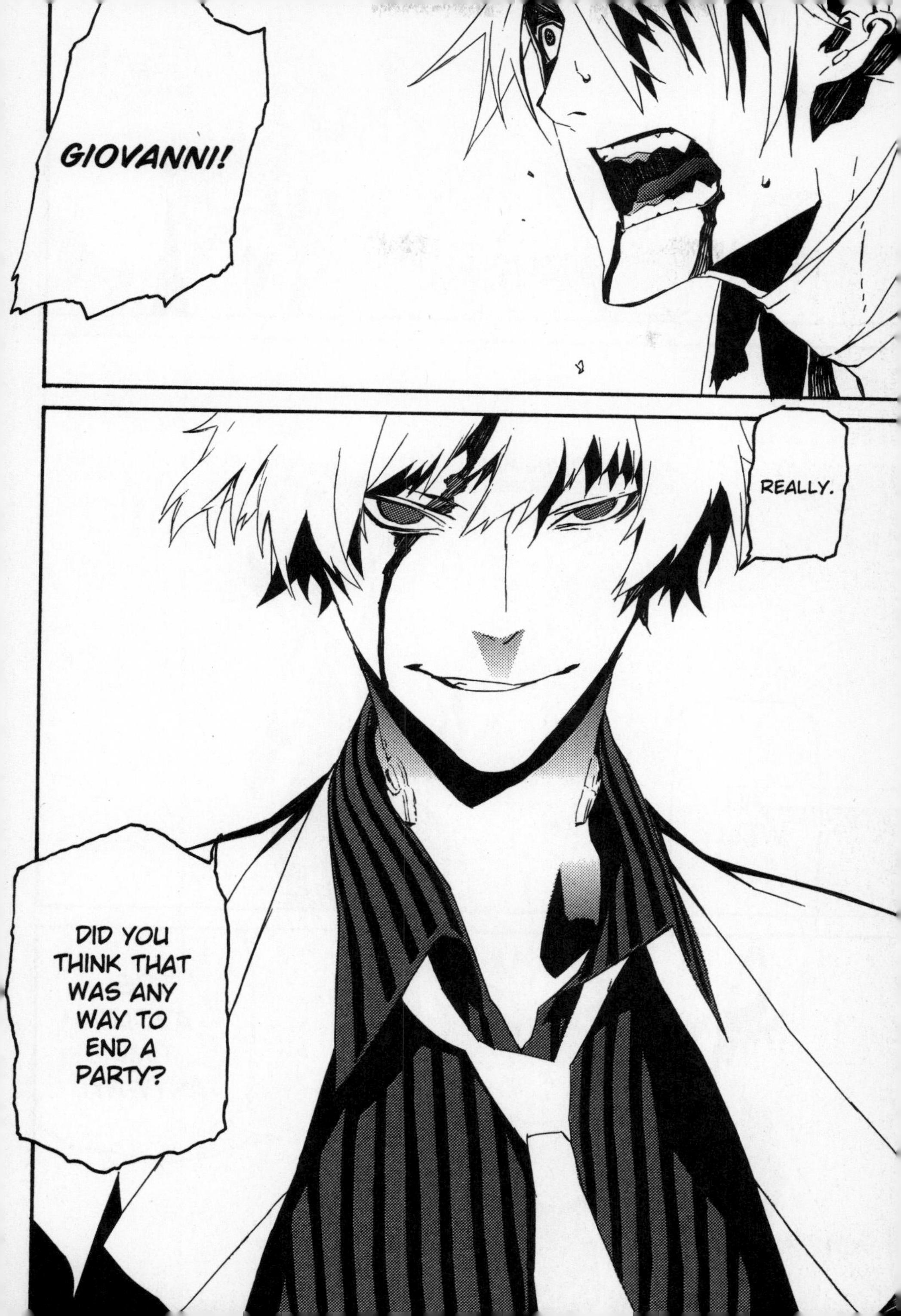
GIOVANNI!
REALLY.
DID YOU THINK THAT WAS ANY WAY TO END A PARTY?

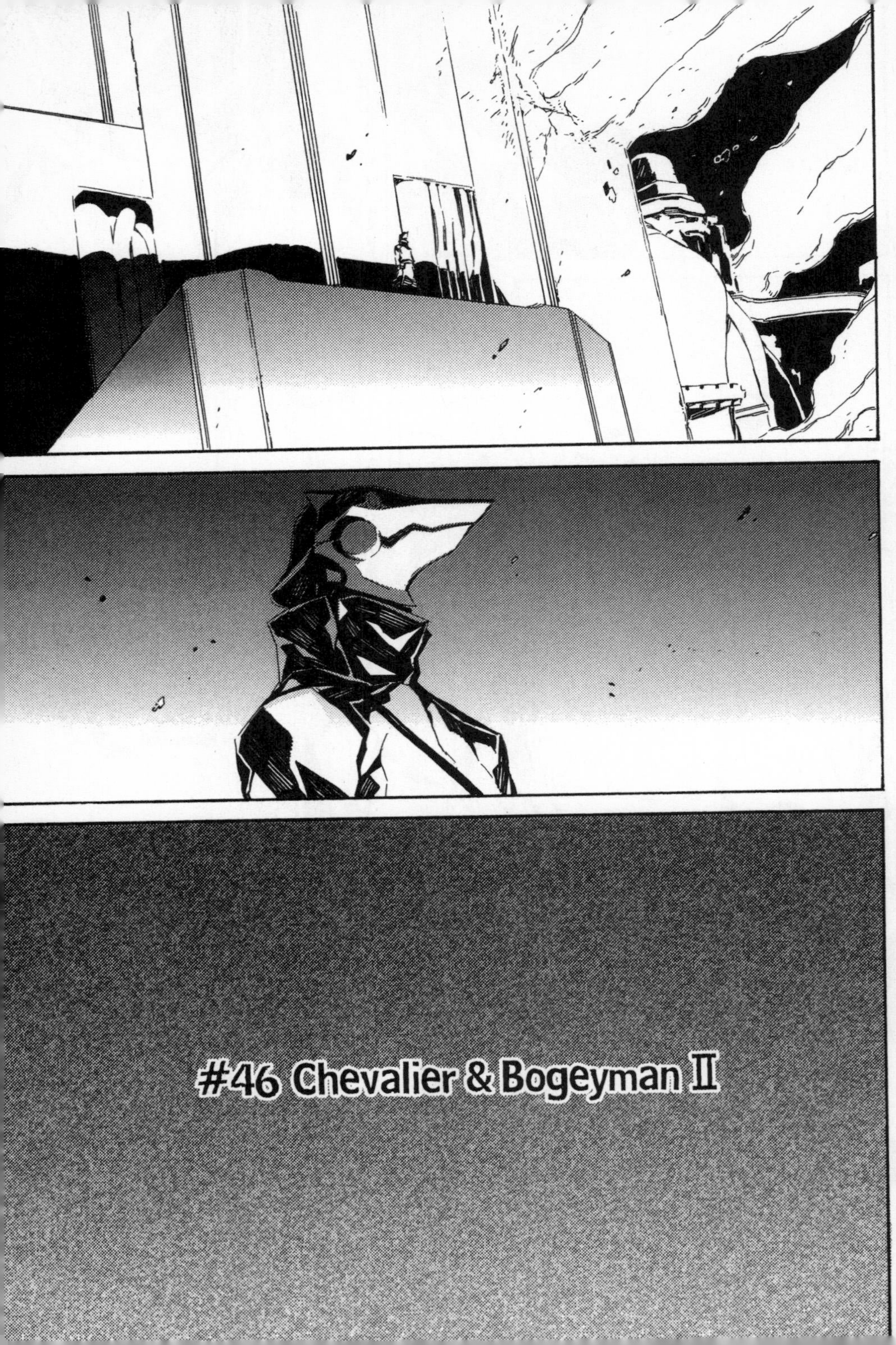
#46 Chevalier & Bogeyman II

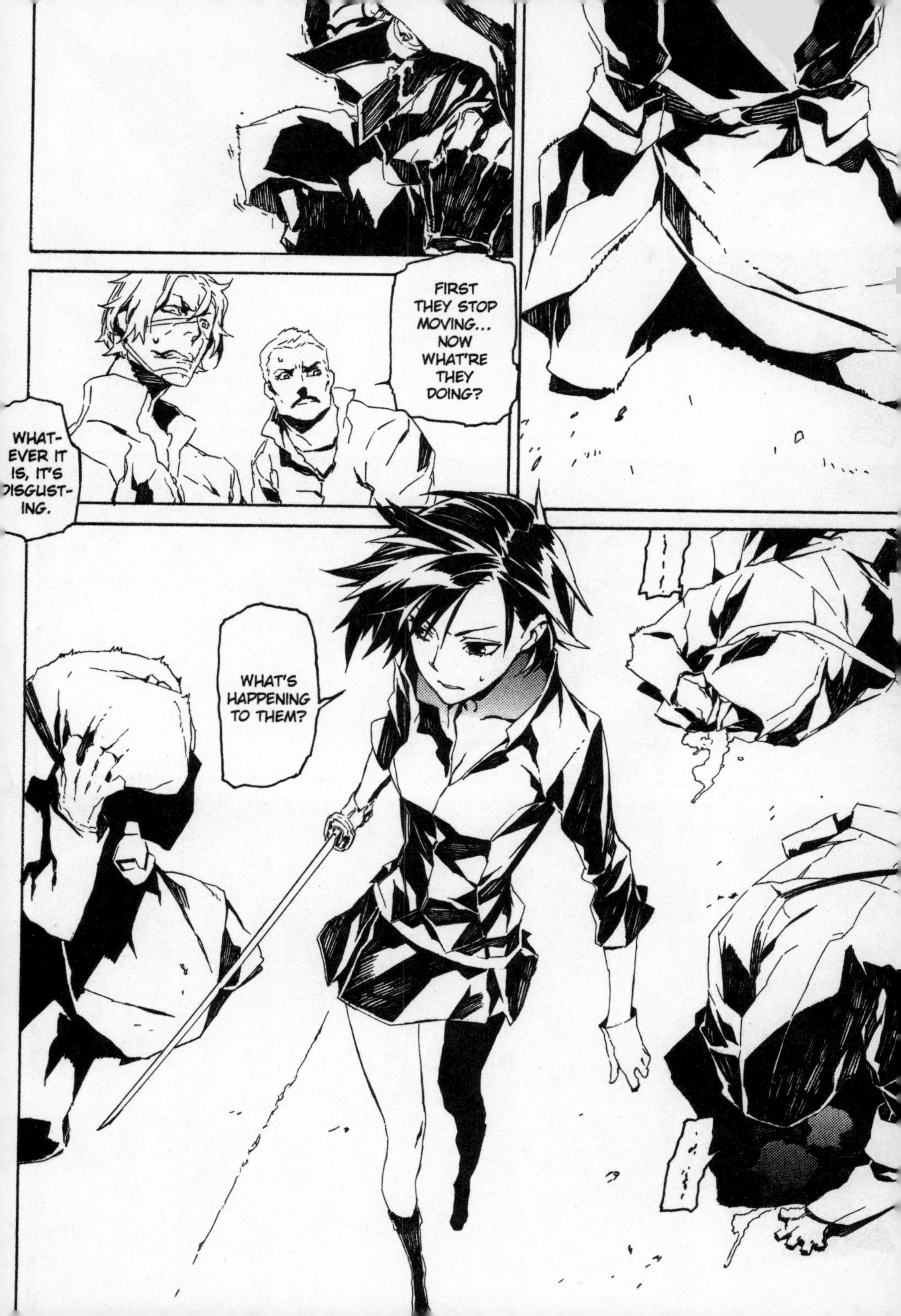
FIRST THEY STOP MOVING... NOW WHAT'RE THEY DOING?
WHATEVER IT IS, IT'S DISGUSTING.
WHAT'S HAPPENING TO THEM?

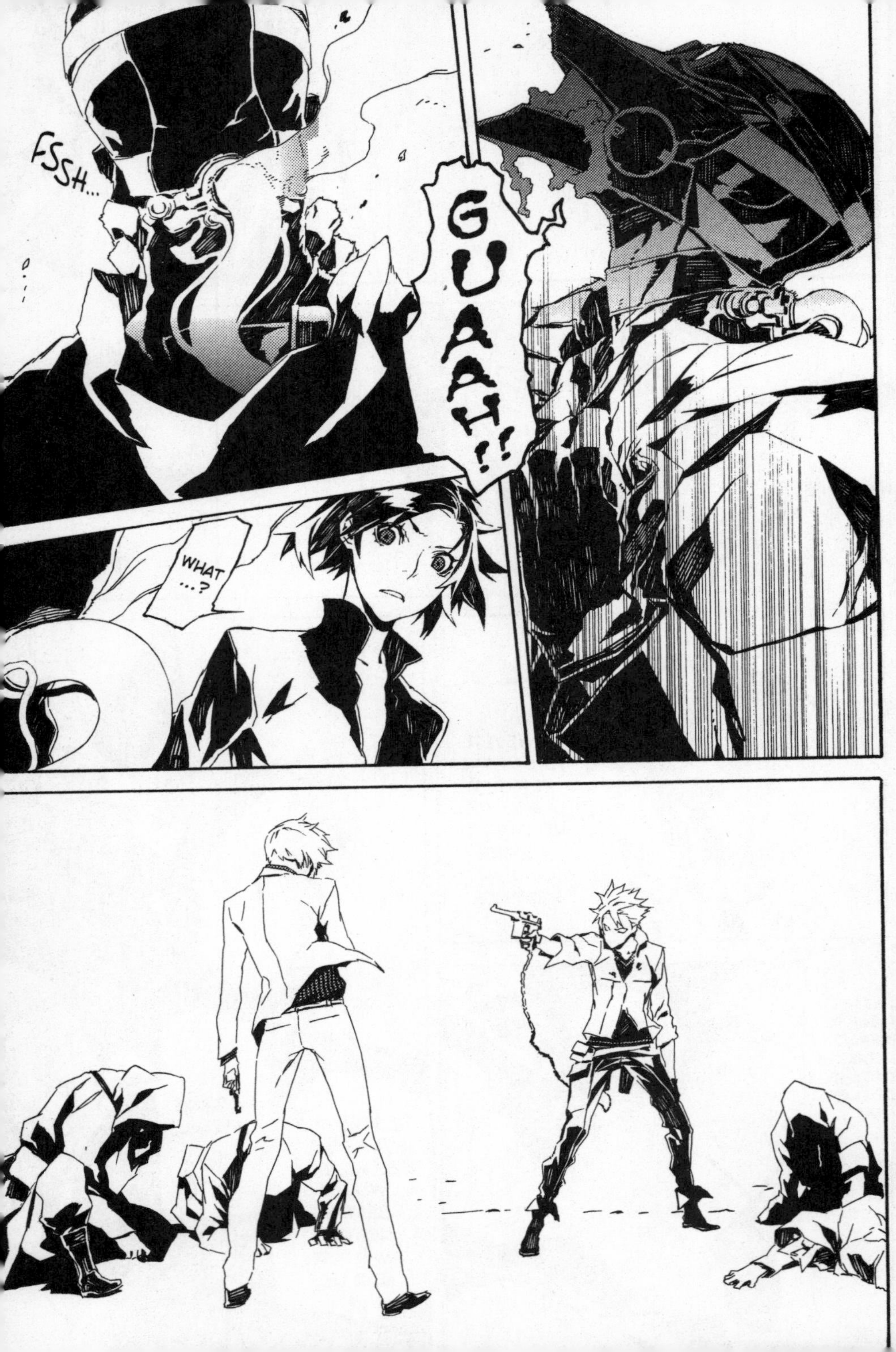
GUAAH!!
FSSH...
...
WHAT ...?

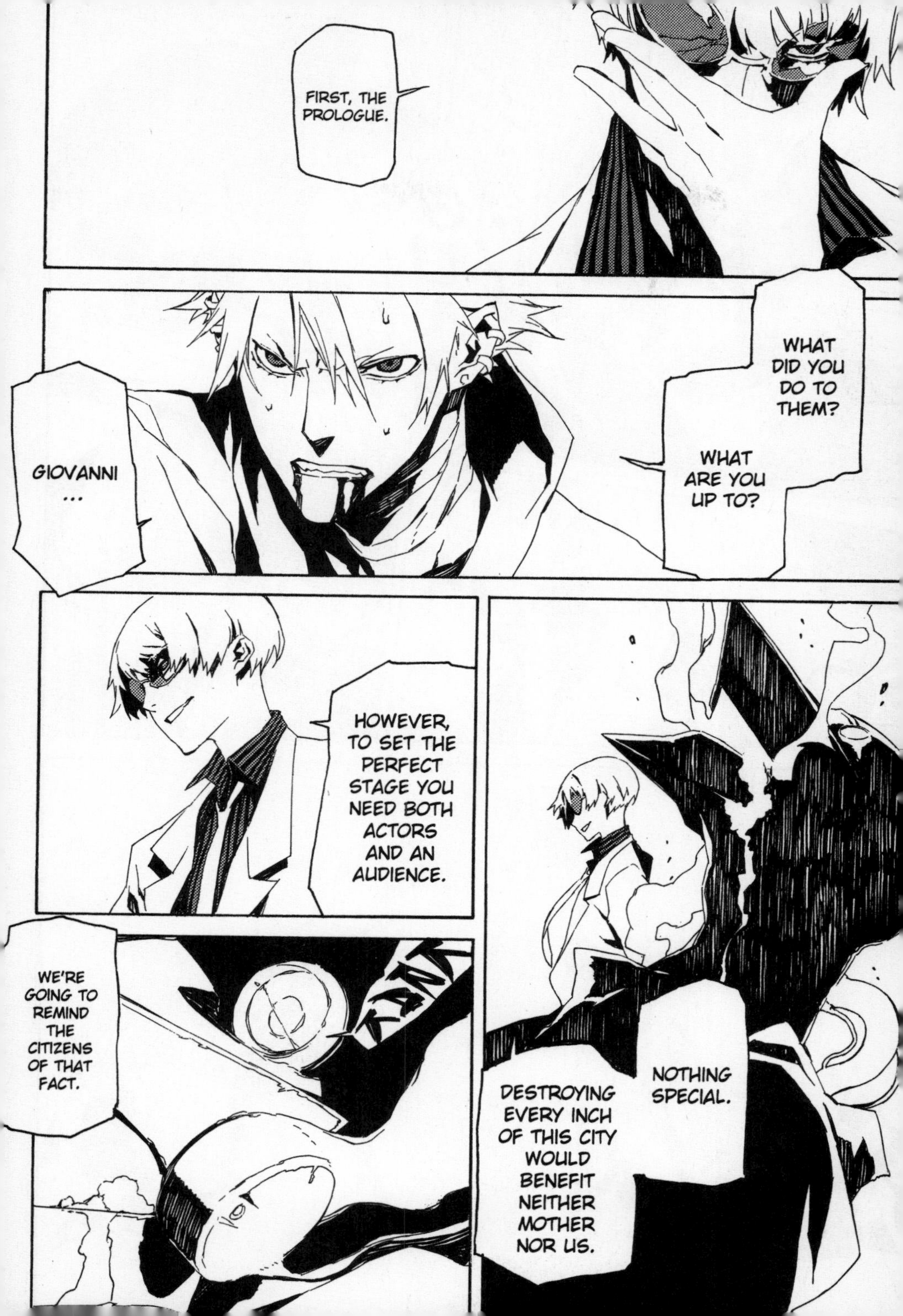
FIRST, THE PROLOGUE.
WHAT DID YOU DO TO THEM?
WHAT ARE YOU UP TO?
GIOVANNI ...
NOTHING SPECIAL.
DESTROYING EVERY INCH OF THIS CITY WOULD BENEFIT NEITHER MOTHER NOR US.
HOWEVER, TO SET THE PERFECT STAGE YOU NEED BOTH ACTORS AND AN AUDIENCE.
WE'RE GOING TO REMIND THE CITIZENS OF THAT FACT.

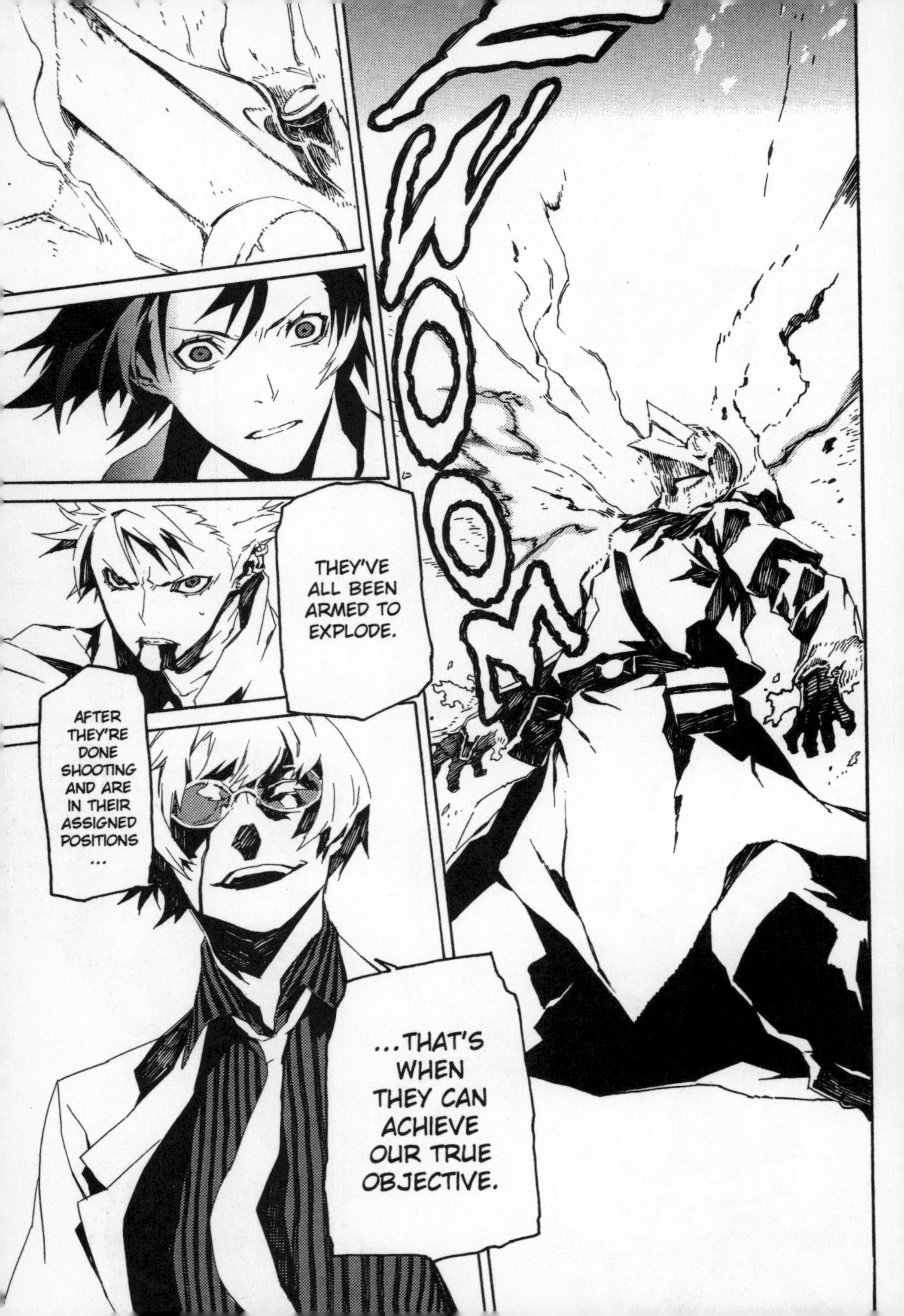
FWOOOM
THEY'VE ALL BEEN ARMED TO EXPLODE.
AFTER THEY'RE DONE SHOOTING AND ARE IN THEIR ASSIGNED POSITIONS ...
...THAT'S WHEN THEY CAN ACHIEVE OUR TRUE OBJECTIVE.

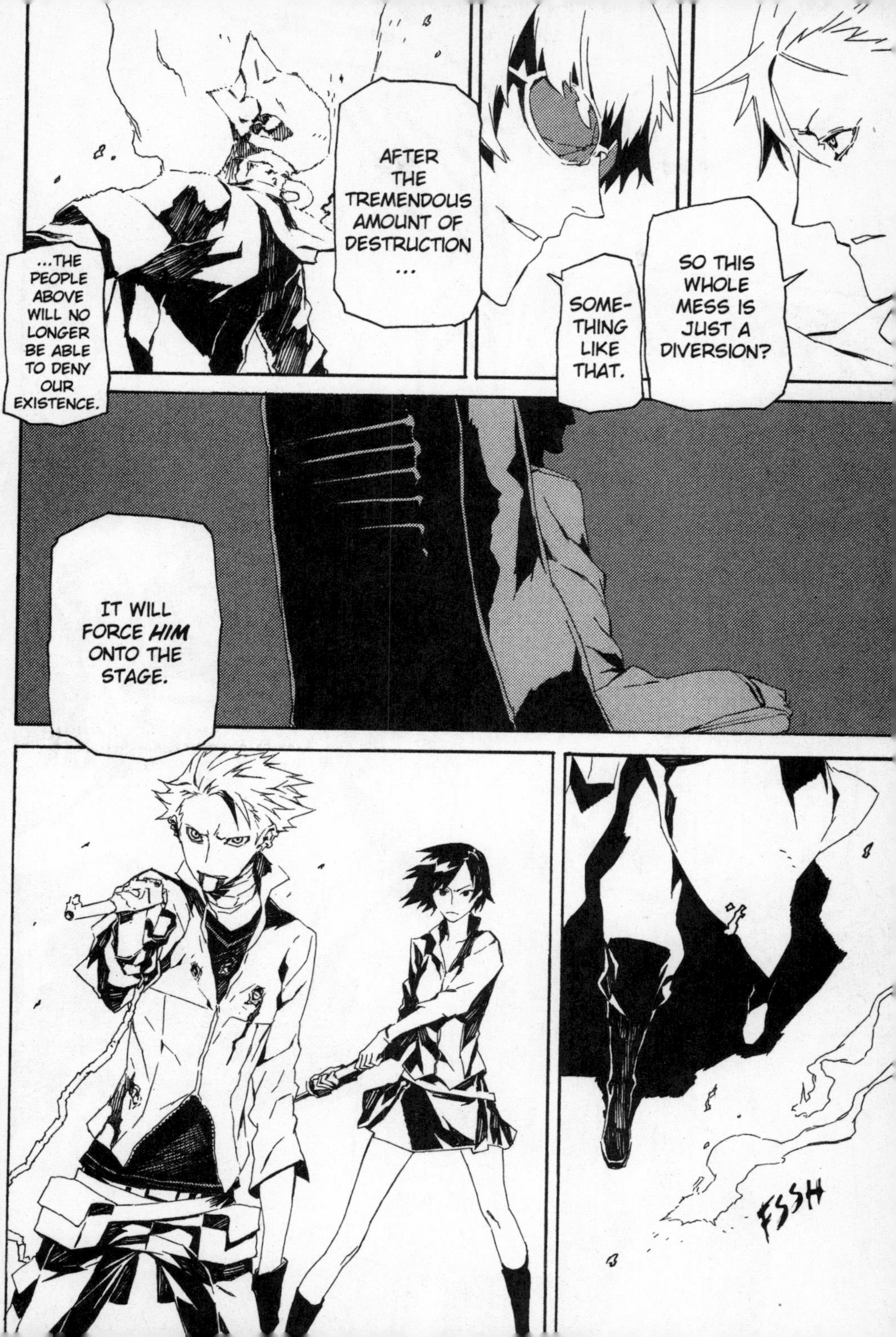
SO THIS WHOLE MESS IS JUST A DIVERSION?
SOME-THING LIKE THAT.
AFTER THE TREMENDOUS AMOUNT OF DESTRUCTION ...
...THE PEOPLE ABOVE WILL NO LONGER BE ABLE TO DENY OUR EXISTENCE.
IT WILL FORCE *HIM* ONTO THE STAGE.
FSSH

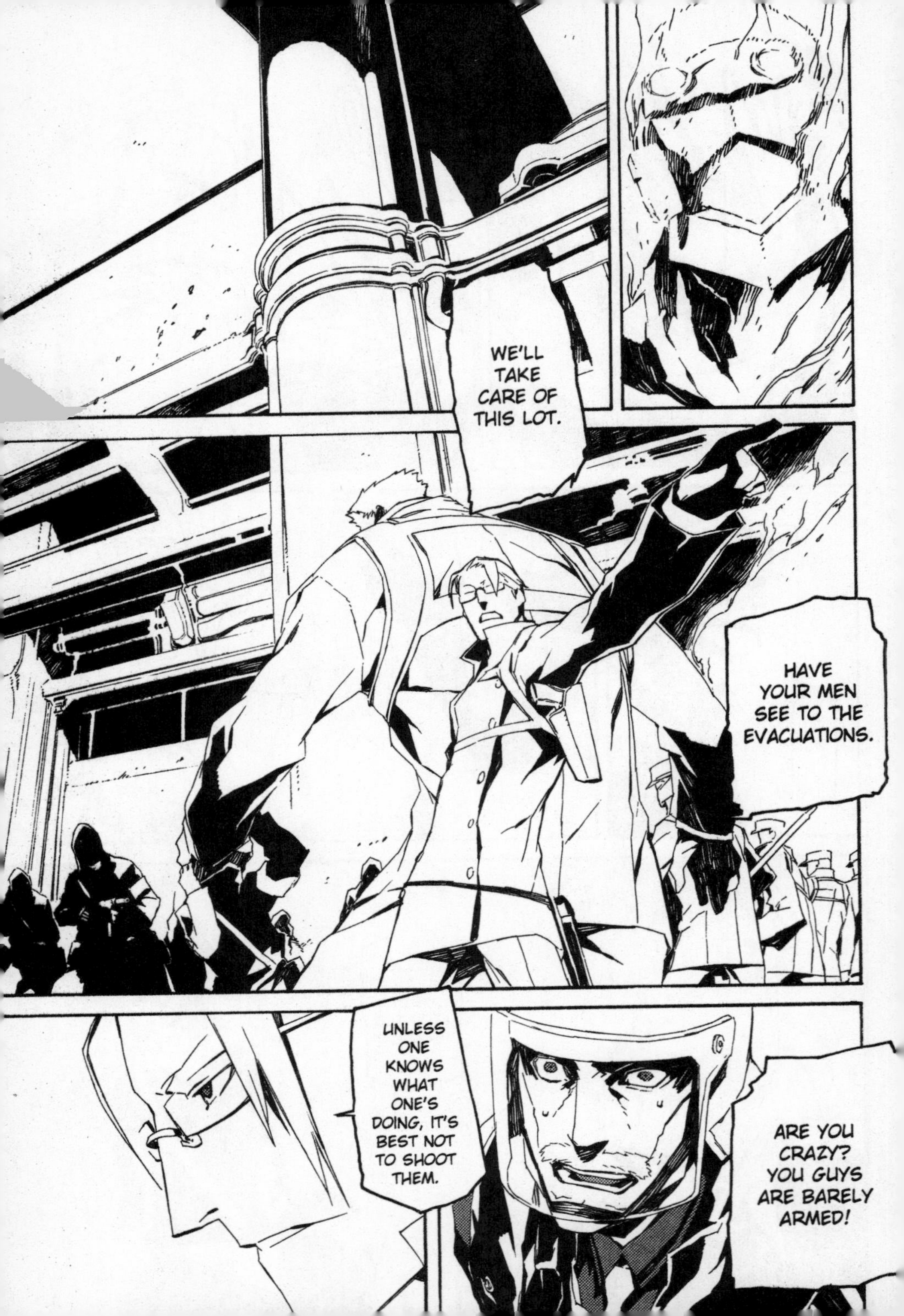
WE'LL TAKE CARE OF THIS LOT.
HAVE YOUR MEN SEE TO THE EVACUATIONS.
ARE YOU CRAZY? YOU GUYS ARE BARELY ARMED!
UNLESS ONE KNOWS WHAT ONE'S DOING, IT'S BEST NOT TO SHOOT THEM.

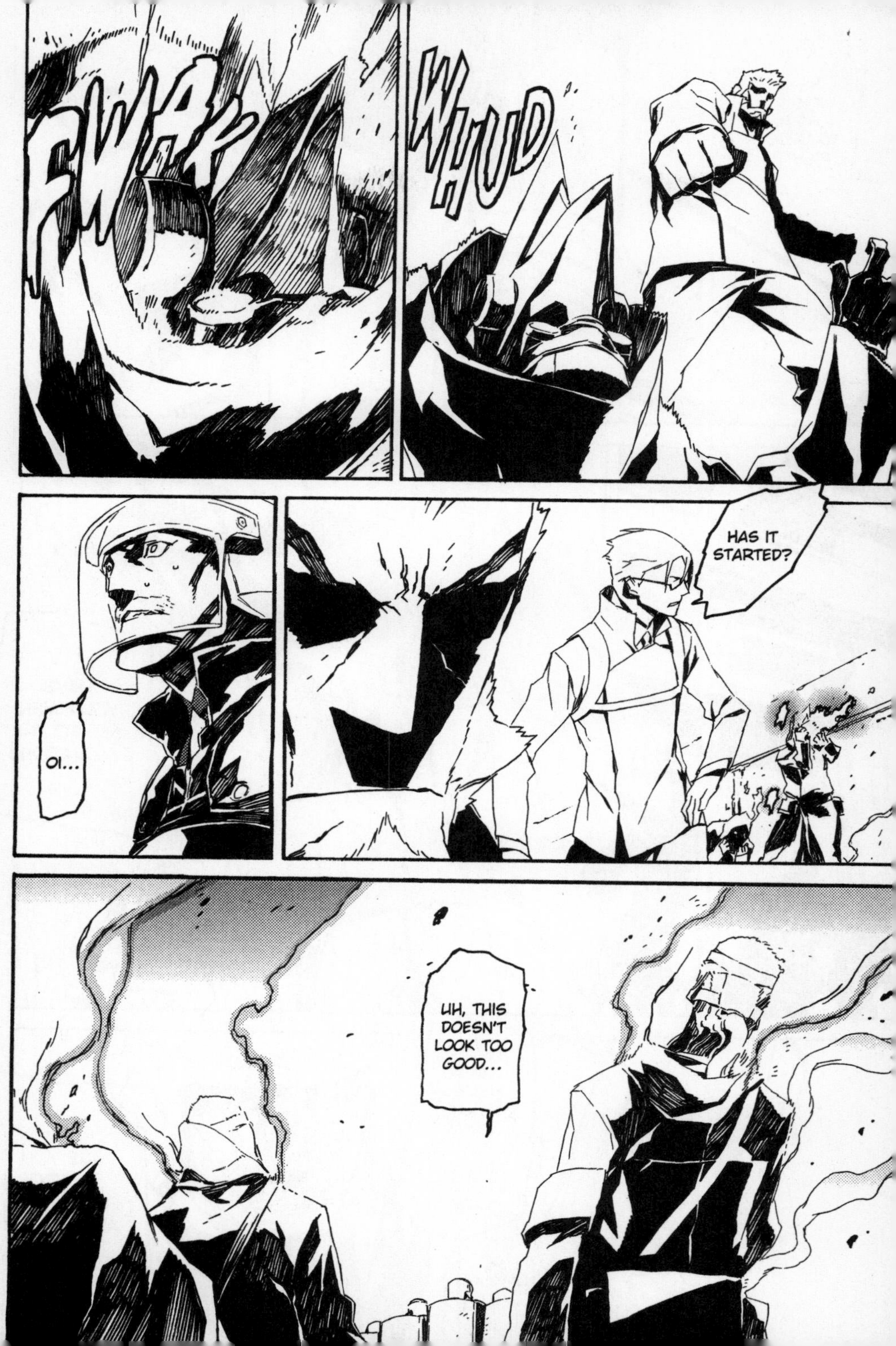
WHUD
FWAK
HAS IT STARTED?
OI...
UH, THIS DOESN'T LOOK TOO GOOD...

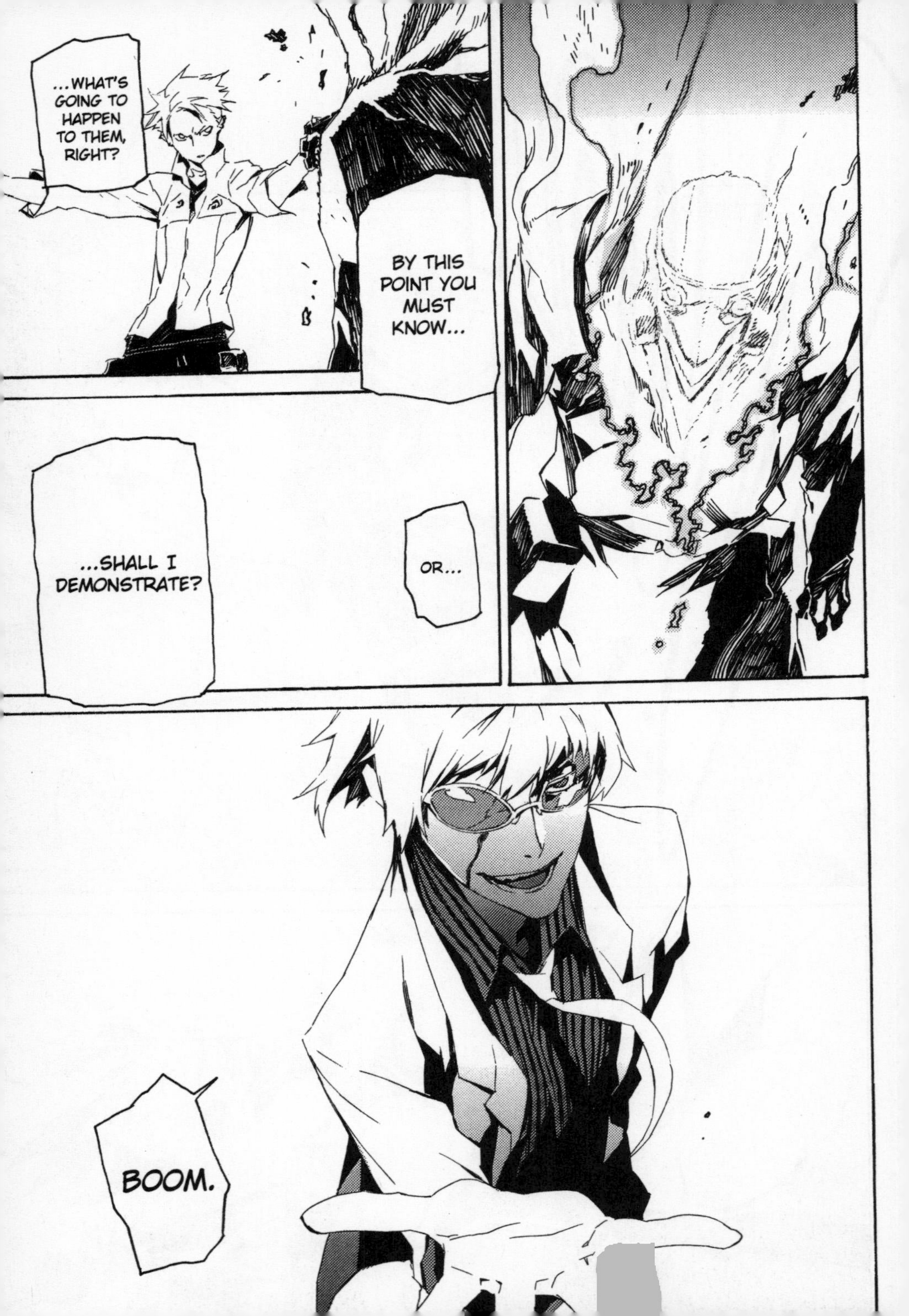
BY THIS POINT YOU MUST KNOW...
...WHAT'S GOING TO HAPPEN TO THEM, RIGHT?
OR...
...SHALL I DEMONSTRATE?
BOOM.

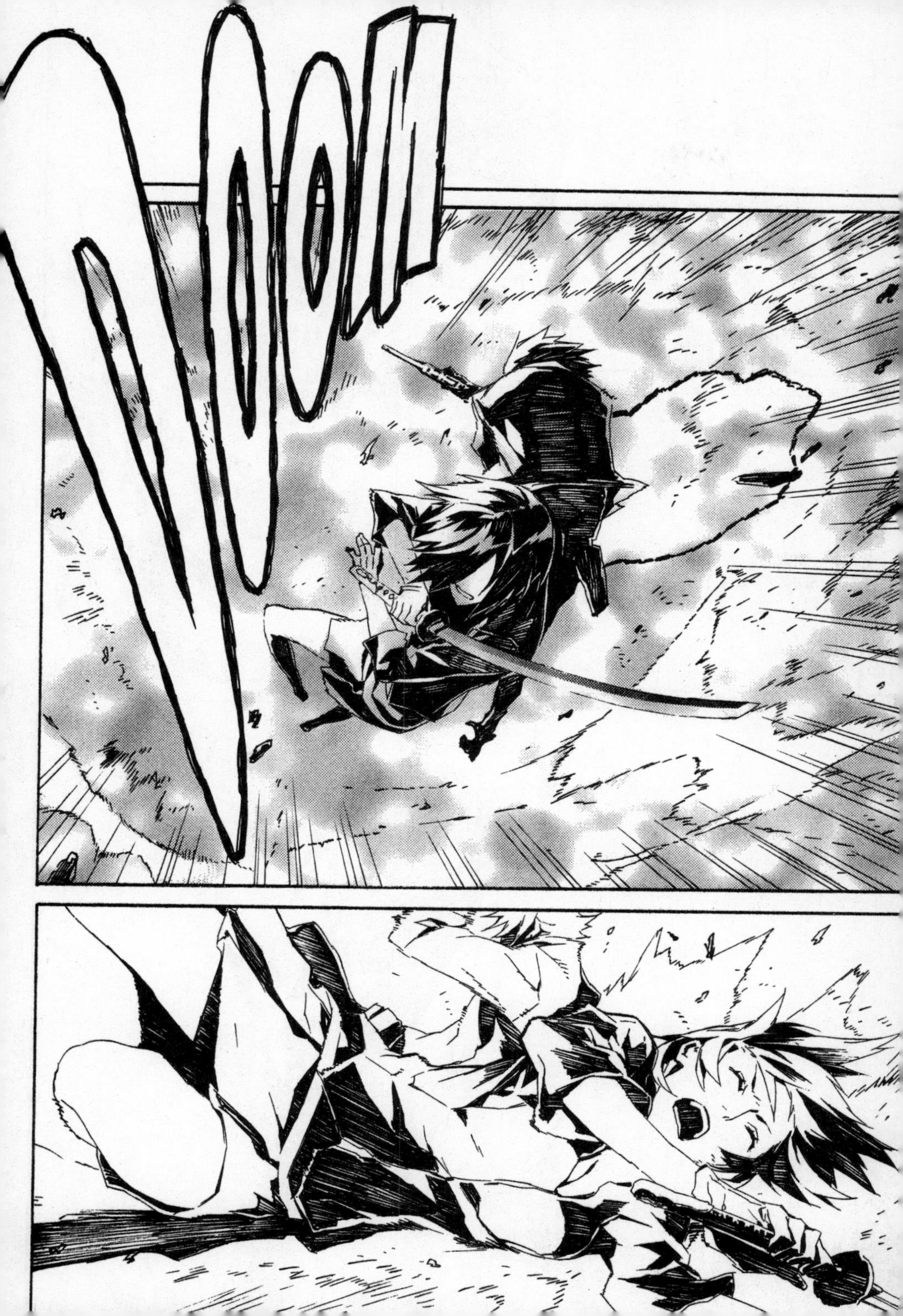
VOOM

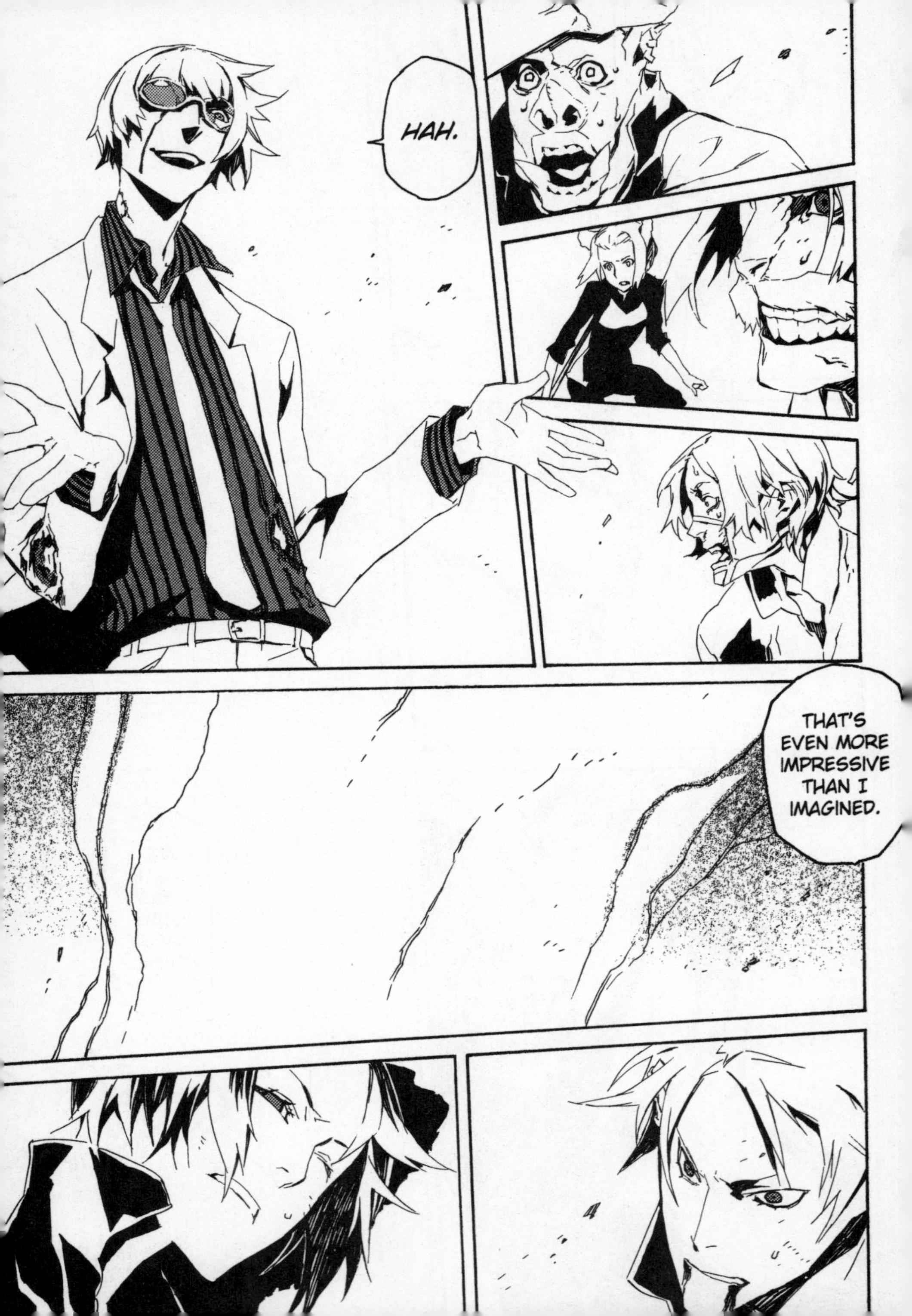
HAH.
THAT'S EVEN MORE IMPRESSIVE THAN I IMAGINED.

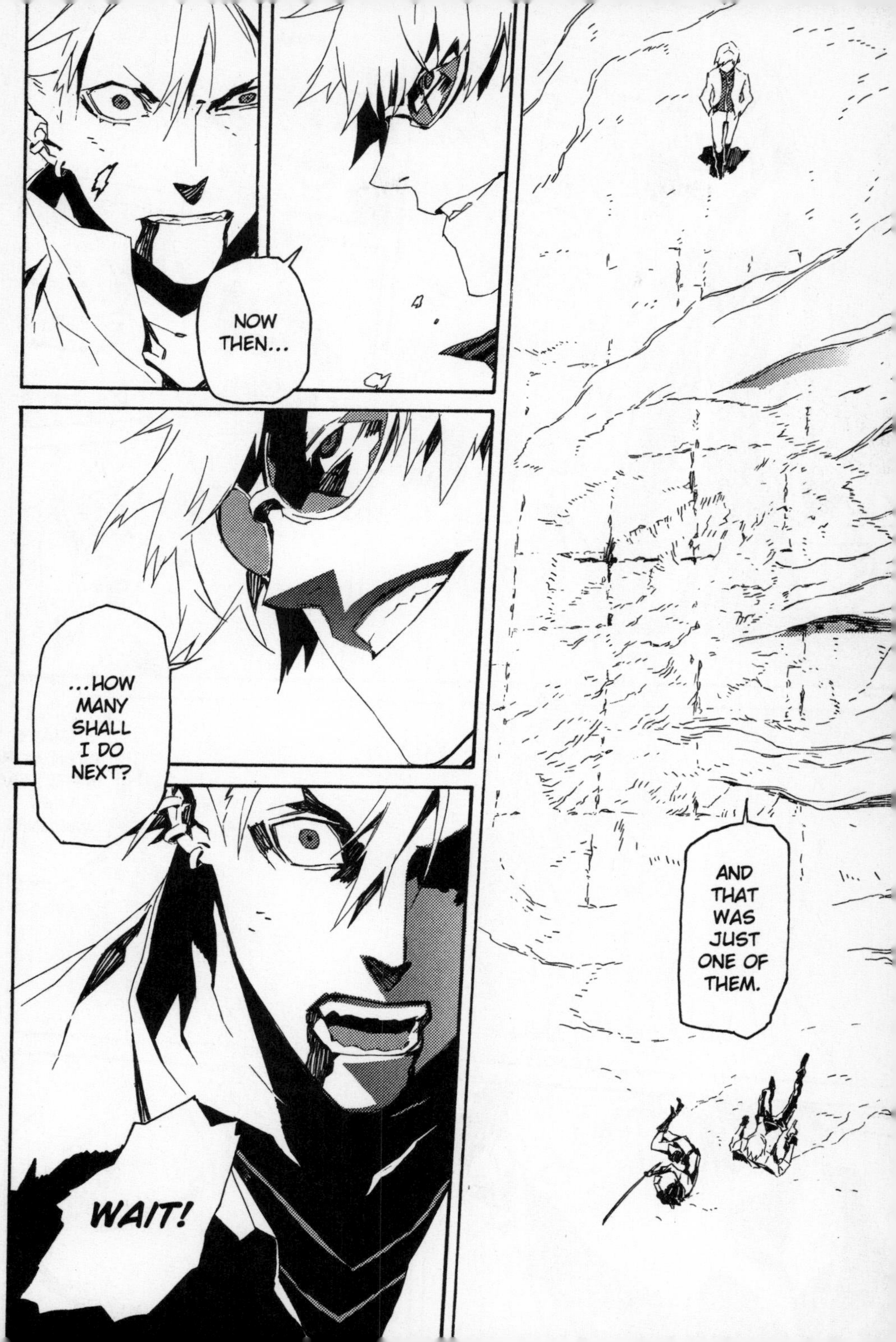
AND THAT WAS JUST ONE OF THEM.
NOW THEN...
...HOW MANY SHALL I DO NEXT?
WAIT!

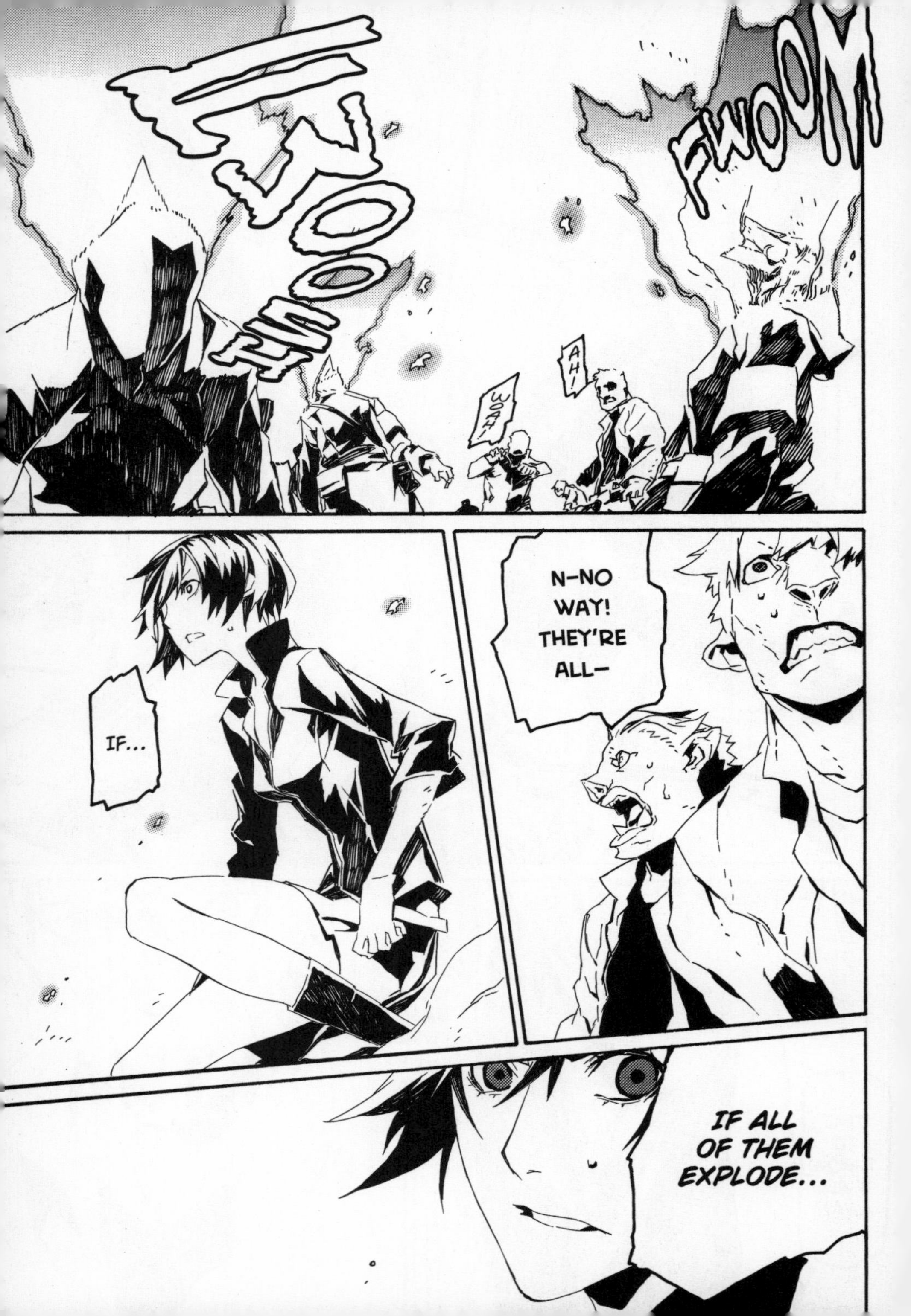
FWOOM
AH!
WOAH!
N-NO WAY! THEY'RE ALL—
IF...
IF ALL OF THEM EXPLODE...

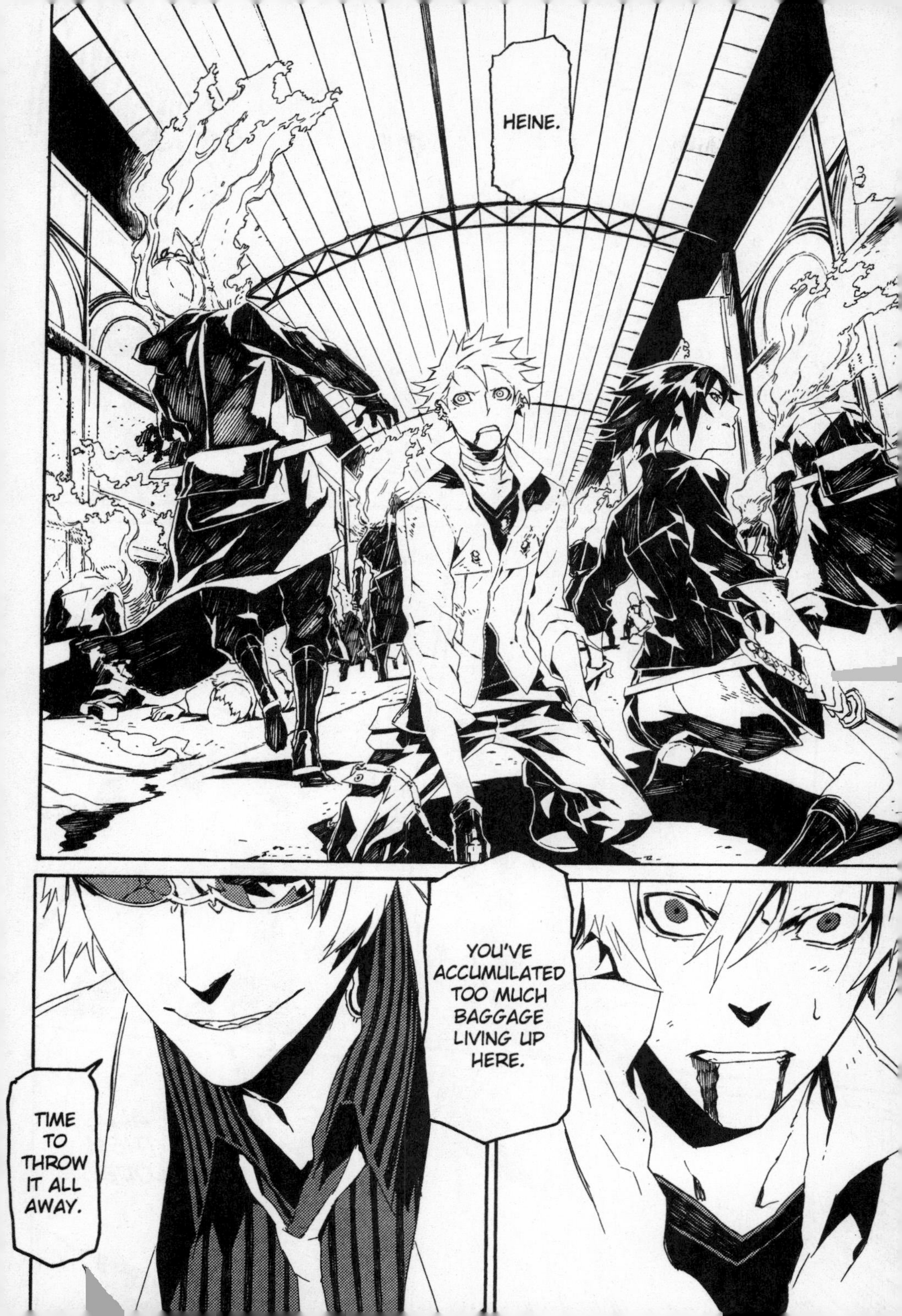
HEINE.
YOU'VE ACCUMULATED TOO MUCH BAGGAGE LIVING UP HERE.
TIME TO THROW IT ALL AWAY.

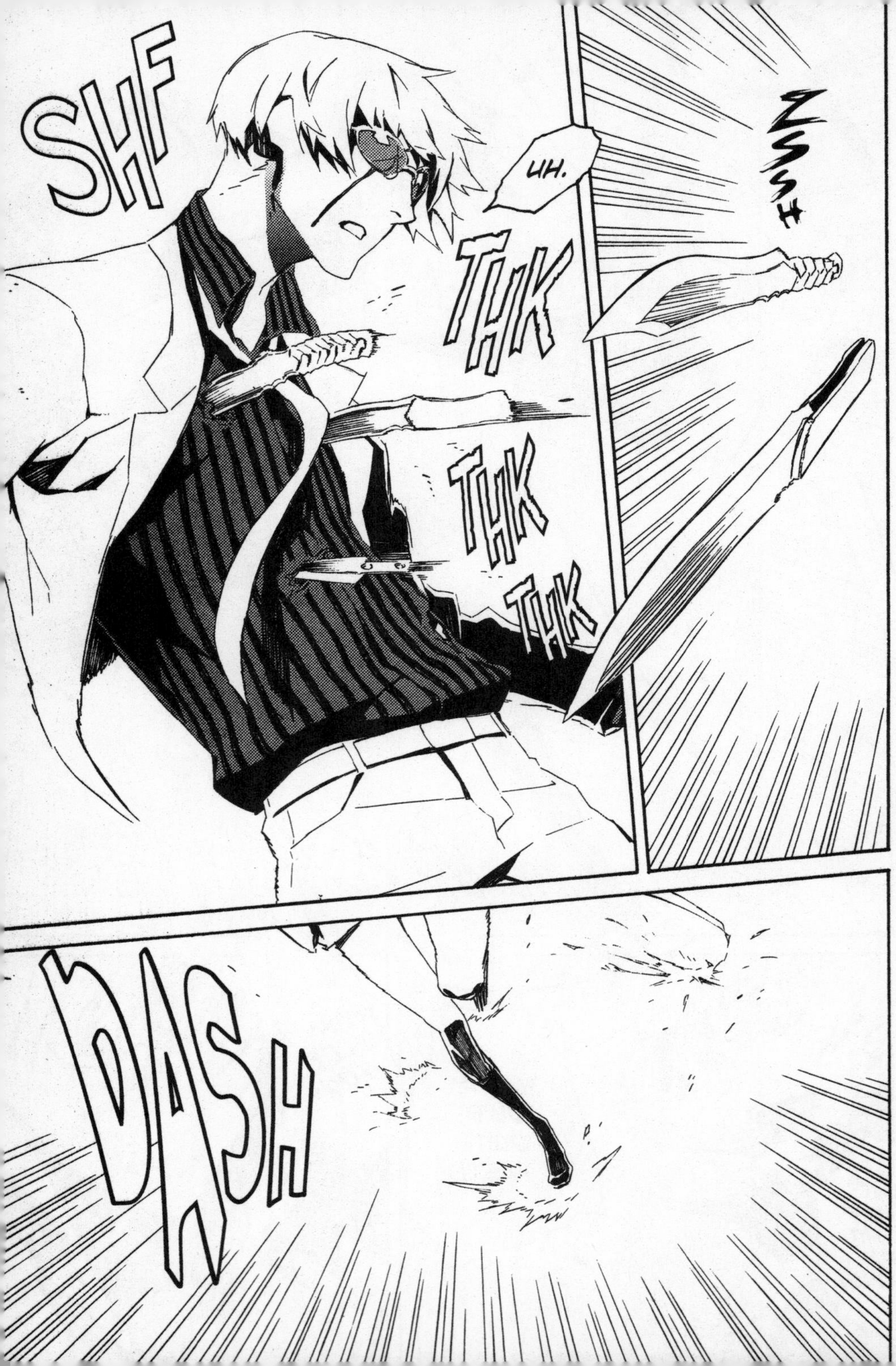
ZSSH
UH.
SHF
THK
THK
THK
DASH

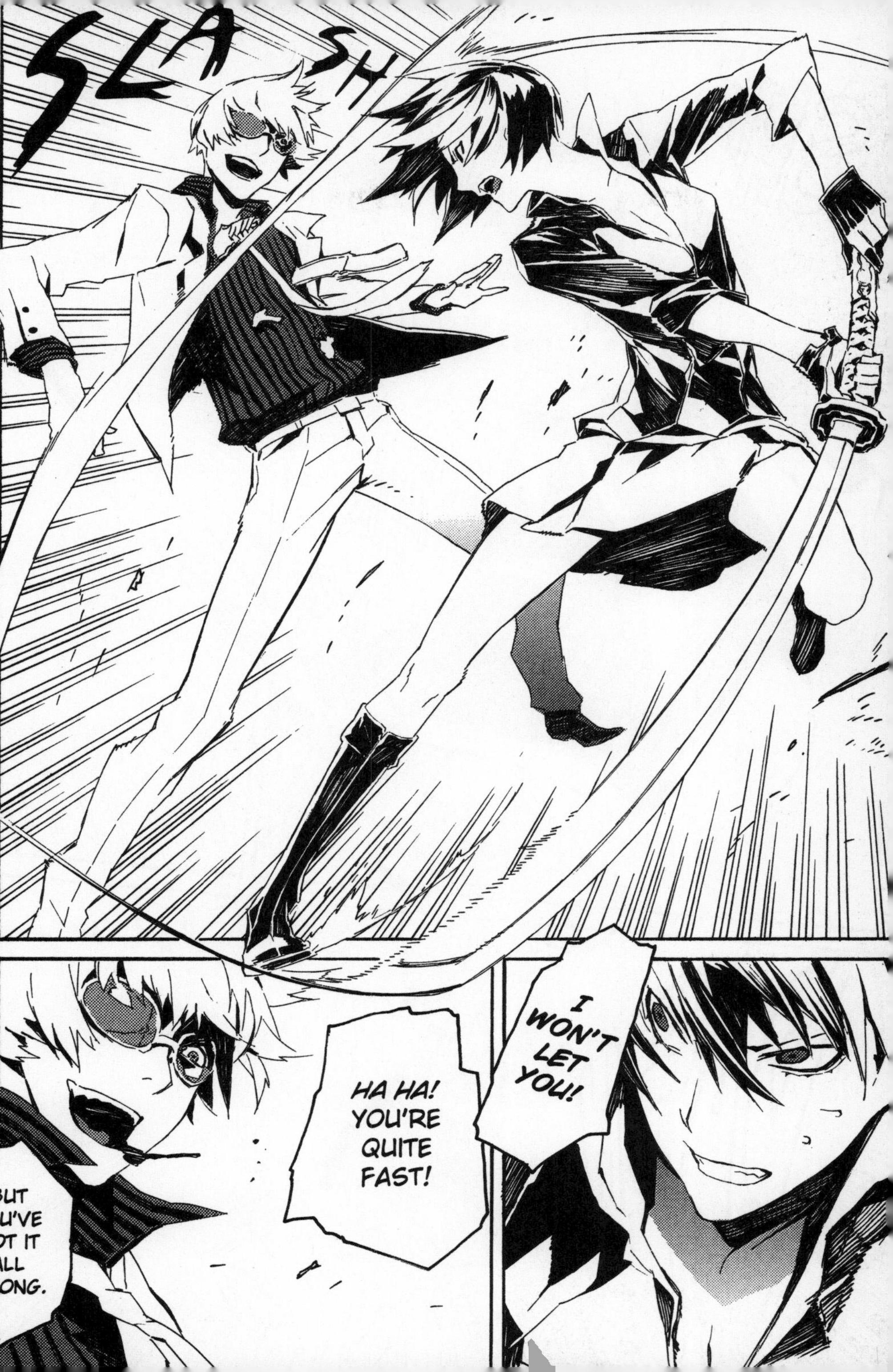
SLASH
I WON'T LET YOU!
HA HA! YOU'RE QUITE FAST!
BUT YOU'VE GOT IT ALL WRONG.

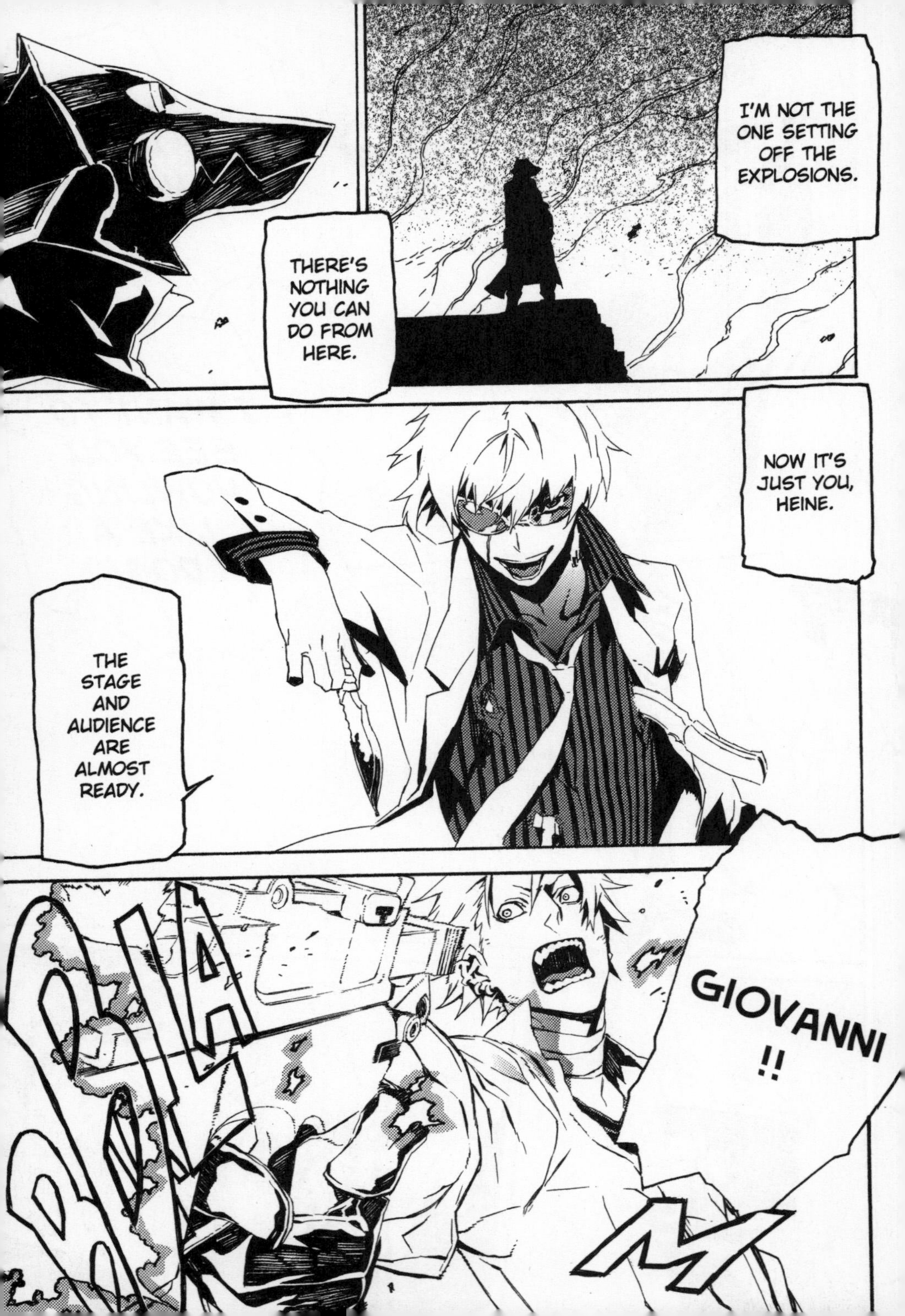
I'M NOT THE ONE SETTING OFF THE EXPLOSIONS.
THERE'S NOTHING YOU CAN DO FROM HERE.
NOW IT'S JUST YOU, HEINE.
THE STAGE AND AUDIENCE ARE ALMOST READY.
GIOVANNI !!

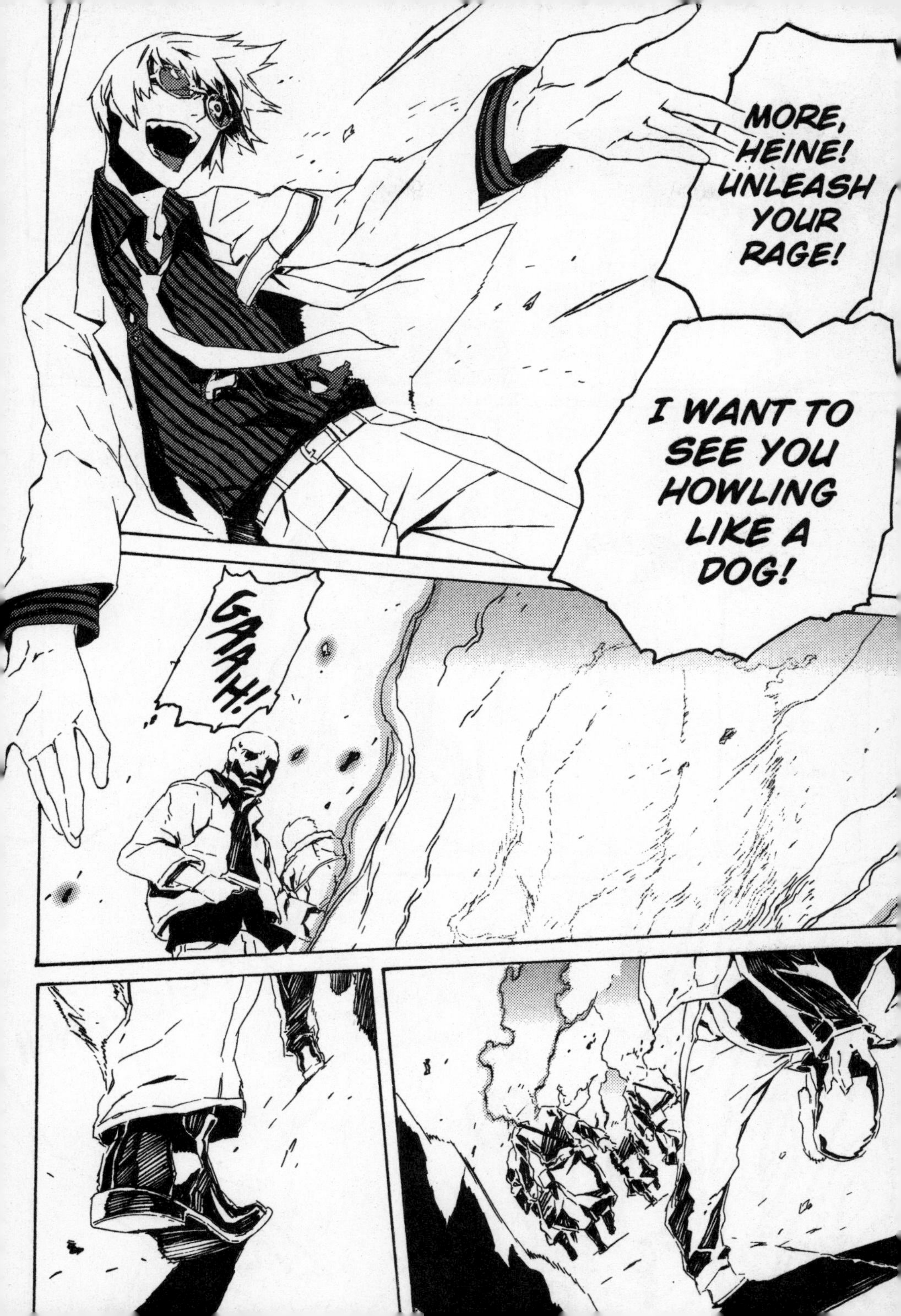
MORE, HEINE! UNLEASH YOUR RAGE!
I WANT TO SEE YOU HOWLING LIKE A DOG!
GRAAH!!

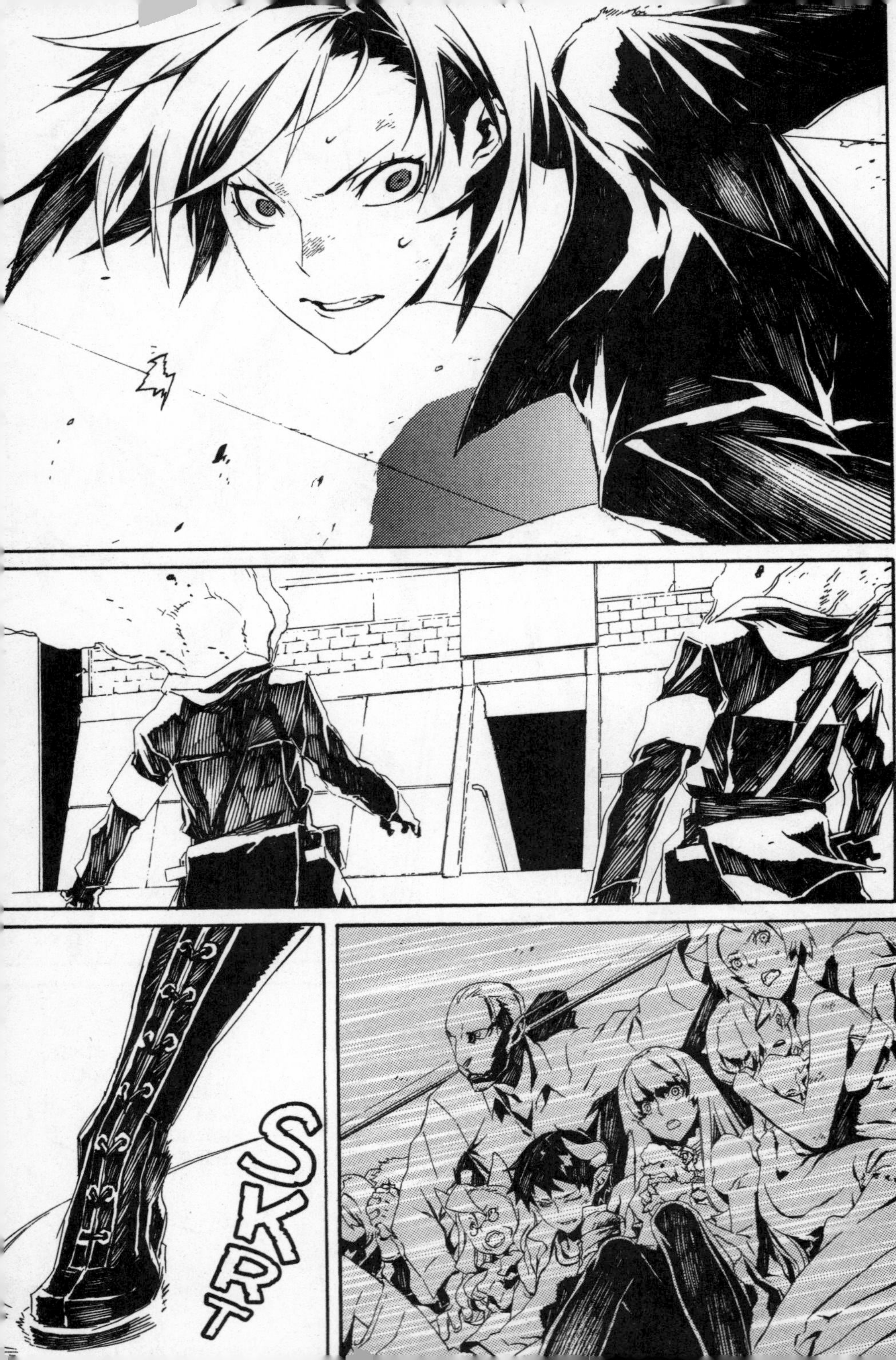
SKRT

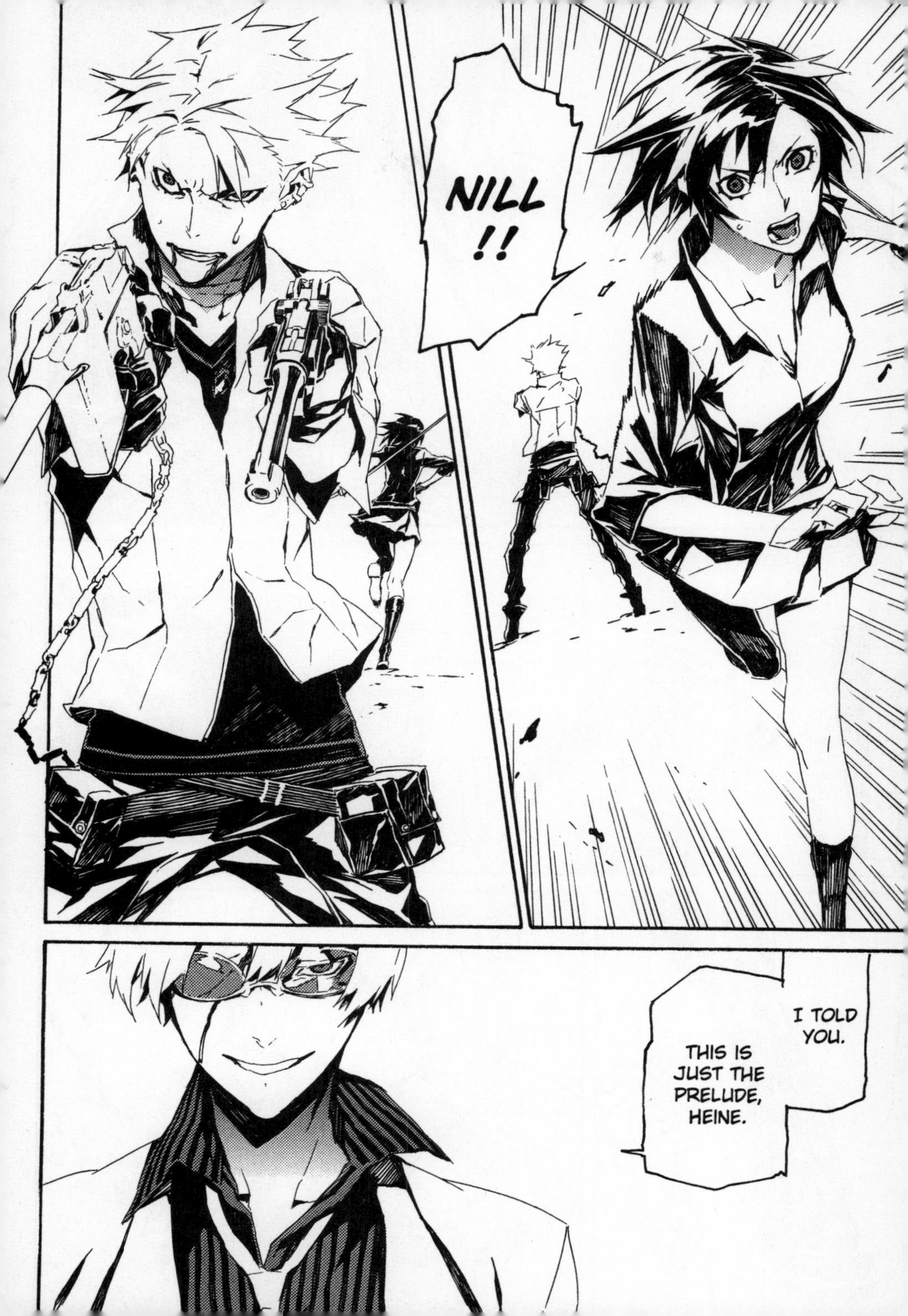
NILL !!
I TOLD YOU.
THIS IS JUST THE PRELUDE, HEINE.

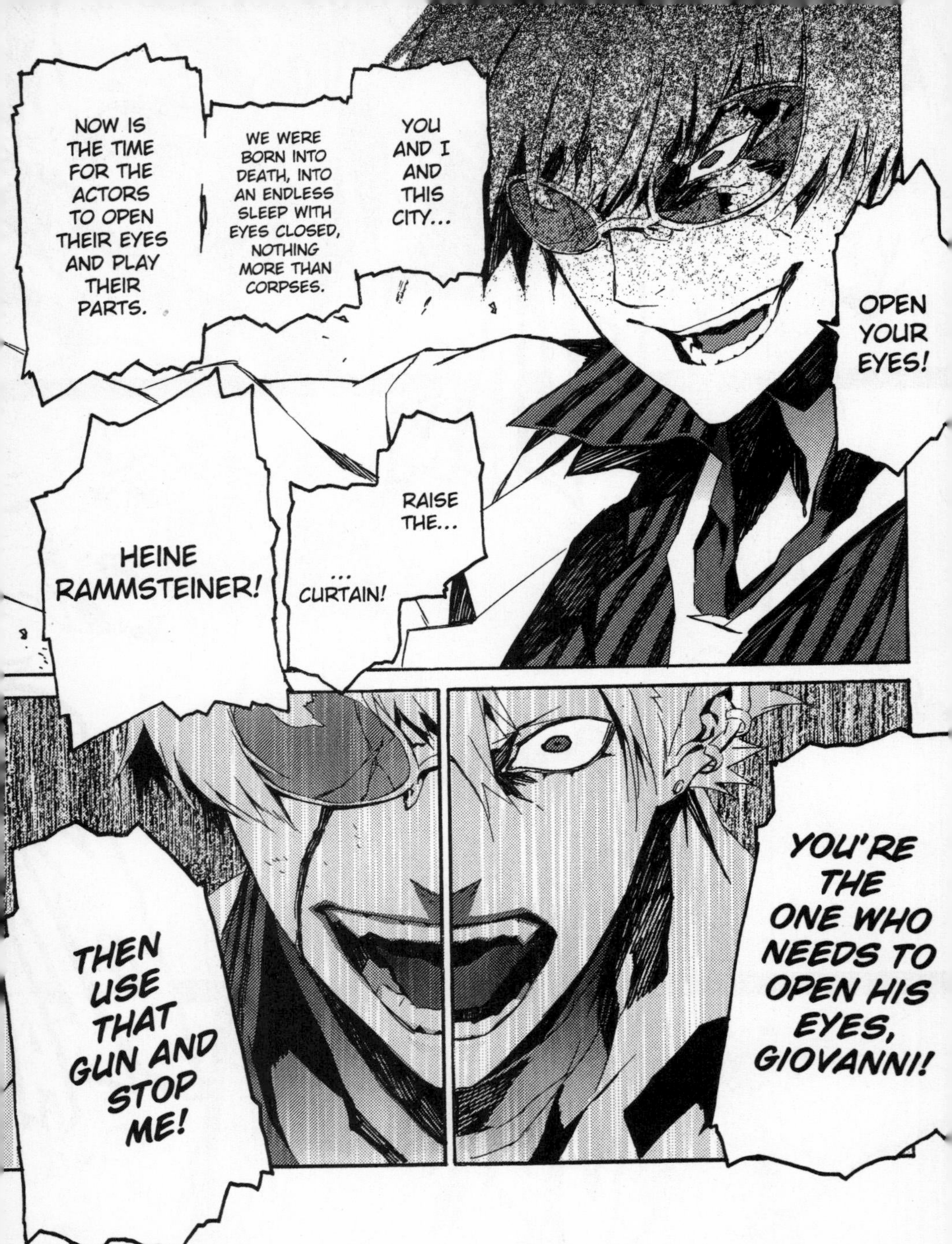
YOU AND I AND THIS CITY...
WE WERE BORN INTO DEATH, INTO AN ENDLESS SLEEP WITH EYES CLOSED, NOTHING MORE THAN CORPSES.
NOW IS THE TIME FOR THE ACTORS TO OPEN THEIR EYES AND PLAY THEIR PARTS.
OPEN YOUR EYES!
RAISE THE...
...CURTAIN!
HEINE RAMMSTEINER!
YOU'RE THE ONE WHO NEEDS TO OPEN HIS EYES, GIOVANNI!
THEN USE THAT GUN AND STOP ME!

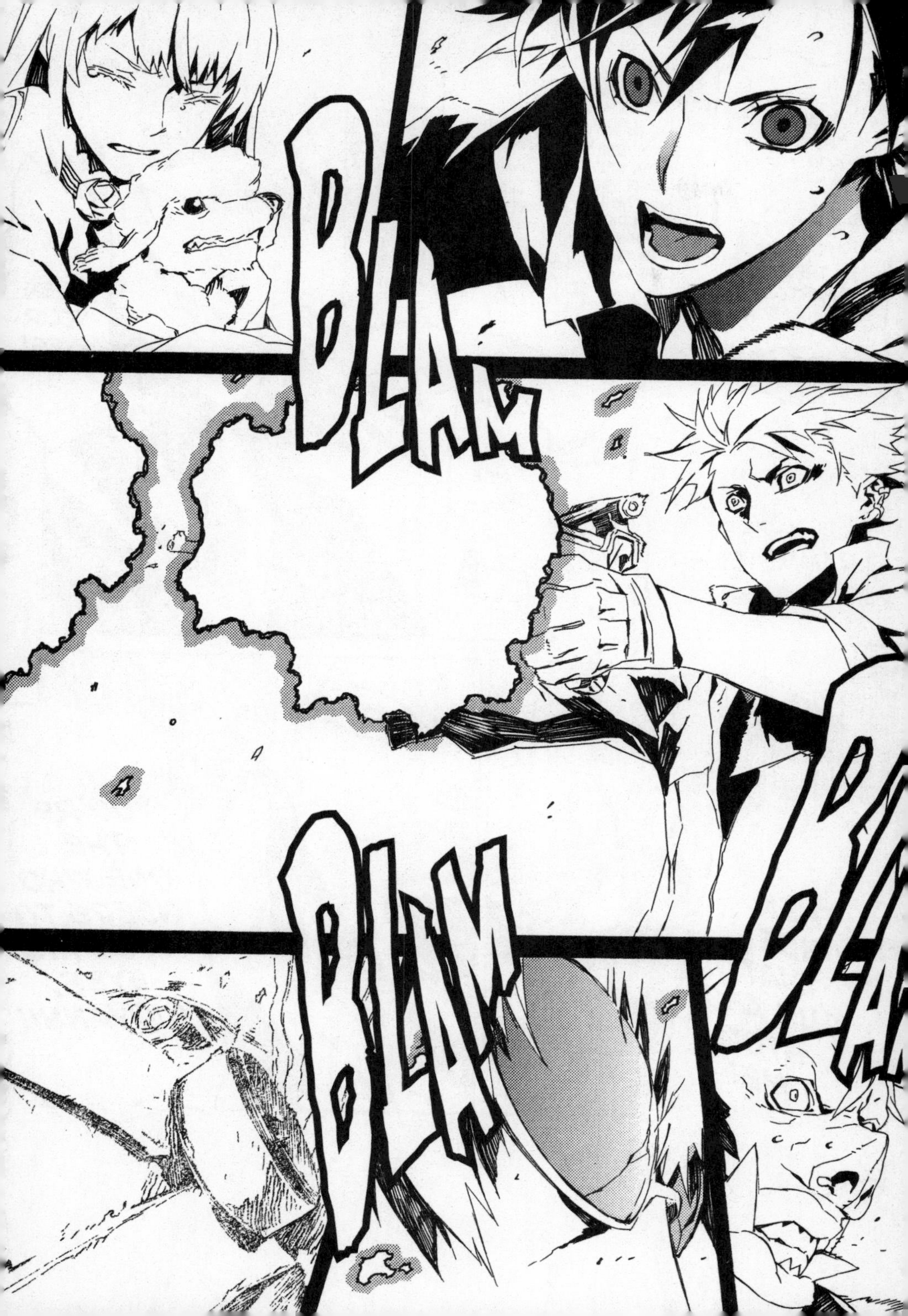
BLAM
BLA
BLAM

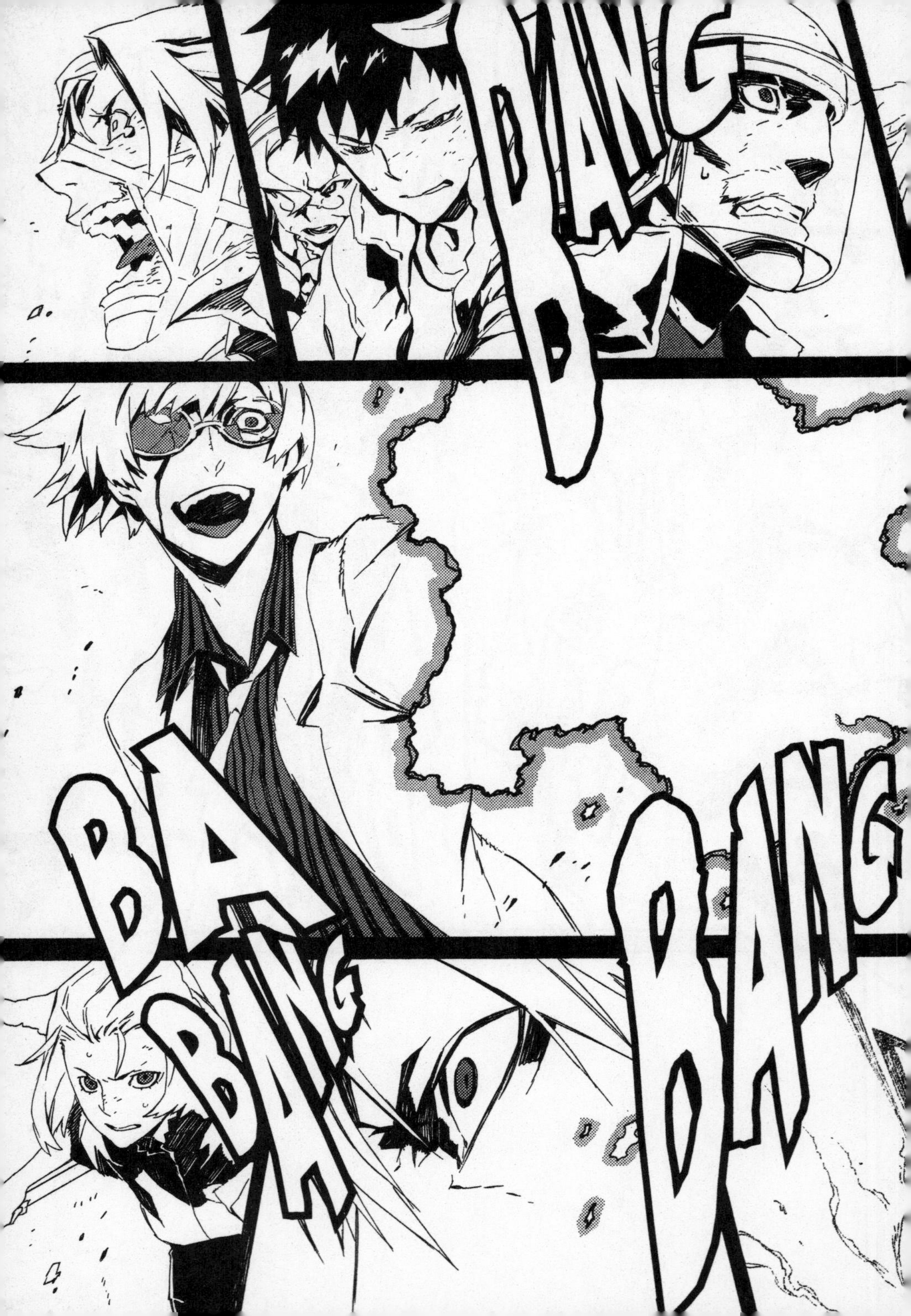
BANG
BANG
BABANG

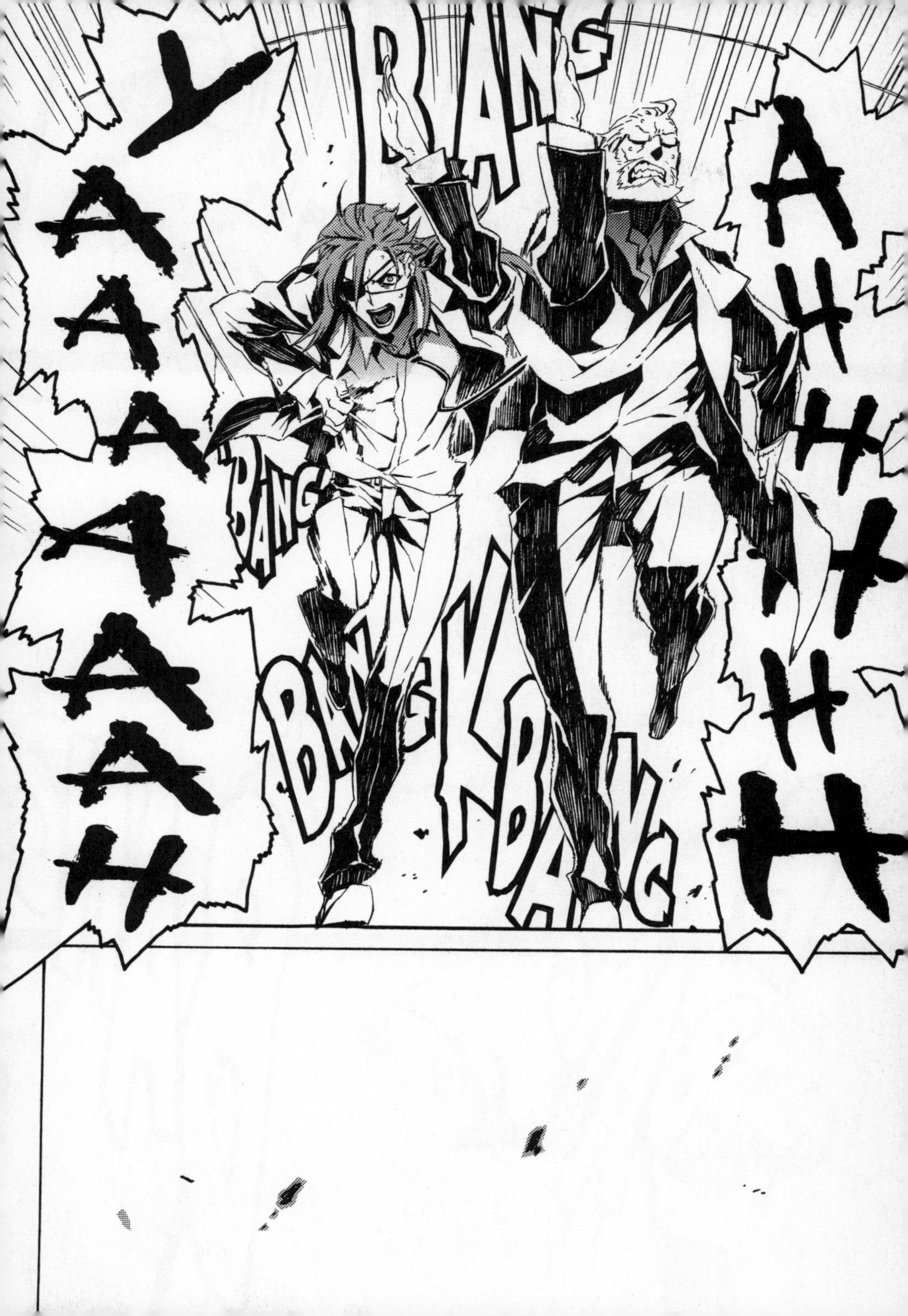

BANG
AHHHHHH
YAAAAAAH
BANG
BANG
BANG
BANG

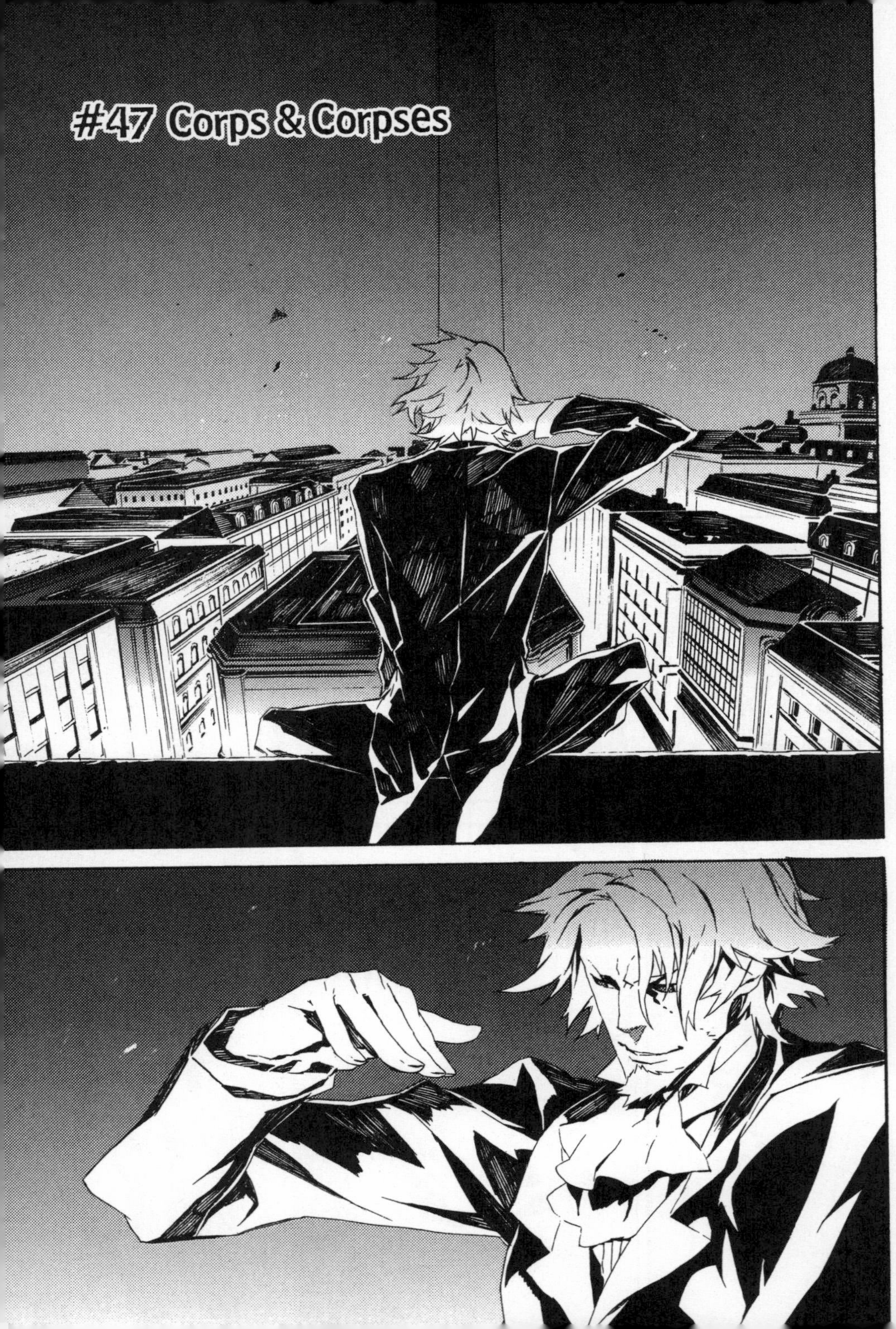
#47 Corps & Corpses

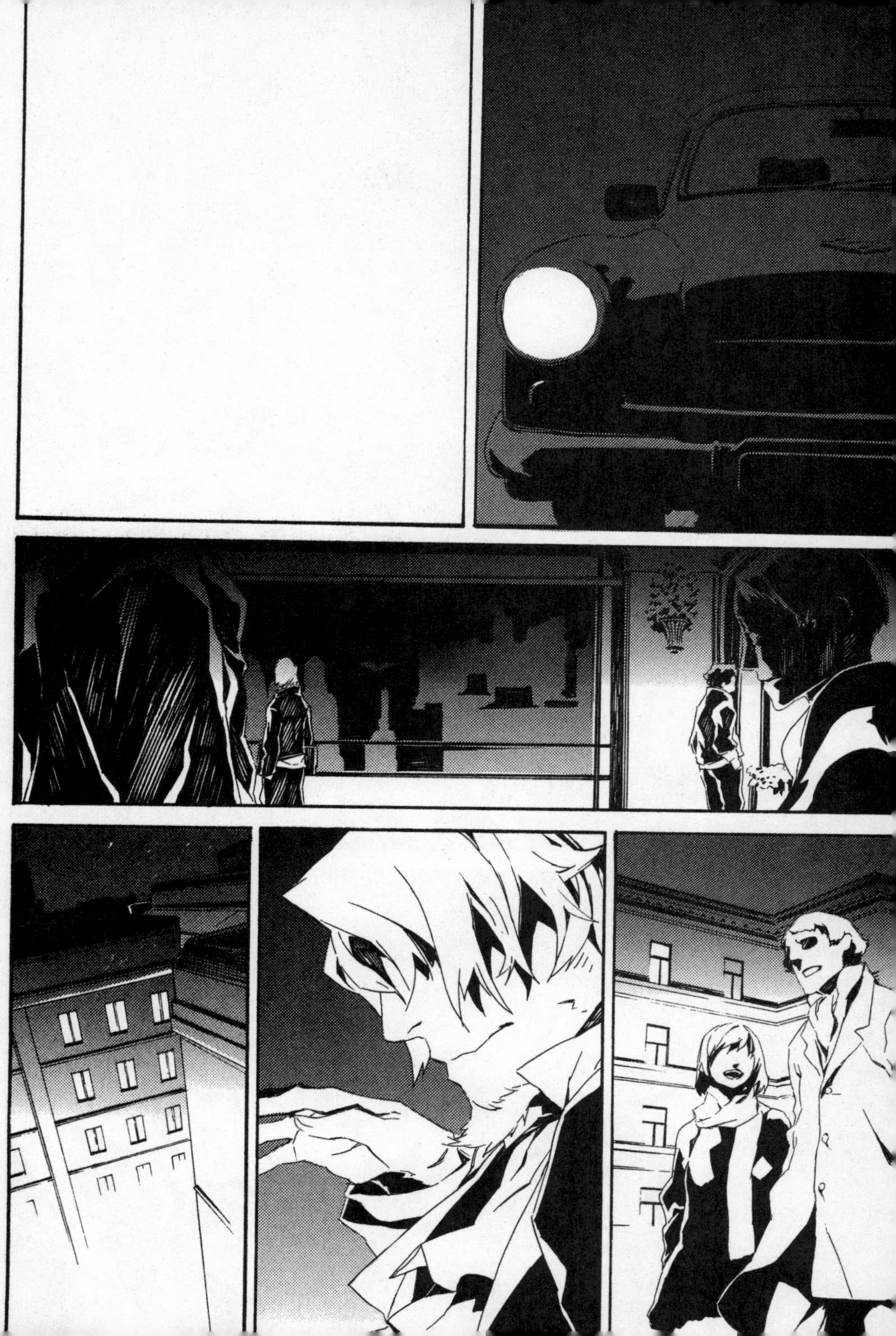

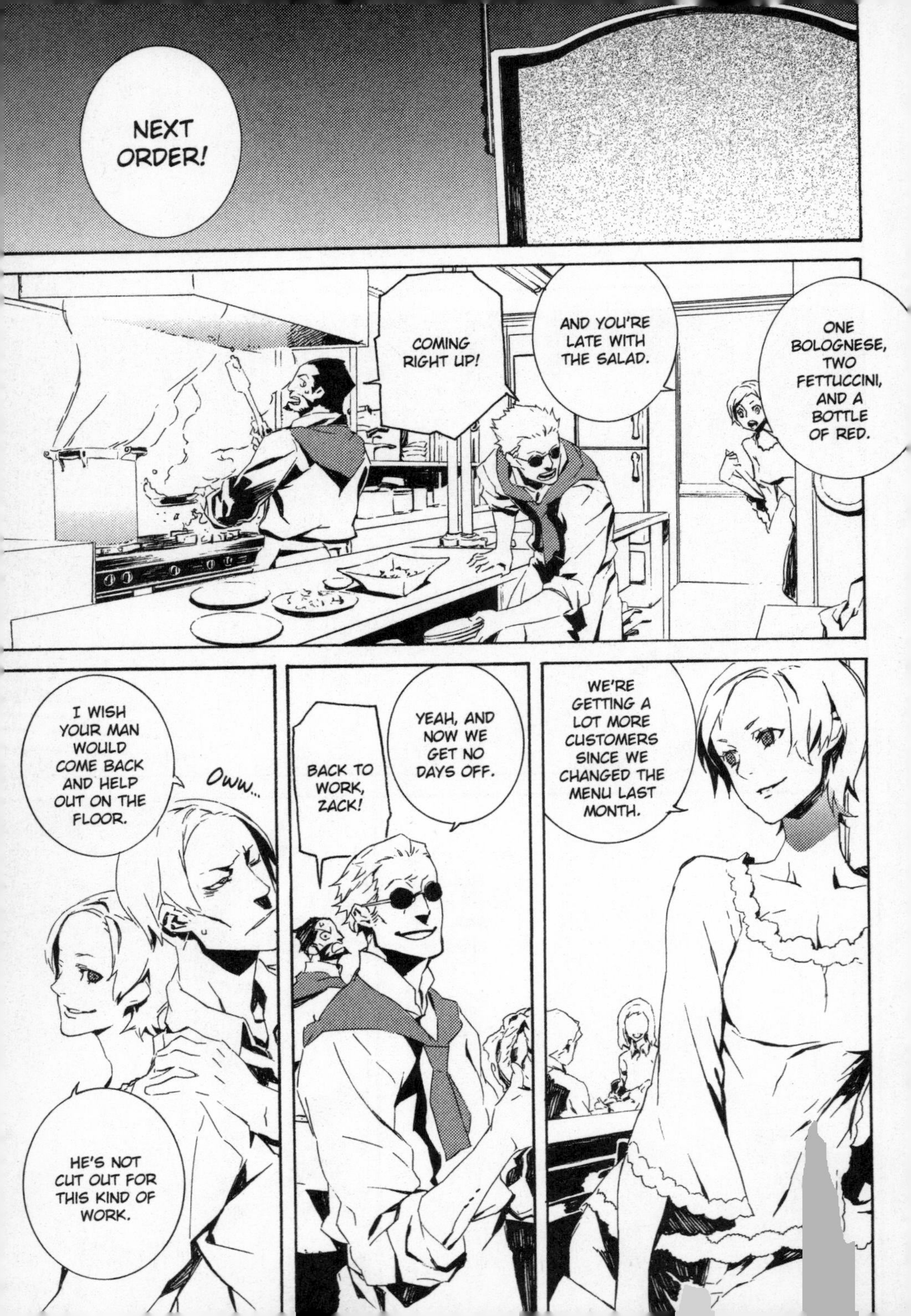
NEXT ORDER!
ONE BOLOGNESE, TWO FETTUCCINI, AND A BOTTLE OF RED.
AND YOU'RE LATE WITH THE SALAD.
COMING RIGHT UP!
WE'RE GETTING A LOT MORE CUSTOMERS SINCE WE CHANGED THE MENU LAST MONTH.
YEAH, AND NOW WE GET NO DAYS OFF.
BACK TO WORK, ZACK!
I WISH YOUR MAN WOULD COME BACK AND HELP OUT ON THE FLOOR.
Oww...
HE'S NOT CUT OUT FOR THIS KIND OF WORK.

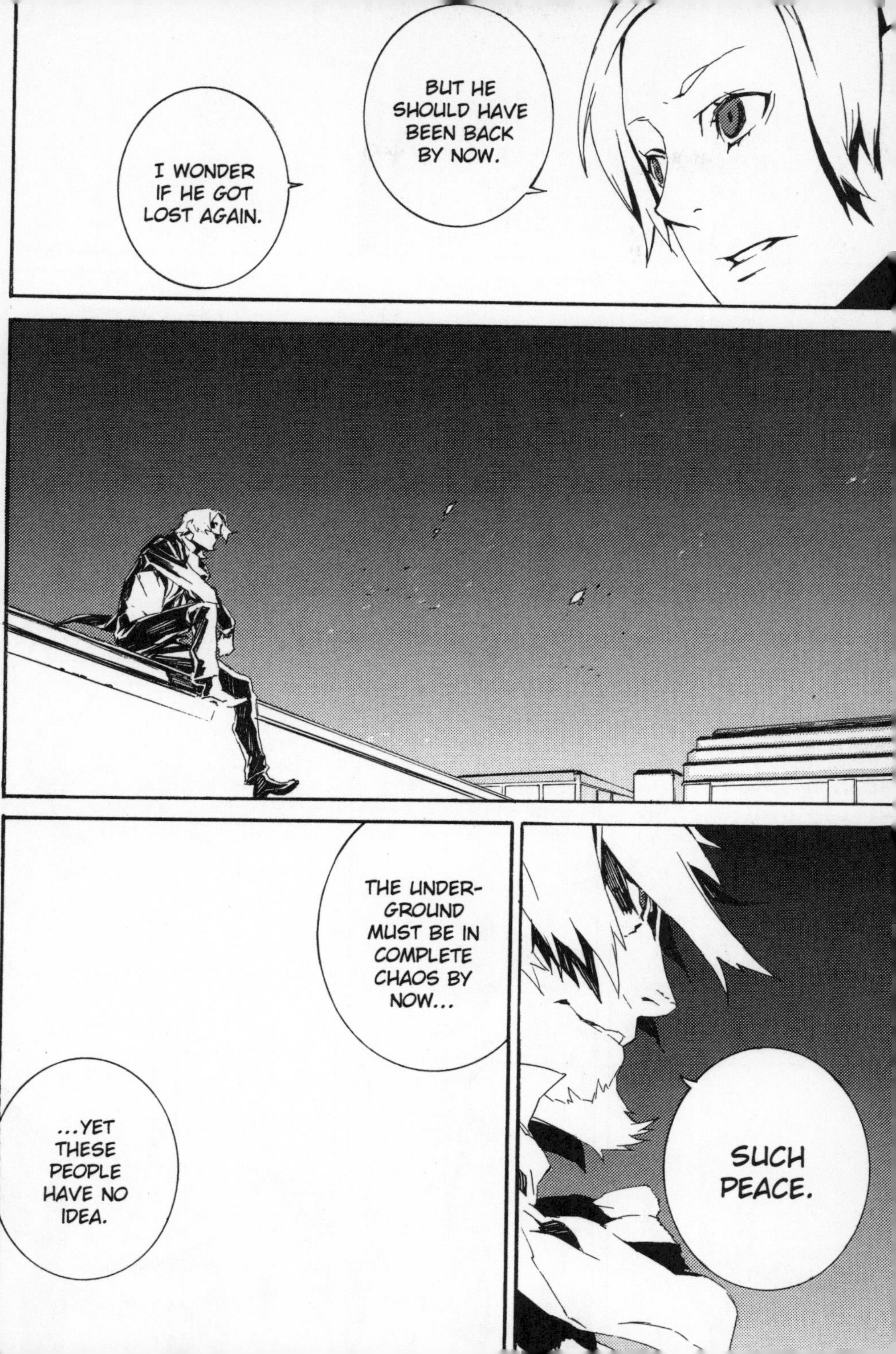
BUT HE SHOULD HAVE BEEN BACK BY NOW.
I WONDER IF HE GOT LOST AGAIN.
SUCH PEACE.
THE UNDER-GROUND MUST BE IN COMPLETE CHAOS BY NOW...
...YET THESE PEOPLE HAVE NO IDEA.

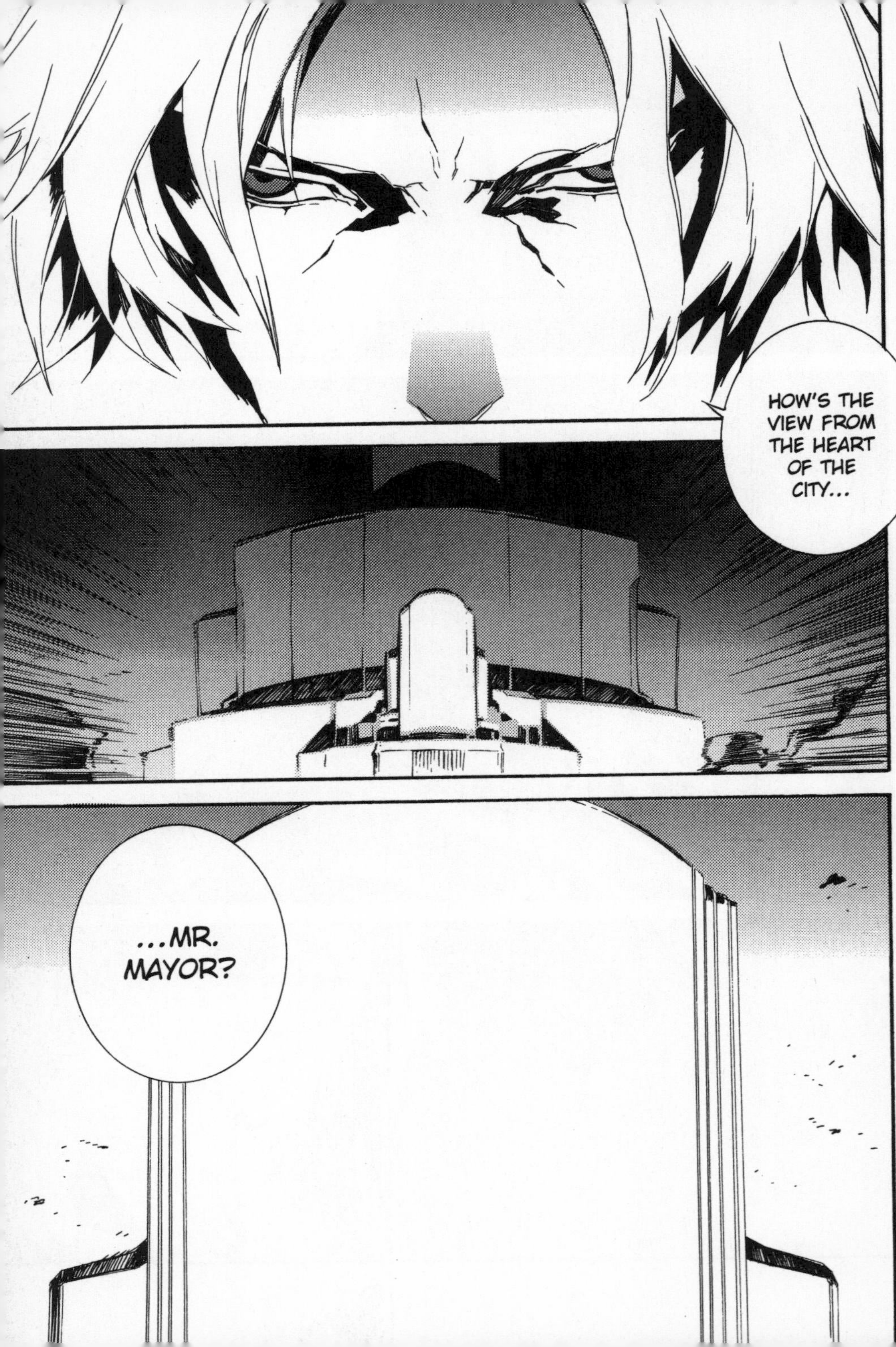
HOW'S THE VIEW FROM THE HEART OF THE CITY...
...MR. MAYOR?

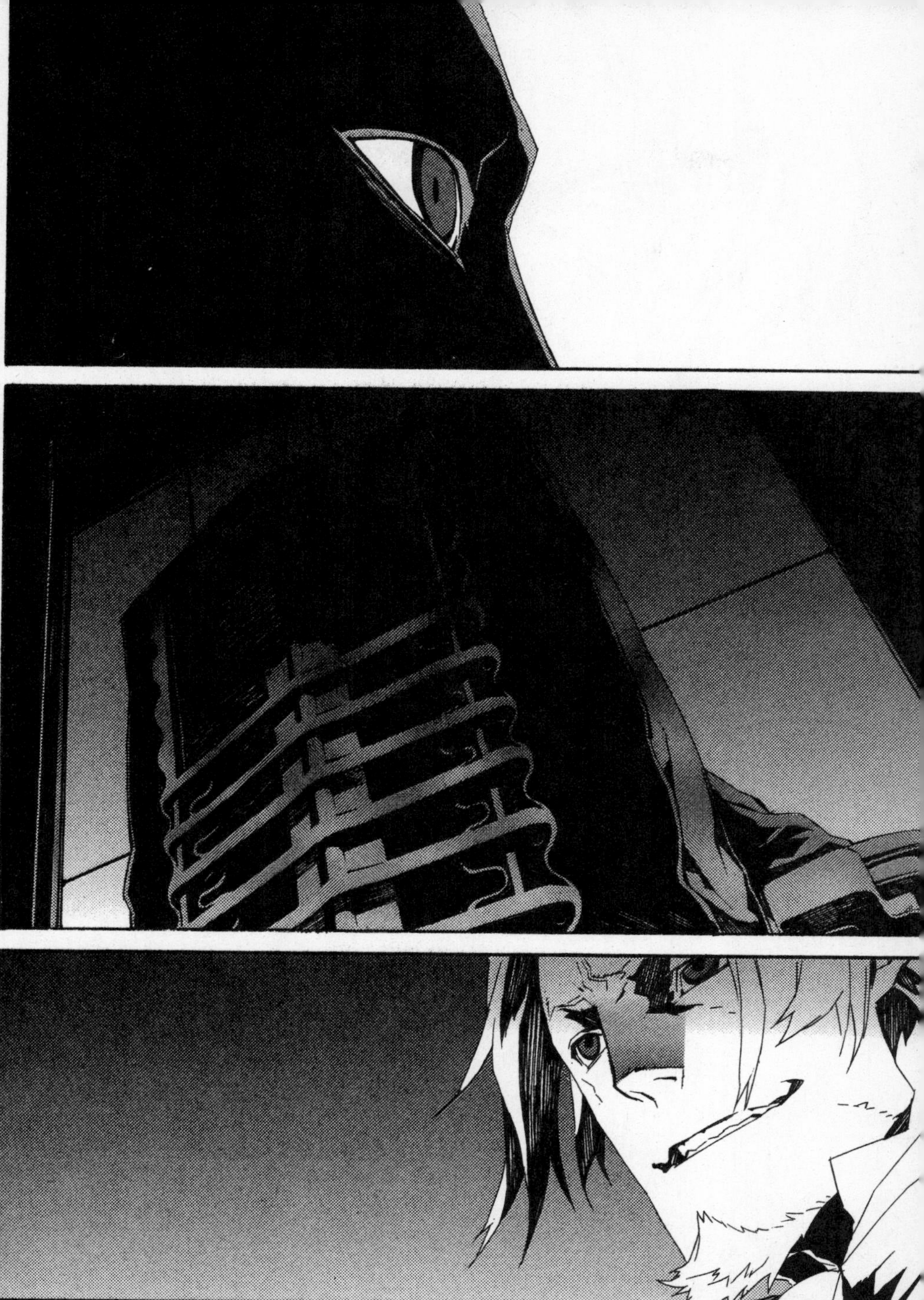

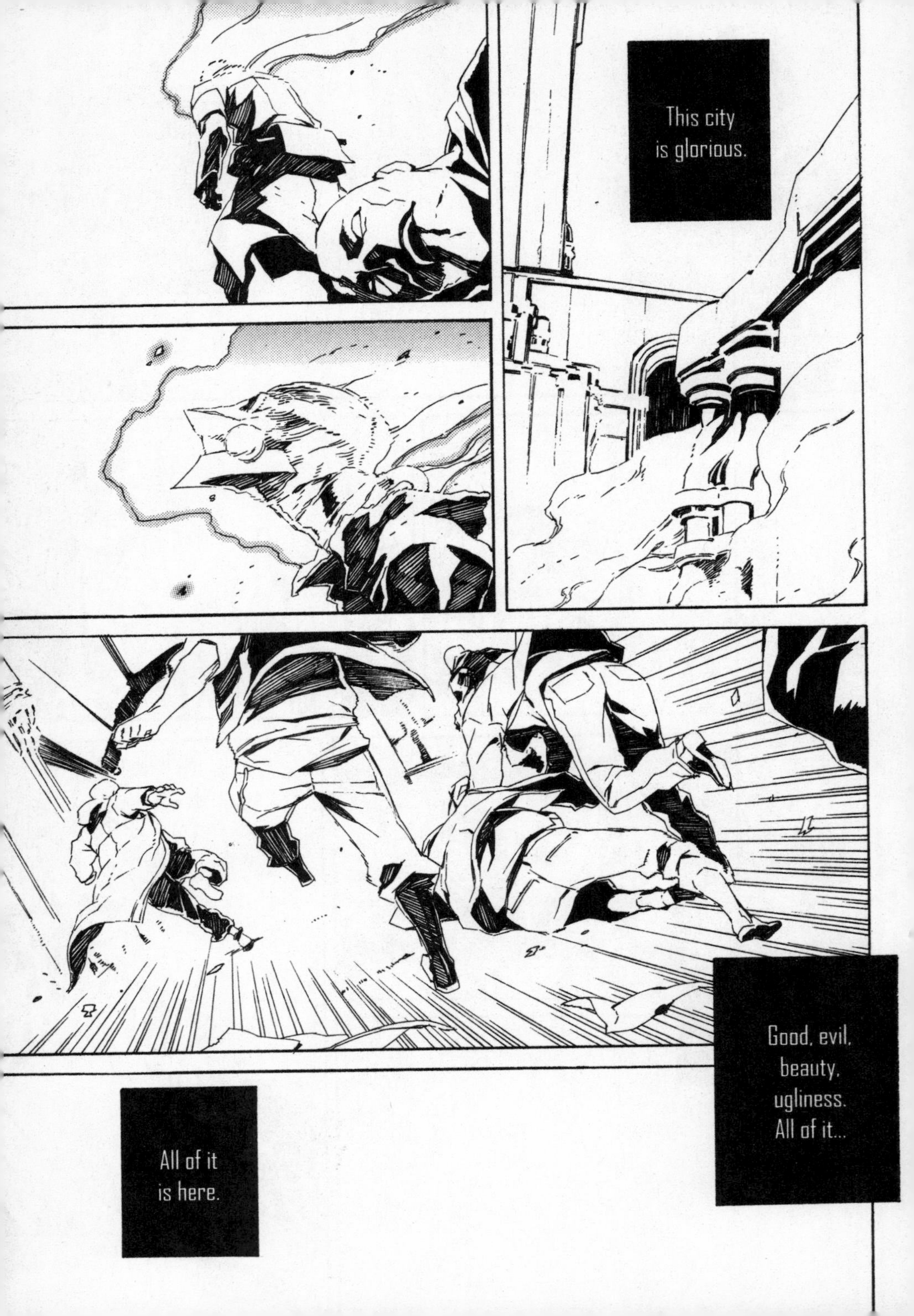
This city is glorious.
Good, evil, beauty, ugliness. All of it...
All of it is here.

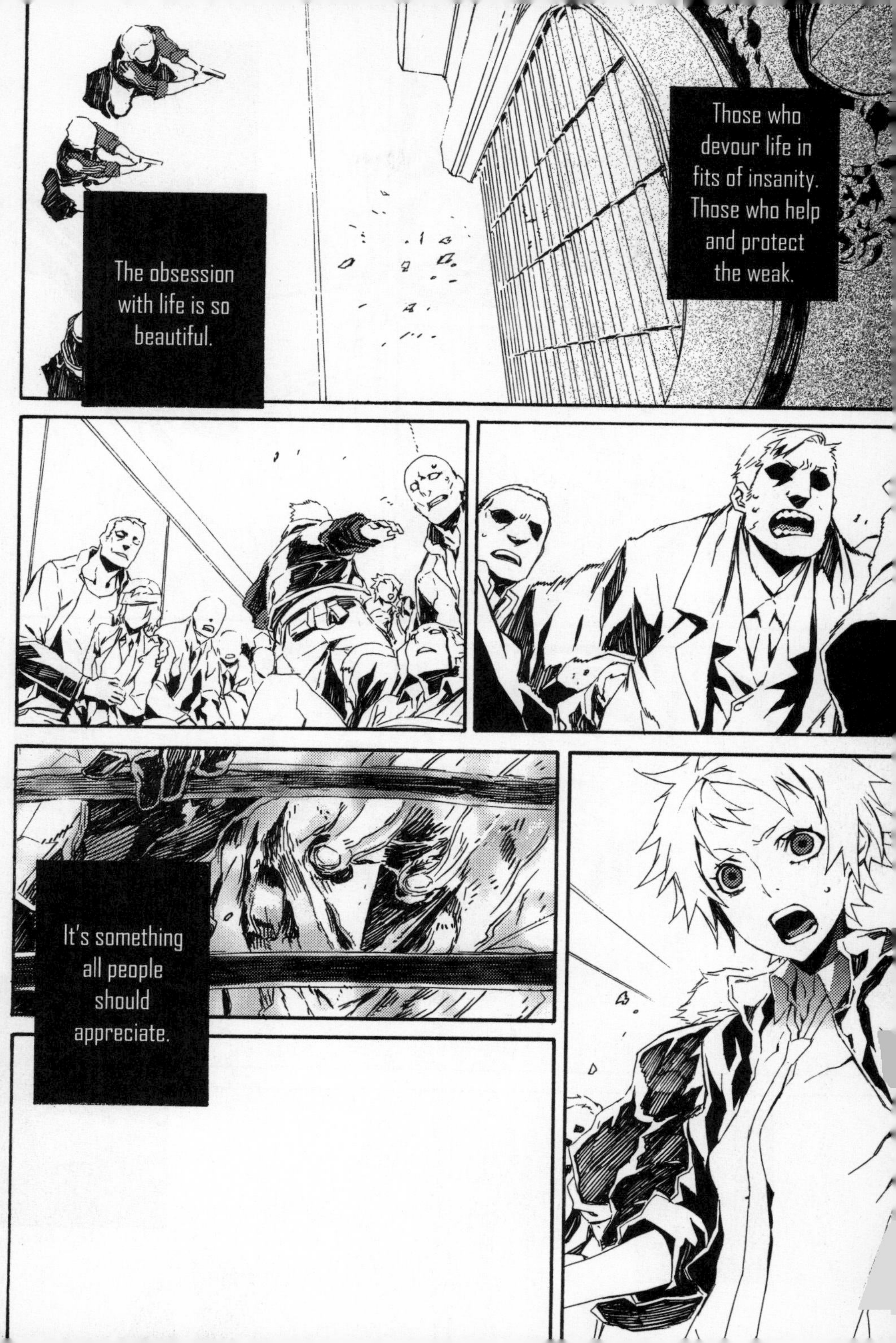
Those who devour life in fits of insanity. Those who help and protect the weak.
The obsession with life is so beautiful.
It's something all people should appreciate.

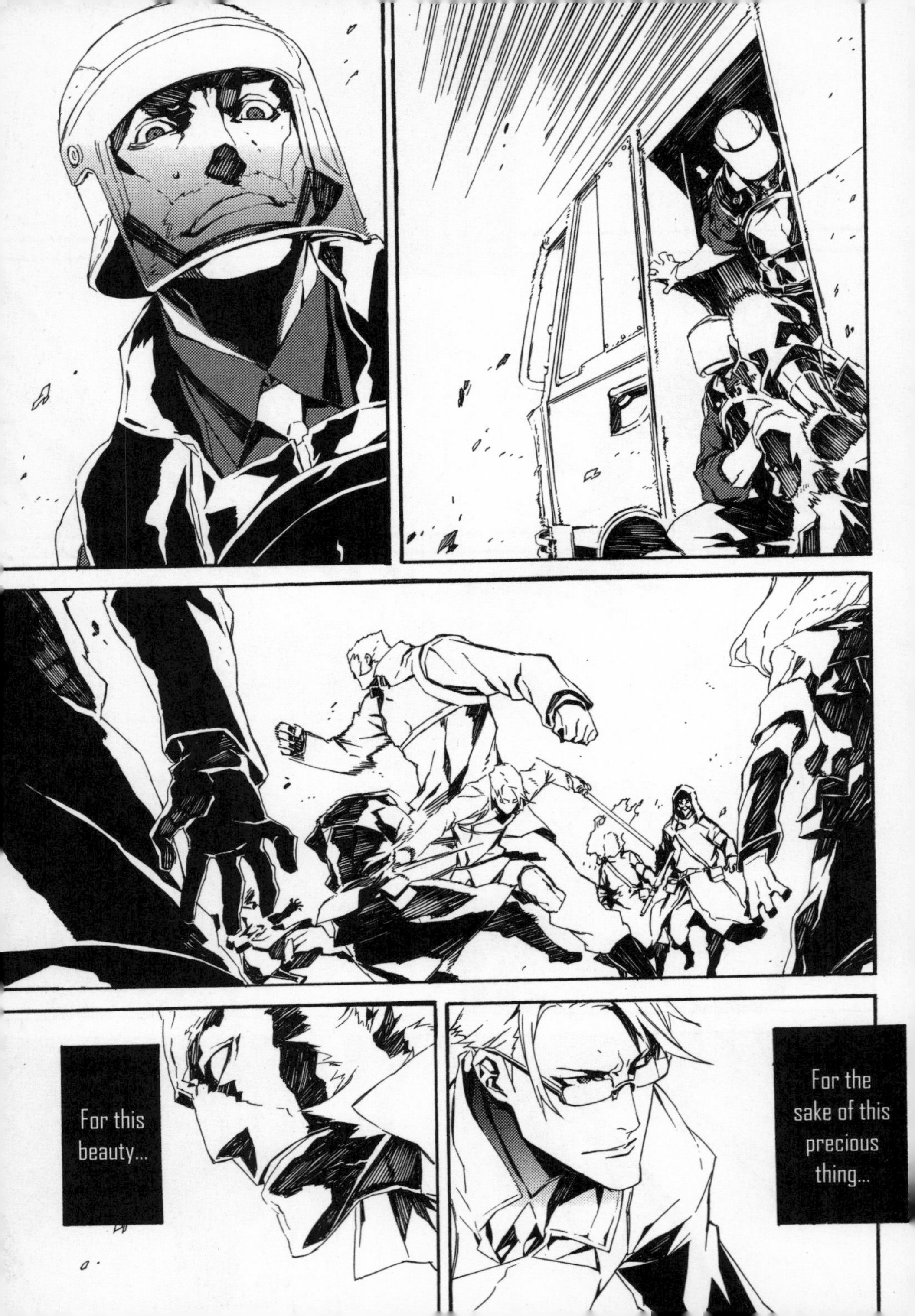

For the sake of this precious thing...
For this beauty...

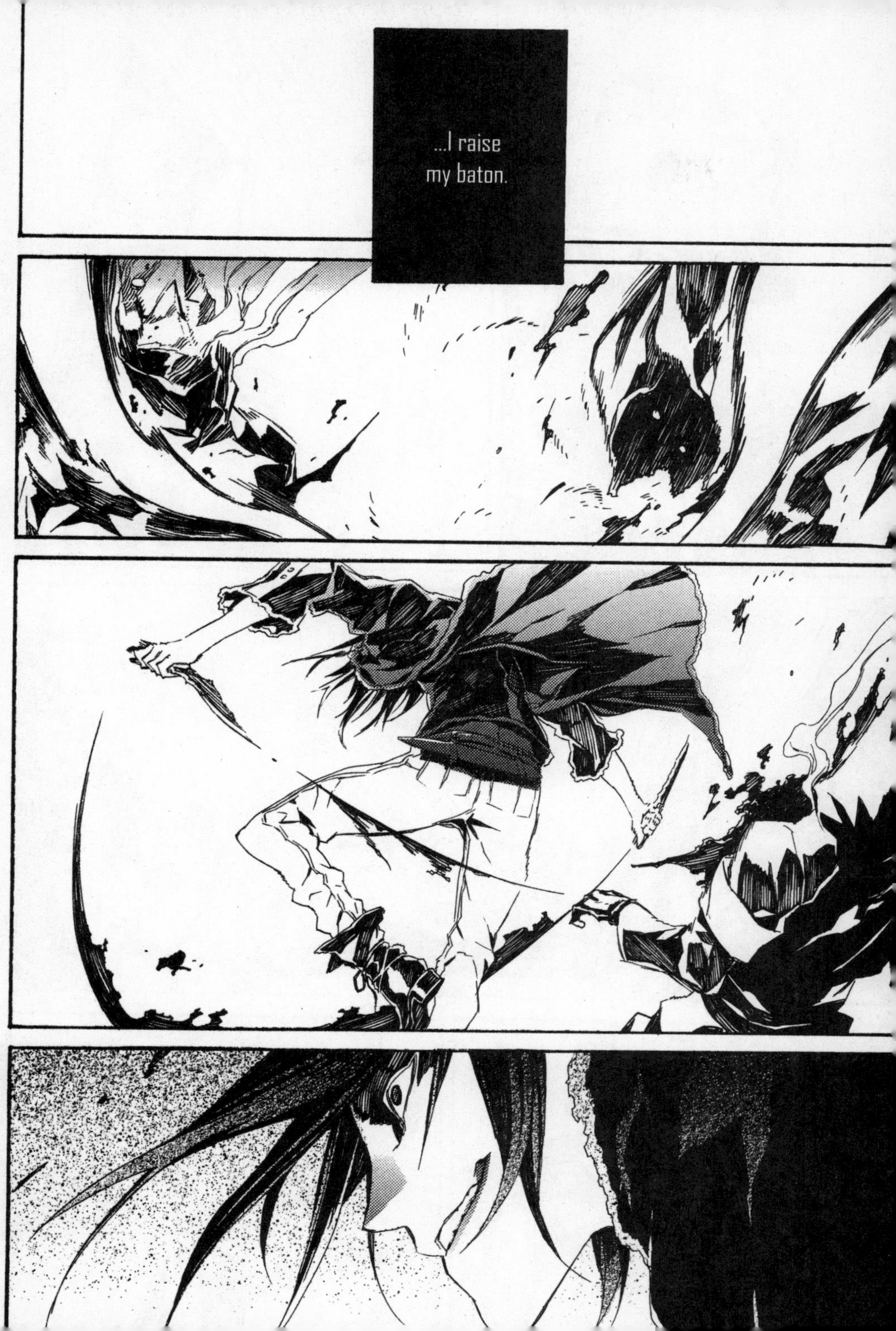
...I raise my baton.

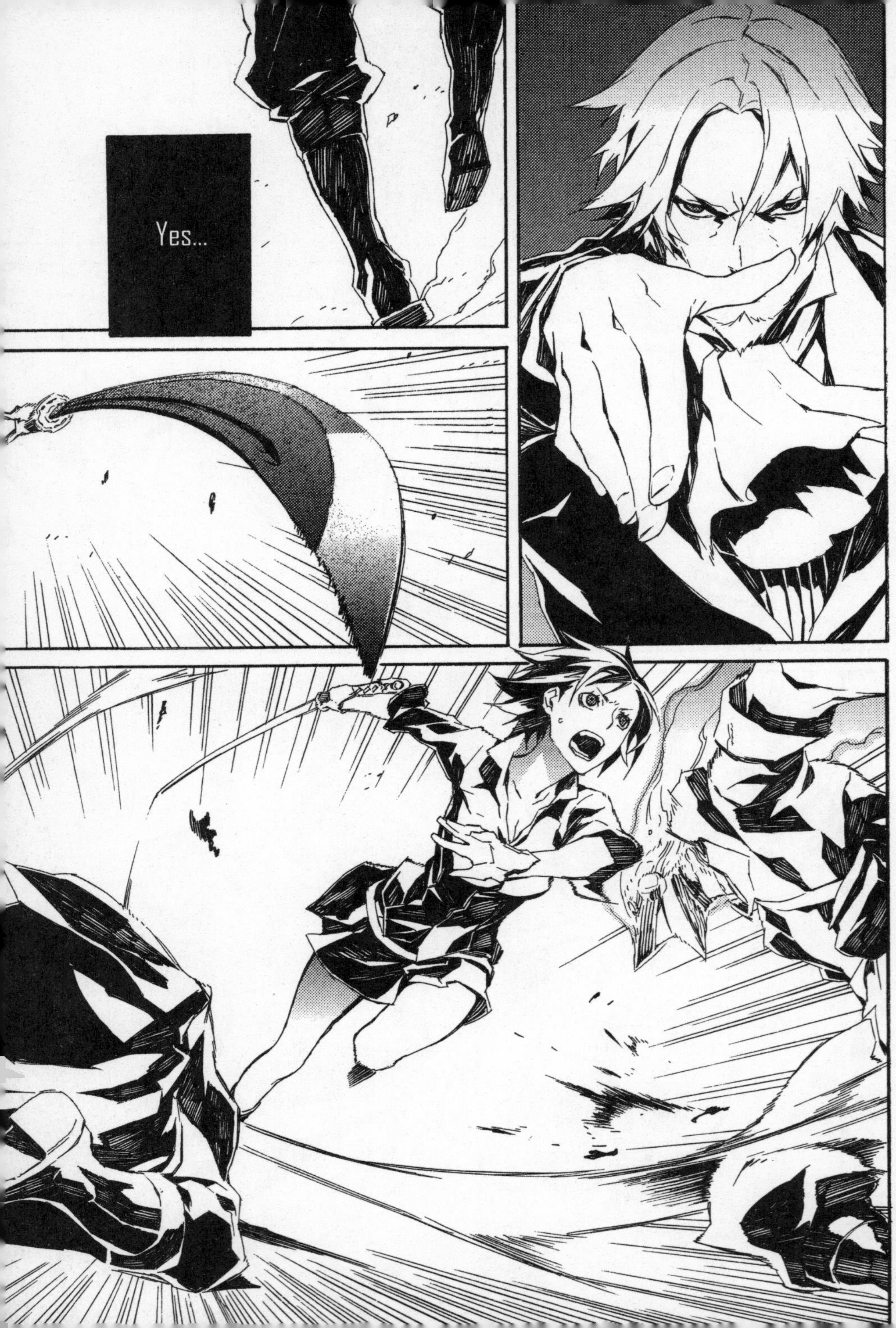
Yes...

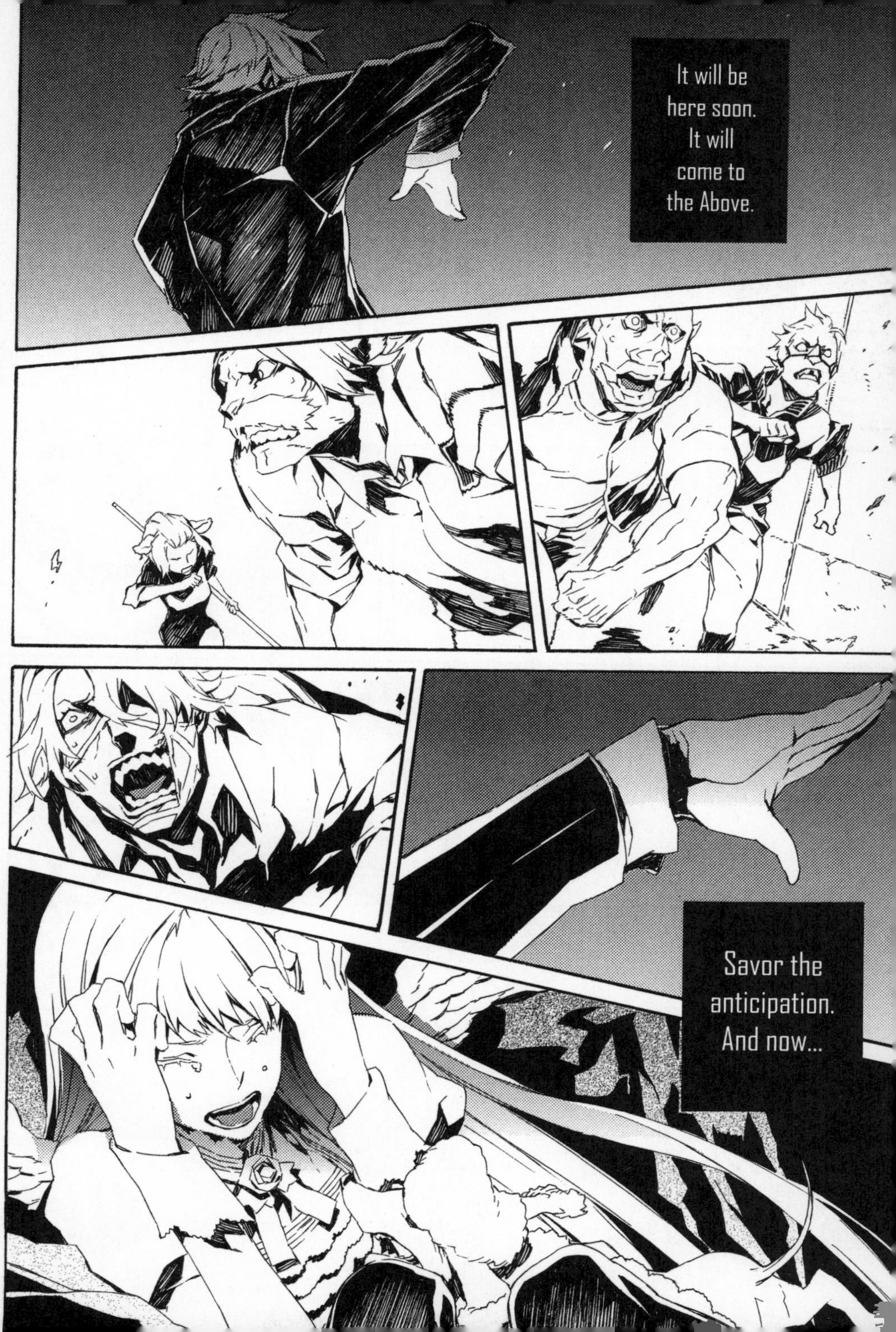
It will be here soon. It will come to the Above.
Savor the anticipation. And now...

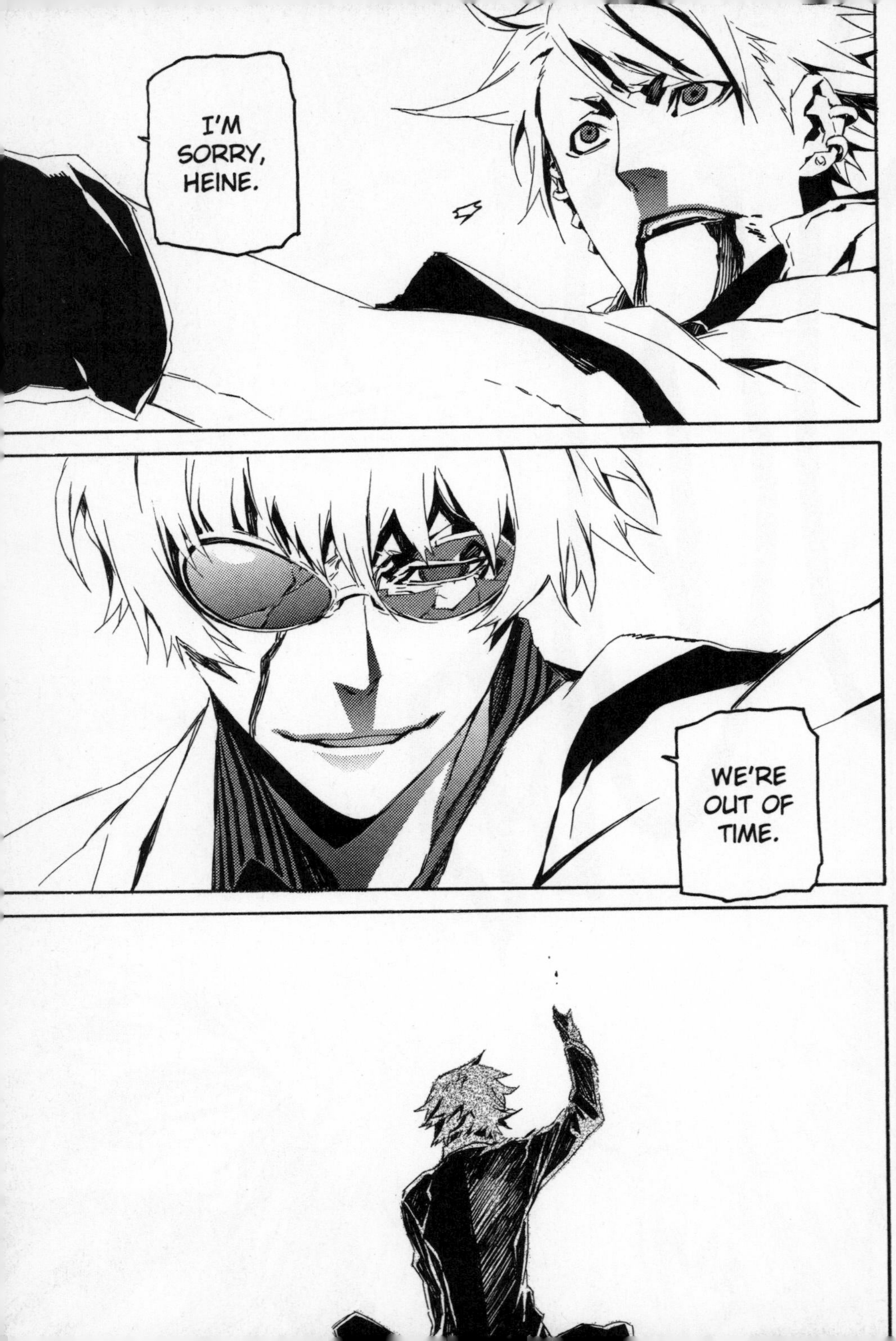
I'M SORRY, HEINE.
WE'RE OUT OF TIME.

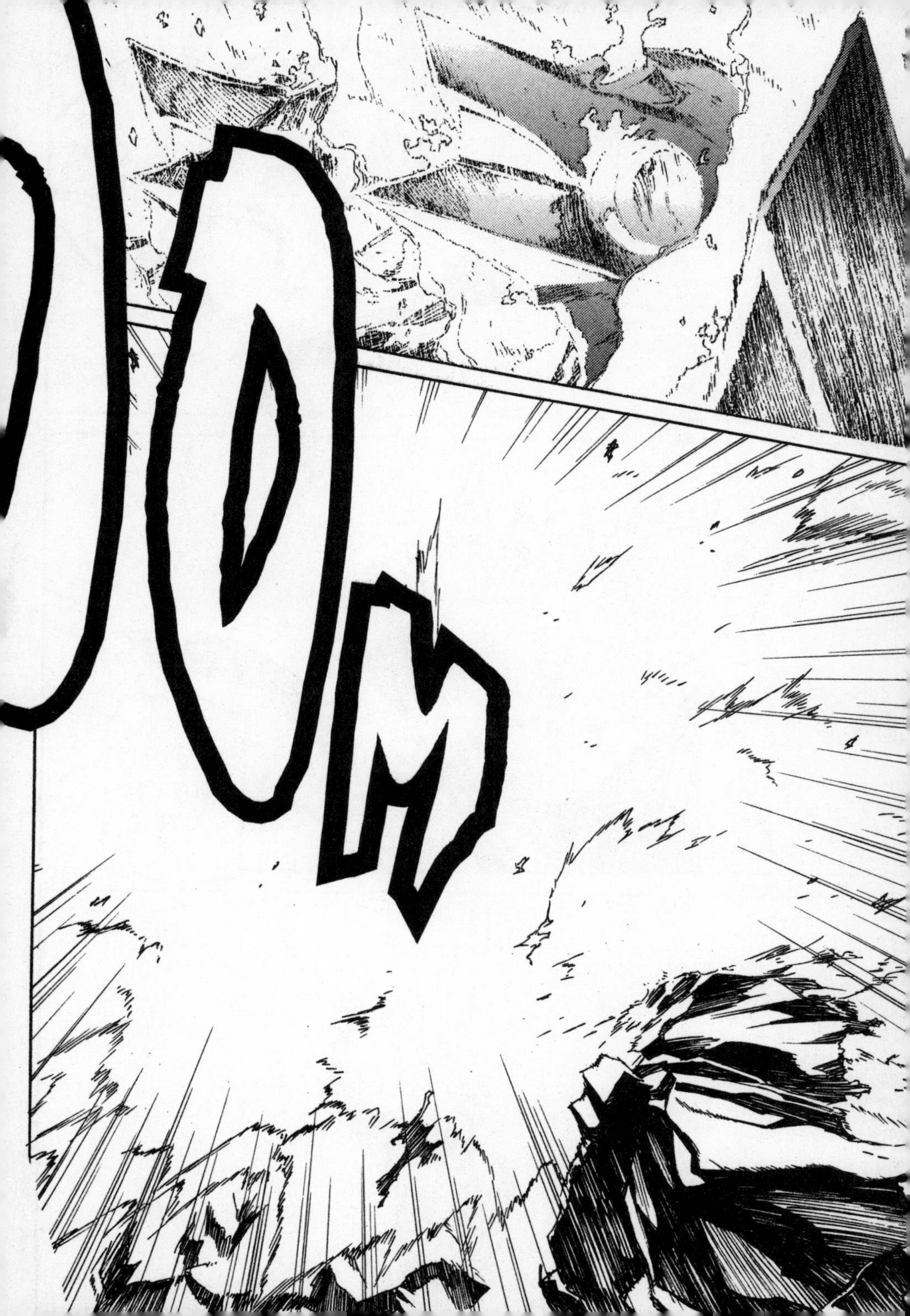
OM

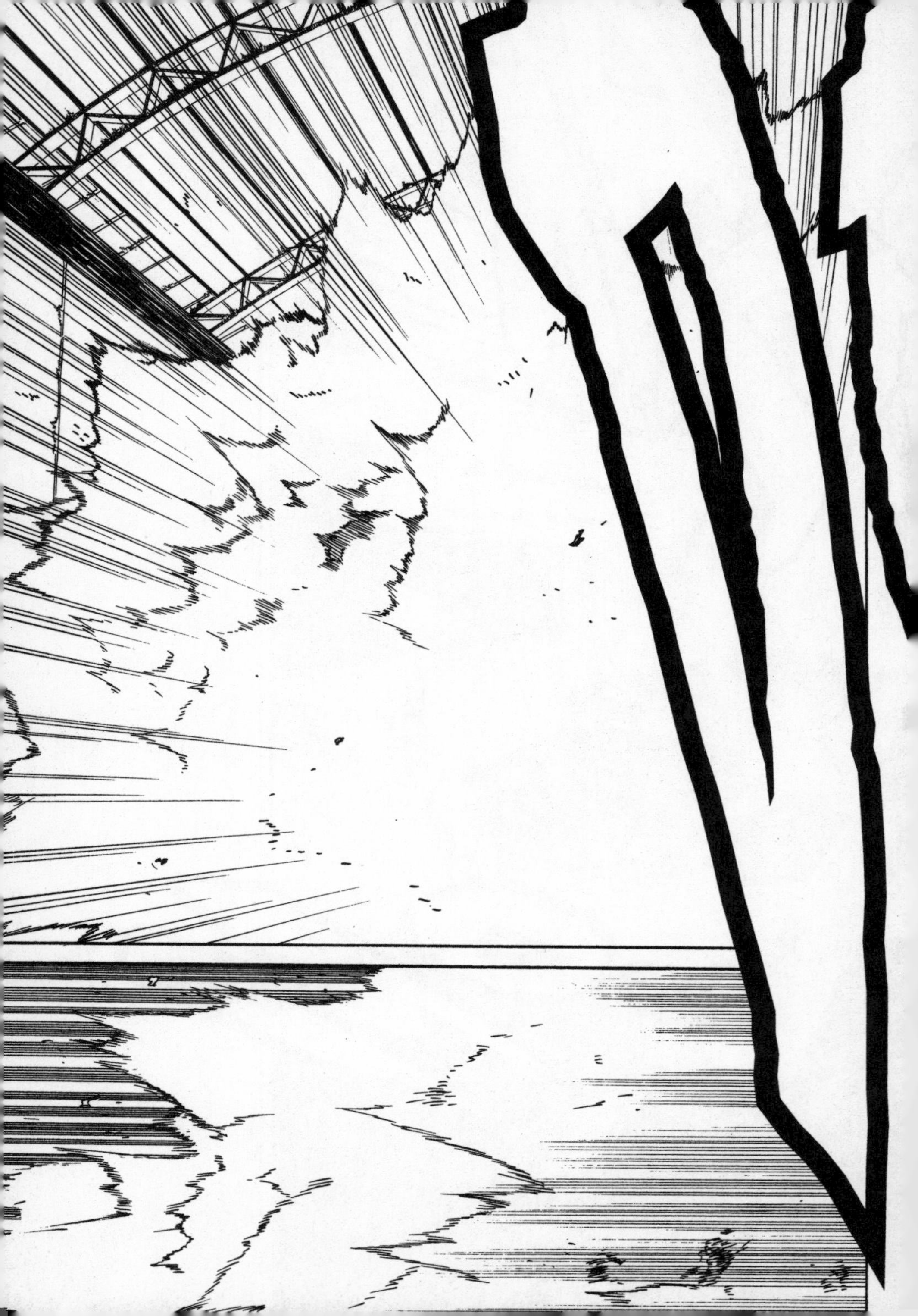

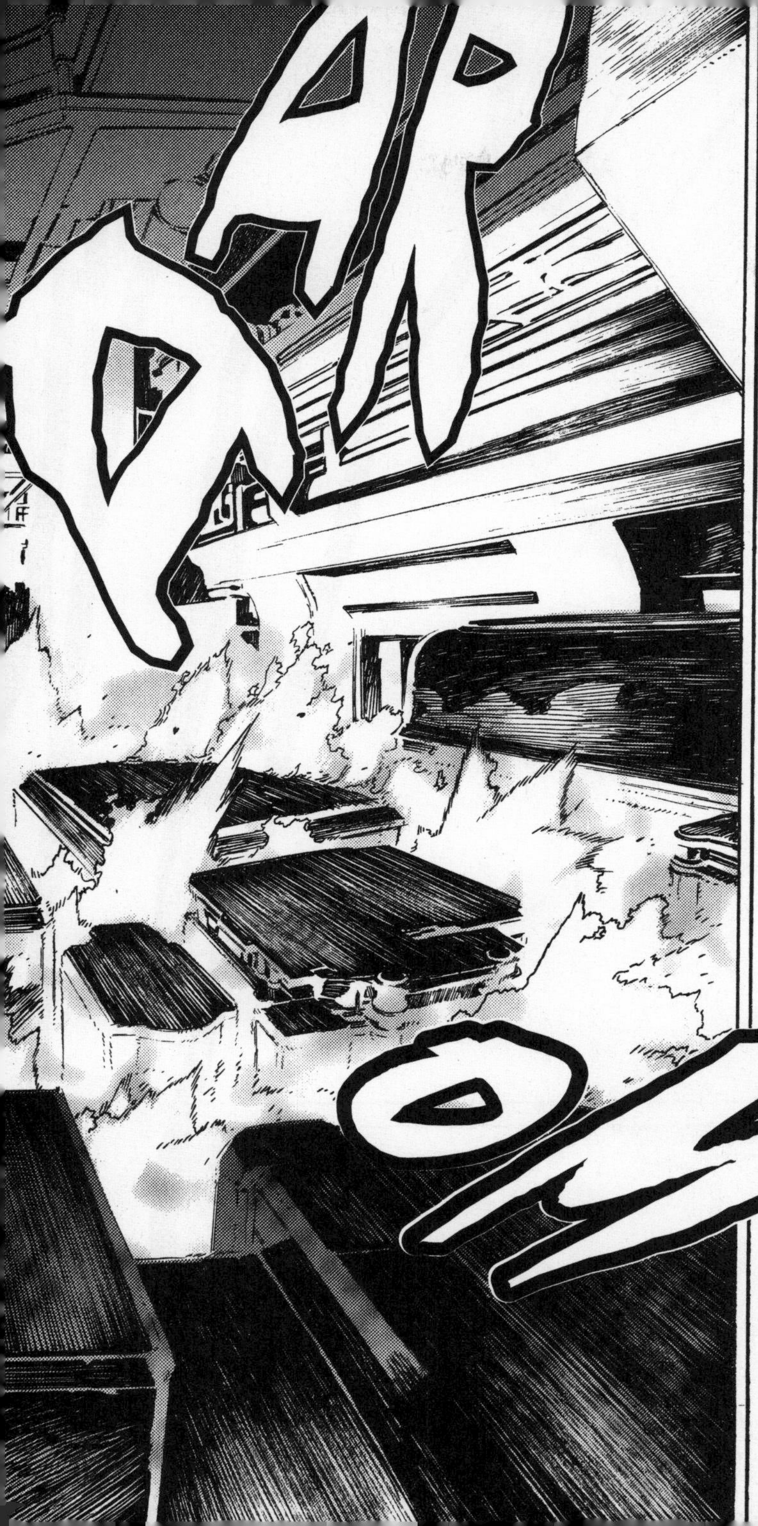

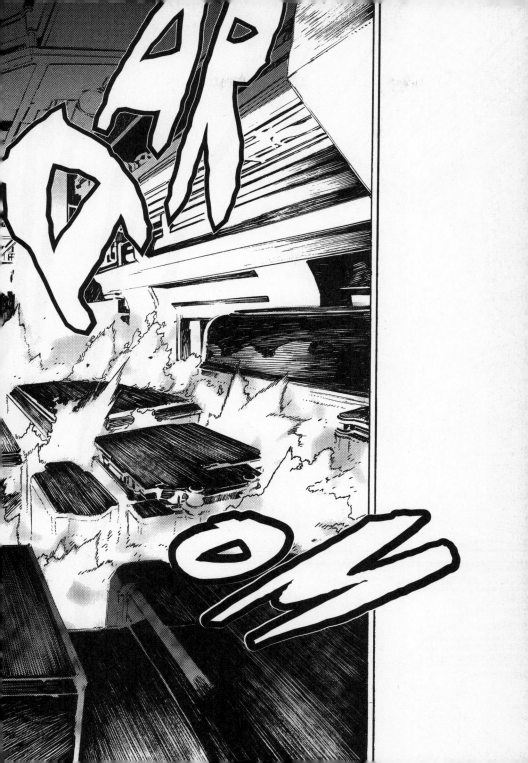

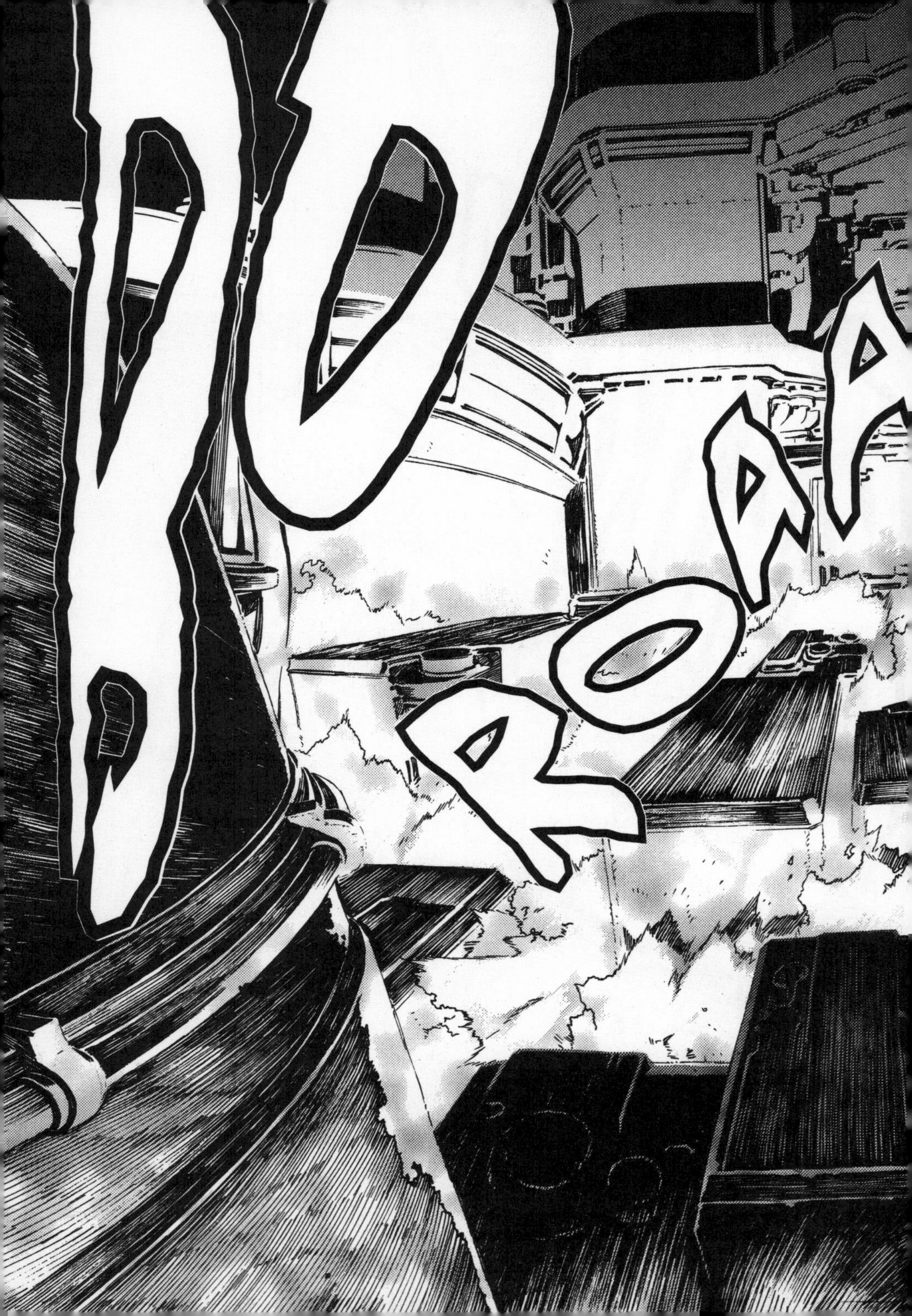
ROAA

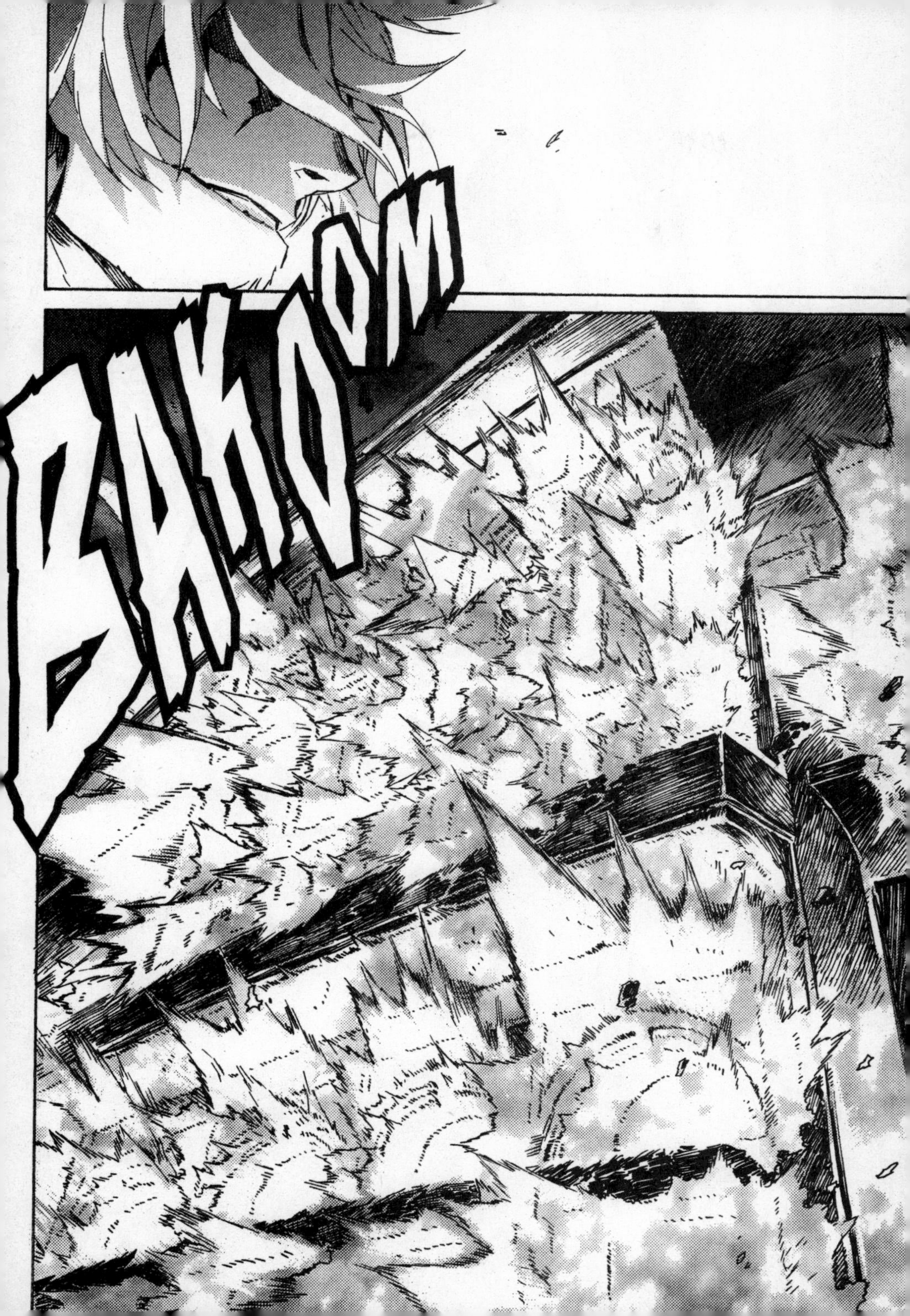
BAHOOM

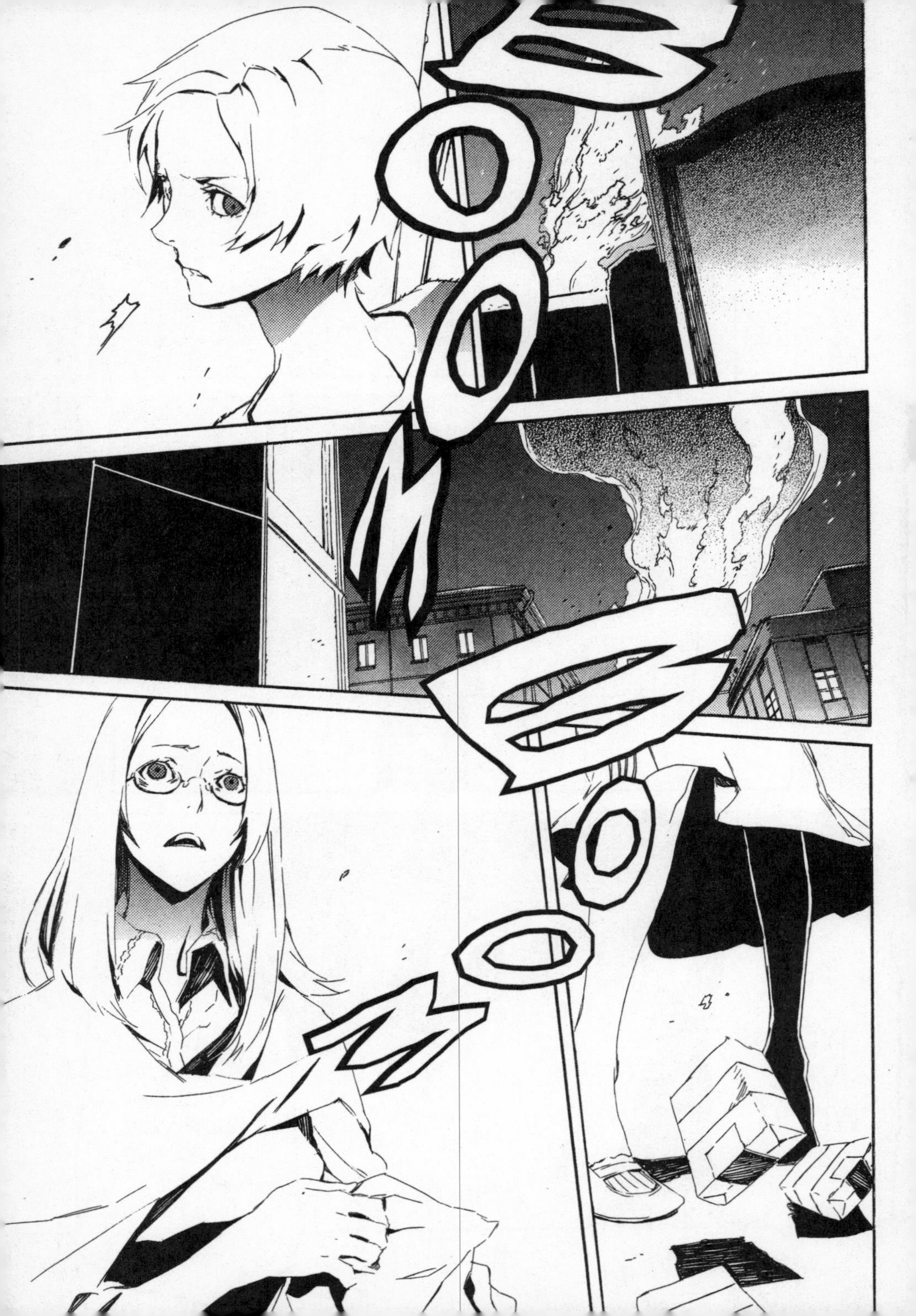
BOOM
BOOM

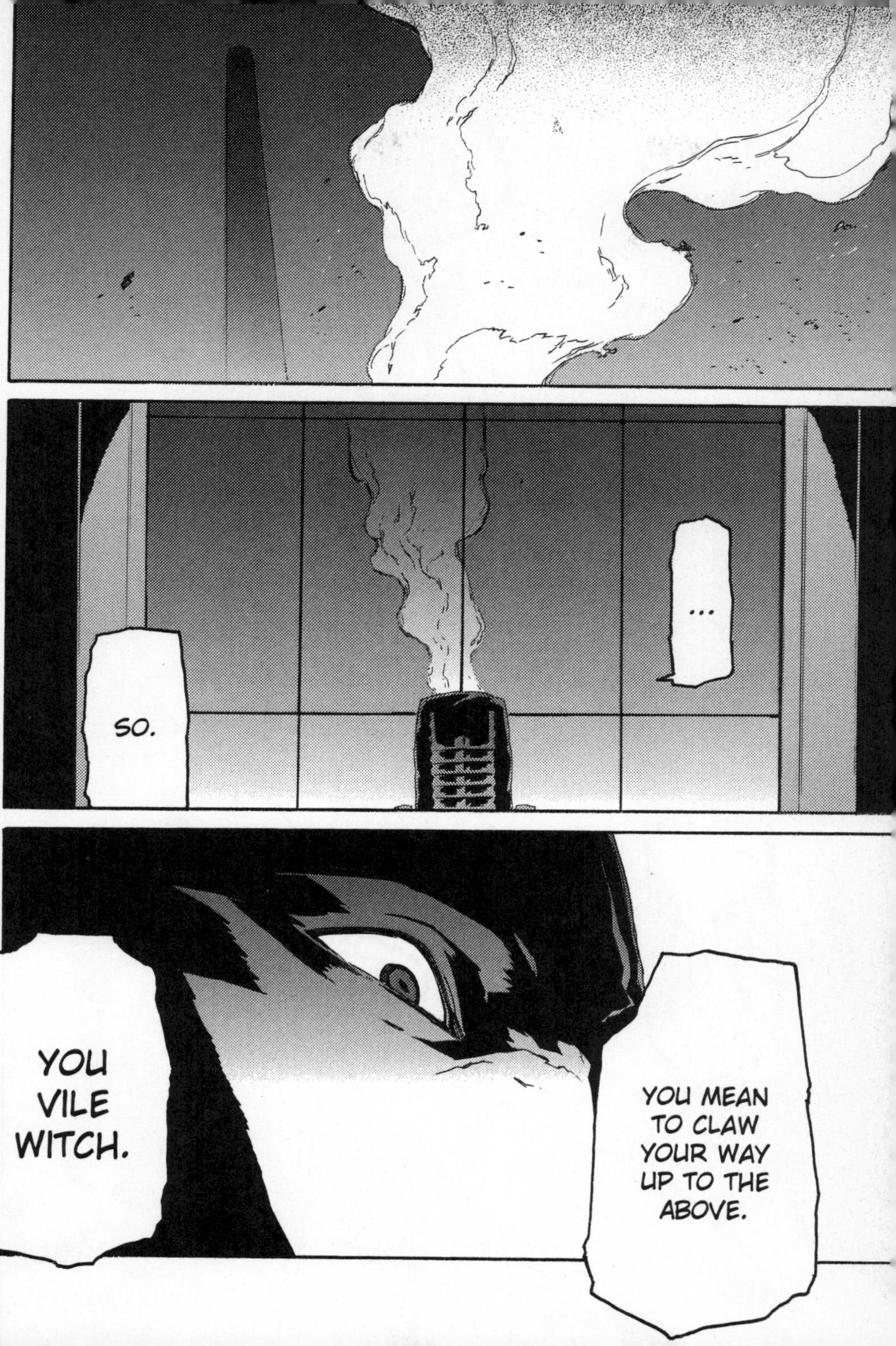
...
SO.
YOU MEAN TO CLAW YOUR WAY UP TO THE ABOVE.
YOU VILE WITCH.

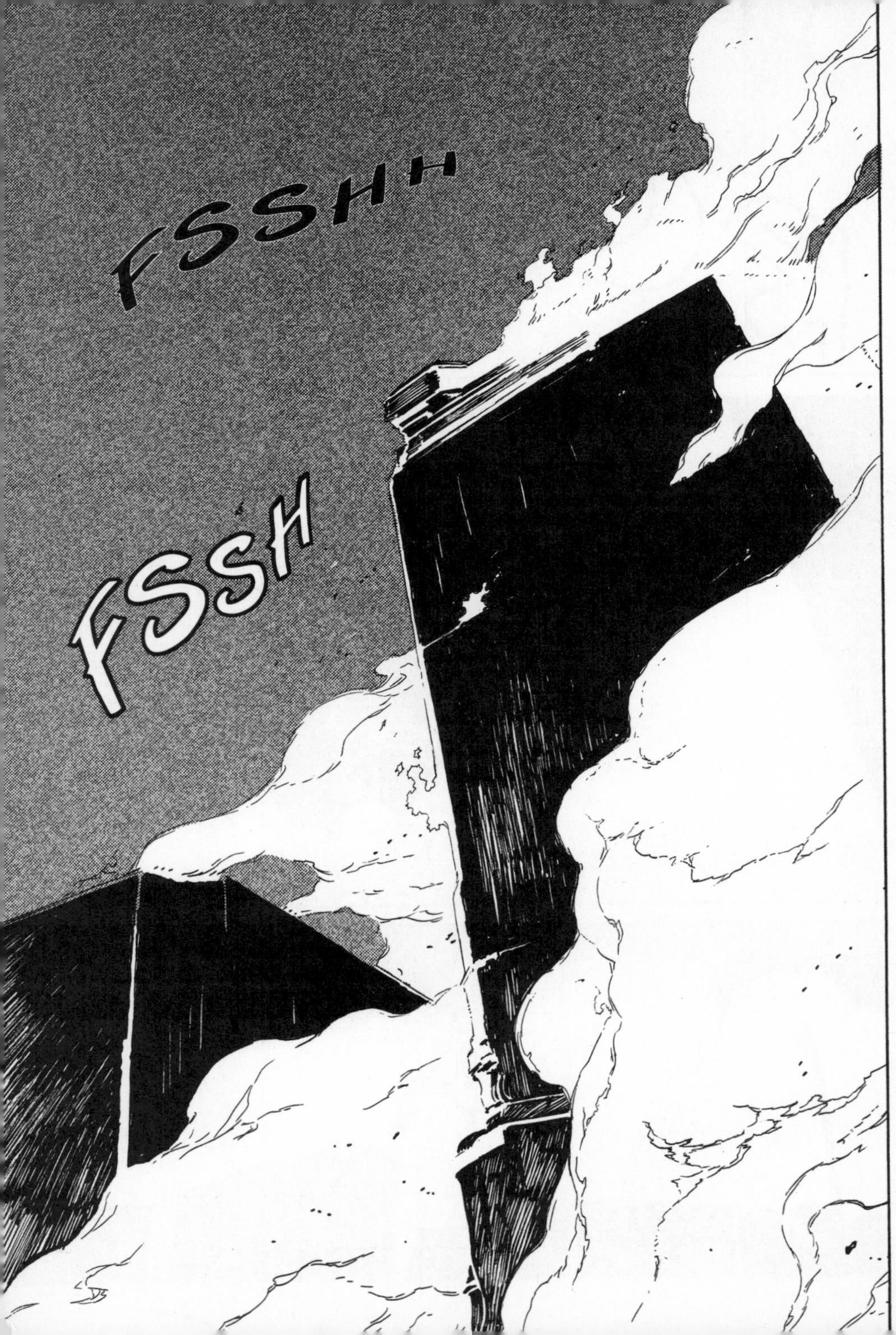
FSSHH
FSSH

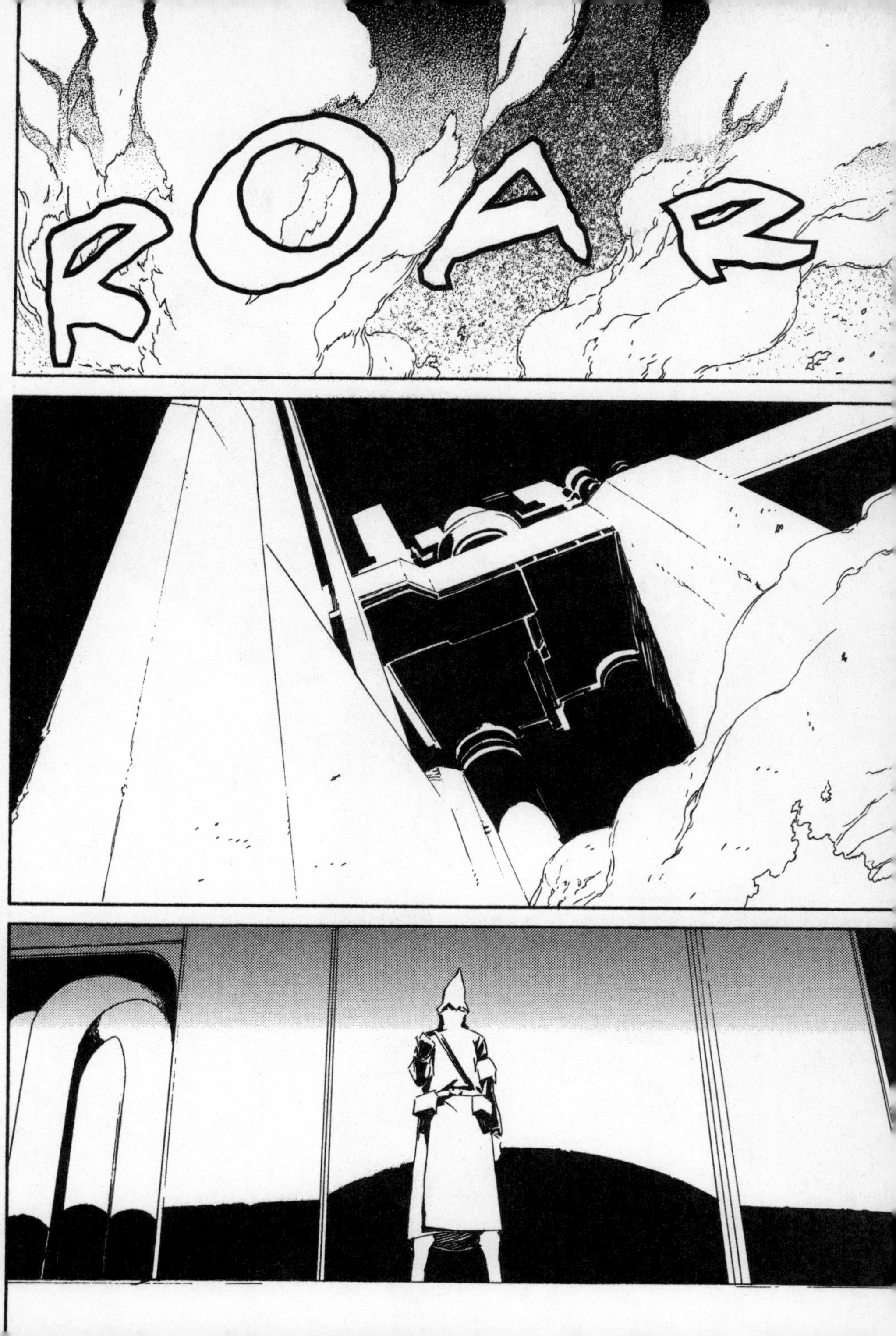
ROAR

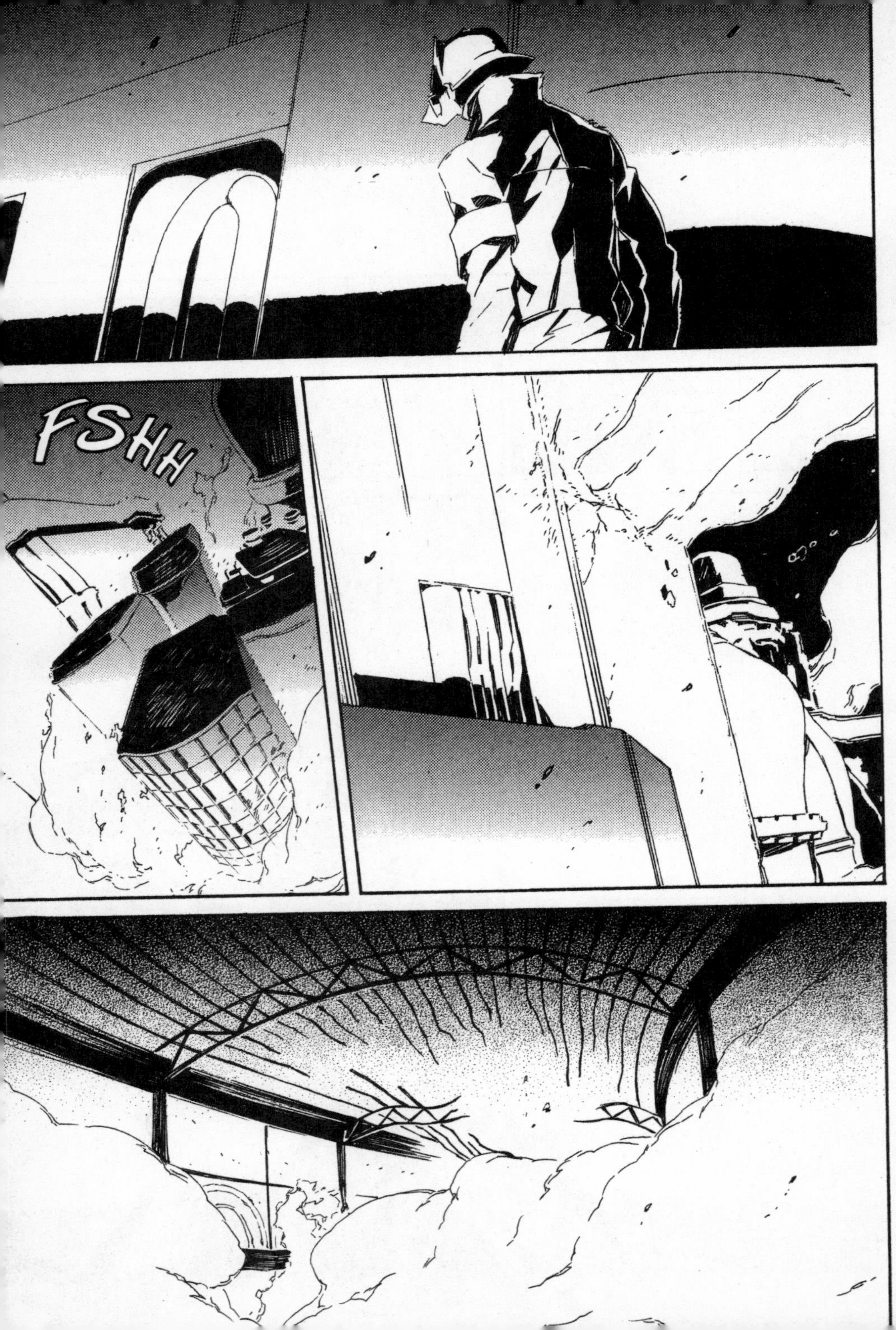
FSHH

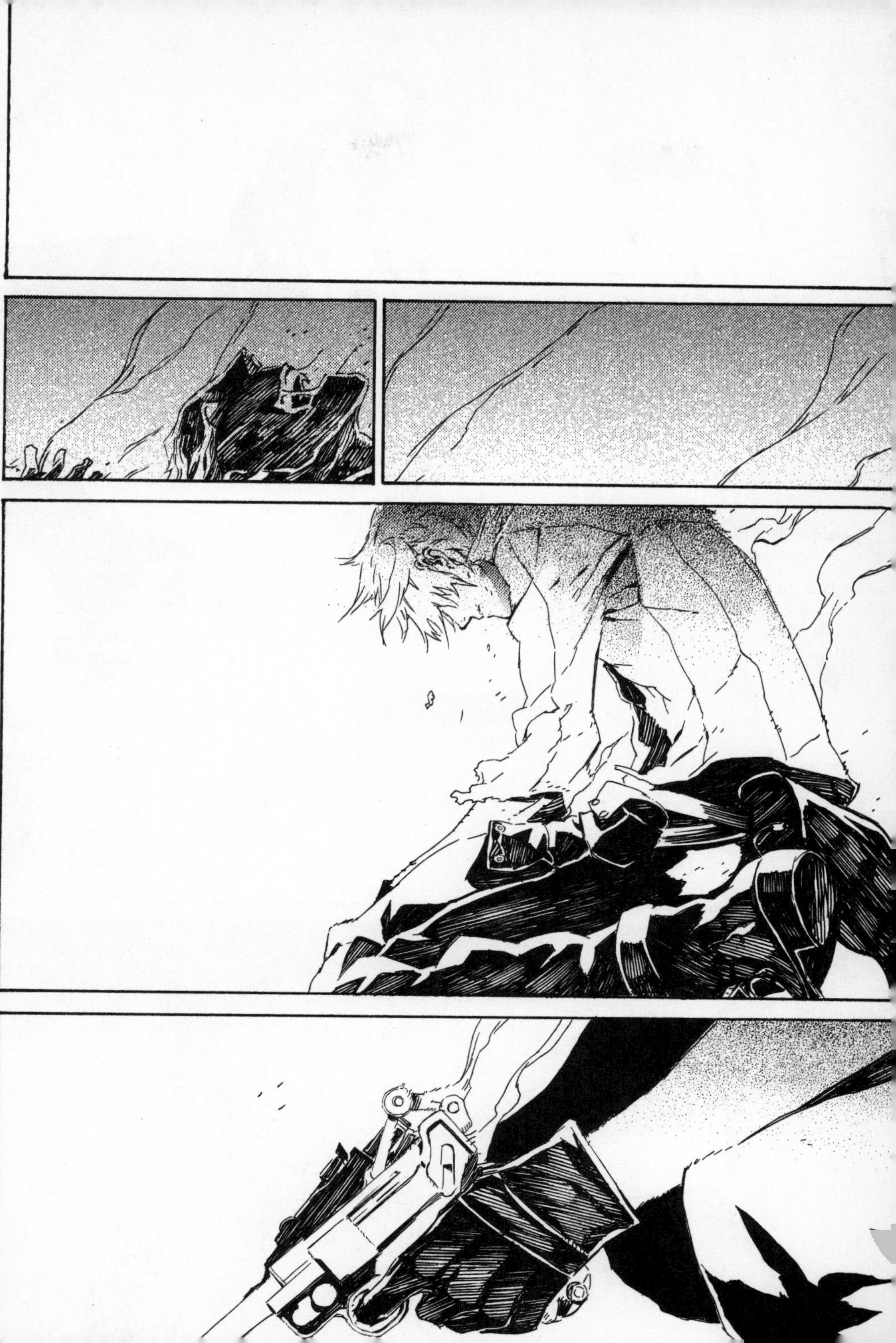

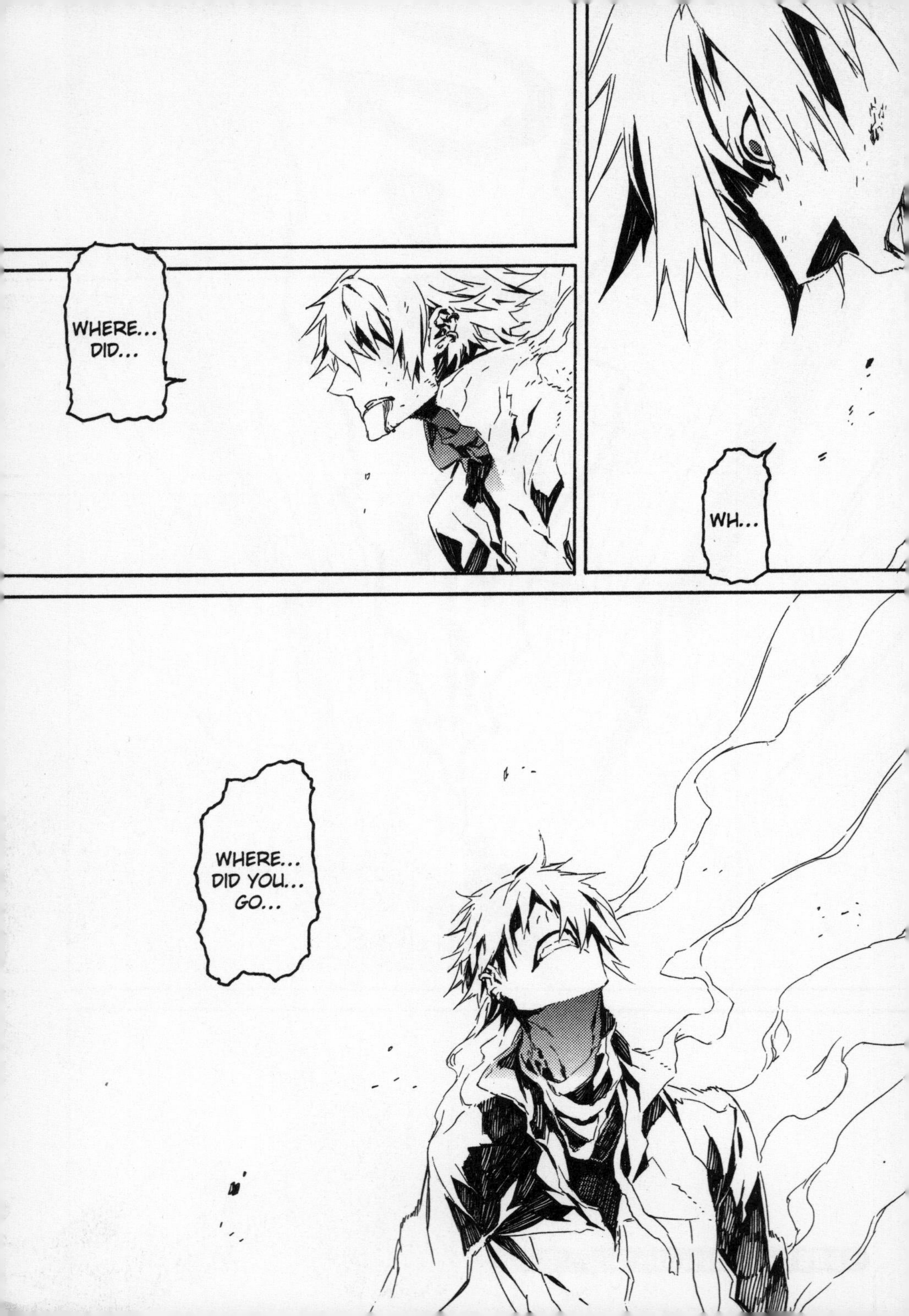
WH...
WHERE... DID...
WHERE... DID YOU... GO...

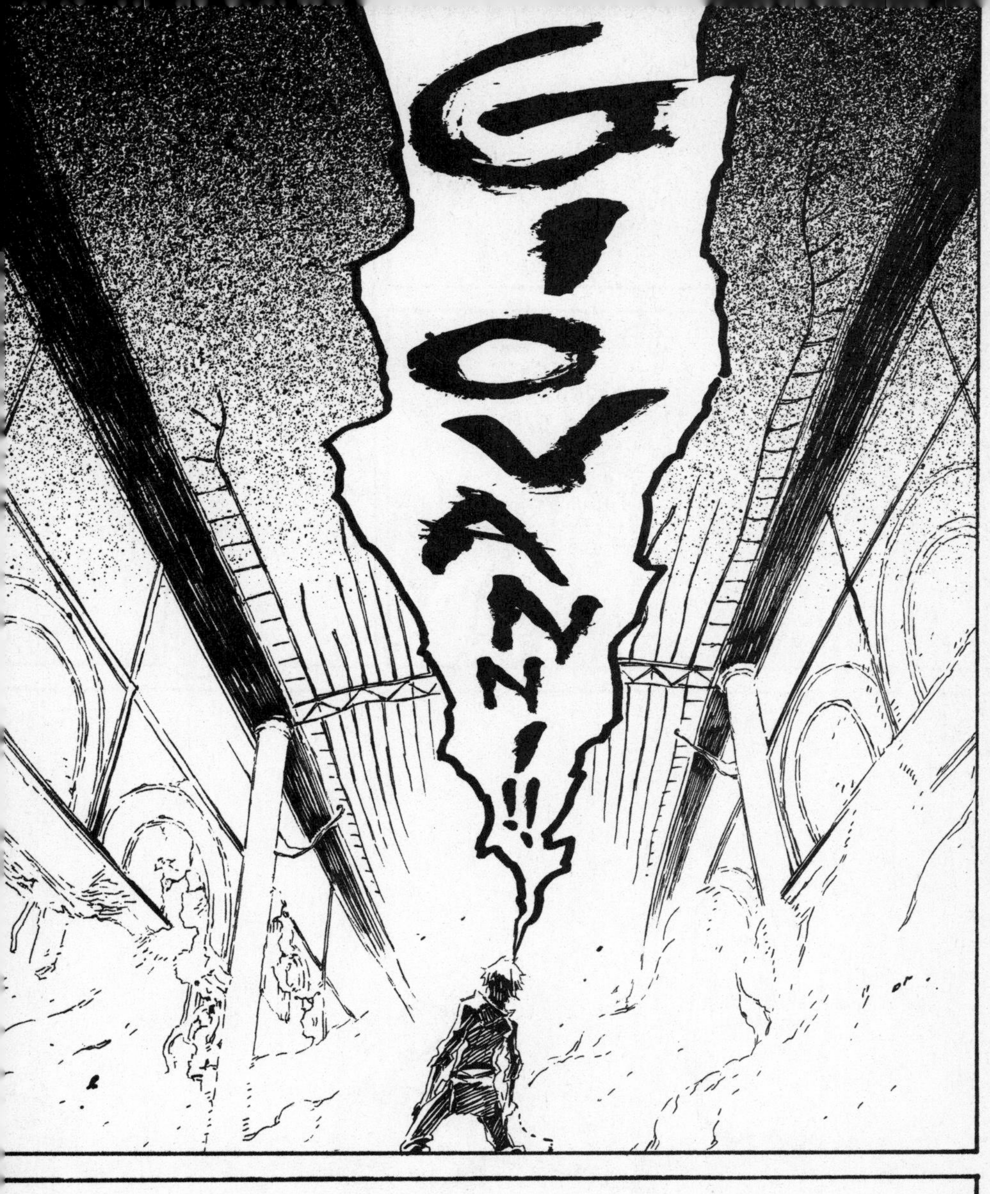

DOGS BULLETS & CARNAGE 5 / END

TO
BE
CONTINUED

SPECIAL THANKS

Iko Sasagawa

U

Suga

SERIES EDITOR

Satoshi Yamauchi

BOOK EDITOR

Jun Kobayashi

ORIGINAL DESIGN

LIGHTNING

ABOUT THE AUTHOR

Shirow Miwa debuted in *UltraJump* magazine in 1999 with the short series *Black Mind*. His next series, *Dogs*, published in the magazine from 2000 to 2001, instantly became a popular success. He returned in 2005 with *Dogs: Bullets & Carnage*, which is currently running in *UltraJump*. Miwa also creates illustrations for books, music videos and magazines, and produces doujinshi (independent comics) under the circle name m.m.m.WORKS. His website is http://mmm-gee.net.

DOGS: BULLETS & CARNAGE
Volume 5

VIZ Signature Edition

Story & Art by
SHIROW MIWA

Translation & Adaptation/Katherine Schilling
Touch-up Art & Lettering/Eric Erbes
Cover & Graphic Design/Sam Elzway
Editor/Leyla Aker

Printed in the U.S.A.

Published by VIZ Media, LLC
P.O. Box 77010
San Francisco, CA 94107

10 9 8 7 6 5 4 3 2
First printing, March 2011
Second printing, August 2012

RATED M FOR MATURE
PARENTAL ADVISORY
DOGS is rated M for Mature and is recommended for mature readers. This volume contains graphic violence and mature themes.
ratings.viz.com

VIZ SIGNATURE

www.viz.com

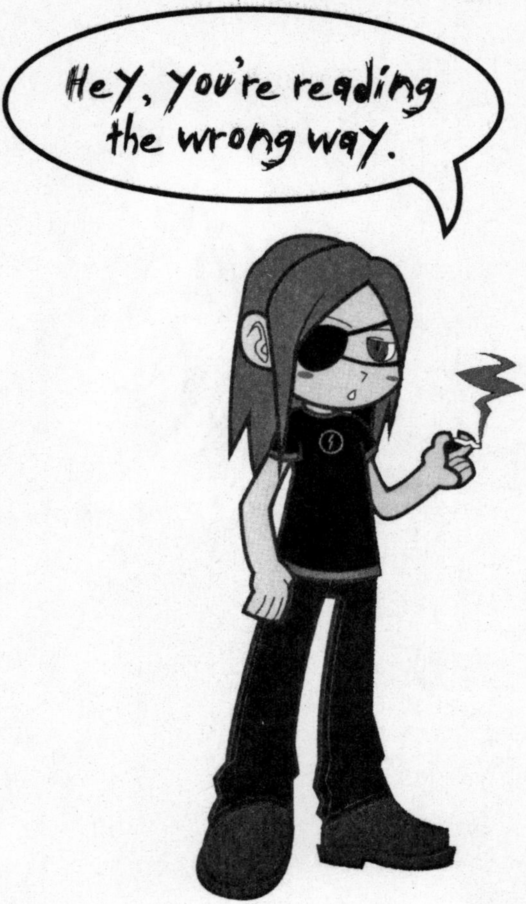
Hey, you're reading the wrong way.

Badou's right—this is actually the end of the book.

To properly enjoy this VIZ graphic novel, please turn it over and begin reading the pages from right to left, starting at the upper right corner of each page and ending at the lower left.

This book has been printed in the Japanese format (right to left) instead of the English format (left to right) in order to preserve the original orientation of the artwork and stay true to the artist's intent. So please flip it over—and have fun.

DOGS
BULLETS & CARNAGE

5

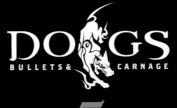

CONTENTS

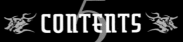

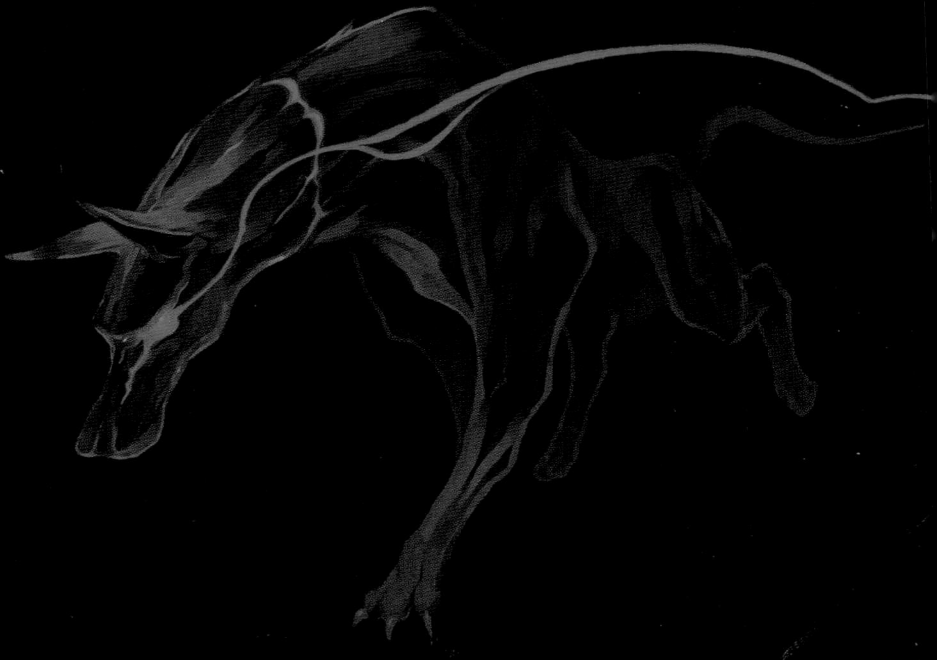

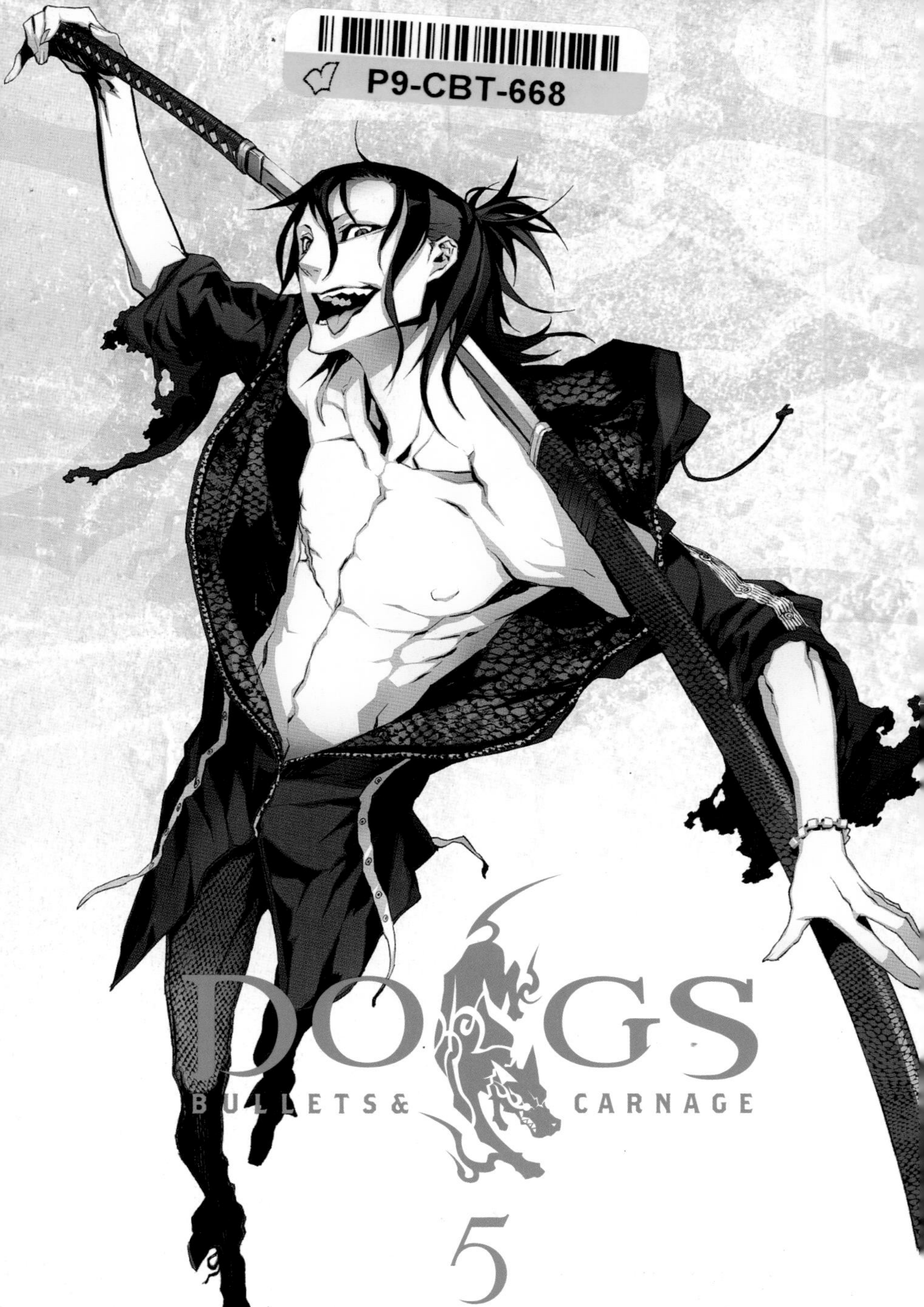

DOGS
BULLETS & CARNAGE

5

SHIROW MIWA